Dr. W. SCHRICKX

SHAKESPEARE'S
EARLY CONTEMPORARIES

THE BACKGROUND OF THE HARVEY-NASHE POLEMIC
AND *LOVE'S LABOUR'S LOST*

ANTWERPEN
DE NEDERLANDSCHE BOEKHANDEL
1956

Library of Congress Cataloging in Publication Data

Schrickx, W
  Shakespeare's early contemporaries.

  Bibliography: p.
  1. Shakespeare, William, 1564-1616--Contemporaries.
2. Mythology in literature. 3. Harvey, Gabriel, 1550?-
1631. 4. Nash, Thomas, 1567-1601. I. Title.
PR2957.S35 1972   820'.9'003   76-144684
ISBN 0-404-05622-9

Reprinted from an original in the collections of The
Wilbur L. Cross Library, University of Connecticut

From the edition of 1956, Antwerp
First AMS edition published in 1972
Manufactured in the United States of America

AMS PRESS INC.
NEW YORK, N. Y. 10003

PREFACE

The importance of mythology to Elizabethan literature is too well known to students of the period to need special emphasis. It has been the habit of scholars and critics to accept mythological references in Elizabethan writers only in their traditional meanings and connotations. Professor Douglas Bush, whose *Mythology and the Renaissance Tradition in English Poetry* (Minneapolis, University of Minnesota Press, 1932) is a standard work on the subject of mythology in Renaissance poetry, has stated that 'myths have appealed to the most diverse minds, have been put to the most diverse uses. They have been the vehicle for sermons on morality, for mystical theology, for obscene burlesque, for decorative tapestry, for human comedy and tragedy, for poems of escape from life, for humanitarian amelioration of life' (p. 4). These, no doubt, are the main uses of mythical stories. But I should like to set forth the proposition that through repeated association with certain events, one idea, one group and, at times, one man, many mythological terms came to have strong topical and personal meanings. There is one period in Elizabethan literature in which these acquired meanings became especially significant, namely in the years wherein the Harvey-Nashe controversy was coming into existence. These accretive meanings, as we will see, were not immutable; in fact, I shall try, at times, to point out the changing course of some applications of myths and study the associations which they evolved. A study of these applications and associations may, I hope, reveal that these accretive meanings gave additional force to certain words, phrases, and, indeed, provide a useful key to the interpretation of many important works of the time. What is more significant, a study of mythological allusions in the early nineties may enable us to shed fresh light on the imaginative and associative processes of the young Shakespeare. There is, therefore, some justification for introducing the present volume with a chapter on allegory and the transmission of mythology.

Our concern with the fruitful literary period of the early nineties has further induced me to write a chapter which deals partly with Shakespeare's early company connexions and partly with the problem of the so-called 'School of Night.' A third chapter, then, attempts to study Chapman's remarkable poem *The Shadow of Night* (1594), a poem which many scholars regard as an extremely important production; the same chapter also draws attention to some peculiarities in Chapman's imagery, peculiarities which, it is suggested, reveal traces of the poet's dependence on the metaphorical machinery employed by Maurice Scève.

From the fourth chapter onwards our main concern will be to study the significance of certain myths prevalent in the years 1590 1593 and to examine their interpretative value. Thomas Nashe, Abraham Fraunce, Robert Greene, Gabriel Harvey, and a few minor writers (chiefly those involved in the Marprelate controversy) are discussed with a view to determining the matrix from which Shakespeare's *Love's Labour's Lost* seems to have issued.

In the course of the preparation of this work I have incurred many obligations which it is pleasant to recall. In the first place, I should like to express my grateful thanks to Professor F. De Backer, who directed this work, for his valuable suggestions and for his permission to use many scarce books from his personal library. His helpful criticisms have greatly encouraged me and it is no small part of my debt to him to state that it is to his encouragement and enthusiasm that the least imperfect pages of my work are probably due. I have also derived much help from Professor De Backer's edition of Shakespeare's *Complete Werken* (Leyden, 1941).

I am also greatly indebted to the Members of the Faculteit der Wijsbegeerte en Letteren of Ghent University, who have always been prepared to help in various ways, and particularly to Professors E. Blancquaert, P. Lambrechts and P. Van de Woestijne. My gratitude also goes to Professors A. Nicoll and C. J. Sisson, who permitted me to attend the winter term of 1952 at the Shakespeare Institute at Stratford-upon-Avon; to Professor R. Apers, former Chief Librarian of the Ghent University Library, and to the members of the staff of that Library for their assistance; to Mr. J. Briley and Mr. E. A. Honigmann, who read a first draft of my work in typescript and made many useful suggestions; to my friend Mr. R. Devadder, who most generously put his time at my disposal to compile an index to my work and who helped me in various ways; and finally, to my friend Dr. A. Van Elslander, whose constant interest in my work I have most warmly appreciated, and whose sound critical judgment has been very helpful to me.

My indebtedness to scholars in the field is acknowledged in the footnotes and in the bibliography and my special debt here to E. K. Chambers, J. Dover Wilson, R. B. McKerrow, and W. W. Greg, and to the American scholars T. W. Baldwin, H. S. Wilson, D. J. McGinn, and many others, will certainly not pass unnoticed.

It is also a pleasure to record my thanks to the Anglo-Belgian Cultural Commission (Ministry of Education) for a grant which enabled me to visit the British Museum during the summer months of 1951; and especially to the Francqui Foundation, Brussels, and the British Council, whose grants enabled me to stay in England for almost six months in 1952, and to visit the British Museum, the Bodleian Library, the Shakespeare Institute and the Birmingham University Library. To the Committee and Trustees of the Patrimonium of the University of Ghent, whose grant made the publication of my work possible, I am also deeply grateful. I am also under an obligation to the Ministry of Education for being granted leave of absence in 1952.

Finally, my thanks go to the Printer to the University of Oxford, who provided a microfilm of John Eliot's *Ortho-epia Gallica* (1593) and photostats of Gabriel Harvey's *New Letter of Notable Contents* (1593) and of a large part of his *Pierces Supererogation* (1593).

In the matter of references and quotations I have usually given full information at the first reference to a work, and when the work is mentioned next it is only referred to by the title in abbreviated form. Quotations from Shakespeare are taken from original editions, the Quarto of 1598 for *Love's Labour's Lost*, and the Folio for other plays, while the line-numeration of the Globe edition is always followed. Other writers are quoted from authoritative modern editions or from editions of the time. The spelling is not modernized, but contractions in Latin extracts have been freely expanded. Unless otherwise stated, italics always derive from the original. I hope the reader will understand my difficulty in quoting from Harvey's works, works which are only to be had with great difficulty on the Continent, if they are to be had at all. I trust he will excuse me if he does not always find a reference to the Harvey edition of A. B. Grosart.

Gentbrugge,   W. Schrickx.
October 15, 1954.

CONTENTS

CHAPTER I

ALLEGORY AND THE TRANSMISSION OF MYTHOLOGY (1)

As it is one of the chief purposes of this volume to examine the significance of mythological allusion in the Elizabethan literature of the early nineties, it may not be amiss first to describe some of the literary trends that were conducive to a renewed interest in classic myth and its allegorical interpretation.

Allegory is a dominant feature of most forms of literature, the metaphor being an allegory in miniature. There are periods in which the allegorizing tendency takes precedence over all others, there are other periods in which it is subordinated to the more elementary or germinal form, the metaphor, and finally there are literary epochs in which a thorough-going rationalism aesthetically stultifies allegory altogether. Although definitions of the concept allegory generally start from those given in Quintilian's *Institutiones*, VIII, vi, 44-59, that it is either an 'inversion' or 'the use of words with more than one meaning,' allegory is often defined as an 'extended' or 'continued' metaphor, a definition which often recurs in the Renaissance theoreticians of literature. But these definitions demand more qualification if they are expected to cover the various uses of allegory, and here we need only refer to the brilliant discussion which C. S. Lewis has devoted to the development of the device (2). If I understand him rightly, Professor Lewis argues that allegory normally rests on some kind of equivalence, on the one hand personifications which represent the virtues and the vices, and,

---

(1) For this chapter I have chiefly drawn on the following works :
D. Bush, *Mythology and the Renaissance Tradition in English Poetry* (Minneapolis, 1932).
M. Praz, *Studies in Seventeenth-Century Imagery* (London, The Warburg Institute, 1939).
J. Seznec, *La survivance des dieux antiques* (London, The Warburg Institute, 1939), transl. as *The Survival of the Pagan Gods* (New York, 1953).
R. Freeman, *English Emblem Books* (London, 1948).
G. Highet, *The Classical Tradition* (Oxford, 1949).
(2) C. S. Lewis, *The Allegory of Love* (Oxford, 1936). Definitions of allegory are discussed on p. 45 f.

on the other, an equivalence which carries a step further than person-ifications in that they are directly applied to ourselves, we being the symbols of abstractions, a mode of thinking which harks back to Plato. The obvious example of the former equivalence is the *Psychomachia* or Soul-Battle of Prudentius, which describes the virtues and the vices battling for the human soul. The latter form can be illustrated from most eminent medieval literary master-pieces, and superbly so in the *Divina Commedia*.

Most great authors have had a secondary meaning imposed upon their works, witness Homer, Vergil, and Ovid. The productions of these writers were soon to be 'interpreted' by those who were no longer content with the barely 'literary' narrative. Though many writers designed their works allegorically, it was above all the search for some mystical meaning that greatly contributed to the growth of the allegorical tendency, and works that did not allow of a purely logical interpretation were pre-eminently liable to an allegorical one. The Bible itself fell victim to a search for mystical meanings at the hands of the Fathers, though not all of them were willing to indulge in 'allegorical' interpretation. The philosopher who ushered in the vogue was Philo Judaeus, who followed in the steps of those who had allegorized Homer. From Alexandria, where he was active, the allegorical tendency conquered the Western Church until the stream of allegorical treatises was checked by the rise of Protestantism. But that is another story and our concern lies elsewhere.

To give a list of all the medieval books which illustrate allegorical tendencies is unnecessary for the purpose we have in mind. Only Fulgentius's *Mitologiarum libri tres*, a comparatively short work written at the beginning of the sixth century (1), and the lengthy poem *Ovide moralisé* of the early fourteenth century (2), need here be mentioned as the outstanding treatises composed with the avowed purpose of exemplifying the allegorical method. The literary art was soon to follow the precepts of these alluring manuals in some way or other. Even great writers such as Dante and Ariosto fell a prey to the prevailing tendency; and the example of Ariosto himself inspired Spenser to use allegory profusely in the *Faerie Queene*.

---

(1) Edition by R. HELM (Leipzig, 1898). JOHN RIDEWALL re-wrote FULGENTIUS about the middle of the 15th century. See also H. LIEBESCHÜTZ, *Fulgentius Metaforalis. Ein Beitrag zur Geschichte der antiken Mythologie im Mittelalter* (Studien der Bibliothek Warburg, 1926).

(2) Edition by C. DE BOER, *Ovide moralisé* (Amsterdam, 1915).

Next to these purely literary attempts, existed the more philosophic achievements of men like Marsilio Ficino, whose endeavours were designed to resuscitate interest in the philosophy of Plato and the allegorically interpreted Platonic myths. The famous Florentine Academy worked in a cooperative effort to restore the prestige of the teachings of the ancients, and so closely was the Ficinian circle wedded to allegory, that Jean Seznec does not hesitate to call the Academy a *foyer de l'allégorie* (1). Considering the enormous influence exercised by Ficino (2) and his fellows on the development of sixteenth century literature generally, it need not surprise us that among poets, the search for correspondences—or equivalences— was given fresh impetus. Ficino's conception of love, his neo-Platonic Christian philosophy, his commentaries on Plato, all these helped to bring about a new literary climate, and Ficino's views are of prime importance to those who wish to gain an adequate understanding of much that is obscure in Renaissance writers. In the field of mythological symbolism, for instance, Ficino's works are able to shed light on many an obscure passage in French sixteenth century literature. The artists of the Renaissance often strove to convey their aspirations in terms of mythology. Once a myth had got hold of an artist's imagination, it was an easy step for him to relate the story to himself and to find himself as a kind of embodiment of the attributes of ancient gods; or again, he was entitled to borrow freely from mythological lore when he was in need of a striking image. Thus Bellorophon symbolized intelligence vanquishing ignorance, and Ganymede stood for the soul rapt to the bosom of God and the contemplation of the divine intelligence. In this way many a mythological hero was furnished with attributes entirely alien to the original sources. Mythological heroes became invested with all kinds of intellectual qualities. Because of the significance of the interpretations of myths it will be necessary to supply a brief survey of the provenance of sixteenth century mythology (3).

The obvious primary sources were the works of Vergil and Ovid, especially the latter, but the part played by the intermediary

---

(1) J. SEZNEC, *Survivance*, p. 88.

(2) On FICINO see P. O. KRISTELLER, *The Philosophy of Marsilio Ficino* (New York, 1943) and G. SAITTA, *Marsilio Ficino e la filosofia dell'Umanesimo* (Florence, 1943); also G. SAITTA's later work, *Il pensiero Italiano sull'Umanesimo e nel Rinascimento*, Vol. I, *L'Umanesimo* (Bologna, 1949), pp. 509-575.

(3) See J. SEZNEC, *Survivance*, pp. 186-222.

transmitters was by no means small. The humanists themselves were not slow to seize on every bit of available information to compile the mythological manuals which the tastes of the time required. Pride of place should be given to Boccaccio's bulky *Genealogia Deorum* (1), a work which was the central occupation of the last twenty-five years of Boccaccio's life. The fifteen books which compose the *Genealogia* touch on a variety of things other than mythology; but it is especially with the first thirteen books that the contemporaries of their compiler were most concerned, since these formed 'the great storehouse from which men of that time drew their knowledge of the details of classical fable' (2). In the *Genealogy* also, in accordance with the universal belief in the value of allegory, the narratives were often furnished with a symbolic interpretation; for instance, Boccaccio gave the allegorical significance of Perseus cutting off the Gorgon's head, and numberless indeed were the poems in which Renaissance poets made use of the elements of that particular fable.

Boccaccio usually follows the three traditional modes of interpretation: the physical or naturalistic, the euhemeristic, and the moral. The naturalistic interpretation generally turns on the idea of generation, a favourite theme with the mythographers, and as such forming a ready device to explain natural phenomena. A myth may also be morally interpreted. The Perseus myth, for example, symbolizes man's victory over sin. The euhemeristic interpretation (3), then, explains how historical characters came to be worshipped as gods, and how from real human beings they developed into mythological deities. It is comprehensible that humanism was going to favour the moral exposition of classical fable, and that sixteenth century mythographers were invariably interested in the elucidation of moral meanings.

Between 1472, the date of the first edition of the *Genealogia*, and 1532, when Georg Pictor's *Theologia mythologica* was published in Antwerp and Freiburg-i.-B., readers with a mythological bent could turn to the medieval mythographers who were being reprinted: Fulgentius, Palaephatus, Macrobius, Martianus Capella,

---

(1) Next to A. HORTIS, *Studij sulle opere latine del Boccaccio* (Trieste, 1879), pp. 155-219, see C. C. COULTER, "The Genealogy of the Gods," in *Vassar Mediaeval Studies* (Yale, 1923), pp. 317-341.
(2) T. R. LOUNSBURY as quoted by C. C. COULTER, *artic. cit.*, p. 323.
(3) See J. D. COOKE, "Euhemerism," *Speculum*, II (1927), 396-410.

Albricus, and so-called 'moralized' Ovids (1). At the beginning of the sixteenth century, however, the need began to be felt for a more systematic and codified treatment of mythology. Ravisius Textor's *Officina*, published in Basle in 1503, is the model of the genre; simultaneously with the ponderous *Officina*, treatises on hieroglyphs and emblems supplied similar kinds of information, but all these efforts in the field were soon outstripped by three widely known Italian manuals: Lilio Gregorio Gyraldi's *De deis gentium varia et multiplex historia* (Basle, 1548), Natalis Comes' *Mythologiae sive explicationum fabularum libri decem* (Venice, 1551), and Vincenzo Cartari's *Le Immagini colla sposizione degli Dei degli Antichi* (Venice, 1556). The last mentioned work, however, was more widely known in the Latin translation made by Verderius and published in Lyons in 1581.

L. G. Gyraldi (1479-1550?), one of the great representatives of humanism, was acclaimed as a man of genius by many of the noblest spirits of his day, and yet the appeal which his *De deis gentium* exercised on poets and artists seems to have been inconsiderable, at least this seems to be the case in England (2). Natalis Comes, however, though intellectually of a much lower order, was widely popular, especially in England. Edmund Spenser, George Chapman, and, oddly enough, Francis Bacon (3) may be mentioned among his debtors. And what is more, John Marston does honor to Comes in mentioning him in the second satire of the *Metamorphoses of Pygmalion's Image* (1598), and thus shows that Comes' *Mythologiae* was highly valued as a storehouse of classic myth.

> O darkness palpable! Egipts black night!
> My wit is stricken blind, hath lost his sight;
> My shins are broke with groping for some sence,
> To know to what his words have reference.
> Certes (*sunt*) but (*non videntur*) that I know;

---

(1) J. Seznec, *Survivance*, pp. 192-5. On p. 193 Seznec gives references to the history of mythographical publications in the 16th and 17th centuries.

(2) George Chapman mentions Gyraldi in one of his glosses to *The Shadow of Night*, but as F. L. Schoell, *Études sur l'humanisme continental en Angleterre* (Paris, 1926). p. 25, note, shows, Chapman was in no way indebted to him.

(3) For mythological lore in these writers and indebtedness to Comes, see : F. L. Schoell, *Études sur l'humanisme continental en Angleterre* (Paris, 1926).
H. G. Lotspeich, *Classical Mythology in the Poetry of Edmund Spenser* (Princeton Univ. Press, 1932).
C. W. Lemmi, *The Classic Deities in Bacon: A Study in Mythological Symbolism* (Baltimore, 1933).

Reach me some poets index that will show.
Imagines Deorum. Booke of Epithites,
Natales Comes, thou I know recites,
And mak'st anatomie of poesie;
Helpe me to unmaske the Satyres secresie;
Delphick Apollo, ayde me to unrip
These intricate deepe oracles of wit—
These dark enigmaes, and strange ridling sence,
Which passe my dullard braines intelligence (1).

Marston makes it clear that for the unravelling of much that
is obscure in Elizabethan literature one may consult Natalis Comes'
manual or Vincenzo Cartari's *Imagines Deorum*, the work to which
Marston is probably also referring. Before leaving Comes, it may
not be superfluous to point out that, like so many others who gave
expression to truly medieval ideas, Comes echoes Boccaccio's statement that the chief reason for a poem's existence is the meaning
hidden *sub cortice* (2). Comes right at the outset of his compendium
claims that he will go beyond the exterior cortex so as to lay bare
the philosophy embodied in fables, *ad mores hominum vel corrigendos
vel informandos* (3).

Comes gets the honour of being mentioned by name in
Marston's satire, but the identity of the author of *Imagines Deorum*
is for the reader to conjecture, a circumstance which, perhaps here
also, relates to the mystery which surrounds the personality of
Cartari. He is, indeed, rarely mentioned by his contemporaries, and
Elizabethans like George Chapman and Abraham Fraunce, who
used his mythological work (4), never mention Cartari by name,
whereas they do refer to Comes. In point of fact, Cartari is cited
as an authority only by his contemporaries G. B. Armenini in 1587
and by G. P. Lomazzo in 1584 (5).

The interests of the Elizabethan world of letters also followed
a variety of other continental currents of thought. Of special relevance to the interpretation of certain sections of English sixteenth
century literature is the vogue of emblem writing. Simultaneously
with the renewed interest in classical literature and Platonic philo-

---

(1) John Marston, *Works*, ed. J. O. Halliwell (London, 1856), III, 218.
(2) C. C. Coulter, art. cit., p. 326. See Boccaccio, *Genealogia*, XIV, 10, 12.
(3) Natalis Comes, *Mythologiae* (Padua, 1616), p. 3.
(4) See D. J. Gordon, "Chapman's Use of Cartari in the Fifth Sestiad of 'Hero and Leander'," *MLR*, XXXIX (1944), 280-5.
(5) J. Seznec, *Survivance*, p. 200.

sophy arose certain new sciences or pseudo-sciences which, under the guise of what may seem to us rather poor and trivial devices, tried to symbolize and represent esoteric doctrines by means of hieroglyphs and emblems. With respect to the dissemination of these sacred signs the following facts are relevant (1). In 1419 a Florentine priest Cristoforo de Buondelmonti, travelling in the island of Andros, bought a manuscript of the *Hieroglyphica* of Horus Apollo, an author presumably Egyptian—he calls himself 'Niliacus'—of the fourth or second century A. D. The translator himself, a certain Philippus is known only by name. The *Hieroglyphica* (2), when brought to Florence, aroused great interest among Marsilio Ficino's circle; the famous printer Aldus Manutius was the first to print Horus' work in 1505, and thus the road was prepared to its enormous influence. Prior to the publication of this work, however, the influence of Horus already displayed itself in Francesco Colonna's *Hypnerotomachia*, written about 1467 and published by Aldus in 1499. It may also be noted, though Mario Praz and Jean Seznec had no need to mention it, that the latter work was translated by 'R. D.' in 1592 (3); it was inscribed 'to the thrise honourable and ever lyving vertues of Syr Phillip Sydney,' before being dedicated to the Earl of Essex. The dedication is in itself significant for the general interests of the Sidney circle. Next to Horus, then, another important treatment of hieroglyphs is represented by the ponderous volume of Pierio Valeriano, *Hieroglyphica sive de sacris Aegyptiorum aliorumque gentium literis* (Basle, 1556).

In addition to the two special studies of Horus and Valeriano, there were of course many other works in which the history of the Egyptians found a place. For instance, Petrus Crinitus also refers to the Egyptian characters in two essays of his *De Honesta Disciplina*, written at the turn of the fifteenth century. Polydore Vergil in *De rerum Inventoribus* (Rome, 1585) only mentions the subject, but more specific references are to be found in the work of Alexander

---

(1) It is especially to the pioneer study of KARL GIEHLOW, "Die Hieroglyphenkunde des Humanismus in der Allegorie der Renaissance," *Jahrbuch der kunsthistorischen Sammlungen des Allerh. Kaiserhauses*, XXXII, pt. I (Vienna, 1915) that all subsequent writers on the subject are indebted. A broad survey of emblems is provided by LUDWIG VOLKMANN's *Bilderschriften der Renaissance. Hieroglyphik und Emblematik in ihren Beziehungen und Fortwirkungen* (Leipzig, 1923).

(2) Modern edition by F. SBORDONE, *Hori Apollinis Hieroglyphica* (Naples, Loffredo, 1940).

(3) The British Museum catalogue and the *Short-title Catalogue* suggest Sir ROBERT DALLINGTON as the translator.

ab Alexandro, *Genialium Dierum libri sex* (Paris, 1565); a later work, not of interest for the present study, is that of Philippus Camerarius, *Operae Horarum Subcisivarum* (Frankfurt, 1602-1609), which frequently refers to Horus and Valeriano (1). It hardly needs saying, of course, that incidental references in Renaissance works are numerous.

Though from the scientific point of view Horus did no more than propagate the false notions about hieroglyphs to be found in Pliny (*Hist. Nat.*, XXXVI, 8-9), Tacitus, Apuleius, Plotinus (*Enneads*, VIII, vi), and others who had no idea of the phonetic nature of the original Egyptian characters, Horus's work did not fail to attract the Italian humanists, who actually believed these signs to represent a revelation of Egyptian wisdom. Marsilio Ficino's specific contribution in this field was that he made this attitude of veneration towards the wisdom of ancient Egypt prevail; it was also associated with the Hermetic cult, Hermes being the reputed inventor of letters. Simultaneously with his translation of Plato in 1483, Ficino brought out *De mysteriis Aegyptiorum*, a work attributed to the neo-Platonic Syrian philosopher Jamblichus. A copy of this work in the Lyons edition of 1577 was not unknown to the Elizabethans: George Chapman, for instance, was in possession of such a copy (2). According to Jamblichus the Egyptians strove to represent the working of the divine will in their pictures of herbs, plants, and animals; in other words, Jamblichus regarded them as intimations of mysterious powers. Similarly Ficino saw nature as a kind of eternal revelation ·of the spirit, an attitude suggested to him by his enthusiasm for the hermetic writings (3). Ficino held that Hermes was *primus theologiae appellatus auctor*, who was followed by Orpheus, Pythagoras, and Philolaos, the master of Plato. As G. Saitta points out, this genealogy, certainly· puerile, nevertheless testifies to the mystical tendencies of Ficino, a philosopher who seems to have found an emotional release in all things clothed in mystery. There is little doubt that the hermetic strain to be found in French literature—notably Maurice Scève—and in English literature—witness Chapman—is to be traced to the Florentine Academy; the more so as the other aspects of Ficino's activity equally found their

(1) See D. C. ALLEN, "Ben Jonson and the Hieroglyphics," *PQ.* XVIII (1939), 290-300.

(2) See J. JACQUOT, *George Chapman* (Paris, 1951), p. 22.

(3) G. SAITTA, *Il pensiero italiano*, I. 510 ff. and 513 ff.

reflection in France and England. There were of course sceptics who rejected the whole fashion of hieroglyphs and the like, and Rabelais' ridicule of it is well known. Before Rabelais, however, the belief in hieroglyphs was so widespread that most humanists could hardly resist the appeal of these 'sacred' pictures.

Once the fashion for 'aenigmatic' and 'sacred' characters had been started, humanists created their counterparts in emblems. As has been shown by Karl Giehlow and Ludwig Volkmann, humanists consciously imitated hieroglyphs in their books of emblems and Andrea Alciati, whose book of emblems was published for the first time in 1531, ushered in the vogue. An emblem book is a book of engravings, each of which is accompanied by a text to explain their meaning. In the seventeenth century the term emblem generally refers to the picture proper, but in the later acceptance of the word it covered the accompanying text—generally an epigram—as well, the epigram being a verbal counterpart to the emblem (1). Owing much to Horus's work, Alciati also drew inspiration from a variety of other sources: the Latin epigrammatists, the *Anthologia Planudea*, and the poetry of Petrarch, who, as Mario Praz (2) indicates, had a peculiarly emblematic turn of mind. Alciati's manual of emblems, the *Emblematum Liber*, was imitated by a countless number of other writers; it went through innumerable editions and in these the number of emblems was often increased, going from a hundred and four to a total of two hundred and twelve. In 1571 the edition was furnished with copious notes by Claude Mignault (1536-1605), and the latter's edition is presumably the one with which the Elizabethans were most familiar. Among Alciati's imitators in Italy was Achille Bocchi, whose *Symbolicarum questionum Libri V* (Bologna, 1555) is a very scarce book. The fashion soon took root in France; eight years after Alciati, Guillaume de la Perrière produced *Le Théâtre des bons Engins* (1539), to be followed by Gilles Corrozet's *Hécatomgraphie* (1540). The former work was apparently translated into English in 1593, since we find *The Theater of fyne Devises conteyninge an hundred morrall Emblemes* mentioned in the Stationers' Register without the author's name; but the translator's name is given as Thomas Combe (3). I may here mention, a point which

---

(1) M. Praz, *Studies*, p. 21.
(2) M. Praz, "Petrarca e gli emblematisti," in *Ricerche Anglo-Italiane* (Rome, 1944), pp. 303-319.
(3) E. Arber, *A Transcript of the Registers of the Company of Stationers of London* (London, 1875), II, 631.

Miss R. Freeman and others have evidently failed to note, that an English translation of de la Perrière may have existed three years earlier, since the Stationers' Register refers to '*Le Theatre des bons Engins & c* to be printed in Englishe' under the date of August 17, 1590 (1). This is not the proper place to give a full-length survey of emblem writing on the Continent, suffice it to mention three Italians, Paolo Giovio, Girolamo Ruscelli and Lucas Contile, whose works were much studied in England.

The development of the 'science' of emblem writing in France and Italy failed to evoke an enthusiasm from the Elizabethans to rival the continental activity. Despite the lack of Elizabethan contributions, the influence of emblem books made itself felt in literature and a few early indications of the interest deserve mention. Sir Philip Sidney, for instance, writing to Languet in 1573 from Venice, promised to send his friend a copy of Ruscelli's *Imprese;* Edward VI owned Giovanni Marquale's Italian version of Alciati of 1549, and Geoffrey Whitney possessed a copy of the 1562 edition of Claude Paradin. The taste for emblems was also reflected in literature, for instance, in the poetry of Edmund Spenser, notably in *The Shepheardes Calender* (1579), a collection of eclogues which actually appeared before the first English emblem book, namely Geoffrey Whitney's *A Choice of Emblems* (Leyden, Plantin, 1586). Another important book in the field, translated and expanded from Paolo Giovio's *Ragionamenti* (1555), was *The VVorthy tract of Paulus Iouius, contayning a Discourse of rare inuentions, both Militarie and Amorous called Imprese* (London, 1585), by Samuel Daniel. In the address to Daniel, signed 'N. W.,' one finds the names of the emblematists Contile, Ruscelli, Domenichi, and Alciati, and, carrying yet further back, 'N. W.' refers to hieroglyphs and names Horus and Valeriano, who are said to have 'shadowed' 'their purposes and intents by figures' (2). A few years later, 'P. S.,' another unknown author, gave a version of Claude Paradin's *Devises Héroiques* (1591) (3).

The prolific Andrew Willet may claim to be the first to have compiled an emblem book in England independent of the continental

---

(1) ARBER, *Transcript*, II, 559.
(2) S. DANIEL, *The VVorthy tract of Paulus Iouius* (London, 1585), sig. A₅. Miss R. FREEMAN, *English Emblem Books*, p. 48, quotes and comments extracts from DANIEL.
(3) Entered on the same day as the translation from G. DE LA PERRIÈRE's work; see ARBER, *Transcript*, II, 558 (August 17, 1590).

example, *Sacrorum Emblematum Centuria Una* (1), undated, but presumably completed about 1592. The taste for emblems soon attracted many poets and playwrights, and numerous are the traces of their influence which scholars have been able to unearth from Elizabethan literature (2). A good testimony to the spread of emblem books is provided by Francis Meres who, in *Palladis Tamia* (1598), contrasting English emblematists with continental writers of like character, maintains that his countrymen do not lag behind: 'As the Latines have these *Emblematists*, Andreas Alciatus, *Reusnerus*, and *Sambucus:* so we have these, *Geffrey Whitney, Andrew Willet*, and *Thomas Combe*' (3).

A subject intimately related to the emblem is that of *imprese*. In this connexion Professor Praz's English translation from a passage in Giovio's *Imprese*, which gives a descriptive definition of the *impresa*, may conveniently be quoted.

In our time, after the descent of King Charles the Eighth and Louis the Twelfth into Italy, whoever followed the military profession imitated the French Captains, and wished to adorn himself with elegant devices, which glittered on the knights, divided company by company with different liveries, because they embroidered with silver-gilt their doublets, their cloaks, and on breast and back they wore the devices of their captains, so that the badges of the soldiers made a dainty and sumptuous pageant, and in the battles one could tell the boldness and bearing of each company (4).

An English imitator, Abraham Fraunce, following Giovio, puts the definition of an *impresa* as follows:

Itali vocant *Imprese*, a verbo *Imprendere:* ita vt sit negotium aliquod, quod quis constanti & confirmato animo obeundum suscepit (5).

Evidently sixteenth century people attached an immense importance to the tenor of the *impresa* or the device adopted by a nobleman. The emblem itself was often accompanied by a device or

---

(1) For WILLET see IRMA TRAMER, *Studien zu den Anfängen der puritanischen Emblemliteratur* (Berlin, 1934).

(2) See especially F. BRIE, "Shakespeare und die Impresa-Kunst seiner Zeit," *Shakespeare-Jahrbuch*, L (1914), 9-30, and M. PRAZ in the appendix on "Emblems and devices in literature," in *Studies*, pp. 187-206. F. BRIE, however, has nothing on SHAKESPEARE. For this see H. GREEN, *Shakespeare and the Emblem Writers* (London, 1870), a book generally discounted by modern scholars.

(3) F. MERES, *Palladis Tamia* (London, 1598), p. 285 v°.

(4) M. PRAZ, *Studies*, pp. 47-48.

(5) A. FRAUNCE, *Insignium* (London, 1588), sig. O_3.

motto, whose chief function was to enforce a moral or to symbolize the principal pursuit of a nobleman's life; *imprese*, after the original etymological meaning of the word, represented 'actions taken in hand,' or 'undertakings.' It is also clear from the Giovio passage quoted above that the fashion for devices and *imprese* is related to heraldry; most noblemen were deeply concerned to live up alike to the general rule of life expressed in their device and to the tenor of their blazon. As will be readily understood, devices or mottos could also serve a variety of other purposes. Queen Elizabeth's courtiers, for instance, often sent lovetokens to their Queen with messages in the form of mottos, a feature also put to account in the drama of the period.

As a typical example of how this type of symbolism had gained ground and of how emblematic conceits permeated literature, a passage from Robert Greene may be quoted, which incidentally brings to light that the more realistically minded were apt to burlesque *imprese*. In *The Spanish Masquerado* (1589), a tale which in its sub-title purports to discover 'the pride and insolencie of the Spanish' under a 'pleasant device' in 'certaine breefe Sentences and Mottoes,' we find that the Spaniards had imagined to be able to gain the victory in the time of the Armada by means of 'Hieroglyphicall Simbols, Emblems, impresses, and deuises' (1).

Let us now turn to a brief consideration of the Elizabethan conception of allegory prevalent in the early nineties, the years with which we will be most concerned. A general survey of the subject can be found in a pamphlet by J. McClennen (2). For our purpose it will suffice to call attention to two significant pronouncements. One is the familiar quotation from Sir John Harington's preface to his translation of Ariosto's *Orlando Furioso* (1591). In the translation itself Harington, on the basis of Simon Fornari's commentary (3), offers us a sustained allegorical interpretation of Ariosto's epic, and so it is not surprising to find the translator stating his opinion on the question of allegory. Considering that a reference to the myth of Perseus and the Gorgon crops up repeatedly

(1) R. GREENE, *Works*, ed. A. B. GROSART (London, 1881-6), V, 271-2.
(2) J. McCLENNEN, *On the Meaning and Function of Allegory in the English Renaissance* (Michigan, 1947).
(3) FORNARI's *Spositione sopra l'Orlando Furioso di M. L. Ariosto* (2 vols., Florence, 1549-50); see T. RICH. *Harington & Ariosto* (Yale, 1940), pp. 148-9.

in the writings of the early nineties, it is of consequence to note that, when referring to that myth, Harington pauses to digress on the purport of the allegorical device.

For the weaker capacities will feede themselues with the pleasantnes of the historie and sweetnes of the verse, some that haue stronger stomackes will as it were take a further taste of the Morall sence, a third sort, more high conceited then they, will digest the Allegorie: so as indeed it hath bene thought by men of verie good iudgement, such manner of Poeticall writing was an excellent way to preserue all kinde of learning from that corruption which now it is come to since they left that mysticall writing of verse (1).

The second statement is to be found in Abraham Fraunce's treatise *The Third part of the Countesse of Pembrokes Yuychurch* (1592), a handbook of mythology which will be discussed in greater detail in a later chapter. Fraunce's opinion, contemporaneous with Harington's but not so often quoted and indeed overlooked by J. McClennen and most commentators, is hardly less significant in that it states even more clearly that allegory is the means of conveyance *par excellence* for hidden mysteries. After having praised Plato for his allegorical discourses and having referred to the hidden multiple meaning of Solomon's song, Fraunce goes on in language which seems to recall Harington's:

He that is but of a meane conceit, hath a pleasant and plausible narration, concerning the famous exploites of renowmed *Heroes*, set forth in most sweete and delightsome verse, to feede his rurall humor. They, whose capacitie is such, as that they can reach somewhat further then the external discourse and history, shall finde a morall sence included therein, extolling vertue, condemning vice, euery way profitable for the institution of a practicall and common wealth man. The rest, that are better borne and of a more noble spirit, shall meete with hidden mysteries of naturall, astrologicall, or diuine and metaphysicall philosophie, to entertaine their heauenly speculation (2).

Both Sir John Harington and Abraham Fraunce declare that allegory is *the* garb in which to shroud mystical treasures, *the* vehicle chosen by a select few to convey divine knowledge, and *the* means to preserve that knowledge from corruption. Whether the claim

---

(1) Quoted from the reprint in *Elizabethan Critical Essays*, ed. G. Gregory Smith (Oxford, 1905, repr. 1950), II, 203.
(2) A. Fraunce, *The Third part* (London, 1592), sig. B$_2$.

was aesthetically justified seems not to have occurred to the m. Obviously, once the secondary meaning has to be detached by relying too much on the reader's intellectual powers, it loses most of its emotional appeal and aesthetic value. Much depends, however, on whether Harington and Fraunce wished to associate allegory with art; and also on whether they were sufficiently aware of the limitations of the allegorical method. For Fraunce at least, himself rather a poor poet, it seems probable that his *Third part* was no more than a mythological manual for prospective writers to use, while parts of it, as we will see, were on occasion pressed into the service of contemporary allusion.

CHAPTER II

THE EARLY NINETIES

THE YOUNG SHAKESPEARE
AND HIS COMPANY CONNEXIONS

Our concern with the relations between Elizabethan writers in the early nineties, renders it necessary to set forth the available evidence regarding Shakespeare's early theatrical activity. With regard to Shakespeare's so-called 'lost' years in London, highly competent critics have held different views. A fresh consideration of the theatrical situation in the years 1589-1592 is perhaps able to clarify part of the mystery which surrounds the history of the actors' companies. The theories here expounded can only hope to contribute something of consequence with regard to Shakespeare's association with Strange's men, while on occasion small bits of evidence will be supplied to confirm the view of other writers on the question. Ferdinando Stanley (born about 1559), summoned to Parliament as Lord Strange on January 28, 1589, succeeded his father as fifth Earl of Derby on September 25, 1593, and died in mysterious circumstances on April 16, 1594. He was presumably a man of high philosophic capacity whose influence on the trend of thought of many poets in the early nineties may have been much stronger than has hitherto been presumed.

If the date 1586 is the best guess for fixing Shakespeare's departure from Stratford-upon-Avon, it remains to study the period stretching from 1586 to the autumn of 1594, when there is documentary evidence that Shakespeare was with the Lord Chamberlain's men, the troupe patronized by Henry Carey, Lord Hunsdon, who had become Lord Chamberlain on July 4, 1585 (died July 22, 1596). In a record of performances given at Court on December 26 and 28, 1594—record dated March 15, 1595—William Shakespeare appears as joint payee with William Kempe and Richard Burbage, and they are mentioned as 'seruantes to the Lord Chamberleyne.' Previous to this date there is only imperfect evidence touching the great dramatist and perhaps this can best be examined chronologically.

Strange's men are mentioned for the first time as a regular company of actors in a letter from Lord Mayor Harte to Lord Burghley, dated November 5, 1589, which states that the Lord Mayor had given order to cancel performances in the city. Both the Lord Admiral's and the Lord Strange's players were summoned, but the latter company contemptuously refused and performed at the Cross Keys' Inn. The very fact that Strange's refused shows that it and the Admiral's company were completely separate organizations, whereas there are reasons for supposing that at a later date there was a partial fusion of the personnel of the two companies. Closely connected with the history of the Admiral's men is the role of Edward Alleyn, the famous actor, who, I believe, retained his status as an Admiral's servant throughout, but who, according to some scholars, temporarily transferred his services to Strange's, although Alleyn's fellow-actors can never be shown to have done so (1). The basis for this temporary association appears to be the fact that 'the reputation of Edward Alleyn about 1592 renders it almost incredible that he was never called upon to appear before the Queen between 1590-1 and 1594-5; and if he did so appear, it can only have been as a 'Strange's' man in 1591-2 and 1592-2' (2). Sir Edmund K. Chambers therefore supposes Alleyn to have been the effective manager of the company, and calls it the 'Alleyn company.' A further examination of the history of the two companies with respect to their association may not be superfluous.

In May 1591 there was a quarrel at the Theatre, the playhouse owned by James Burbage, where the two companies were playing together. Strange's men left and probably went to play at the Curtain, which was an 'easer' to the Theatre (3). A few months later Philip Henslowe began his famous *Diary* and the first company with which we find him connected is that of Lord Strange. From February to June 1592, and again from December to January 1593, Strange's players acted, probably at the Rose; so far as the extant records go, they started on February 19 with the play *Fryer Bacune*, that is Robert Greene's *The Honorable Historie of frier Bacon, and frier Bongay*. It should be noted that Henslowe's initial entry runs 'Jn the name of god Amen 1591 beginge the 19 of febreary my lord

---

(1) See W. W. GREG, "The Evidence of Theatrical Plots for the History of the Elizabethan Stage," *RES*, I (1925), 265.

(2) E. K. CHAMBERS, *William Shakespeare* (Oxford, 1930), I, 48.

(3) E. K. CHAMBERS, *The Elizabethan Stage* (Oxford, 1923), II, 393.

strangers mene a ffoloweth 1591' (1), which can hardly be considered good evidence for Strange's acting with the Admiral's. Several small items of the theatrical evidence, however, help the critics to assume an amalgamation between the two actors' companies. For instance, on June 10, 1592, Henslowe records the performance of 'A Knacke to Knowe a Knave,' preceded by the letters *ne* (generally interpreted as 'new'), and this play was published in 1594 with the mention on the title-page: 'sundrie tymes played by Ed. Allen and his Company.' Unfortunately, the company is not named, so that the Admiral's men may also have performed it, on the assumption that both companies of actors possessed a common stock of plays. Be that as it may, the actual position of Alleyn remains with the Admiral's, and he cannot with certainty be considered a servant of Strange's; in point of fact, his position may have changed and may have depended on the type of play that was put on the boards.

The description of Edward Alleyn's company connexions in 1592 is here set forth in some detail because his activity may have a bearing on the interpretation of Shakespeare's career in that year. Shakespeare apparently wrote for Strange's troupe, for Henslowe recorded on March 3, 1592, the performance of 'harey the vj,' which is almost certainly Shakespeare's *Henry the Sixth, Part I*. It must be stressed that this entry is the only direct evidence for Shakespeare's writing for Strange's. The play was a great success for it was performed thirteen or fourteen times before the theatrical season ended, and Thomas Nashe gives us further witness to its popularity (2). Another play, performed ten times in Henslowe's theatre, was 'tittus & vespacia'—first performance as a new play on April 11, 1592—and it is possible that Shakespeare was somehow indebted to, or concerned with, this piece, because it may eventually have become *Titus Andronicus*. The 1594 quarto title-page of *Titus Andronicus* indeed lends confirmation to this view for it states that it was played by 'the Earle of Darbie, Earle of Pembrooke, and Earle of Sussex their Seruants,' the Earl of Derby being of course identical with Lord Strange. In connexion with this question two other items of the theatrical evidence deserve notice.

The plague having made acting within the city impossible, the Privy Council issued a travelling license to the players, dated

(1) W. W. GREG, ed. *Henslowe's Diary* (London, 1904), I, 13.
(2) THOMAS NASHE, *Works*, ed. R. B. MCKERROW (London, 1910), I, 212.

May 6, 1593, of which the portion relevant to our discussion runs:

Whereas it was thought meet that during the time of the infection and continewaunce of the sicknes in the citie of London there shold no plaies or enterludes be usd, for th' avoiding of th' assemblies and concourse of people in anie usual place apointed nere the said cittie, and though the bearers hereof, Edward Allen, servaunt to the right honorable the Lord Highe Admiral, William Kemp, Thomas Pope, John Heminges, Augustine Phillipes and George Brian, being al one companie, servauntes to our verie good Lord the Lord Strainge, ar restrained their exercize of playing within the said citie and liberties thereof . . . (1)

The inclusion of Alleyn among the servants of Lord Strange depends on the interpretation of the phrase 'being al one companie' in relation to the context. It can of course be construed in two ways. My view is different from that of Chambers: I believe that the phrase only covers the five actors that appear immediately before it and that Alleyn receives specific mention because he was the prominent actor of the Admiral's and could hardly be dispensed with in provincial performances. The warrant by no means implies that they acted together in London or before the Queen; 'being al one companie' may mean no more than that the actors did not form one company when playing in the city, as those who drew up the warrant seem to have been aware.

Another interesting item with regard to the composition of the early acting companies is furnished by one of the documents now preserved at Dulwich College, namely the 'plot' of a play with the inscription *The Booke and Platt of the second part of the 7 deadly sinns* (2). The play itself was probably acted about 1590 by Strange's men at the Curtain. In this Plot the names of twenty actors are preserved and have their roles assigned, while for the parts of Henry VI and Lydgate no performers are indicated. Twelve of these are fully named: Mr. Pope, Mr. Phillips, Mr. Brian, Richard Burbage, Richard Cowley, John Duke, Robert Pallant, John Sincler, Thomas Goodale, William Sly, John Holland, and T. Belt. Most of these performers later appear in the Lord Chamberlain's troupe, with which Shakespeare was closely associated. Because of Alleyn's

---

(1) E. K. CHAMBERS, *Shakespeare*, II, 313 gives the full document.
(2) See especially W. W. GREG, *Dramatic Documents from the Elizabethan Playhouses* (Oxford, 1931). The term 'Plot' is here used as a highly technical term of the Elizabethan stage; it is the name of a document which gives a skeleton outline of plays, scene by scene, for use of the prompter on the stage.

eminent qualities as an actor it is peculiar that he should not be explicitly mentioned in the cast of the *Seven Deadly Sins*. This circumstance led Sir Walter Greg (1) to the inference that the Plot belonged to Strange's men alone, a view I believe to be correct. Now, three of the actors named have the honorific prefix Mr., which probably emphasizes their status as sharers. When we examine the names mentioned in the Plot and those given in the warrant, we notice that of the five actors mentioned in the previously quoted document two do not appear in the cast of the *Seven Deadly Sins*, namely William Kemp and John Hemings. For this reason we are perhaps entitled to infer that it was they who filled the unassigned roles (2). Sir Walter Greg, however, considers this improbable since Will Kemp was a clown of recognized position and it is almost inconceivable that he should have taken the part of either Henry VI or Lydgate, another clown being chosen to act 'Will Foole' (John Duke). Sir Walter then goes on to suggest that Lydgate was played by Hemings and Henry VI by Shakespeare, and though he concedes that it is a mere guess, I do not believe him to be wrong. With regard to the actual actors of the *Seven Deadly Sins* the authorship question is also of interest. Contemporary references in Gabriel Harvey's *Foure Letters* (1592) and Thomas Nashe's *Strange Newes of the Intercepting Certaine Letters* (1592), point to the famous comic actor Richard Tarlton as the writer, and since he was a prominent member of the Queen's men, a company whose fortunes were shattered by Tarlton's death in 1588, it is reasonable to think that they were the original performers of the *Seven Deadly Sins*. This affords yet another reason for thinking that the Queen's men merged after Tarlton's death into Strange's, and for thinking that Shakespeare was originally a Queen's man as well (3).

Several other indications point to Shakespeare's association with the Queen's men. George Peele, author of the *Old Wives' Tale* written for 'the Queenes Maiesties players,' also wrote *The Famous Chronicle of Edward I*, published in quarto in 1593. Unfortunately

---

(1) W. W. GREG, *RES*, I (1925), 261-2.

(2) E. K. CHAMBERS, *Shakespeare*, I, 52 takes it that Sir WALTER GREG suggested that they were filled by HEMINGES and KEMPE. But this rests on a misunderstanding since W. W. GREG, ed. *Henslowe's Diary*, II, 374 and *Dramatic Documents*, pp. 21, 46, follows the line of argument developed above.

(3) See A. W. POLLARD's introduction to P. ALEXANDER's *Shakespeare's 'Henry VI' and 'Richard III'* (Cambridge, 1929), pp. 1-28. A. W. POLLARD apparently subscribes to GREG's view concerning SHAKESPEARE's acting in the *Seven Deadly Sins*, see p. 16.

the title-page of that play does not tell us which company played it, but there is at any rate a nearness of date which makes it reasonable to think that it was also a Queen's play. Now, in this play there is a possible allusion to Shakespeare which may perhaps be accepted as evidence for Shakespeare having performed the part of Baliol. King Edward having assigned the crown of Scotland to Baliol, Queen Elinor addresses the latter as follows:

> Now, brave John Baliol, Lord of Galloway
> And King of Scots, shine with thy golden head;
> Shake thy spears, in honour of his name,
> Under whose royalty thou wear'st the same (1).
>
> (Edward I, Sc. iii, 70-73.)

Sir Edmund Chambers says that the evidence for Shakespeare's acting is not very convincing (2), but Professor A. W. Pollard holds that 'the flatness of the rhyming couplet is so glaring that [he] doubt[s] whether Peele at his worst could have written it, save for the sake of a friendly pun on the name of the actor who (subsequently known for his favour of royal parts) was playing Edward I' (3). The case for connecting Shakespeare with the Queen's men finds further support from the fact that three old Queen's plays formed the basis of three Shakespearean plays: they are *The Troublesome Reign of King John*, imprinted for Sampson Clarke in 1591; *The most famous chronicle historye of Leire King of England*, performed by the Queen's and Sussex' men in April 1594 (earliest extant edition, 1605); and *The famous victories of Henrye the Fyft*, licensed for publication on May 14, 1594. It is probable that Shakespeare used these plays because he knew them from his having acted in them or from performances by others.

The tantalizing feature of all this evidence is the anomalous fact that Shakespeare was possibly connected with the Queen's men, and probably wrote for Strange's—assuming that 'harey the vi' refers to Shakespeare's play—but he is never mentioned as an actor for either company, his name being listed for the first time as a servant to the Lord Chamberlain, together with Kemp and Burbage, in the Court record for December 1594. It is at this point that we must turn our attention to a play whose significance for the

---

(1) G. PEELE, *Works*, ed. A. H. BULLEN (London, 1888), I, 117.
(2) E. K. CHAMBERS, *Eliz. Stage*, III, 460.
(3) A. W. POLLARD, *Intr.*, p. 19.

reconstruction of theatrical events may have been insufficiently realized, namely Robert Greene's *Orlando Furioso*.

Greene's play, which presents interesting problems many of which were analysed by Sir Walter Greg in his *Two Elizabethan Stage Abridgements: The Battle of Alcazar & Orlando Furioso* (Oxford, 1923), was staged about 1592 and printed in a garbled version by John Danter in 1594. The evidence for ascribing the play to Greene is in fact indirect as *The Historie of Orlando Furioso* was published anonymously. In an anonymous pamphlet entitled *Defence of Cony-Catching* (1) Greene is attacked as follows: 'Aske the Queens Players, if you sold them not *Orlando Furioso* for twenty Nobles, and when they were in the country, sold the same Play to the Lord Admirals men for as much more. Was not this plaine Conny-catching Maister R. G. ?' This ascription of the play is supported by Allot, who assigns five out of the six quotations to Greene in *England's Parnassus* (1600). As Greene owes something to Sir John Harington's translation of Ariosto's *Orlando Furioso*, published in 1591 and entered in the Stationers' Register on February 26, 1591, it is highly probable that Greene wrote his drama in the autumn of 1591 (2). From Henslowe's *Diary* we learn that a play called 'orlando' was acted in February 1592 by Lord Strange's men at the Rose theatre. Just at this time the most famous actor of the Admiral's company, Edward Alleyn, may have allied himself temporarily with Strange's men and this apparently explains the charge of the anonymous pamphleteer of Greene's having sold the play to the Admiral's. The entry of performance at the Rose does not indicate that the play was new and the absence of a subsequent entry justifies the belief that the play was not a success. Before *Orlando Furioso* came to be printed it was twice entered in the Stationers' Register, on December 7, 1593 and on May 28, 1594 (3). But besides the quarto we possess a manuscript of the part of the actor to whom the role of Orlando was assigned (4). The corrections which this part bears are all in the hand of Edward Alleyn; he therefore studied the part, which was presumably written out for his use.

(1) *Defence* (1952), sig. C₃; see GREENE, *Works*, XI, 75. It was entered in the Stationers' Register on April 21, 1592; see ARBER, *Transcript*, II, 609.

(2) See W. W. GREG, *Two Elizabethan Stage Abridgements: The Battle of Alcazar & Orlando Furioso* (Oxford, 1923), p. 127.

(3) ARBER, *Transcript*, II, 641, 650.

(4) This actor's part is now at Dulwich College (MS. I, item 138, fols. 261-271); it is unfortunately incomplete and mutilated, but still contains the speeches of Orlando for some two-thirds of the play. It was fully studied by W. W. GREG.

When we examine the repertory of Strange's men it appears that three plays by Greene were put on the boards: *Friar Bacon and Friar Bungay*, *Orlando Furioso*, and *A Looking Glass for London and England;* the last-named play was written in collaboration with Thomas Lodge. Robert Greene had become acquainted with the Stanley family at an early date, having dedicated *The Myrrour of Modestie* (1584), *Penelopes Web* (1587) and *Ciceronis Amor* (1589) to Strange. It is therefore worth noting that the grumblings about more successful dramatists which we discern in Greene's writings after 1589 (1), probable owe their origin to his unsuccessful attempts to ingratiate himself with the Stanley family. And here the drift of Greene's famous pamphlet, *A Groatsworth of Wit*, written shortly before his death on September 3, 1592, may acquire fresh significance. Every student of Shakespeare has the passage by heart in which Greene sends a warning to his 'olde consorts, which haue liued as loosely' as himself, and yet, with apologies to the reader, I must perforce quote the relevant portions again. Having addressed the 'famous gracer of Tragedians,' unquestionably Marlowe, Greene admonishes young Juvenal, probably a reference to Thomas Nashe, and George Peele, after which comes the now famous allusion to Shakespeare as a 'Shake-scene' and an 'upstart crow'.

With thee I ioyne yong *Iuuenall*, that byting Satyrist, that lastly with mee together writ a Comedie. Sweet boy, might I aduise thee, be aduisde, and get not many enemies by bitter wordes: inueigh against vaine men, for thou canst do it, no man better, no man so well: thou hast a libertie to reprooue all, and name none; for one being spoken to, all are offended; none being blamed no man is iniured. Stop shallow water still running, it will rage, or tread on a worme and it will turne: then blame not Schollers vexed with sharpe lines, if they reproue thy too much liberty of reproofe.

And thou no lesse deseruing than the other two, in some things rarer, in nothing inferiour; driuen (as my selfe) to extreme shifts, a litle haue I to say to thee: and were it not an idolatrous oth, I would sweare by sweet S. George, thou art vnworthy better hap, sith thou dependest on so meane a stay. Base minded men all three of you, if by my miserie you be not warnd: for vnto none of you (like mee) sought those burres to cleaue: those Puppets (I meane) that spake from our mouths, those Anticks garnisht in our colours. Is it not strange, that I, to whom they all haue beene beholding: is it not like that you, to whome they all haue beene beholding, shall (were yee in that case as I am now) bee both at once of them forsaken? Yes trust them not: for there is an vpstart Crow, beautified with our feathers, that with his *Tygers hart wrapt in a Players*

---

(1) See R. Pruvost, *Robert Greene et ses romans (1558-1592)* (Paris, 1938), p. 335.

hyde, supposes he is as well able to bombast out a blanke verse as the best of you: and beeing an absolute *Iohannes fac totum,* is in his owne conceit the onely Shake-scene in a countrey. O that I might intreat your rare wits to be imploied in more profitable courses: & let those Apes imitate your past excellence, and neuer more acquaint them with your admired inuentions. I knowe the best husband of you all will neuer proue an Vsurer, and the kindest of them all will neuer proue a kind nurse: yet whilest you may, seeke you better Maisters; for it is pittie men of such rare wits, should be subiect to the pleasure of such rude groomes (1).

The phrase 'Tygers hart wrapt in a Players hyde' is, as everyone knows, a parody of the line

O tiger's heart wrapt in a woman's hide!

which occurs in 3 *Henry VI,* I, iv, 137, and in the corresponding place in *The True Tragedy of Richard Duke of York* (1595). It may be noted that the line parodied appeared in the very trilogy which, as acted by Strange's men, had scored such a great success at the Rose.

A few current interpretations of Greene's admonishments must now be referred to. In the first place, everybody has inferred from the outburst that Shakespeare must be numbered among the leading dramatists of the years 1590-1592, the playwright who threatened to eclipse the fame of the University Wits. Furthermore, eminent Shakespearean scholars such as Professor Peter Alexander, Sir Walter Greg and Sir Edmund Chambers have all interpreted the phrase about the 'upstart Crow,' 'beautified with our feathers' as a reference to Shakespeare the actor, because this was Greene's as well as Nashe's customary phraseology to vent their grievance against the acting profession (2). For instance, in Nashe's preface to Greene's *Menaphon* (1589), we hear about gentlemen who have 'trickt vp a companie of taffata fooles with their feathers' (3), and in Greene's *Never too Late* (1590), Cicero is represented as rebuking the actor Roscius thus: 'Why, Roscius, art thou proud with Aesop's crow, being prancked with the glorie of others' feathers? Of thy selfe thou canst say nothing, and if the cobbler hath taught thee to say 'Ave Caesar,' disdain not thy tutor because thou pratest in a king's chamber' (4). The aforementioned critics also hold that Greene's

---

(1) R. GREENE, *A Groatsworth of Wit,* ed. G. B. HARRISON (London, 1923), pp. 44-6.

(2) As far as I know, attention was first drawn to this similarity by R. SIMPSON, *The School of Shakspere* (London, 1878), II, 384.

(3) NASHE, *Works,* III, 323-4.

(4) GREENE, *Works,* VIII, 132.

words do not convey any charge of plagiarism, an interpretation first advanced by Edmond Malone and which held the field for more than a century until modern scholars utterly demolished it. There is, however, one eminent dissenter, Professor J. Dover Wilson who, in a recent article (1), has endeavoured to re-establish the claim originally put forward by Malone, that Shakespeare had been a former collaborator of Greene's. Both Dover Wilson and the interpreters he attacks are, however, at one in wondering why Greene was so angry with Shakespeare in August 1592, and why Shakespeare should have been denounced as a thief when, on the testimony of the master-printer Henry Chettle in *Kind-Heart's Dream* (published in December, 1592), we are informed that Shakespeare was gentle and known for his 'uprightness of dealing.' Greene's and Chettle's statements are indeed so incompatible as to exclude the interpretation of Greene's words in this sense that Shakespeare falsely appropriated other dramatists' plays.

We may now return to the former stages of this discussion and consider the bearing of Greene's *Orlando Furioso* on the interpretation of the pamphleteer's dying words. Professor Dover Wilson, in the article mentioned above, also hazards the suggestion that the final cause of Greene's ruin was the fact that he sold *Orlando Furioso* to two different acting companies in succession. It is possible that certain features of Alleyn's Orlando impersonation were offensive to Lord Strange, or perhaps, to other contemporary writers. The clues in the play are extremely vague and elusive, and chapter IV of the present volume attempts to furnish a few. But did other dramatists know Lord Strange?

The two fellow-playwrights who took most offence at Greene's admonishment have been generally identified as Marlowe and Shakespeare, Peele and Nashe being 'handled in a more friendly spirit,' as Sir Edmund K. Chambers puts it (2). Both Greene and Shakespeare can be shown to have had connexions with Strange, but Marlowe's case is different. The latter's *Jew of Malta* was indeed repeatedly put on by Strange's players, but most of Marlowe's plays were written for the Admiral's men, except *Edward II*, which is described on the title-page as a Pembroke play. Professor P.

---

(1) J. Dover Wilson, "Malone and the Upstart Crow," *Shakespeare Survey*, 4 (1951), 56-68.

(2) E. K. Chambers, *Shakespeare*, I, 59.

Alexander (1) uses this as evidence to connect Thomas Kyd, Marlowe, and Shakespeare as writers for the Pembroke company about 1590, and with respect to Shakespeare he may be right. For Marlowe, however, the interpretation is bound up with the identity of the noble lord, Kyd's patron, who had also engaged Marlowe. In June 1593 Thomas Kyd was arrested on suspicion of heterodoxy and to exonerate himself from the charge, Kyd wrote a letter to Sir John Puckering, from which we learn that two years earlier he had been writing in one room together with Marlowe.

My first acquaintance with this Marlowe, rose upon his bearing name to serve my Lord although his Lordship never knewe his service but in writing for his players; for never could my Lord endure his name or sight when he had heard of his conditions, nor would indeed the form of divine prayer used duly in his Lordship's house, have quadred with such reprobates (2).

Several noblemen (3) have been suggested as the person here referred to, but C. F. Tucker Brooke points out that Ferdinando Stanley, Lord Strange is the only satisfactory candidate for the identification, because Strange was probably sensitive to the Privy Council's opinion of his religious orthodoxy (4).

Thus we see that there is every reason to suppose that Greene may have had special motives for venting his wrath against his two former fellow-dramatists, of whom only Shakespeare had been able to be on friendly terms with the company's patron. And the obvious interpretation of the latter part of Greene's admonishment, quoted above, is surely that Greene's companions should seek another patron: 'whilest you may, seeke you better Maisters; for it is pittie men of such rare wits should be subiect to the pleasure of such rude groomes,' the 'groomes' being, of course, the actors. A fairly recent interpretation of Greene's celebrated passage is that offered by Karl Wentersdorf (5), who suggests that Greene had the Queen's men

---

(1) P. ALEXANDER, *Shakespeare's Life and Art* (London, 1939, repr. 1946), pp. 56-7.
(2) Quoted in full by C. F. TUCKER BROOKE, *The Life of Marlowe* (London, 1930), pp. 103-106.
(3) F. S. BOAS, ed. *The Works of Kyd* (Oxford, 1901), p. lxiv; W. W. GREG, ed. *Henslowe's Diary*, II, 79, and E. K. CHAMBERS, *Eliz. Stage*, II, 92-96 suggest ROBERT, FIFTH EARL OF SUSSEX.
(4) C. F. TUCKER BROOKE, *The Life of Marlowe*, p. 47. He is followed by P. KOCHER, *Christopher Marlowe* (North Carolina, 1946), p. 24.
(5) K. WENTERSDORF, "Shakespeares erste Truppe," *Shakespeare-Jahrbuch*, 84/86 (1948/1950), 114-130.

in mind, Greene having actually cheated that company and having thus abandoned the very company for which he and Shakespeare had formerly been writing. It looks more probable, however, knowing that the fortunes of the Queen's men had failed since 1590, that Greene was only ruminating on the recent disillusionments suffered in his connexions with Strange's players. It would thus seem that there is little doubt that the performance of *Orlando Furioso* in conjunction with the unscrupulous sale of the manuscript of the play was the cause of Greene's ruin. In an indirect way the foregoing argument also confirms the view that Shakespeare was writing, or trying to write, for Strange's men in the early months of 1592.

THE SCHOOL OF NIGHT

Literary historians need labels for their pigeon-holes and ever since Arthur Acheson in his work *Shakespeare and the Rival Poet* (London, 1903), supported the 'School of night' reading in *Love's Labour's Lost*, IV, iii, 254-56, many students of that play have accepted the phrase as a convenient designation to cover a society of noblemen and poets who entertained heretical views in religion and who indulged in speculations of an occult character in the early nineties. The presumable leader of this School was the brilliant courtier Sir Walter Ralegh, who, at almost any time of his eventful career, was the rival of Robert Devereux, Earl of Essex. The textual foundation of the phrase is to be found in the original Quarto reading:

> O paradox, Blacke is the badge of Hell,
> The hue of dungions and the Schoole of night:
> And beauties crest becomes the heauens well.
>
> (IV, iii, 254-56.)

Various critics since Acheson have supported the quoted version and they have pointed out that Shakespeare had Sir Walter Ralegh's society in mind here. Thus Professor J. Dover Wilson in the New Cambridge edition of *Love's Labour's Lost* (Cambridge, 1923), Miss M. C. Bradbrook in her book *The School of Night* (Cambridge, 1936) and Miss Frances A. Yates in *A Study of Love's Labour's Lost* (Cambridge, 1936) have all in various ways attached credence to the theory, although they may not have argued all the points. Recent students, however, approaching the problem from different angles, have thrown doubt on the correctness of the 'Schoole' reading, and have especially impugned the validity of the theories developed by the aforementioned critics with regard to whether Shakespeare's comedy is a satire on the school. Although I am aware of the questionable nature of the evidence, I must join with the originators of the School of Night theory, and I have already presented the reasons why the grounds for emendation suggested by E. A. Strathmann (1) are not imperative. The textual argument on which this is based need not be repeated here.

In the present section it is proposed to furnish an account of the external evidence for the existence of the School of Night. This will establish its reputed membership and expose the links between its adherents.

The contemporary documents which require examination are the following:

a) The Baines note, printed in C. F. Tucker Brooke's *Life of Marlowe*, pp. 98-100.

b) Thomas Kyd's letter to Sir John Puckering (British Museum, Harleian 6849, fol. 218), a portion of which has already been quoted.

c) Thomas Kyd's unsigned note to Puckering (Brit. Mus., Harleian 6848, fol. 154) also printed in C. F. T. Brooke's *Life of Marlowe*, pp. 98-100.

d) A *Responsio ad Elizabethae Edictum* written in 1592 by the Jesuit priest Robert Parsons under the pseudonym D. Andreas Philopater in answer to the edict of 1591 directed against Catholics (2); a summary in English was issued shortly after.

e) George Chapman's dedicatory epistles to *The Shadow of Night* (1594) and *Ovids Banquet of Sence* (1595).

Next to this direct testimony, there is, of course, the material which can be extracted from plays, poems and tracts written by the various members of the School of Night, but as can be readily understood, this indirect testimony can never be universally accepted,

---

(1) E. A. STRATHMANN, "The Textual Evidence for 'The School of Night'" *MLN*, LVI (1941), 176-86. See W. SCHRICKX, "Shakespeare and the 'School of Night,'" *Neophilologus*, XXXIV (1950), 35-44.
(2) Printed by G. B. HARRISON, ed. *Willobie his Avisa* (London, 1926), pp. 207-8. A copy of this *Responsio* is in the Ghent University Library. On PARSONS, see E. A. STRATHMANN, "Robert Parsons' Essay on Atheism," in *Joseph Quincy Adams Memorial Studies* (Washington, 1948), pp. 665-681.

since much will depend on the willingness of the individual critic to accept inferences from purely literary documents.

Sir Walter Ralegh employed Thomas Harriot, a mathematician of European renown, as his mathematical tutor. The earliest evidence to this effect occurs in the preface the navigator Richard Hakluyt wrote for Peter Martyr's *Decades Octo* (*Eight Decades*, Paris, 1587). The preface is addressed to Ralegh and contains recommendations for setting up an *institutus*.

Cum vero artis nauigatoriae peritia, praecipuum regni insularis orna-mentum, Mathematicarum scientiarum adminiculis adhibitis, suum apud nos splendorem posse consequi facile perspiceres, Thomam Hariotum, iuuenum in illis disciplinis excellentem, honestissimo salario iamdiu dona-tum apud te aluisti, cuius subsidio horis successiuis nobilissimas scientias illas addisceres, tuique familiares duces maritimi, quos habes non paucos, cum praxi theoriam non sine fructu incredibili coniugerent. Ex quo pul-cherrimo & sapientissimo instituto tuo, quid breui euenturum sit, qui vel mediocri iudicio volent, facile proculdubio diuinare poterunt. Vnum hoc scio, vnam & vnicam rationem te inire, qua primo Lusitani, deinde Castel-lani, quod antea toties cum non exigua iactura sunt conati, tandem ex animorum Votis perficerunt. Perge ergo Spartam quam nactus es ornare, perge nauem illam plusquam Argonauticam, ille cuparum fere capacem, quam sumptibus plane regiis fabricatam iam tandem foeliciter absoluisti, reliquae tuae classi, quam habes egregie instructam, adiungere (1).

From this extract one may reasonable deduce that Harriot had been Ralegh's close friend long before the time Hakluyt wrote his preface.

About seven years later, the famous navigator Captain John Davis, in the dedication of his book, *The Seamens Secrets* (1595), to Lord Charles Howard, Baron Effingham (whom Hakluyt called a second Neptune of the Ocean, in a passage not quoted above), also testified to the reputation enjoyed by Harriot, Thomas Digges, and John Dee and claimed that the English contribution to the science of astronomy was in no way inferior to that of continental scientists (2).

Besides Ralegh and Harriot, several poets and noblemen have been associated with the School of Night, namely George Chapman,

---

(1) See E. G. R. TAYLOR, ed. *The Original Writings & Correspondence of the two Richard Hakluyts* (London, 1935), Works issued by the Hakluyt Society, 2nd Ser., LXXVI. 359 ff.

(2) See F. R. JOHNSON, *Astronomical Thought in Renaissance England* (Baltimore, 1937), p. 226.

Christopher Marlowe, Matthew Roydon, and among noblemen, Ferdinando Stanley (Lord Strange), Henry Percy (ninth Earl of Northumberland), and Sir George Carey (afterwards Lord Hunsdon and patron of Shakespeare), a list which may not exhaust the number of possible members. In the view of some critics the persons just mentioned formed a close group which united the rivals of the Essex-Southampton circle, and it is in connexion with this rivalry that Shakespeare's *Love's Labour's Lost* is perhaps to be interpreted. Let us now examine some of the evidence itself.

George Chapman's dedicatory epistle to *The Shadow of Night* will be given first attention, because it is regarded as a sort of manifesto of the School by such critics as Miss M. C. Bradbrook and Miss F. A. Yates and because it may contain a reference to Shakespeare as a 'heavenly familiar.' In this epistle, addressed 'To my deare and most worthy friend master Mathew Roydon,' occurs the following passage:

> But I stay this spleene when I remember my good *Mat.* how ioyfully oftentimes you reported vnto me, that most ingenious *Darbie*, deepe searching *Northumberland*, and skill-imbracing *heire of Hunsdon* had most profitably entertained learning in themselues, to the vitall warmth of freezing science, & to the admirable luster of their true Nobilitie, whose high deseruing vertues may cause me hereafter strike that fire out of darknesse, which the brightest Day shall enuie for beautie (1).

Matthew Roydon (fl. 1580-1622), Chapman's good friend, was a minor poet of whom we know almost nothing, except that he is noted for having belonged to Sir Walter Ralegh's company, and for having written a poem on Sidney entitled *Elegie, or Friends passion for his Astrophill*, which appeared in the *Phoenix nest* (1593). 'Darbie' of course refers to Ferdinando Stanley, fifth Earl of Derby, and his mention is highly interesting, first for fixing the publication of Chapman's poem in early 1594, since 'Darbie' died on April 16, 1594; and second, because, as has been pointed out before, the Earl was somehow connected with Shakespeare's early theatrical activity. Furthermore, *Love's Labour's Lost* itself seems to reveal textual features which point to the Earl's concern with that play. The next person Chapman mentions is 'Northumberland,' that is

---

(1) GEORGE CHAPMAN, *The Poems*, ed. P. B. BARTLETT (New York, Modern Language Assoc. of America, 1941), p. 19. All subsequent references to CHAPMAN's poems will be to this edition.

Henry Percy, ninth Earl of Northumberland (1564-1632), chiefly known as a scholar and mathematician, whose reputation was such that contemporary gossip described him as the 'wizard earl.' About 1594 Northumberland married Dorothy Perrot, *née* Devereux, the sister of Penelope Devereux, Sidney's 'Stella,' and of the Earl of Essex; the marriage was unhappy from the first, and the violent quarrels of the couple formed the talk of the town. An interesting document has come down to us that reveals the Earl's aversion to marriage. Miss Frances A. Yates has discovered, in the Public Record Office, a manuscript copy of an essay by the Earl of Northumberland, which the official who calendared the document in the Calendar of State Papers (1) supplied with the title 'On the entertainment of a Mistress being inconsistent with the pursuit of Learning.' This was apparently a favourite theme of the Earl's, and, of course, it was also one of the well-known controversies among Renaissance thinkers; as late as 1605 the Earl of Northumberland bought a treatise *Inferiorita della Donna* (2), which again testifies to his general attitude towards women. The Earl of Northumberland's essay has been examined by Miss Yates, who concludes that it is the theme of Shakespeare's *Love's Labour's Lost*, reversed. This, then, is a further reason to believe in the existence of the School of Night.

The 'heire of Hunsdon' is George Carey, second Lord Hunsdon (1547-1603), who succeeded to the peerage in 1596. In his function of Lord Chamberlain (March 1596/97) he was patron of Shakespeare's company. To his wife, Lady Elizabeth Carey, Thomas Nashe dedicated *Christ's Tears Over Jerusalem* (1593) and *The Terrors of the Night* (1594), and these dedications, in view of Nashe's possible connexions with Shakespeare, again bid us suspect that artists in the days of Elizabeth were very much alive to each other's literary undertakings.

Another piece of evidence is Thomas Kyd's letter to Sir John Puckering. It will be remembered that Kyd had denounced Marlowe's atheism. In Kyd's letter we find the following interesting passage (contractions are expanded):

Ffor more assurance that J was not of that vile opinion, Lett it but please your Lordship to enquire of such as he conversd withall, that is

(1) Reprinted by Miss F. A. YATES, *A Study of Love's Labour's Lost* (Cambridge, 1936), pp. 206-211.

(2) See E. B. DE FONBLANQUE, *Annals of the House of Percy* (London, 1887), II, 350.

(as J am geven to vnderstand) with Harriot, Warner, Royden, and some stationers in Paules churchyard, whom J in no sort can excuse nor will excuse by reson of his companie, of whose consent if J had been, no question but J also shold haue been of their consort, for ex minimo vestigio artifex agnoscit artificem.

Thomas Kyd here mentions as associates Thomas Harriot, a certain unidentifiable Warner—unidentifiable because there are several—and Matthew Roydon, whose acquaintance we have already made. Harriot's great mathematical work *Artis Analytica Praxis*, edited by his disciples in 1631, ten years after the author's death, was dedicated to the Earl of Northumberland, and, considering that Harriot was Ralegh's mathematical tutor and that Roydon was mentioned by Chapman, it seems quite natural to assume that all these persons knew each other intimately. But was Chapman also an adherent of Ralegh's 'school of atheism'? It is not inconceivable that Chapman, Roydon, Harriot and Ralegh could meet each other on the common ground of scientific interests, but objections have of course been raised against the theory of an outspoken association between the poets and Ralegh, notably by P. Kocher in the introductory chapter of his book on Marlowe.

The chief external evidence for Ralegh's atheism is that in March, 1594, a commission was appointed to inquire into heresies in the county of Dorsetshire, Ralegh living at Sherborne, an estate granted him by Queen Elizabeth in January 1592. The commission met at Cerne Abbas and its depositions and interrogatories shed a valuable light on religious doctrine in Elizabethan times. The depositions have been fully transcribed by Professor G. B. Harrison for his edition of *Willobie his Avisa*. Only the *Responsio* (1592) by the Jesuit Robert Parsons deserves to be partly quoted here, and not any of the passages from the interrogatories held at Cerne Abbas, because these were probably held long after the completion of *Love's Labour's Lost*, and therefore of little use to the present argument.

Et certe si Gualteri quoque Raulaei schola frequens de Atheismo paulo longius processerit, (quam modo ita notam & publicam suis in aedibus habere dicitur, Astronomo quodam necromantico praeceptore; vt iuuentutis nobilioris non exiguae turmae, tam Moysis legem veterem, quam nouam Christi Domini, ingeniosis quibusdam facetijs ac dicterijs eludere, ac in circulis suis irridere didicerint, si haec inquam schola radices ac robur caeperit, & ipse Raulaeus in senatum delectus fuerit, . . .

In the English issue of the *Responsio* this runs:

> Of Sir Walter Rauleys schoole of Atheisme by the waye, and of the Conjurer that is M. thereof, and of the diligence vsed to get young gentlemen to this schoole, where in both Moyses, and our Sauior; the olde, and new Testamente are iested at, and the schollers taught amonge other thinges, to spell God backwarde.

From these extracts it is clear that Ralegh and his tutor Harriot had achieved notoriety as atheists and conjurers; and it may not be superfluous to point out that, according to the Latin testimony, they are accused of dabbling in necromancy, a feature also conspicuous in Chapman's early poem *The Shadow of Night*. Furthermore, it is evident that Ralegh's associates formed a 'school' in the popular mind, and that the terms used in the pamphlet and *Love's Labour's Lost* happen to coincide.

Another very important document is the so-called Baines note. About the time of Thomas Kyd's arrest a warrant was issued (May 18, 1593) to bring Marlowe before the Privy Council. A certain Richard Baines, hitherto unidentified (1), drew up 'A note Containing the opinion of on [sic] Christopher Marly Concerning his damnable opini Judgment of Religion, and scorn of Gods word.' The note (2) says that Marlowe 'affirmeth that Moyses was but a Jugler & that one Hariots being Sir W Raleighs man Can do more then he.' Does this mean that Marlowe knew Thomas Harriot intimately, or is Baines simply availing himself of the generally propagated rumours about Ralegh's heretical views and is Baines trying to accuse Marlowe by associating him with the notorious atheist's school? As it stands there is no clue for a confident decision, although Marlowe's profound interest in astronomy strongly suggests that the dramatist studied Harriot's speculations.

The question also arises whether Chapman shared Marlowe's views. Chapman's continuation of *Hero and Leander* (1598) indicates some friendship between both, but the date of publication reduces the significance of this fact for the interpretation of the religious situation in the early nineties. There are, however, four lines in Marlowe's *Doctor Faustus* which are perhaps not entirely worthless

---

(1) See F. S. BOAS, "Informer against Marlowe," *TLS*, Sept. 16, 1949, p. 608.

(2) Since P. KOCHER made such an extensive use of the BAINES note, its questionable validity has been tentatively established by L. and E. FEASY, "The Validity of the Baines Document," *NQ*, 194 (1949), 514-517.

with regard to a possible interdependence of the two poets. The quotation is from the 1616 quarto text (Faustus speaks).

> Now that the gloomy shadow of the night,
> Longing to view *Orions* drisling looke,
> Leapes from th' Antarticke world vnto the skie,
> And dyms the *Welkin*, with her pitchy breathe:
>
> (I, iii, 1-4.)

The 1604 quarto has in the first line 'shadow of the earth,' but the reading 'shadow of the night' is doubtless right since it appears together with the three other lines in the anonymous play *The Taming of A Shrew*, published in 1594. Sir Walter Greg (1) has drawn attention to this similarity, but other students have surely independently noted that the phrase 'shadow of the night' happens to coincide with the title of Chapman's earliest publication. It seems rather dangerous to attach any importance to the appearance of the phrase in Marlowe, though there may well be some connexion with Chapman. As will subsequently be shown, the stellar constellation Orion here mentioned is also one of the symbols Chapman uses in *The Shadow of Night*. For the time being it is not necessary to interpret Marlowe's lines as topical allusions, but I suggest that the appearance of 'shadow of the night' and Orion together was once meaningful in a special sense to Elizabethan readers and spectators, a meaning hidden to us in what appears to be merely rhetorical embellishment. Later investigators may be better equipped to reveal the full significance of these suggestive lines.

Be that as it may, Ralegh and Harriot were certainly intimates and so were Chapman and Roydon, but the precise position of Chapman, Marlowe and Shakespeare is bound to remain uncertain. Chapman's association with Ralegh is especially questionable, the only known link being the tenuous one with Roydon. It is of course tempting to group all the noblemen and the artists in a 'School of Night' or a 'School of Atheism' and posit their identity as Professor J. Dover Wilson and Sir Arthur Quiller-Couch have done (2); but it is perhaps more prudent to keep them apart, especially since we are in considerable doubt as to Shakespeare's early relations to Marlowe.

---

(1) W. W. GREG, ed. *Marlowe's 'Doctor Faustus'* (Oxford, 1950), pp. 310-311.
(2) J. DOVER WILSON and Sir A. QUILLER-COUCH, ed. *Love's Labour's Lost* (Cambridge, 1923), p. xxxii.

This seems to me an important objection to the identity of both schools, since Shakespeare's allusion to the 'School' can hardly be a gibe at Marlowe—actually the most prominent atheist according to contemporary gossip—for Shakespeare apparently held his 'dead shepherd' in very high esteem (1). Besides, there is no point at all in the reference to 'night' as far as Marlowe is concerned, and Miss M. C. Bradbrook has maintained (2) that Marlowe in his later writings repudiated the doctrine of the School, while her argument suggests that Marlowe may have been in a position quite different from that of the other adherents of the School. On the other hand, Chapman's religious attitude, as far as this can be determined, cannot be said to have been tainted by atheism; neither does any of his poems reveal that urge to shake off the bonds of religious convention which led the more ardent supporters of Ralegh into difficulties with Her Majesty's Commissions of Justice. And Chapman's *Shadow of Night*, which from its date should have displayed affinities with atheist thought, fails to do so in any respect. Then, too, the Earl of Derby, whom Chapman addresses, seems to have felt uneasy about any taint of heresy, for he entertained Catholic convictions of a kind and, through his mother Margaret Clifford, was a possible claimant to the throne, forming the centre of a plot in 1593-1594.

For the reasons just discussed I am inclined to believe that there were actually two groups, one centering in Sir Walter Ralegh and the other embracing those mentioned by Chapman in the epistle to Roydon. That there must have been points of contact seems hardly disputable. The whole Renaissance period was, indeed, one of amalgamation and literary contacts, and the two groups could not but know of each other's pursuits. Paul Kocher's strictures on the alleged uniformity of doctrine seem fully justified; 'the only discoverable principle of unity among the several individuals is an earnestness of desire for knowledge,' says Kocher, and I agree, with the restriction, however, that the Earl of Northumberland's process of thinking *is* closely akin to Chapman's. Anyone who takes the trouble to examine the Earl's essay and Chapman's *Shadow of*

---

(1) This is based on the generally accepted reference to MARLOWE in *As You Like It*, III, v, 82-83 :

> Dead shepherd, now I find thy saw of might,
> 'Who ever loved that loved not at first sight?'

This is the 'only fellow-poet to whom Shakespeare directly refers in his plays' says Sir EDMUND K. CHAMBERS, *Shakespeare*, I, 69.

(2) M. C. BRADBROOK, *The School of Night* (Cambridge, 1936), pp. 120-21.

Night will notice a striking affinity between the two minds. And Kocher, apparently, does only scant justice to Miss Yates' chapter on the Earl of Northumberland and Stella's sister, a chapter which reveals how the Earl's essay is related to contemporary thought (1).

The presumable doctrine of the School may now be briefly sketched. Any uniformity being out of the question, it is only possible to describe some aspects of the general background of sixteenth century thought. The best exponents of the thought of the School would have been Harriot and Ralegh, but, as I have confined myself to a study of the writings of the early nineties, their works are not of much use to the present survey. It is regrettable that, the succinct treatment by Miss M. C. Bradbrook excepted, no other information is at present accessible. For the philosophy of Ralegh a few publications, mentioned in the footnote below, are instructive (2).

As worthy exponents of a truly Renaissance spirit the adherents of the School seem to have conceived a novel enthusiasm for the sciences which gradually unsettled the stability of medieval thinking: astronomy, mathematics and alchemy were beginning to interest an ever-growing number of questioning minds, while those of a more philosophic bent were the admirers of some form of Stoicism or neo-Platonism. In the field of astronomy, Copernicus (1473-1543), Tycho Brahe (1546-1600) and Johann Kepler (1571-1630) need only be mentioned as the celebrated astronomers of the age; their findings were eagerly discussed and made accessible to Elizabethan readers by such able scientists as Robert Recorde and John Dee (3). The former was the first in England to give an account of the Copernican system in *The Castle of Knowledge* (1556), and the latter, Queen Elizabeth's famous astronomer, numbered Tycho Brahe among his continental friends. John Dee's pupil, Thomas Digges, was the author of a treatise entitled *Perfit Description of the Caelestiall Orbes*,

---

(1) See PAUL H. KOCHER, *Christopher Marlowe. A Study of his Thought, Learning and Character* (North Carolina, 1946), Chap. I, *passim;* and F. A. YATES, *A Study of Love's Labour's Lost*, pp. 137-151.

(2) C. F. T. BROOKE, "Sir Walter Ralegh as Poet and Philosopher," *JELH*, V (1938), 93-112. Reprinted in *Essays on Shakespeare and other Elizabethans* (Yale, 1948), pp. 121-144; E. A. STRATHMANN, "Sir Walter Ralegh on Natural Philosophy," *MLQ*, I (1940), 49-61; and E. A. STRATHMANN's latest contribution, *Sir Walter Ralegh, A Study in Elizabethan Skepticism* (New York, 1952).

(3) See E. B. KNOBEL, "Astronomy and Astrology," in *Shakespeare's England* (Oxford, 1916), I, 444-461; F. R. JOHNSON, *Astronomical Thought in Renaissance England* (Baltimore, 1937) and D. C. ALLEN, *The Star-Crossed Renaissance* (North Carolina, 1941).

a work which enjoyed an enormous popularity, as is evident from the no less than seven editions which appeared from 1576 to 1605. The dissemination of mathematical and astronomical knowledge was especially encouraged because the findings of astronomers could be applied practically by the explorers of the seas.

In matters of philosophy the adherents of the School were advocates of Stoicism in relying upon reason to a much greater extent than religious decency permitted. This Stoical attitude entailed a disdain of the mob, a feature which crops up frequently in the writings of the School. Their disdain sprang from the arrogant belief that they exceeded the ordinary run of mortals, and their inborn haughtiness and pride was a matter of common knowledge.

Stoicism was also accompanied by the revival of some form of Platonism, historically traceable to the famous Florentine Academy of the Quattrocento, as whose distant offshoot the School of Night might, in a way, be regarded. Nor are the similarities merely external. Chapman, for instance, was well acquainted with Ficino's commentaries on the Platonic dialogues; and the School seems to have shared Ficino's enthusiasm for Hermetic teaching as well, for in the writings of the early nineties the authority of Hermes is frequently invoked. The type of Hermetic doctrine by which some of the members of the School were probably tainted can only be determined with difficulty. In its essence Hermetic doctrine expounds that it can liberate man from the slavery of the body, matter being the root of evil. The spread of Hermetic teaching, for which Ficino was partly responsible, went hand in hand with an ever-growing tendency towards the obscure in literature, and it is therefore not entirely accidental—as has already been pointed out—that French sixteenth century writers, among them Marguerite de Navarre, Lefevre d'Etaples, and Rabelais, show occasional traces of allegiance to Hermes Trismegistos (1). Knowing that it is possible to speak of a French Renaissance in England (2), it need not surprise us that

(1) See A. LEFRANC, "Le platonisme et la littérature en France à l'époque de la Renaissance" and "Marguerite de Navarre et le platonisme de la Renaissance," in *Grands Écrivains de la Renaissance* (Paris, 1914), pp. 63-249. LEFRANC, p. 94, also suggests that it is not impossible that the famous Lyons group of artists had its own academy on the model of that of Florence.

J. FESTUGIÈRE, *La philosophie de l'amour de Marsile Ficin et son influence sur la littérature française au XVIe siècle* (Paris, 1941) shows the indebtedness of the Lyons group to FICINO. One of its poets, SYMPHORIEN CHAMPIER took a profound interest in HERMES (see pp. 67, 69, 76).

(2) See SIDNEY LEE, *The French Renaissance in England* (Oxford, 1910).

the adherents of the School of Night should have inherited a reverence for Hermes from French sixteenth century artists, and that they should be indebted to Hermes for their spiritual attitude. The Earl of Northumberland and his followers also dabbled in the occult sciences, another claim to esoteric supernatural powers and a device for stressing the fact that they belonged to an intellectual élite.

CHAPTER III

CHAPMAN'S *THE SHADOW OF NIGHT* AND SOME NOTES ON CHAPMAN'S IMAGERY

One of the most baffling and recondite poems of Elizabethan literature, *The Shadow of Night* has received its due as far as interpretations are concerned (1), not so much because this poem possesses extraordinarily poetical qualities as because its language offers wide scope for interpretative conjecture. That there is method in Chapman's madness has been fully laid bare in a brilliant article by R. W. Battenhouse; this poem, obscure though it may be, does reveal a meaning after long and assiduous scrutiny. *The Shadow of Night* was published in a quarto edition in the early months of 1594; it had been entered in the Stationers' Register on December 31, 1593, so that the poem may be said to have existed in its entirety at the latest by the end of 1593. The title-page informs us that *The Shadow of Night* consists of two hymns, the *Hymnus in Noctem* and the *Hymnus in Cynthiam*, titles which, of course, tell us that Chapman is going to celebrate and extol the virtues of the 'Night' and the 'Moon' (2). Most critics have noted that Chapman's entire composition turns on the contrast between night and day, moon and sun, the sole logical element in a heap of bewilderingly confusing elaborations. Also the dedicatory epistle to Matthew Roydon, which precedes the hymns, reveals this fundamental distinction.

Those who wanted to attach a meaning to the poem were confronted with a wilfully obscure style and had to work their way through Chapman's far-fetched mythological similes. Swinburne first

---

(1) J. SPENS, "Chapman's Ethical Thought," *ESEA*, XI (1925), 149-169.
F. L. SCHOELL, *Études sur l'humanisme continental*, p. 36 ff.
E. HOLMES, *Aspects of Elizabethan Imagery* (Oxford, 1929), pp. 72-101.
M. C. BRADBROOK, *The School of Night*, pp. 127-150.
D. BUSH, *Mythology and the Renaissance Tradition*, pp. 199-215.
R. W. BATTENHOUSE, "Chapman's *The Shadow of Night*: An Interpretation," *SP*, XXXVIII (1941), 584-608.

(2) It may be of some use to note something that the critics do not deem noteworthy. RONSARD wrote a *Hymne à la nuit*, which is paraphrased from the *Hymnus in Noctem* by JOAN. JOV. PONTANUS, to be found in the latter's *Amores* (Paris edition of 1791, p. 149). The theme of these poems, however, is the exact reverse of that of CHAPMAN's hymns.

voiced these feelings of disgust when he said that there was no perceptible centre towards which Chapman's ravelled lines of thought converged. The poet was enticed by the antithesis day-night, and he was forced to work it to death by attaching to this central pair a variety of allied notions, which can only be determined from a repeated examination of the hymns. 'Night' thus stands for purity, or reason, whereas 'Day' is regarded as the root of all evil, whoredom and lust.

In the matter of interpretation the mythological handbook of Natalis Comes, as Professor F. L. Schoell points out, may be of material assistance. As the subsequent argument will certainly appear disconnected, I may plead in excuse that Chapman's poem itself is characterized by an utter lack of coherence. The main, indeed the only, burden of the poem is that the glories of night are unequalled, that night embodies our highest aspirations, and that its empire is being usurped by an enemy and debaucher who can best be named by the common denominator 'day'. These are the obvious themes, but they are most of the time developed with the help of very elaborate and far-fetched mythological similes. My main purpose in the following pages has been to establish points of contact with kindred writers, Elizabethan and otherwise, and to elucidate the mythological references.

Chapman opens his first hymn with an invocation to night couched in the 'hermetic' language of the prophet.

> Great Goddesse to whose throne in Cynthian fires,
> This earthlie Alter endlesse fumes exspires,
> Therefore, in fumes of sighes and fires of griefe,
> To fearefull chances thou sendst bold reliefe,
> Happie, thrise happie, Type, and nurse of death,
> Who breathlesse, feedes on nothing but our breath,
> In whom must vertue and her issue liue,
> Or dye for euer; now let humor giue
> Seas to mine eyes, that I may quicklie weepe
> The shipwracke of the world: or let soft sleepe
> (Binding my sences) lose my working soule,
> That in her highest pitch, she may controule
> The court of skill, compact of misterie,
> Wanting but franchisement and memorie
> To reach all secrets: then in blissfull trance,
> Raise her (deare Night) to that perseuerance,
> That in my torture, she all earths may sing,
> And force to tremble in her trumpeting

Heauens christall temples: in her powrs implant
Skill of my griefs, and she can nothing want.

(*Hymnus in Noctem*, 1-20.)

The influence of Comes' *Mythologiae* is widespread throughout
this poem. It occurs at the very start. In the gloss appended to
the first line of the above-quoted extract, Chapman explains that
Cynthian fires are those of Cynthius or the sun, and Schoell shows
that the gloss itself is derived from the *Mythologiae*, III, 12, *De
Nocte*, whence the poet also borrows the comparison of the earth
to an altar. Part of this gloss runs: 'That the earth is cald an aulter,
Aratus in *Astronimicis* testifies in these verses.' There are two writers
whose thought bears some resemblance to Chapman's. First there is
Thomas Hill, one of the opponents of Copernicanism in Elizabethan
times, who has the following statement in his posthumously published
textbook *The Schoole of Skil* (1599): 'The celestiall figure named the
Aulter, doeth *Aratus* place in heauen, under that beast called the
Wolfe, neare to the South, and standing under the taile of
Scorpius' (1). Though Hill's sense does not tally with Chapman's,
it looks as though Hill was also familiar with Comes' work, and it is
even possible that he belonged to Chapman's associates, a suspicion
strengthened by the fact that Hill's textbook reveals other points of
contact with Chapman's poem which will be mentioned in due course.

On the other hand, Thomas Edwards' *Cephalus and Procris*
(1595), entered in the Stationers' Register as early as October 22,
1593—note that this precedes the date of entry of *The Shadow of
Night* by two months—contains a dedicatory poem to Thomas Argall,
Esquire, in which occurs the following distich:

What were it then for me to praise the light?
When none, but one, commendes darke shady night.

Mrs. C. C. Stopes (2) seems to be quite right when she suggests that
Edwards resembles Shakespeare in having a little grudge against
Chapman; and in view of Chapman's contrasting day and night
it is surely worth noting that Edwards, in his humility, states in the
same poem that he does not wish to 'straine foorth' his pen 'to tilt
against the Sunne.' The initial lines of the second stanza of Edward's

---

(1) THOMAS HILL, *The Schoole of Skil* (London, 1599), pp. 89-90.
(2) See C. C. STOPES, "Thomas Edwards, Author of 'Cephalus and Procris'," *MLR*,
XVI (1921), 209-223.

poem are even plainer in maintaining that day is the true preserver of art.

> Then as the day is made to shame the sinner,
> To staine obscuritie, inur'd supposes,
> And mainetaine Artes inestimable treasure,
> To blind-fold Enuie, barbarisme scorning (1).

And from the prose dedication 'The the Honorable Gentlemen & true fauorites of Poetrie' the following passage may be cited in support:

> How many when they tosse their pens to eternize some of their fauourites, that although it be neuer so exquisite for the Poeme, or excellent for memoriall: that either begin or end not with the description of blacke and ougly night, as who would say, my thoughts are obscur'd and my soule darkened with the terrour of obliuion.

Edwards, however, is at one with Chapman in regarding Cynthia, the Great Goddess who relieves Chapman in his distress, as the true embodiment of science.

> Base necessitie, which schollers hate as ignorance, hath beene Englanddes shame, and made many liue in bastardy a long time: Now is the sap of sweete science budding, and the true honor of *Cynthia* vnder our climate girt in a robe of bright tralucent lawne: Deckt gloriously with bayes, and vnder her faire raigne, honoured with euerlasting renowne, fame and Maiesty.

Though Edwards is surely thinking of Queen Elizabeth, it is probable, in view of the existence of similar praises of Cynthia in the literature of the early nineties, that a large group of Elizabethans attached a secondary meaning to 'Cynthia' as a symbol attracting the worshippers of divine knowledge. Compare Edwards' phrase 'Cynthia vnder our climate girt in a robe of bright tralucent lawne' with a few lines at the end of Chapman's *Hymnus in Noctem*, 394-5, where Luna, or Cynthia for that matter, is hailed as

> great Hyperions horned daughter drawne
> Enchantresse-like, deckt in disparent lawne...

'Disparent,' of course, means either 'disappearing' or 'of various

---

(1) The British Museum copy of EDWARDS' work is unfortunately incomplete. The full text was edited by W. E. BUCKLEY in the Roxburghe Society Reprints (1882).

appearance' ('dis' in the sense 'diversely'), the latter sense being the more probable here. Schoell thinks that Chapman derived the lines just quoted from Comes' chapter *De Aurora* (*Mythologiae*, VI, 2), but this is slightly incorrect since in that case great Hyperion's daughter would be Aurora, not Luna. The source, therefore, is the chapter *De Luna* (III, 17), where the lines from Hesiod given by Chapman in his own glosses are also quoted. This is an example of the transmission of mythology that may profitably remind us that mythographers generally were far from consistent in their genealogies.

A few further points of contact between Chapman and Edwards remain to be mentioned. Edwards, like Chapman, begins his poem in praise of

> Faire and bright *Cynthia*, Ioues great ornament,
> Richly adorning nightes darke firmament, . . .

Edwards in this place gives a marginal gloss 'A pariphrisis of the Night,' which echoes Chapman's 'This *Periphrasis* of the Night he vseth' in gloss 10 to the *Hymnus in Noctem;* a point of incidental interest is that it seems to have been a favourite with poets, since it also occurs in the margin of Marlowe's *Hero and Leander*, First Sestiad, 190.

It is generally recognized that *Cephalus and Procris* seems to have been consciously designed to emulate *The Shadow of Night* by the employment of an analogous theme and by borrowing from Chapman's phraseology. The topical interest of Edwards' poem is shown by the fact that Shakespeare, as many scholars believe, refers to it in *A Midsummer-night's Dream*, V, i, 200-201 :

> *Pir.* Not *Shafalus* to *Procrus*, was so true,
> *This.* As *Shafalus* to *Procrus*, I to you.

Let us now turn back to Chapman's initial stanza, quoted before. The poet besought soft sleep to bind his senses in order to allow his working soul the fullest scope of activity. This emphasis on the suppression of the senses as a necessary preliminary to the penetration into the eternal mysteries happens to coincide with certain aspects of the Hermetic doctrine. In *Poemander*, 30, Hermes states in language closely similar to Chapman's :

Ego autem Poemandri beneficium inscripsi penetralibus animi, atque adeptus, quae petieram omnia, in gaudio requieui. corporis enim somnus, animi sobrietas extiterat: oculorum compressio, verus intuitus: silentium meum, bonitatis foecunda praegnatio: sermonis prolatio, bonorum omnium genitura. Haec mihi contigerunt ex mente haurienti, id est ex Poemandro diuinae potentiae verbo. vnde ipse diuino afflatus spiritu, veritatis compos effectus sum (1).

The obliteration of the senses is here clearly conveyed as necessary to the intuition of truth. Chapman's thought is also coloured by Platonism: the poet's soul is wrought to its highest pitch and can only penetrate all secrets with the aid of liberty and memory. In the first stanza of the *Hymnus in Noctem*, then, Chapman's flamboyant mind has woven together several threads of thought. The occult atmosphere which characterizes the first stanza pervades the whole composition; the language in which Chapman 'hollows up' his 'confusions' is involved, ecstatic and prophetic, and the poet thus intimates that the cult of night can be celebrated only by those who have been initiated.

In the course of his composition Chapman frequently develops closely connected themes. One of these may perhaps be further explored because Comes' Latin treatise may shed light on it. The notion of 'humor' finds particular favour with our poet. It would be tedious to enumerate all the instances in which this reference crops up, but the theme is presented for the first time in the initial stanza:

> now let humor giue
> Seas to mine eyes, that I may quicklie weepe
> The shipwracke of the world:

One wonders what Chapman means by 'humor'; at lines 376-77 of the *Hymnus in Noctem*, however, occurs a couplet which may explain part of its meaning and apparently indicates the place from which it is derived.

> No pen can any thing eternall wright,
> That is not steept in humor of the night.

The phrase 'humor of the night' is perhaps traceable to Comes, who states in his chapter *De Nocte* (III, 12):

(1) The translation here quoted is that made by FICINO, who translated the *Poemander* after MS. Laurentius, 71, 33, in 1463. Edition used: *Mercurii Trismegisti Poemander* (Paris, A. Turnebus, 1553). The Hermetic writings are now put together under the name *Corpus Hermeticum*; recent edition by J. FESTUGIÈRE and A. D. NOCK (Paris, 1945), see vol. I, p. 17.

Dicta est eadem mater omnium, quia rerum omnium partum ante-
cesserit, & a nocendo Nox dicitur, vt quidam voluerunt, quia noctis
humor infestus sit hominibus, quod vel in laborantibus scabie, vel febre,
vel aliis morbis patet; qui quidem grauiores fiunt, magisque infestant per
noctem (1).

Though the *De Nocte* chapter has left many traces in Chapman's
composition, it is noticeable that the poet merely picks out a phrase
from a context and deviates from the interpretation his authority
offers, Comes expressly stating that the mists of night are harmful
to mankind. As far as I have been able to gather from the *Mythologiae*,
Comes hold a more favourable view of the humour of the night
in the *De Somno* (III, 14), where it is also linked with the idea of
generation, issue, or birth, a great favourite with the mythographers.

Cum enim noctis humor stomachi vapores ad supremas partes corporis ascendentes augeat, qui postea facti frigore cerebri frigidiores des-
cendunt inferius, atque ita gignant somnum, iure optimo Somnus dictus
est Noctis filius. Ab illo maxime plantarum & animalium omnium fit
incrementum, quibus per aetatem id licet, quod accidit nocturni humoris
beneficio: cum vis diurni caloris interim tanquam occulta vis fermenti
in corporibus lateat, dum nox superueniat (2).

Though Comes applies his interpretation to the vegetative life only,
Chapman's view of the beneficence of the humour of the night
runs parallel with that of Comes, except that the English poet regards
this humour as a furtherer of his contemplative leanings.

Two passages remain for consideration. After having deplored
that 'Night' has allowed 'Day' to disturb her serene rule, Chapman
winds up his lament by referring to the myth of the nymph
Amalthea (lines 105-111). Chapman doubtless allegorizes Amalthea
as the horn of plenty (cornucopia); but, Chapman maintains, she
is unable to confer her benefits upon mankind, even though she was
transferred to heaven by Jupiter. Such is the miserable condition
of the universe that even divine beings cannot work their 'kindnesse
in our hearts.' Chapman then refers to the ship of the Argonauts,
which Jupiter did not exclude from heaven either. And the examples
just cited are held up by the poet as a warning to 'stone-peasants.'

---

(1) COMES, *Mythologiae* (Padua, 1616), p. 120. See also W. SCHRICKX, "George
Chapman's Borrowings from Natali Conti," *English Studies*, XXXII (1951), 107-112.
(2) COMES, *Mythologiae*, p. 123.

> The sencelesse Argiue ship, for her deserts,
> Bearing to Colchos, and for bringing backe,
> The hardie Argonauts, secure of wracke,
> The fautor and the God of gratitude,
> Would not from number of the starres exclude.
>
> (Lines 112-116.)

Again Chapman's authority is Comes, and again it is noteworthy that Thomas Hill in his *Schoole of Skil* supplies an analogous interpretation.

> The long *Ship* (named *Argo*) not the whole forme of it is described or seene among the stars (in that it is deuided from the fore part unto the mast) that may signifie to men litle to dispayre although the Shippe happen to breake (1).

All this argues the prevalence of the allegorizing tendency. And seeing that Richard Hakluyt, in the preface to Peter Martyr's *Decades Octo* (quoted in the second chapter), had used the particular imagery of the Argonauts to refer to Ralegh's maritime exploits, it is probable that Chapman may have had Ralegh in mind in his own poem also.

At 328-333, the second passage to be considered, Chapman exhorts his fellows to

> Come to this house of mourning, serue the night,
> To whom pale day (with whoredome soked quite)
> Is but a drudge, selling her beauties vse
> To rapes, adultries, and to all abuse.
> Her labors feast imperiall Night with sports,
> Where Loues are Christmast, with all pleasures sorts:

In view of Professor J. Dover Wilson's belief that *Love's Labour's Lost* was performed at Christmas, it is tempting to suppose that the last line here quoted might refer to this (2); and one wonders whether there is any significance in the fact that 'Loues are Christmast' occurs in the 333rd line, obviously a magic number.

With the *Hymnus in Cynthiam* Chapman enters upon a new and important phase of his argument. It has already been mentioned that to Elizabethan poets in the early nineties the figure of Cynthia

---

(1) HILL, *The Schoole of Skil*, p. 91.
(2) See J. D. WILSON, ed. *Love's Labour's Lost* (Cambridge, 1923), p. 127.

was the embodiment of a kind of divine Platonic idea which the poets longed to attain. Chapman incorporates this figure in his nocturnal symbolism, and Cynthia exercises her divine powers wherever night has obliterated 'outward bravery' and created that kind of hypnotic trance which alone permits 'insight' into the divine mystery. As has often been observed, this otherworldly aspiration was associated with the veneration of Queen Elizabeth, a Cynthia who, parallel to the Platonic cosmic soul, ruled her subjects, she being a kind of fecund principle from which Elizabeth's courtiers derived their whole existence. The result of such a conception was the association of the sacred and the profane sphere, deliberately fostered by the revival of Platonism in the sixteenth century (1). The theme of Cynthia in this role is consistently developed by Chapman: she rules the fates, she commands the spirits of every region, and by her eternal beauty she has the power of 'scorching the wings of time.' The only disturber of Cynthia's inspiring 'forces of the mind' is again 'love,' an idea also developed in the first hymn.

> So since that adamantine powre is giuen
> To thy chast hands, to cut of all desire
> Of fleshly sports, and quench to Cupids fire:
> Let it approue: no change shall take thee hence,
> Nor thy throne beare another inference.
>
> (*Hymnus in Cynthiam*, 26-30.)

After this succinct outline of the intellectual mood of the *Hymnus in Cynthiam* a few connexions with contemporary literature may be pointed out. As many critics have noted, lines 162-165:

> Presume not then ye flesh confounded soules,
> That cannot beare the full Castalian bowles,
> Which seuer mounting spirits from the sences,
> To looke in this deepe fount for thy pretenses:

distinctly recall the Ovidian motto Shakespeare prefixed to *Venus and Adonis* (1593).

> Vilia miretur vulgus; mihi flavus Apollo
> Pocula Castalia plena ministret aqua.
>
> (Ovid, *Amores*, I, 15, 35-36.)

---

(1) The question arises, however, whether any reference whatever to Cynthia may be so interpreted. Indeed, the unanimity of critics has never made allowance for a different view, and one often has a feeling that not all references to Cynthia, or Diana for that matter, allude to QUEEN ELIZABETH.

The change from 'ye' to 'thy' in Chapman's lines is surely tell-tale, and the two extracts have often been quoted to support the theory that Chapman is the Rival Poet of the Sonnets. We may also expect Shakespeare to have been aware of the significance of his motto and it certainly throws light on the poet's artistic ideals.

The passage at 410-417, however, is one which no critic of *The Shadow of Night* has ever given adequate attention.

> Come Goddesse come, the double fatherd sonne,
> Shall dare no more amongst thy traine to runne,
> Nor with poluted handes to touch thy vaile:
> His death was darted from the Scorpions taile,
> For which her forme to endlesse memorie,
> With other lamps, doth lend the heauens an eye,
> And he that shewd such great presumption,
> Is hidden now, beneath a little stone.
>
> (*Hymnus in Cynthiam*, 410-417.)

As Schoell (1) shows, this passage is derived from Comes, *Mythologiae*, VIII, 13, *De Orione*, while gloss 22 which Chapman appends to 'double fatherd sonne' is also traceable to the Italian mythographer. But Schoell does not give the extract from Comes corresponding to Chapman's gloss, so that the significant changes introduced by the English poet have escaped the notice of all commentators. Let us, therefore, compare Chapman's gloss with its source (italics original).

> The double-fathered sonne is Orion, so cald since he was the sonne of Ioue and Appollo, borne of their seede enclosed in a Bulls hide, which abhorreth not from Philosophie (according to Poets intentions) that one sonne should haue two fathers: for in the generation of elements it is true, since *omnia sint in omnibus*.

> Orion fuit Neptuni & Iouis & Apollinis filius, ex horum semine nimirum in pellem bouis incluso natus. Quid hoc est monstri Dii boni ? an potest vnus esse multorum parentum filius ? haec in elementorum generatione vera esse possunt, cum omnia sint in omnibus (2).

In Chapman's particularly close translation two things are remarkable: first, he drops Neptunus and retains Jove and Apollo, and second, he tampers with Comes' genealogy by translating *multorum* by *two*, Comes explicitly stating that Orion is the son of *many*

---

(1) F. L. Schoell, *Études*, pp. 190-191. The chapter indication from Comes is twice misprinted as VIII, 12.
(2) Comes, *Mythologiae*, p. 459.

fathers. Nowhere in the whole chapter Comes devotes to Orion do we find a reference to a double-fathered Orion. From this confrontation between the passages from Comes and Chapman, one may conclude, almost with certainty, that Chapman must have had good reasons to alter his source in this manner. In the last resort I must of course leave the interpretation of Chapman's tag to the Chapman specialists, but I am not unwilling to suggest that our poet may have had Shakespeare in mind here (1). The 'traine' reference in the line under discussion carries the obvious implication that Cynthia is venerated by a train of followers, or, to use Thomas Nashe's words in *Pierce Penilesse*, by 'bright stars of Nobilitie, and glistering attendants on the true *Diana*' (2). 'Train' references, moreover, are scattered all over Chapman's composition (see *Hymnus in Noctem*, 231, 241, 386, 400; *Hymnus in Cynthiam*, 410, 482). It is therefore not entirely beyond the bounds of probability that, when Chapman requests Cynthia to allow the double-fathered son no longer among her train, he thereby suggests that Shakespeare should no longer be regarded as a genuine worshipper of the only true Cynthia, metaphysical speculation. The general drift of *Love's Labour's Lost*, by the way, is precisely that learning is a power far inferior to love, a circumstance which supports the interpretation here advanced.

Finally, let us proceed to consider another higly important passage in the *Hymnus in Cynthiam*, namely lines 456-474:

> The minde in that we like, rules euery limme,
> Giues hands to bodies, makes them make them trimme:
> Why then in that the body doth dislike,
> Should not his sword as great a vennie strike?
> The bit, and spurre that Monarcke ruleth still,
> To further good things, and to curb the ill,
> He is the Ganemede, the birde of Ioue,
> Rapt to his soueraignes bosome for his loue,
> His bewtie was it, not the bodies pride,
> That made him great Aquarius stellified:
> And that minde most is bewtifull and hye,

---

(1) I may hazard the suggestion that 'double-fathered' might refer to Hamlet, who is indeed furnished with two fathers in both *Der bestrafte Brudermord* and the 'bad' quarto of *Hamlet* (1603), in both of which Hamlet addresses Claudius as 'father.' Note also that in the good quarto Hamlet's father is in turn compared to Hyperion (= Apollo) at III, iv, 56 and to Jove at III, ii, 294, allusions not represented by the bad quarto. If there is anything in my suggestion, it is obvious that this CHAPMAN allusion has a bearing on the authorship of the old *Hamlet*, a play about which we hear from NASHE in 1589, and which was on the boards of HENSLOWE's theatre in 1594.

(2) NASHE, *Works*, I, 242.

And nearest comes to a Diuinitie,
That furthest is from spot of earths delight,
Pleasures that lose their substance with their sight,
Such one, Saturnius rauisheth to loue,
And fills the cup of all content to Ioue.
　　If wisedome be the mindes true bewtie then,
And that such bewtie shines in vertuous men,
If those sweet Ganemedes shall onely finde,

After this line the poem breaks off abruptly, and Chapman starts
on a new idea with the next. Professor Schoell again points out
the poet's indebtedness to a passage from Comes, which, though
inordinately long, may also be reproduced here on account of its
'allegorical' importance (irrelevant passages are omitted).

Hic cum esset eximiae & prope inauditae pulchritudinis, ob eam
dignus habitus est, non qui ad libidinem, vt crediderunt plerique raperetur,
sed qui pocula Ioui ministraret, vt scripsit Homerus lib. υ. Iliadis . . .

Alii vero inter quos fuit Xenophon vt scripsit in Symposio, Ganymedem propter animi pulchritudinem & prudentiam potius, quam propter
formam corporis, in coelum ascitum esse voluerunt: nam hi dictum fuisse
Ganymedem putarunt non a γάνυμι. quod conuiuari & genio indulgere
significat: sed potius ab his dictionibus in vnum compositis ad praestantiam
prudentiae & consilii exprimendam, ἄγαν, & νὺ, & μῆδος. nam illae cum
intensionem & incrementum significent, extrema est consilium. Enim-
uero diuinum quidpiam sub hac fabula contineri ita inquit Cicero lib. I.
Tusculanarum Disputationum: Nec Homerum audio, qui Ganymedem
a Diis raptum ait propter formam vt Ioui pocula ministraret. Non iusta
causa, cur Laomendonti tanta fieret iniuria. Fingebat hace Homerus &
humana ad Deos transferebat quidam ad solatium coniunctorum ipsi
Ganymedi hanc fabulam fictam esse tradiderunt, cum is clam raptus
fuisse inter venandum: atque illis persuasum denique Ganymedem inter
sidera relatum esse, & in id signum quod dicitur Aquarius (1).

A beautiful mind, both Chapman and Comes maintain, is assured of
its place in heaven, while body and earth alike are the trammels of
our noblest aspirations. The myth that most fittingly symbolizes
man's noble pursuits is that of Ganymede, an allegorization which
Comes describes with an almost childish delight. The commonness
of the conceit can be illustrated—as I will show in the next chapter—
from several Elizabethan writers. But one instance of its currency
must now be quoted. Thomas Hill, whose *Schoole of Skil* has already

---

(1) COMES, *Mythologiae*, IX, xiii, *De Ganymede*, pp. 518-519.

revealed points of contact with Chapman, has a statement which is reminiscent of both Chapman and Comes; it is such as to render it likely that his treatise emanated from one of the adherents of the School of Night; and, considering that this is the third point of contact with *The Shadow of Night*, one sees a really characteristic meaning in Hill's title (compare also Chapman's 'court of skill' in his *Hymnus in Noctem*, 13).

The figure named the Eagle (whereon *Aquarius* seemeth to fly) which many affirm to be *Ganimedes*, *Ptholomie* doth deck with nine stars, of the second, third, fourth, and fifte bignesse . . . (1)

Despite the commonplace character of the myth of Ganymede, a special significance seems, for several reasons, to attach to its use by Chapman. It has already been hinted before that Ganymede was regularly allegorized in Renaissance literature as the human soul aspiring after the immersion into the divine essence, and Chapman does little more than exemplify how this particular myth could be put to use in poetry. What does strike the reader, however, is that Chapman finds it necessary to append a gloss to interpret it: 'The bewtie of the minde being signified in *Ganemede*, he here by *Prosopopoeia*, giues a mans shape vnto it.' It seems to me that 'giues a mans shape vnto it' intimates clearly that Ganymede is exemplified in a living Elizabethan, who, as will be shown more fully in the next chapter, is the Earl of Derby, one of those praised for their nobility in the epistle which prefaces *The Shadow of Night*. The same mythological comparison is used by Nashe who, eulogizing the Earl of Derby (at that time Lord Strange) in *Pierce Penilesse*, hails him as 'Ioues Eagle-borne Ganimed' (2).

One realizes that this identification may have a bearing on many aspects of Elizabethan literature. Consider Shakespeare's *Love's Labour's Lost*, for instance: Ferdinand, King of Navarre, at the very beginning of the play puts in an eloquent plea for the founding of an academy with a view to discovering things 'hid and barred from common sense.' When it is remembered that no King of Navarre known to history ever bore the christian name Ferdinand, it is not improbable that Shakespeare may have had Ferdinando

---

(1) HILL, *The Schoole of Skil*, p. 83.
(2) NASHE, *Works*, I, 243. NASHE's phrase and HILL's statement, by the way, probably explain the symbolism of the *Hymnus in Cynthiam* at line 49 : 'Ioues thundring Eagles featherd like the night.'

Stanley, Lord Strange, in mind when planning his comedy. And, considering the marked contrast between the general atmosphere of *The Shadow of Night* and *Love's Labour's Lost*, Shakespeare, like Chapman, may have attempted to incorporate the intellectual attitude of the Earl in his play. It looks as though the significance of the Earl of Derby in the critical years 1590-1593 has never yet been properly appreciated. It is therefore of interest to note that Thomas Edwards' *Cephalus and Procris*, a poem emanating from a sphere of thought related to that of Chapman, may contain an allusion to the Earl of Derby as the 'center poet'. In the Envoy to the volume occur the following stanzas:

> Eke in purple robes distaind,
>   Amid the center of this clime,
> I haue heard say doth remaine,
>   One whose power floweth far,
> That should haue been of our rime,
>   The only object and the Star.

> Well could his bewitching pen
>   Done the Muses obiects to us,
> Although he differs much from men,
>   Tilting under Frieries,
> Yet his golden art might woo us
>   To haue honored him with baies.

Mrs. C. C. Stopes (1) points out that F. J. Furnivall in 1882 asked all the literary men of England who could be meant by this 'center poet', and that no two answers agreed. The only person who seems to Mrs. Stopes possible is the Earl of Derby, the authority for her opinion being Nashe's panegyric at the end of *Pierce Penilesse*. From various quarters, then, there comes evidence that the Earl of Derby was a person of singular intellectual eminence. Spenser, Nashe, Chapman, Greene, Shakespeare, Marlowe, all these artists had at one time in their careers come across this 'center poet'; and as patron of an actors' company the Earl was no doubt acquainted with the leading dramatists of the day. And, incidentally, such is the Earl of Derby's importance that Professor Abel Lefranc (2), a heretic in matters Shakespearean, has been prepared to suggest

---

(1) C. C. STOPES, *MLR*, XVI (1921), 219-220. The stanzas quoted above are taken from Mrs. STOPES' article.

(2) A. LEFRANC, *A la découverte de Shakespeare* (Paris, 1945).

William Stanley, Ferdinando's brother, as a fitting candidate for the authorship of Shakespeare's plays.

* *
*

We may now proceed to consider a few aspects of Chapman's imagery, and since this imagery will partly be taken from the Homer translations, it will be necessary to supply some relevant information (1). Chapman's earliest translations to be published were the *Seaven Bookes of the Iliades*, printed by John Windet in 1598. This volume contained the first two books and the seventh through the eleventh in a consecutive numbering. Later in the year Windet printed *Achilles Shield*, a rendering of part of the *Iliad*, book XVIII; at the end of this volume came a poem 'To *M. Harriots*, accompanying *Achilles Shield*,' inscribed 'to my admired and soule-loved friend, Mayster of all essentiall and true knowledge, *M. Harriots*.' Next appeared the *Twelve Bookes of his Iliades*, undated, but usually catalogued as of 1610, but presumably published the year before, as Miss P. B. Bartlett argues. A complete edition of the *Iliads* appeared in 1611, to be followed by the *Whole Works* in 1616. When he prepared his 1609 translation, Chapman undertook considerable revisions and cut out many of the interpolations present in the 1598 version. Miss Bartlett has shown that the greater number of these were taken from the annotated Latin Homer translation by Johannes Spondanus, published in 1583 and several times reprinted. Certain interpolations, however, cannot possibly be traced in Spondanus's Homer version (2). Spondanus dedicated his Homer translation to Henry III of France, a monarch who took learning particularly to heart. This monarch's intellectual attitude was certainly a determining factor in the spread of the academic movement in the sixteenth century, for Henry III founded an academy on the model of that of Florence for the purpose of disseminating classical learning and science. French intellectual circles inherited the Ficinian tradition through Henry's academy. Spondanus, a scholar familiar

---

(1) See articles by Miss P. B. BARTLETT, "Chapman's Revisions in his *Iliads*," *JELH*, II (1935), 92-119; "The Heroes of Chapman's Homer," *RES*, XVII (1941), 257-280; "Stylistic Devices in Chapman's *Iliads*," *PMLA*, LVII (1942), 661-675. More recent is H. C. FAY, "Chapman's Materials for his Translation of Homer," *RES*, New Ser., II (1951), 121-128.

(2) See also F. L. SCHOELL, *Études*, pp. 162-177. On SPONDANUS see JEAN DE SPONDE, *Poésies*, ed. F. RUCHON and A. BOASE (Genève, 1949), with a biographical study and a critical estimate.

with Ficino, thus forms a link in the chain which ties Chapman to Ficino's ideas.

When is Chapman's Homer translation to be dated? Professor Schoell has remarked that the earliest attempts might well belong to a period much earlier than that of publication, and he has suggested a date somewhere about 1590 (1). On the assumption that Chapman was translating Homer in these years, it need not surprise us that *Achilles Shield* and the poem to Harriot should also belong to a sphere of ideas characteristic of the School of Night.

The poem to Harriot reveals in each of its lines a particular aspect of Chapman's philosophy, a philosophy whose general Platonic provenance has been ably discussed by Jean Jacquot (2). In Chapman's metaphorical machinery, however, there is one striking image that deserves further attention. It is that of the Sphere of fire to which the poet aspires, and, connected with it, that of two varieties of fire. It is clearly in line with the great importance attached to myths generally, that Chapman introduces this symbol of the Sphere of fire into *Achilles Shield*, a Homer rendering which, from the very nature of its metaphors, belongs to the great sixteenth century tradition of scientific poetry as this was produced especially in France. Let us now compare the two versions of the *Iliad*, book XVIII, with a few of Chapman's lines to Harriot.

> Brightfooted *Thetis* did the Spheere aspire,
> (Amongst the Immortals) of the God of fire,
> Starrie, incorruptible, and had frame
> Of ruddie brasse, right shaped by the lame.
> (*Achilles Shield*, 1-4.)

> And now the silver-footed Queen had her ascension made
> To that incorruptible house, that starry golden court
> Of fiery Vulcan, beautiful amongst th'immortal sort,
> Which yet the lame god built himself.
> (*Iliad*, XVIII, 328-32.)

In the description of Thetis' entrance into Vulcan's house, Chapman in his second version excised the comparison which represents Vulcan's smithy as a sphere of fire. Of course, in Homer's text there is nothing of the sort, and Spondanus's Latin translation did not provide the sphere image either.

---

(1) F. L. SCHOELL, *Études*, p. 176.
(2) J. JACQUOT, *George Chapman*, pp. 199-231.

Sic hi quidem talia inter se loquebantur:
Vulcani .a. peruenit ad domum Thetis argentipes,
Incorruptam, stellatam, decoram inter immortales,
Auream, quam quidem ipse fecit claudus (1).

And here are a few lines of Chapman's commendatory poem to Harriot.

To you whose depth of soule measures the height,
And all dimensions of all workes of weight,
Reason being ground, structure and ornament,
To all inuentions, graue and permanent,
And your cleare eyes the Spheres where *Reason* moues;
                    (To *M. Harriots*, accompanying *Achilles Shield*, 1-5.)

Rich mine of knowledge, ô that my strange muse
Without this bodies nourishment could vse,
Her zealous faculties, onely t'aspire,
Instructiue light from your whole Sphere of fire:
                                        (31-34.)

Chapman is here developing the theme that the ascension of the soul is towards a sphere, the fire of which ministers learning and instruction to mankind. In the Homer translation the reference is only prompted by the current association of Vulcan with fire and nothing more, but it is nevertheless illustrative of the poet's love of sphere and fire imagery. The sequence of thought is decidedly Platonic, but Chapman slightly diverges from Platonism in that he substitutes reason for the immutable idea of beauty, though another term for reason, such as learning or science, would represent Chapman's meaning as well. According to the true Platonic tradition the soul resides only temporarily in the body, and longs to attain the realm of the ideas, where love and beauty reign supreme. But love and beauty are not the primary aims of Chapman's ascent, for his soul strives after an ultimate immersion into a sphere of instruction, from which 'instructive fire' (compare *Bussy D'Ambois*, V, i, 44) is hurled into the universe. The shift from the Platonic idea of beauty to the notion of learning would seem to have been an intentional one, for Chapman preserves the whole of the symbolic requisites by which genuine Platonists convey their ideas. For example, there is the adamantine nature of learning which attracts its worshippers ir-

---

(1) J. Spondanus, *Homeri quae exstant omnia* (Basle, 1606), p. 338.

resistibly, a well-worn metaphor of neo-Platonic thinking; further, the soul is animated by a sort of glowing heat, a warm zeal, brought about by the splendour of learning, the beams of which strike the onlookers with awe and wonder; and, another important metaphor, the soul's liberation is a kind of new birth, a delivery from the oppression of matter.

From a poet with such marked reiterative habits, one may expect that the fire image will recur in a few other poems as well. In *Euthymiae Raptus; or The Teares of Peace* (first published in 1609), a poem 'linked to *The Shadow of Night* by its numerous references to the evil effect of day' (1), there occurs a passage characterized by a development of thought remarkably analogous to that of Chapman's lines to Harriot. *The Teares of Peace* is written in the form of a dialogue between Peace and an Interlocutor, who seems to stand for the author himself. At one time, at 872-885, the Interlocutor states the fire imagery in the following terms:

> But; as Earths grosse and elementall fire,
> Cannot maintaine it selfe; but doth require
> Fresh matter still, to giue it heate, and light;
> And, when it is enflam'd; mounts not vpright;
> But struggles in his lame impure ascent;
> Now this waie works, and then is that waie bent,
> Not able, straight, t'aspire to this true Sphere
> Where burns the fire, eternall, and sincere;
> So, best soules here; with heartiest zeales enflam'd
> In their high flight for heauen; earth-broos'd and lam'd
> Make many faint approches; and are faine,
> With much vnworthy matter, to sustaine
> Their holiest fire; and with sick feathers, driuen,
> And broken Pinions, flutter towards heauen.

Chapman posits a marked opposition between 'Earths grosse and elementall fire' and the 'fire, eternall, and sincere' which burns in the true sphere to which 'best soules' aspire; or, in other words, ordinary inhabitants of the earth are feeding a fire singularly wanting in aspiring qualities. Chapman, in the above lines, voices his fundamental creed that those who secure merely terrestrial triumphs are eclipsed by those engaged in the ardent pursuit of knowledge.

One may reasonably suspect that, in the way of symbolism, Chapman may have inherited much from the scientific poets of

---

(1) J. SPENS, *ESEA*, XI, 166.

sixteenth century France (1). There are at least two French writers whose works present close spiritual affinities with Chapman's poetry. The following items are not offered as actual sources, but only as evidence of the parallel development of certain currents of thought in France and England. The concept of the two varieties of fire can of course be incorporated with the Platonic doctrine of the ideas, while the contrast Chapman makes between matter and mind seems to anticipate Descartes' dualism. However that may be, it is noteworthy that in the *Mantice* (1558), an attack on judicial astrology, by Pontus de Tyard, there is a statement closely similar to Chapman's. The marginal gloss Tyard gives is a summary of the theme: 'Le Feu materiel ayant source du superieur.'

Le Feu materiel accomodé à nostre vsage, procede du Feu superieur: & toutefois il tient ses qualitez beaucoup empirées: Car le superieur est durable, non esteignable, salutaire & conseruateur des choses engendrées & de leur generation: au contraire, le materiel est peu durable, esteingnable, requerant pour l'entretien de sa durée nourriture continuelle, dont il est dommageable & ruineur de tout ce qui tombe dessous sa deuorante force. Le superieur est tout lumineux: & le materiel tousiours accompagné de fumée tenebreuse. Donques de la puissance ignée, qui de là haut se communique çà bas, & rejaillit sur nous, ne nous reste que ie ne sçay quel feu abastardy, qui neantmoins ne doit tacher la source de l'ignée purité d' aucune marque d'imperfection (2).

Chapman's points of contact with Maurice Scève (1501-1560), who may be regarded as a disciple of Tyard, are even more striking. So far as I know, no student of Chapman has ever noticed that Chapman's whole symbolism of night with its detailed panoply of notions such as the funeral mantle and the like, is curiously reminiscent of the metaphorical machinery employed by Maurice Scève, the most prominent of the scientific poets. Especially one poem in Scève's collection of *dizains*, entitled *Delie, object de plus haulte vertu* (first published in 1544), deserves consideration. To set poems by Chapman and Scève side by side is to become aware of the cardinal importance of literary ancestry. Just after the passage with the 'whole Sphere of fire' reference, quoted before, Chapman goes on:

---

(1) See A.-M. SCHMIDT, *La poésie scientifique en France au seizième siècle* (Paris, 1938).
(2) PONTUS DE TYARD, *Discours philosophiques* (Paris, 1587), pp. 182-183. The TYARD edition by MARTY-LAVEAUX (1875) contains only the poetry and a few prose extracts.

But woe is me, what zeale or power soeuer
My free soule hath, my body will be neuer
Able t'attend: neuer shal I enioy,
Th'end of my happles birth: neuer employ
That smotherd feruour that in lothed embers,
Lyes swept from light, and no cleare howre remembers.
O had your perfect eye Organs to pierce
Into that Chaos whence this stiffled verse
By violence breakes: where Gloweworme like doth shine
In nights of sorrow, this hid soule of mine:
And how her genuine formes struggle for birth,
Vnder the clawes of this fowle Panther earth;

(To *M. Harriots*, 35-46.)

Compare with this Scève's *dizain* CCCLV.

L'Aulbe venant pour nous rendre apparent
Ce, que l'obscur des tenebres nous cele,
Le feu de nuict en mon corps transparent,
Rentre en mon coeur couvrant mainte estincelle,
    Et quand Vesper sur terre universelle
Estendre vient son voile tenebreux,
Ma flamme sort de son creux funebreux,
Ou est l'abysme a mon cler jour nuisant,
Et derechef reluit le soir umbreux,
Accompaignant le Vermisseau luisant.

Although Scève is surely a far greater artist and shows more restraint than the slightly pathetic Chapman, the affinity between the two poets is conspicuous. In the second half of the *dizain* the poet describes that when night has spread its veil, his flame leaves its funeral abode, the very place where is the abyss obnoxious to his lucidity of mind; and from that moment onwards shady night sparkles anew in the company of the shining glow-worm. In spite of Chapman's shifting the emphasis in that his poignant lament strikes a strongly subjective note, he does resemble Scève in conveying this lament by the aid of an analogous symbolism. Either poem represents the soul's inner fire as emprisoned in a kind of chaos or abyss from whence, to ensure the soul's growth into full consciousness, it has to be liberated. The soul of either poet is unable to engage in a sustained flight only because its fervour has so much worn off by day that it is reduced to embers. Chapman, at the end of the above quotation, beseeches Harriot to free him from the abysmal chaos whence his verses have to break asunder.

It is surely illuminating to note that both Chapman and Scève use the glow-worm simile to describe their emotional situation at the moment night has enveloped the earth. A kind of light has in fact proceeded from darkness. E. Parturier, the learned editor of Scève's *Delie*, has traced the simile of the *vermisseau luisant* to Serafino dell'Aquila (1466-1500), one of the knottiest poets of the Italian Renaissance (1). This fact might lead us to surmise that the glow-worm simile was commonplace. But V.-L. Saulnier (2), the latest investigator of Scève who is continually at pains to demonstrate the commonplace character of Scève's imagery and who attempts a wholesale demolition of Parturier's thesis as to the poet's indebtedness to Italy, is apparently unable to cite something parallel to this particular comparison elsewhere. The conceit of the glow-worm is probably of emblematic origin. Professor Mario Praz (3), in his discussion of the emblems in literature, points out that in John Marston's *Antonia and Mellida*, V, i, several devices are mentioned, one of which runs 'A glowe worme, the word?—*Splendescit tantum tenebris.*' Professor Praz, however, is only able to refer to an example of this conceit as recorded in Picinelli's *Mondo Simbolico* (Milan, 1653). From the examples here adduced it is satisfactorily clear that it was of much longer standing, and might derive from the peculiarly emblematic poetry of Scève and Serafino.

Nor does this exhaust the elements of parallelism between Chapman and Scève, and there is little doubt that an investigation of Chapman's indebtedness to French sixteenth century scientific poetry generally would be worth while. In the first place, Chapman and Scève frequently refer to the 'funeral' character of their aspirations—it forms, of course, an obvious part of nocturnal symbolism and can be related to sixteenth century necromancy—an instance

---

(1) M. Scève, *Delie*, ed. E. Parturier (Paris, 1916). Parturier quotes Serafino, but gives only two lines from the poem with the 'lucciola.' It is perhaps best to quote the full stanza :

> Inuisibil neuo per piaggie e campi
>   Chel fumo del mio ardor mi tien nascosto,
> E se talhor del petto escono i uampi
>   Mi fan parer qual lucciola d'agosto,
> Gran marauiglia è pur che in foco io campi
>   Ne segno o bruscio il loco, oue me acosto.
> Poi me ritrouo un hom di ghiaccio al Sole
>   Gran miracol non è cio che amor vuole.
>   (ed. 1548, fol. 153 r⁰)

(2) V.-L. Saulnier, *Maurice Scève* (Paris, 1949), I, 260-270.
(3) M. Praz, *Studies*, p. 196.

of this propensity for using funeral imagery already occurs in the *dizain* here quoted. In the second place, both poets regard Love as the enemy of Reason—or Learning—a debate which occupies the *dizains* CLXXIX-CLXXXIV (1); and their treating of a lunar myth, brilliantly analysed by V.-L. Saulnier in discussing Scève, may be a further point of contact. But to suggest Chapman's dependence upon Scève, in the absence of any external evidence, would surely put a strain upon the credulity of critics, and they will argue that it is hardly ever possible to fix the boundaries of real originality or to segregate what is unique from what is commonplace. However that may be, we are here confronted with two poets who stand somewhat apart from literary tradition, and that in an age where imitation was the basic tenet of literary composition. Once it has become plausible that Scève and Chapman are somehow related, however, one may perhaps infer that they relied on some common system of thought.

When Chapman's poetry is considered in its relation to that of contemporary France it becomes easier to interpret his Sphere of fire concept. In the first place, spheres are often used in the scientific poetry of France (2); in the second, spheres may voice a kind of consciousness of the recurrent cyclical pattern of human development, and might in point of fact serve as a fitting symbol to convey Chapman's insistent preoccupation with the idea of eternity; and, perhaps, there is also a relation of some sort or other to circles, things so often toyed with by mathematicians and alchemists. And in view of Chapman's adherence to Hermetic speculation, it may be of use to note that a sphere could stand for the encyclopaedic character of knowledge, and symbolize the achievements and pursuits of the seven liberal arts. Such an interpretation may receive support from Pierio Valeriano's handbook on the hieroglyphs, in which it is stated that a sphere symbolizes eternity (3), a fairly common sixteenth century conceit, or from Ficino who has an interesting reference to *sphaera ignis* to describe the upward urge of the mind (4). The sphere

(1) See V.-L. SAULNIER, *Maurice Scève*, I, 238.

(2) A.-M. SCHMIDT, *La poésie scientifique*, p. 33.

(3) P. VALERIANO, *Hieroglyphica* (Basle, 1556), p. 288, says of 'aeternitas' : 'Itaque recte cum per hieroglyphicum sphaerae Deum intelligerent, aeternitatem quoque eadem figura descripserunt,' and further on, 'Apud Romanos quoque perpetuitas est per sphaeram indicata, ut in sphaera. . . .'

(4) FICINO, *Theologia platonica* (Paris, 1559), Lib. X, cap. 5 (p. 155): 'Exprimi vero oportuit aliquam in natura formam deo simillimam : si modo diuinus artifex materiam sit superaturus vt Plato tradidit in Timaeo. Talem vero esse vult mentem quae est in corpore,

is only one of the many symbols used by Chapman; the fire image, however, is such a basic feature of his poetry and characteristic of the poets in some way associated with the School of Night, that Jean Jacquot (1) has been able to regard this as the tie which unites the members of the School.

What has become clear, I believe, is that Chapman expresses himself in imagery which reminds us of the more unfamiliar poets of sixteenth century France, but in a style characterized by an obtrusive disjunctiveness. The same symbols and properties appear over and over again till the reader grows weary of the iteration. If one wishes to account for the persistent confusion so characteristic of his poetry, it cannot be too strongly insisted that, like the French scientific poets, Chapman wished to make his impact upon a comparatively small circle of Elizabethan readers apparently equipped with the necessary key words to grasp his meaning.

---

a mente quae est extra corpora, delibatam, quasi quendam mentis illius vultum in subli-mioris materiae speculo relucentem. Considera ad quantam sui similitudinem ignis materiam extollat, & quibus gradibus. Sphaera ignis qualitatem triplicem possidet : calorem, lumen, & leuitatem ad superiora vergentem. Mouet sphaera illa corpora infima : & crassissimis ineptissimisque corporibus calorem infundit solum : vt plerunque sit in lapidibus.' — See P. O. KRISTELLER, *The Philosophy of Marsilio Ficino* (New York, 1943), pp. 79, 209.

(1) J. JACQUOT, *George Chapman*, pp. 19, 75.

CHAPTER IV

ABRAHAM FRAUNCE, ROBERT GREENE, AND THOMAS NASHE

Although one of the minor figures of Elizabethan literature, Abraham Fraunce nevertheless deserves a place in the literary movement of his time, not because of the value of his artistic contribution, but because his works shed fresh light on some of the mythological references to be found in his immediate contemporaries. Fraunce is also an important figure in Renaissance rhetoric, as Miss Ethel Seaton shows in her recent edition of Fraunce's treatise, *The Arcadian Rhetorike* (Oxford, 1950). His efforts to determine the principles of rhetoric form part of the general theoretical interest in literature characteristic of the group around Gabriel Harvey. A few words of introduction to Fraunce may not be out of place (1).

Fraunce was born at Shrewsbury about 1558-1560, and visited Shrewsbury School where his name is to be found in the pupils' register in January 1571/2, and though he may have entered school at an earlier time, he probably did not come into contact with Philip Sidney who had left in 1568. Owing to the patronage of the Sidney family, Fraunce was sent to St. John's College, Cambridge, that great seat of learning where so many Elizabethan men of letters were educated. He matriculated there on May 26, 1576, becoming Fellow in 1580 and M. A. in 1583. He probably made the direct acquaintance of Philip Sidney about 1583. He passed from Cambridge to Gray's Inn, the Pension Book of the Inn recording his call to the bar on February 8, 1588; after that he practised as a lawyer in the court of the Marches of Wales. After Sidney's death in 1586 he became a member of the circle of Sidney's sister, Mary, Countess of Pembroke, and dedicated each of his works to one of the members of the family. Of Fraunce's subsequent career nothing is known, and apart from Spenser's probable reference to him as 'Corydon' in *Colin Clouts Come Home Again* (line 382) and from

---

(1) The best biography of FRAUNCE is still that by G. C. MOORE SMITH in his edition of FRAUNCE's Latin drama *Victoria*, in the *Materialien zur Kunde des älteren Englischen Dramas*, XIV (1906).

a few other casual references in contemporaries, he is lost sight of for almost forty years. Then in 1628-30 there is evidence that he entered the service of Lord Bridgewater and remained there till 1633, the year in which he presumably died. The significance of Fraunce's works, however, more than counterbalances the scant details of his biography. His literary career stretches only from 1587 to 1592, but these are crucial years indeed for the development of Elizabethan literature.

In 1587 Fraunce's first literary venture was published under the title *The Lamentations of Amyntas for the Death of Phillis, paraphrastically translated out of Latine into English Hexameters*, printed by John Wolfe for Thomas Newman and Thomas Gubbin. Thomas Nashe, a former scholar of St. John's College, was the first to praise this hexameter rendering of Thomas Watson's Latin *Amyntas* (1585), when, after apparently discounting Stanyhurst's earlier endeavours in the same metre, he exclaimed in the preface to Robert Greene's *Menaphon* (1589), that 'our peaceable Poets' were kept from 'intermedling hereafter with that quarrelling kind of verse, had not sweet Maister *France*, by his excellent translation of Maister *Thomas Watsons* sugred *Amintas*, animated their dulled spirits to such high witted endeuours' (1). As in a few other fields, Fraunce was probably following Gabriel Harvey's lead, who in course of time came to be ridiculed by Thomas Nashe as the confirmed champion of hexameter verse, Harvey himself producing the poor specimens preserved. Next came *The Arcadian Rhetorike* (entered in the Stationers' Register on June 11, 1588, and published in the same year), a work based on the *Rhetorica* of Audemarus Talaeus (Omer Talon, died 1562), the close collaborator and friend of the notorious Petrus Ramus (1515-1572) (2).

More ambitious was the scope of Fraunce's *Insignium, Armorum, Emblematum, Hieroglyphicorum, et Symbolorum, quae ab Italis Imprese nominantur explicatio: Quae Symbolicae philosophiae postrema pars est*. It was entered in the Stationers' Register on May 20, 1588, and printed by Thomas Orwin for Gubbin and Newman. The treatise is divided into three books, *De Insignibus*, *De Armis*, and *De Symbolis, Emblematicus, & Hieroglyphicis*, and was dedicated to Robert Sidney, the poet's brother. The title of the treatise sufficiently describes what

---

(1) THOMAS NASHE, *Works*, ed. by R. B. McKerrow (London, 1910), III, 320.
(2) The best authority for both is CHARLES WADDINGTON, *Ramus* (Paris, 1855). See also E. SEATON, ed. *The Arcadian Rhetorike* (Oxford, 1950), p. x.

it deals with, but one passage from it needs to be quoted, for it gives a striking testimony to the general spread of emblem-books.

Exordiemur autem a Paulo Iouio: Nam is primus est, qui praecepta tradidit, constituitque; nouam quandam symbolorum quasi disciplinam; deinde quid Hieronymus Russellus, Alexander Farra, Lucas Contiles, Scipio Bargaglius, adiecerunt, subiungemus. Nam & Paradinus, & Lodouicus Dominicus, & Gabriel Simeon, caeterique minuta quaedam exempla obtrudunt potius, quam rei naturam inuestigant. Sic igitur Iouius (1).

Abraham Fraunce's next work, *The Lawiers Logike*, links up with *Insignium* through its incidental reference to the fact that

. . . fine Vniuersity men haue been trained vp in such easie, elegant, conceipted, nice, and delicate learning, that they can better make new-found verses of Amyntas death, and popular discourses of Ensignes, Armory, Emblemes, Hieroglyphikes, and Italian Impreses, than apply their heads to the study of the Law . . . (2)

Fraunce also appends Vergil's Eclogue to *The Lawiers Logike*, and adds a translation in hexameters and a logical analysis of the poem, after which follow the so-called logical analyses of the Earl of Northumberland's case and of Stanford's crown pleas.

The works produced by Fraunce in the years 1591-2 are specially deserving of notice. In 1591 appeared *The Countesse of Pembrokes Yuychurch* and *The Countess of Pembrokes Emanuel*, entered together in the Stationers' Register on February 9, 1590/1 (3). The former work, to be presently examined, falls into two parts: *Amyntas Pastorall*. *The first part of the Countesse of Pembrokes Yuychurch* is translated from Tasso's pastoral play *Aminta* (4), while the second part *Phillis Funerall* is in part a republication of the *Lamentations* of 1587. In the dedication to Mary, Countess of Pembroke, Fraunce makes amends to his readers for the omission of his sources in 1587 in stating: 'J haue somewhat altered S. *Tassoes* Italian, & M. *Watsons* Latine *Amyntas*, to make them both one English,' and then embarks upon a defence of hexameters against rhymed verses, rewriting the preface of 1587. Also in the course of his own poetical effusions

---

(1) A. FRAUNCE, *Insignium* (1588), sig. M$_2$ v⁰.
(2) A. FRAUNCE, *The Lawiers Logike* (1588), sig. q.$_2$ r⁰.
(3) ARBER, *Transcript*, II, 575.
(4) For TASSO translations in general see E. KOEPPEL, "Die englischen Tasso-Übersetzungen des 16. Jahrhunderts," *Anglia*, XI (1888), 11-38; and XII (1889), 103-142.

Fraunce takes every opportunity of reviling the rhymers. The first and second parts of Fraunce's 'Yvychurch' composition, just referred to, were followed in 1592 by a third part, entitled *The Third part of the Countesse of Pembrokes Yuychurch*, a work, as we will see, too much neglected by students of Elizabethan literature.

The following discussion attempts first, to study the nature of a few mythological references in Fraunce, Greene, and Shakespeare and, after that, to assemble from Elizabethan literature some allusions using Ganymede as a descriptive name for Ferdinando Stanley, Lord Strange; and second, to establish the currency of Cerberus as an allegorical sobriquet for Thomas Nashe in the early nineties. The latter identification is especially significant, since, if it is correct, it provides an important key to passages in Nashe's own writings and to the interpretation of works connected with Nashe.

I

Amyntas Pastorall follows Tasso's *Aminta* pretty closely, but Fraunce has allowed himself many licences. When these are studied several interesting points come out. Emil Koeppel has drawn attention to the translator's expansions and cuttings but was unable to appreciate their significance. The characters of the Italian drama all appear in the English version but Fraunce has changed two names: Amyntas's 'coy mistress' is not called Silvia but Phillis, while the shepherdess who falsely informs Amyntas of Phillis' death is called Fulvia, instead of Nerina. He also suppresses the chorus at the end of the fourth act, but, on the other hand, he adds a second scene to the fifth act which in the original consists of one scene only. When the English is compared with the Italian version two, possibly three, points of some interest with respect to the early Shakespeare emerge. In the first place, there is a curious verbal similarity noticeable between the expansion undertaken by Fraunce in I, ii of *Aminta* and a few lines in *Love's Labour's Lost*, to which Emil Koeppel (1) had already drawn attention, a similarity previously (and still at present) neglected by Shakespeare's editors.

---

(1) E. KOEPPEL, *Anglia*, XI, 19. The two next extracts here quoted are taken from KOEPPEL's article, pp. 19, 21.

Am. Ma mentre io fea rapina d'animali,
Fui, non so come, a me stesso rapito (1).

(I, ii.)

But when Amyntas thus bestow'd himself on his angling,
Other baytes and hookes tooke secreate hould of Amyntas:
Whilst that Amyntas thus layd trapps and snares for a Redbrest,
White-brest layd new snares and hidden trapps for Amyntas:
Whilst that Amyntas I say ran pricking after a Pricket,
Farre more poysned darts have prickt hart-roote of Amyntas.

Compare *Love's Labour's Lost*, IV, ii, 57-58:

The preyfull Princesse pearst and prickt
a prettie pleasing Pricket, . . .

It is noteworthy that Fraunce uses the image of the buck again in
a passage where it does not appear in his source.

Tirsis. L'innamorato Aminta, che ciò intese
Si spiccò com' un dardo, ed io seguillo.

(III, i.)

Lover Amyntas leapt as a Rowe-buck prickt with an arrow,
At these woords, and flew, and quickly I hastened after.

Another example of free adaptation, though less outspoken, occurs
in the chorus at the end of Act II in which the great power of love
is celebrated.

Amore, in quale scuola,
Da qual mastro s'apprende
La tua sì lunga e dubbia arte d'amare?
Chi n'insegna a spiegare
Ciò che la mente intende,
Mentre con l'ali tue sovra il ciel vola?
Non già la dotta Atene,
Nè 'l Liceo nel dimostra;
Non Febo in Elicona,
Che sì d'Amor ragiona
Come colui che impara;

O Heart-ennobling great loue, where shall wee bee learnyng
These thy sacred lawes? in what schoole must wee be trayned
Vp to thy high conceipts? or what soe skilful a mayster
Possibly may vnfould those supreame thoughts of a louer

---

(1) The Italian quotations are from T. Tasso, *La Gerusalemme liberata e l'Aminta*
(Paris, 1882).

Which his soule possesse, whilst with thy wings in a moment
His mynde mounts to the skies, and Christall-mantled *Olympus?*
  Neyther learned *Athens,* nor great fame-worthy *Lycaeus.*
Could loues force espresse, or loues perfection vtter;
Neither *Castalian* Muses, nor great-God *Apollo,*
Nor rymewright singers could once aspyre to the thousandst
Part of those ioys, which in a louers brest be abounding:
Their voyce is not a voyce of fire, they sing a cold song,
Song and voyce vnfit for loues vnspeakable ardor (1):
                                                    (II, iii.)

But the chorus from which a quotation was given above also happens
to describe a situation paralleled in two plays performed or written
about, or shortly after, the time the translation was completed.

> Amor, leggan pur gli altri
> Le Socratiche carte,
> Ch'io in due begli occhi apprenderò quest'arte:
> E perderan le rime
> Dell penne più saggie
> Appo le mie selvaggie,
> Che rozza mano in rozza scorza imprime.

>   Nay, those silent looks, and louely regards of a Louer
> More, than a thousand words, expresse those pangs of a Louer.
> Let those famous Clercks with an endles toyle be perusing
> *Socraticall* writings; twoo faire eyes teach mee my lesson:
> And what I read in those, I doe write in a barck of a beech-tree,
> Beech-tree better booke, than a thousand *Dainty deuises.*

The device of carving love's lesson upon the bark of a tree, as appears
from the Italian, derives from Tasso. But it also occurs in two plays
whose singular connexion has already been noted by Professor
J. Dover Wilson (2), namely Greene's *Orlando Furioso* and
Shakespeare's *As You Like It.*

The New Cambridge Shakespeare editor has pointed out the
various similarities between the two plays. At one time Orlando in
As You Like It hangs verses upon the boughs of trees while the

---

(1) A. FRAUNCE, *The Countesse of Pembrokes Yuychurch* (1591), sig. D$_2$ v^o. Does part
of the above quotation anticipate SHAKESPEARE's Ovidian motto to *Venus and Adonis?*

    Vilia miretur vulgus; mihi flavus Apollo
    Pocula Castalia ministret aqua.

FRAUNCE's 'Castalian Muses' are not in TASSO, but their association with Apollo is, of
course, common. But there is perhaps more in FRAUNCE's depreciation of 'rymewright
singers' who cannot aspire to the joys of love.

(2) J. DOVER WILSON, ed. *As You Like It* (Cambridge, 1926, repr. 1948), p. 134.

lady's name is carved upon their barks and the same incident occurs in *Orlando Furioso;* in Greene's play, however, the work is accomplished by an enemy of Orlando's, namely Sacripante, to inspire him with jealousy. Dover Wilson further observes that the incident is prefaced in both dramas by an impassioned invocation to some heavenly body: in Greene to Venus, in Shakespeare to Phoebe, the latter deity also being named by Greene. As to the device of carving names upon the barks of trees, we know already that it also occurs in Fraunce's *Aminta* rendering. But Greene, it is true, need not have borrowed the device from Fraunce, for he presumably took it from his source, Ariosto's *Orlando Furioso,* XXIII, 108-109, though the poems themselves are entirely different (1). Only Shakespeare may have been indebted to Fraunce or Greene, or even Ariosto, though the invention of such an incident is surely not beyond Shakespeare's imagination. By relying on mythological data there is, I think, a possibility of partly solving the connexion between the plays of Greene and Shakespeare, and of that between Alleyn's player part of Orlando and the Orlando role in Greene's printed play as well.

In *As You Like It* Orlando hangs verses upon the boughs and is made to say:

> *Orl.* Hang there my verse, in witnesse of my loue,
> And thou thrice crowned Queene of night suruey
> With thy chaste eye, from thy pale sphere aboue
> Thy Huntresse name, that my full life doth sway.
>
> (III, ii, 1-4.)

The thrice crowned queen of night is, of course, 'triple Hecate,' the moon, and therefore Orlando is speaking at night; in the prose-sequel, however, it is day-time, which is one of the reasons advanced by Dover Wilson for suggesting that the play is of uneven date, an early version belonging to 1593. It will be recognized that such a date-ascription is of interest because it reinforces the probability of a connexion between the plays of Greene and Shakespeare. On the other hand, Greene also has Orlando invoke a heavenly body, commonly believed to be Venus, but it is remarkable that this Venus is said to be a gladsome lamp waiting on Phoebe's train, consequently attending on the moon.

---

(1) See J. Schoembs, *Ariosts Orlando Furioso in der englischen Litteratur des Zeitalters der Elisabeth* (Soden a. T.), p. 72.

Orl: Faire Queene of loue, thou mistres of delight,
Thou gladsome lamp that waitst on Phoebes traine,
Spredding thy kindnes through the iarring Orbes,
That in their vnion praise thy lasting powres.
Thou that hast staid the fierie Phlegons course,
And madest the Coach-man of the glorious waine
To droop, in view of Daphnes excellence (1).

(*Orlando Furioso*, 590-596.)

In his textual commentary on this passage Sir Walter Greg (2) observes that there seems some confusion in line 591, for the planet Venus attends on the sun not the moon, and he proposes to read 'Phoebus', saying that the connexion is pursued in what follows. But this comment seems to be beside the mark since Venus is implored to stay the fiery Phlegon's course, and she further makes the coachman of the glorious wain to droop, no doubt a reference to Phaethon's driving the sun-carriage. It is more reasonable to think that Greene, or the man responsible for the text of the 1594 quarto, is not to be convicted of error. In the first place, there is the coincidence of the association of love or Venus with the *moon* in both Greene and Shakespeare, but secondly, in connexion with this coincidence it is no doubt significant that Fraunce, albeit on the authority of the *Aminta*, states that Apollo, the *sun*-god, has nothing to do with love. And, be it noted, Fraunce reinforces his statement by coupling it with a reference to the Castalian Muses' inability to express love's aspirations, a reference not in Tasso which may have originated from Ovid. A final consideration of a portion of *Orlando Furioso* may further show that Greene, for some reason or other, was quite right when making Venus attend on Phoebe, since in the remarkable lines introductory to the poet laureate passage in the play, Orlando likens his love to swans that gallop by the coach of Cynthia. Apollo, on the other hand, receives specific mention because Orlando, as a poet, is making verses for Angelica.

Orl: Orgalio, is not my loue like those purple coloured swans,
That gallop by the Coach of Cynthia.
Org: Yes marry is shee my Lord.
Orl: Is not her face siluerd like that milke-white shape,
When Ioue came dauncing downe to Semele.

---

(1) Quotations from the Malone Society Reprint, ed. W. W. GREG (1907). ALLEYN's Orlando player part will be quoted from the edition by W. W. GREG, *Alcazar & Orlando*.
(2) W. W. GREG, *Alcazar & Orlando*, p. 213.

Org: It is my Lord.
Then goe thy waies and clime vp to the Clowds,
And tell Apollo that Orlando sits,
Making of verses for Angelica.

(*Orlando Furioso*, 1169-1178.)

The 'purple coloured swans,' as Churton Collins noted (1), are clearly borrowed from Horace, *Odes*, IV, i, 10, 'purpureis ales oloribus,' and though this may seem an additional reason for thinking that 'Cynthia' in the above quotation must be wrong, as Greg holds (2), I have no doubt that Greene actually wrote 'Cynthia,' because other elements of his text would seem to vindicate the correctness of the original reading, consider only Orlando's invocation to 'love' as an attendant upon Phoebe's train, which runs parallel to Orlando's later saying that his love gallops like swans by Cynthia's coach. We are here confronted with logically developed correspondences, and the textual evidence betrays a singular awareness of these in the poet.

It is difficult to suggest a reason why Orlando in Greene's play associates his invocation to love with Cynthia or Phoebe instead of offering his love exclusively to some earthly creature. The somewhat analogous situation revealed by other texts, probably contemporary with *Orlando Furioso*, suggests that such an association was not uncommon, and that it may have arisen from the theory of Platonic love.

Orlando's peculiarly contemplative leanings are still more in evidence in the version of his role preserved in the Alleyn manuscript. Edward Alleyn's part of Orlando is remarkable in two respects: first, its mythology, much reduced in the printed text, lends confirmation to the view just argued that Orlando is a worshipper of wisdom, but second, many burlesque phrases, not represented in the printed text either (or at least softened down considerably), seem to have been so contrived as to derogate from Orlando's lofty aspirations. On the assumption that Alleyn's player part represents Greene's original composition, these textual features suggest that Greene was pouring ridicule on a contemporary writer, especially since Orlando is at one time described as a 'poet laureate for geometry' (Alleyn manuscript, lines 224-6; 1594 quarto, ll. 1175 ff.). A particularly instructive example of these features occurs at

---

(1) J. C. COLLINS, ed. *The Plays & Poems of Robert Greene* (Oxford, 1905), I, 317.
(2) W. W. GREG, *Alcazar & Orlando*, p. 233.

lines 844-848. At the point where Orlando enters attired like a madman, the quarto text only has:

Orl: Woods, trees, leaues; leaues, trees, woods: tria sequuntur tria. Ho Minerua, salve, God morrow how doo you to day? Tell me sweet Goddesse, will Ioue send Mercury to Calipso to let mee goe. Will he? why then hees a Gentleman euerie haire a the head on him.

but the Alleyn manuscript runs:

woodes, trees, leaues, leaues, trees, woodes. *tria sequuntur tria, ergo optimus vir, non est optimus magistratus*, a peny for a pott of beer, & sixe pence for a peec of beife. wound-e what am I the worse. *o minerua salue*, god morrow how doe you to day, sweet goddesse now I see thou louest thy vlisses, louely Minerua tell thy vlisses, will Ioue send Mercury to Calipso to lett me goe. Will he, why then he is a good fellow, nay more he is a gentlem˜, euery haire of the head of him, . . .

The quarto text, in its compression, leaves the reference to Calypso unexplained; it is made clear, however, through Alleyn's part which informs us that Orlando twice compares himself to Ulysses; in this connexion it should be noted that nowhere in the printed version do we find references to Ulysses, so that it looks as if some person saw to it that these were removed from the composing-frame before the *Orlando* play was finally struck off in Danter's printing-office. In the portion of the Alleyn manuscript quoted above the reader further notes that Orlando twice invokes Minerva, the Roman goddess of wisdom, while the printed text preserves 'Minerva' only once. Nor are the lines just quoted the only ones which contain a 'Ulysses.' Twice elsewhere do we find Homer's hero mentioned. One is in the particularly corrupt passage which follows lines 1190-1 of the printed version (Alleyn manuscript, line 285), and is comparatively unimportant, but the other occurs in a passage where we again find the goddess Minerva. Where the quarto only preserves the line 'But ho Orgalio, where art thou boy?' the manuscript has:

> but soft you minerua, whats a clock, you
> lye like a <h e   >ne is <   <vlisses.
> I am orland <   >ty pala<   >, ner be
> so bragg, tho <ugh> you be Min<   >. I knowe
> who buggard Iupiters brayne, when you wer
> begotten. Argalio, Argalio,
> farewell good Minerua, haue me recomended
> to vulcan, & tell him I would fayne see him
> daūce a galyard

But the portrayal of Orlando, next to involving a more elaborate use of classical imagery, is also distinct from that to be found in the printed version in that Orlando is described as a 'poet laureate' (Alleyn MS., ll. 224-6; 1594 quarto, ll. 1175 ff.).

> tell me Argalio, what sayes charlemayne
> his nephew Orlando palantyne of fraūce
> is poet laureat for geometry.

A few lines further down the phrase 'poet laureate' is used again, when Orlando tells Argalio that he wears the badges of a crowned poet (Alleyn MS., 240 ff.).

> loue, whate loue vilayne, but the bastard of mars
> the poyson of venus, and yet thou seest I wear
> badges of a poet laureat.

The nature of the difference between the two Orlando parts leads us to infer, with Greg, that some very important agent stands between the printed and the acted version. Sir Walter Greg (1) suggests that John Danter, the printer of the 1594 quarto of *Orlando Furioso* who also aided and abetted Thomas Nashe in the latter's pamphlet-war against Gabriel Harvey, perhaps enlisted Nashe's services to keep an eye on the correctness of the classical names throughout. But if it could be assumed that Nashe was entrusted with the office of adapting Greene's play as well, one wonders whether Nashe's cuttings were not designed to soften down an Orlando impersonation that was offensive to a contemporary writer (2).

Finally, let us examine a few mythological references in Shakespeare's *As You Like It*. Shakespeare's portraiture of Orlando, it is true, hardly reveals anything that might point to that character's leanings toward contemplation. Shakespeare, however, may well have made up for this lack in that he has Orlando fall in love with Rosalind, who adopts the garb of a shepherd under the name Ganymede. In Renaissance symbolism Ganymede, as we shall presently

---

(1) W. W. Greg, *Alcazar & Orlando*, p. 357.
(2) I tentatively suggest that certain phrases in the Alleyn manuscript might bear on Gabriel Harvey : as we will see, 'poet laureate' fits him, while the so-called proverbial phrase (not listed elsewhere by Greg) 'three blue beans in a blue bladder, rattle bladder rattle' (Alleyn MS., 136) also occurs in George Peele's *Old Wives' Tale*, printed in 1595 (Malone Society Reprint, ll. 819-20), in a conversation between Zantippa and Huanebango. The latter character, as many critics recognize, was a caricature of Gabriel Harvey.

see from a significant example, designated the contemplative mind rapt to the divine intelligence, and it is in this light that Orlando's pursuit of Rosalind's love may perhaps be viewed. To determine the provenance of the mythological reference is, of course, difficult and one has to bear in mind that Thomas Lodge's *Rosalynde* (1590) actually supplied Shakespeare with a Ganymede. But whatever be the origin of the name, a few textual features in *As You Like It* suggest that Shakespeare developed the myth of Ganymede consistently. Ganymede, so the myth tells us, was carried up into heaven by an eagle and became cup-bearer to the gods, in other words, a page to Jupiter. Now, Celia in *As You Like It*, though adopting the name of Aliena, is occasionally regarded as a Jupiter by Rosalind, a circumstance insufficiently recognized by Shakespeare's editors. Compare:

Cel. If I had a thunderbolt in mine eie, I can tell who should downe.
(I, ii, 226-7.)

Ros. Ile haue no worse a name than *Ioues* own Page,
And therefore looke you call me *Ganimed*.
(I, iii, 126-7.)

Ros. O *Iupiter*, how merry are my spirits.
(II, iv, 1.)

Ros. *Ioue, Ioue*, this Shepherds passion,
Is much vpon my fashion.
(II, iv, 61-2.)

Ros. O most gentle *Iupiter*, what tedious homilie of Loue haue you wearied your parishioners withall, and neuer cri'de, haue patience good people. (III, ii, 163-166.)

Three of the above quotations, it is true, do not *necessarily* imply that Rosalind outsteps the limits of the conventional symbolism inherent in her being a Ganymede, while her exclamations may be merely conventional ones as well. But Celia's expression 'If I had a thunderbolt in mine eie, I can tell who should downe,' seen in connexion with the myth of Ganymede, intimates clearly that Celia is only an imperfect or reputed Jupiter, one who is not equipped with a thunderbolt. These considerations are of importance because they help us, at least in one instance, to establish the merits of the First Folio reading. At III, ii, 163-166 (the last passage above quoted) most, if not all, editors of *As You Like It* give the word 'pulpiter' for the Folio's 'Iupiter,' an emendation first introduced by Spedding. On this emendation Professor J. Dover Wilson comments: 'Spedding's emendation, now adopted by most edd., fits the context perfectly. The epithet 'gentle,' ludicrous as applied to Jupiter, is obviously directed to Celia, while 'tedious homily' and 'parishioners' lend 'pulpiter' strong support. We may add that there is no serious difficulty from the graphical point of view, since an 'English' p might be mistaken for a capital I if the loop were blind' (1). To my mind there is little doubt that this ingenious argument is invalid and that Spedding's emendation had better be discarded. The Ganymede-Jupiter symbolism, too, perhaps affects another emendation at II, iv, 1, where Rosalind says (Folio text): 'O *Iupiter*, how merry are my spirits.' Most editors, following Lewis Theobald's emendation, read 'weary spirits' instead of 'merry spirits,' and they point out that this fits the context. On the assumption that Rosalind is 'Jove's own page,' however, she is perfectly entitled to be 'merry,' for, under Jupiter's influence, she may have a 'Jovial' and merry complexion.

To conclude this section I wish to call attention to the re-vitalizing of the Ganymede myth as this appears in a few contemporary writings. A first reference, from Fraunce's *Amyntas Pastorall*, is not very significant. It will be remembered that the second scene of the last act of *Amyntas Pastorall* was a conclusion to the Tasso translation that was entirely of Fraunce's invention. Phillis and Amyntas are shown courting, though Phillis is still unwilling to grant her favours. Here is Amyntas' final request and Phillis' answer:

> *Amyntas.*
> Let come fayre *Helene, Troys* tribulation.
> Or braue *Endymions* sweete speculation
> Or Nymph *Idalian* friendly to passion:
> None but *Phillis* alone holdeth *Amyntas* hands:
> None but *Phillis* alone pleaseth *Amyntas* eyes:
> None but *Phillis* alone woundeth *Amyntas* hart.

> *Phillis.*
> Let come that prety boy, fonde of his owne image,
> Or Goddesse mynion kylde by an ougly Boare,
> Or youthfull *Ganymede* rapt by the thunderer;

---

(1) J. DOVER WILSON, ed. *As You Like It* (Cambridge, 1926, repr. 1948), p. 137.

> *Phillis* stretcheth alone hands to *Amyntas* hands,
> *Phillis* turneth alone eyes to *Amyntas* eyes,
> *Phillis* ioyneth alone hart to *Amyntas* hart (1).

The appearance of mythological or astrological embroidery—the two are obviously connected—is, of course, extremely common in Elizabethan and Renaissance literature generally, but this does not mean that mythology was merely fortuitously used, Greene's consistency in the practice being a case in point. Though Fraunce's lines which compare Amyntas to a youthful Ganymede rapt by Jupiter do not intimate much of the author's concern with the allegorical significance of his comparison (but note the phrase '*Endymions* sweete speculation'), we are fortunate in possessing other evidence which shows convincingly that Fraunce was thoroughly familiar with the Renaissance allegorization of Ganymede as the pure mind which finds joy in heavenly contemplation. Fraunce's statement occurs in his treatise *The Third part of the Countesse of Pembrokes Yuychurch* (1592) and must be fully quoted.

> Others, by the rauishing of *Ganymede* by Iupiter, vnderstand the lifting vp of mans minde from these earthly toyes, to heauenly conceipts: that *Ganymedes* may be derived of γάνυμι to ioy and reioyce, and μήδεα, signifying aduice & counsaile, as though mans soule thus rauished by *Ioue*, might wel be sayd to enioy his heauenly comfort and counsaile, γαννύθαι μήδεσι τοῦ διὸς (2).

Fraunce leaves his source unmentioned at this point, but he simply translates from the Latin explanations which Claude Mignault appended to Alciati's *Emblematum Liber*. Critics have already noticed (3) that Fraunce's treatise *The Third part* is indebted to Cartari and Comes, but nobody, to my knowledge, seems to have drawn attention to Fraunce's use of Alciati. To explain *Ganymedis nomen vnde* Mignault says:

> *Consilium, mens atque Dei*, &c. μυθολογία est, in qua aduertendum, quam graphice & commode Ganymedei nominis vim exprimat. γάννυμι enim, vel γάννυμαι, laetor est: respondetque his quae dixit, Gaudia praestant: & μήδεα consilia. vnde γάννυσθαι μήδεσι τοῦ διὸς Emblematis & figmenti sensum explanat.

---

(1) FRAUNCE, *The Countesse of Pembrokes Yuychurch* (1591), sig. F₄.
(2) FRAUNCE, *The Third part of the Countesse of Pembrokes Yuychurch* (1592), sig. I₂.
(3) See DOUGLAS BUSH, *Mythology and the Renaissance Tradition*, p. 308.

In the body of Alciati's text itself we also find a passage containing the source of Fraunce's initial words.

. . . , per Ganymedem ab aquila raptum, animam humanam intelligimus, quae, vt ait Plotinus, tum condere caput intra caelum dicitur, cum relicta quasi corporis secretione, caelestia mentis oculo contemplatur: quod sane absque raptu quodam fieri minime potest (1).

The emblematic engraving which accompanies Alciati's text shows us Ganymede borne aloft by an eagle, his face turned upwards to contemplate the divine image.

The prevalence of the Ganymede myth in several contemporary works and Fraunce's conferring this name upon Amyntas raise the further question whether Fraunce and others did not think of a particular nobleman as a new Amyntas. A collection of a few relevant allusions may afford us a key to this person's identity. The most striking reference is supplied by Thomas Nashe. He dedicates his *Pierce Penilesse His Supplication to the Devil* (published in 1592, entered in the Stationers' Register on August 8, 1592) to

. . . the matchlesse image of Honor, and magnificent rewarder of vertue, *Ioues Eagle-borne Ganimed*, thrice noble *Amyntas*. In whose spirit, such a Deitie of wisdom appeereth, that if *Homer* were to write his *Odissea* new (where, vnder the person of *Vlysses*, he describeth a singular man of perfection, in whom all ornaments both of peace and warre are assembled in the height of their excelence), he need no other instance to augment his conceipt, than the rare carriage of his honorable minde (2).

Thomas Nashe has spared no pains to accumulate precisely such epithets as emphasize the supreme intellectual gifts of Amyntas. A dedication is admittedly conventional in tone, but it is here once more the mythological simile which sets one thinking. Amyntas, as in Fraunce, is also a Ganymede, carried aloft by an eagle, and one may conclude, almost with certainty, that Nashe's conceit goes back to Alciati's handbook of emblems. The coincidences just discussed stamp Amyntas as a singular example of intellectual beauty, and Nashe further stressed this by comparing his patron to Ulysses. But who was this patron ?

R. B. McKerrow (3), the distinguished editor of Nashe's works,

---

(1) ALCIATI, *Emblemata* (Leyden, 1591), pp. 51, 49.
(2) NASHE, *Works*, I, 243.
(3) R. B. McKERROW, ed. *Nashe*, IV, 150-1.

following Edmond Malone, suggests an identification of Amyntas with Ferdinando Stanley, Lord Strange, Earl of Derby, the nobleman, it will be remembered, whose troupe of actors performed Greene's *Orlando Furioso* at the Rose. In another poem, written about the same time, the Earl of Derby is probably referred to under the same pastoral name, namely in Edmund Spenser's *Colin Clouts Come Home Again* (1595), lines 434-5:

> *Amyntas* quite is gone and lies full low,
> Hauing his *Amaryllis* left to mone.

With regard to Nashe's use of 'Ganymede' for his patron, it must be recalled that among those mentioned in George Chapman's *The Shadow of Night* figured 'most ingenious *Darbie*,' and it is therefore illuminating to find corroboration for the currency of the symbolism of Ganymede in that poem to signify 'bewtie of the minde.' It is, of course, conceivable that Chapman may have inserted a passage about Ganymede to celebrate intellectual beauty without any personal reference; but this is apparently not the case since, as I have already pointed out, Chapman expressly states that he gives a man's shape to Ganymede. The employment of similar symbolic imagery suggests that both Chapman and Nashe regard the Earl of Derby as an outstanding representative of wisdom, as a person whom it was customary to cast for the part of Ganymede (1). A third poet, George Peele, also uses the imagery of Jove's eagle in connexion with Lord Strange, and though Ganymede is not named, it is not impossible that Peele's imagery also harks backs to the symbolism associated with that myth. In *Polyhymnia, describing the honourable triumph at Tylt* (1590), by George Peele, we find Ferdinando Stanley described as follows:

> The Earl of Derby's valiant son and heir,
> Brave Ferdinand Lord Strange, strangely embark'd
> Under Jove's kingly bird the golden eagle,
> Stanley's old crest and honourable badge,
> As veering 'fore the wind in costly ship,
> And armour white and watchet buckled fast,
> Presents himself; . . . (2)

---

(1) See also R. W. Battenhouse, "Chapman's *The Shadow of Night*: An Interpretation," *SP*, XXXVIII (1941), 606 footnote.
(2) Peele. *Works*, ed. A. H. Bullen (London, 1888). II. 289.

Peele, Nashe, and Chapman may all three be said to confirm the view that Lord Strange was a kind of Ganymede, the very incarnation of divine wisdom.

Reviewing the allegorical imagery current in or about 1592, it cannot escape our notice that several artists of the period, when they were anxious to describe intellectual aspirations, often employed the symbolism connected with some specific classic myth; Greene, Nashe, and Chapman, in their different ways, testified to their being attracted by mythological symbolism made serviceable to personal allusion. Shakespeare, as ever, seems to have held aloof from using, as indiscriminatingly as his contemporaries, the ready-made devices supplied by the mythographers. Attracted by mythology Shakespeare certainly was, but he never deemed it necessary to press it into the service of contemporary allusion. To determine how this type of allusion affected Thomas Nashe personally will be our next concern.

II

Though the bearing on Ferdinando Stanley of *Amyntas Pastorall* is far from being proved—indeed it merely depends on a casual allusion to Ganymede—the texts of the second and third parts of Fraunce's *Yuychurch* composition do indicate that at various moments Fraunce had Nashe, and perhaps also Ferdinando Stanley, in mind. Abraham Fraunce's so-called 'second part' of the Countess of Pembroke's *Yuychurch* is entitled *Phillis Funerall*. It is largely a republication of the *Lamentations* of 1587, but the eclogues, instead of eleven, now number twelve. What is called 'The last Lamentation and the death of Amintas' in the earlier publication, now becomes the song of the twelfth day, to which are appended another sixteen lines. Fraunce has thus added an 'eleventh day,' except lines 65-68 which are lifted bodily from the originally last eclogue of the 1587 *Lamentations*. This 'eleventh day' is an interesting production, because, as I will endeavour to show, it contains an allusion to Nashe in connexion with his patron 'Amyntas.' It is also of some interest to note that this eclogue also refers to the fact that lovers' names are carved upon the barks of trees, while nothing of the sort appeared in the *Lamentations*.

> Farewell knife at last, whose poynt engrau'd in a thousand
> Barcks of trees that name, sweet name of my bony *Phillis*,
> And hard by that name, this name of Louer *Amyntas*:

Soe that in euery ash, these names stood, *Phillis Amyntas,*
And each Beech-tree barck, bare these names, *Phillis Amyntas:*

(The eleuenth day, ll. 82-80)

Finally, we come to consider Fraunce's most important publication, namely *The Third part of the Countesse of Pembrokes Yuychurch: Entituled, Amintas Dale; Wherein are the most conceited
tales of the Pagan Gods in English Hexameters together with their
ancient descriptions and Philosophicall explications,* At London, for
Thomas Woodcocke, 1592. The work was entered in the Stationers'
Register on October 2, 1592 (1), and, bearing in mind that Nashe's
Pierce Penilesse had been entered on 8th August and Greene's
Groatsworth of Wit on 20th September of the same year, we need
not be surprised to find and allusion to Nashe in Fraunce's *Third
part.* This work was again dedicated to Mary, Countess of Pembroke.
It is a sort of mythological handbook as the sub-title states. Fraunce's
knowledge in the field of mythology is drawn from many contemporary sources. The author shows acquaintance with the writers of
his day in quoting Remy Belleau, Natalis Comes, Pontanus, while he
also refers to Dante. *The Third part* is connected with the other
'parts' through the use of the names Thirsis and Elpinus, two
characters from Tasso's *Aminta.* Fraunce, through the mouth of
Thirsis, first gives a description of the genesis of the world, while
Elpinus adds his commentary in the form of 'philosophicall explications.' Fraunce's view concerning allegory—this has already been
referred to—ushers in the explanations.

Before tackling the passage which probably refers to Nashe,
I wish to point out that Professor Douglas Bush (2) observes that
Fraunce's treatise contains the story of Venus and Adonis, of which
he quotes 'some lines which in tone are not unlike Shakespeare's
poem.' On the other hand, *The Third part* also contains the story
of Salmacis and Hermaphrodite, which, as students of *Venus and
Adonis* know, Shakespeare was also to incorporate in his epic poem.
We know already that for his classical learning Fraunce leans
heavily on the mythographers Comes and Cartari, while another part
of his allegorical matter seems to be compiled from an annotated

---

(1) Arber, *Transcript,* II, 621.
(2) See D. Bush, "Notes on Shakespeare's Classical Mythology," *PQ,* VI (1927),
295-302, esp. p. 299.

edition of Ovid (Cambridge, 1584), from Leo Hebraeus (1), as well as from Alciati's *Emblemata.*

Having quoted the *Aeneid,* VI, 237-242, Fraunce, drawing on Comes, explains Cerberus thus:

Cerberus is *Plutoes* dog, with three heades, watching that none goe out, but ready to let all in; fawning on these, deuouring those, according to his name. For κρεόβορος, and, by a more easie contraction of the word, κέρβερος, is a deuowrer of flesh, of κρεάς and βορᾶν: wherefore some vnderstand by him, the all-deuowring earth, eating and consuming all earthly bodies. Others, by *Cerberus,* intend mans bodie, prest and appliable to all sensuall lust, but repugning and abhorring vertue and contemplation. His three heads be taken of some to represent those three necessarie euills, which withdraw men from contemplation, I meane, hunger, thirst, and sleepe: to all which, we must offer a morsell, as *Sybilla* taught *Aeneas* in Virgil, we must yeeld, but not too much; so much only, as thereby nature may be susteined. *Natalis Comes* expoundeth it thus: *Cerberus* is Couetousnes: and a couetous man laughes when hee sees gold come in; but it greeues his heart to lay out one penie. His three heads note the manifold guiles and deceites of couetous men, *Qui omnes pecuniae vias norunt,* know all the waies in the world how to scrape coyne. *Cerberus* lyes in an hellish dungeon: a myser lurketh in corners, turning his rustie groates, without either profit to others, or pleasure to himselfe. *Hercules* drew him out of Hell, for, who can be a *Hercules,* and accomplish great matters, without money? Or thus, *Hercules* bound and brought out *Cerberus,* that is to say, he bridled and kept vnder concupiscence, and therefore returned safe from Hell: but *Pyrithous* going thither of purpose to ravish *Plutoes* Queene, and so to satisfie sensualitie, was deuoured of *Cerberus:* or, lastly, Hercules is a learned and absolute Philosopher: hee draweth the three-throated *Cerberus* out of Hell, by bringing to light the tripertite mysteries of Philosophie, naturall, morall, and dialecticall. *Cerberus,* for spite and rage, strugling with *Hercules* did let his poysoned foame fall on the earth, whence proceeded the deadly *Aconitum,* for, what but rancor, can come from a rancorous heart? Historically, as *Pausanias* reporteth, there was in a darke dungeon in *Taenarus,* leading to Hell, as the fame went, for the deepenes thereof, an hydeous and terrible serpent, which for his deadly poyson, and fearefull aspect, was called the Diuels dog, and was by *Hercules* drawne forth, and brought to King *Euristheus* (2).

The above quotation is largely made up from scraps out of Comes' chapter *De Cerbero* (*Mythologiae,* III, v), scraps which may be cited in the order in which they occur in Fraunce.

Ipsum siquidem nomen significat sepulchrum esse cerberum, quia κρέας caro est, βορῶ autem voro.

---

(1) See D. Bush, *Mythology and the Renaissance Tradition,* p. 308.
(2) Fraunce, *The Third part,* sig. H₁v°.

Qui ad mores, vitaeque humanae institutionem haec transtulere, cerberum auaritia esse, diuitiarumque cupiditatem arbitrantur: quae non nisi malis cogitationibus oritur: cum nemo vir bonus diues breui euadat.

Dictus est cerberus in obscura spelunca habitare, quoniam omnium prope vitiorum stultissimum sit auaritia: cum neque sibi prosit, nec reliquis nec sibi vel posteris gloriam comparare studeat, sed semper inter sordidos & obscuros homines versetur. At Hercules, quae virtus est animi magnitudo, cerberum in lucem extraxit, sibique perpetuam gloriam comparauit. Quis enim sine opibus facilem esse sibi viam ad perpetuitatem nominis affirmauerit?

Iubebantur cum Cerbero prius pugnare, qui Proserpina nuptias peterent: qui victi laniabantur, hanc Theseus cum Pirithoo per insidias rapere conati sunt, quos cum non vt procos, sed vt raptorem accessisse intellexit Aidoneus, in vincula coniecit, ac Pirithoum cani statim vorandum exposuit.

Alii fabulati sunt illum ab inferis eductum fuisse ab Hercule, per eam speluncam, quae non procul distat a Taenaro, qui cum primum lucem sensisset, vomuit; ex quo vomitu spumaque oris natum est aconitum, . . .

Atqui cum nullos esse inferos putarent antiquorum nonnulli, scriptum reliquit Pausanias in Laconicis non solum nulla esse Deorum regna subterranea, quo animae deuenirent, vbi e vita excesserint, sed Cerberum etiam tetrum ac immanem serpentem fuisse, qui lustrum haberet in spelunca quadam apud Taenarum: qui quecumque momordisset, continuo vis veneni interimebat, vt sensit etiam Hecataeus Milesius, quare dictus est canis inferorum (1).

On the other hand, the interpretation of Hercules as a philosopher seems to me to owe much to Valeriano's handbook of hieroglyphs, an authority Fraunce leaves unmentioned. To explain *Cerberi mythologia* Valeriano says:

Hieroglyphicum & Cerberus argumentum habet: Graecorum enim nonnulli non incongrue forsan existimarunt, abstractum Herculis opera ex obscuris Erebi penetralibus tricipitem Cerberum, patefactam ab Heroë Philosophiam, quae prius in arcanis delitescebat, indicare. Ea vero vna ceruice contenta, tribus distinguitur capitibus, quorum vnum Rationi, Naturae alterum, tertium Moribus inseruit (2).

Here, no doubt, is the origin of Fraunce's phrase 'Philosophie, naturall, morall, and dialecticall.'

The reasons for thinking that in the years 1590-1592 'Cerberus' was in certain circles an 'allegorical' sobriquet for Thomas Nashe

---

(1) COMES, *Mythologiae* (1616), pp. 104-106.
(2) VALERIANO, *Hieroglyphica* (ed. 1556), p. 41.

have to be collected from a number of Elizabethan writers. Taken singly, these pieces of evidence may not appear particularly convincing, but when they are surveyed as a whole they will render it highly probable that many Elizabethans thought of Nashe as a Cerberus vomiting poisoned foam upon the earth, 'whence proceeded the deadly *Aconitum.*' The word aconite or aconitum occurs fairly frequently in Elizabethan literature, especially in Greene, but it may be noted in passing that Shakespeare uses it only once, in a passage to be considered later. The aconite is a genus of poisonous plants, also called monk's-hood or wolf's-bane; aconite may also refer to the extract of this plant, used as a poison, while figuratively it merely means deadly poison. If there is evidence to regard Nashe as a Cerberus, it does not necessarily follow that every mention of Cerberus in Elizabethan literature therefore refers to Nashe. Before considering the works of Nashe and Gabriel Harvey, writers who are obviously best qualified to give information on the subject, we may begin with Fraunce's passage itself.

On the whole Fraunce merely follows the allegorical interpretation indicated by his sources, but he does make a few additions; for instance, when he tells us that only rancour can come from a rancorous heart he makes a reflection which may have been prompted by some contemporary incident. On the other hand, he slightly deviates from the source in translating *canis inferorum* as 'the Diuels dog.' Of course, in themselves these changes are of very little consequence in an attempt to find in Cerberus an allusion to Nashe, and it must be conceded that Fraunce 'allegorizes' other details which could hardly apply to Nashe. It must be borne in mind, however, that *Pierce Penilesse*, the most popular of Nashe's works, had just been given to the public; it went through three editions in 1592, while it was again in demand in 1593 and 1595. Nashe's readers must especially have been struck by the fact that it was a 'supplication' to the 'Devil,' certainly something exceptional even to Elizabethans; and that this was really the case appears from the fact the printer of Nashe's tract termed the title 'strange and in it selfe somewhat preposterous.' And Gabriel Harvey's description of the tract as 'the notorious Diabolicall discourse of the said *Pierce*, a man better acquainted with the Diuels of Hell, then with the Starres of Heauen' (1), indicates how tellingly that feature struck

---

(1) HARVEY, *Foure Letters*, ed. G. B. HARRISON (London, 1922), p. 49.

Nashe's readers. An association of Nashe with the devil could thus quite naturally be made, and so we find Nashe regarded as a kind of devil's dog. Furthermore, the allegorization Fraunce gives fits in admirably with what we know of Nashe's finances, for Nashe, to quote Harvey's words again, was a man 'cruelly pinched with want, vexed with discredite, tormented with other mens felicitie, and ouerwhelmed with his own misery' (1). Let us now examine Nashe's writings themselves.

As an important reference to Cerberus occurs in his *Summers Last Will and Testament*, a comedy probably composed at Croydon in September or October, 1592—note the date, something very important with regard to the matter in hand—we had best first discuss the circumstances of its production (2). From certain allusions in *Summers Last Will and Testament* it appears that the performance probably took place in Croydon, while the description (line 1879) of the house in which it was played can apply only to the Archbishop's palace. One may therefore conclude, with a high degree of probability, that the comedy was acted before John Whitgift, Archbishop of Canterbury. Whitgift had been raised to the dignity of Archbishop in 1583, and, untiring opponent of Puritanism as he was, he soon began to enforce Queen Elizabeth's ecclesiastical policy rigorously. After the excommunication of the Queen in 1570, and especially after the successful overthrow of the rising of the Northern Earls, the ecclesiastical government was allowed an entirely free hand to interfere with the religious convictions of England's subjects. The Anglican bishops were engaged in fighting two enemies, the Roman Catholics on the one hand, and the Puritans on the other. Whitgift's policy was to stamp out Puritanism by force; a great many Puritans were emprisoned and had their goods confiscated, while many others paid their conviction with their lives. This kind of ecclesiastical rule was soon to call forth a reaction from the puritan camp in the form of satirical attacks, first conducted by church ministers and then by a writer under the name 'Martin Marprelate.' This writer's identity, though long suspected, has now been conclusively established (3). Martin was

---

(1) HARVEY, *Foure Letters*, p. 44.
(2) See R. B. McKERROW, ed. *Nashe*, I, 21 and IV, 416-419.
(3) See DONALD J. McGINN, "The Real Martin Marprelate," *PMLA*, LVIII (1943), 83-107.

a certain John Penry (1559-1593), a Welsh puritan, who was hanged on the charge of exciting rebellion by his writings.

The first Marprelate tract, known as *The Epistle*, was printed by Robert Waldegrave and issued about the end of October 1588; other tracts followed and after some time the strength of the movement in favour of Martin and Puritanism generally became such that, by the summer or autumn of 1589, Whitgift decided upon new methods of warfare and enlisted the professional writers of the day to defend the episcopal cause. In this way John Lyly, Robert Greene, and probably Thomas Nashe were commissioned to reply to the Martinist attacks. It was perhaps in that capacity that the nickname Cerberus became first attached to Nashe, though, with the possible exception of one mention, I have failed to discover any relevant allusion. Cerberus might have been a fitting name for one who was able to ferret out Martins (= a popular nickname for an ape) (1). R. B. McKerrow, though considering it practically certain that the Martin Marprelate Controversy formed an important episode in Nashe's career as a writer, points out that his precise connexion with it is vague (2), so much so that it is difficult to attribute any of the anti-Martinist pamphlets to him. Recently, however, Professor Donald J. McGinn (3) has convincingly attributed the anti-Martinist tract *An Almond for a Parrat* (probably published in February-March, 1590) to Nashe. This tract is also Nashe's first work containing a reference to Cerberus. Let us first examine that to be found in *Summers Last Will and Testament*.

---

(1) Cerberus's ability to ferret out Martins is well conveyed in an anonymous pamphlet of 1642, suggested by a tract by JOHN TAYLOR, *Differing Worships* (1640). In this anonymous pamphlet, entitled *Tom Nash his Ghost*, occurs a set of verses on the back of the title from which the following lines may be quoted :

> *I* then did gall their *Galls*, and spight their spight,
> *I* made the Nests of *Martins* take their flight;
> But first they had disperst their fond opinions,
> *In* sundry places of the Queenes Dominions,
> Which (like *Impostumes*) not well cur'd at first,
> Corrupted ever since, doth now out-burst.
> Wherfore my ayery *Ghost* shall undertake
> Once more to try a perfect Cure to make;
> For (being now invisible, a Spirit)
> I cut through th'Ayre, and in the Earth can ferrit,
> And in an Augure hole my selfe can hide,
> And heare their knaveries and spie vnspide.

The whole text is quoted by R. B. McKERROW, ed. *Nashe*, V, 46.

(2) R. B. McKERROW, ed. *Nashe*, V, 49.

(3) D. J. McGINN, "Nashe's Share in the Marprelate Controversy," *PMLA*, LIX (1944), 952-984.

If we recall the circumstances of the comedy's production, the following passage from *Summers Last Will* (lines 1255-1264) may have acquired a topical meaning for its original spectators. It is spoken by 'Winter' :

> When Cerberus was headlong drawne from hell,
> He voided a blacke poison from his mouth,
> Called *Aconitum*, whereof inke was made :
> That inke, with reeds first laid on dried barkes,
> Seru'd men a while to make rude workes withall,
> Till *Hermes*, secretarie to the Gods,
> Or *Hermes Trismegistus*, as some will,
> Wearie with grauing in blind characters,
> And figures of familiar beasts and plants,
> Inuented letters to write lies withall.

McKerrow, annotating this passage, refers to Pliny, *Hist. Nat.*, XXVII, 2, where Pliny describes the properties of aconite ; Cerberus, however, is not mentioned by Pliny. There are, of course, many ancient authors who can inform us that Cerberus's foam gave rise to aconite, see for instance Ovid, *Metamorphoses*, VII, 413 ff. It is a little peculiar that Nashe skips a stage in the production of this poison, for he simply identifies Cerberus's foam with aconite, which is surely unwarranted by any ancient authority. One sixteenth century mythographer, Comes, for instance, says that aconite is born of Cerberus's vomit, not identical with it. Nashe further declares that ink was made of it, and this statement is a second product of Nashe's invention, and here, surely, one may suspect an allusion to the quantities of ink he had to waste, first on the Martin Marprelate controversy, and second, on his unsavoury quarrels with Gabriel Harvey ; for, no ancient authority will be found to specify that Cerberus vomited a black poison of which ink was made (1).

Given a Nashe-Cerberus association, one can hardly feel surprised that the pamphlets written by Gabriel Harvey, Nashe's great enemy in the years 1592-1593, often reproach Nashe with being a dog. The passages in which this kind of insult occurs are so numerous that it would be tedious to enumerate them. Such insults, if they stood alone, might of course be explained away as just extremely common terms of abuse, but, considering Nashe's associ-

---

(1) Compare HARVEY, *Foure Letters*, p. 64 : 'and although his incke, be not pitch, or poison, yet it is incke' is an indirect confirmation of the fact that NASHE's ink is a black poison, which HARVEY wants to refute.

ation with Cerberus, they must be recognized as literary epithets probably related to that particular myth. Conclusive evidence on this question is, however, provided by a passage in Harvey's last known contribution to his famous controversy with Nashe, namely *A New Letter of Notable Contents*, published in 1593. In the course of this pamphlet Harvey upbraids Nashe thus: 'It was his glory, to be a *hellhounde incarnate*, and to spoile Origen of his egregious praise: *Vbi benè, nemo melius: vbi malè, nemo peius*' (1). Harvey's own italics are significant; 'dog' is a very common term of abuse indeed, but 'hellhounde incarnate' is certainly not. It completely coincides with a Nashe who glories to be the very incarnation of Cerberus.

The style of Nashe's *An Almond for a Parrat* is so much loaded with imagery that it becomes difficult to give as satisfactory an interpretation of the satirist's first reference to Cerberus. Yet I believe it to be relevant to the present discussion. Having upbraided his countrymen for their simplicity, Nashe proceeds to attack John Penry, the redoubtable 'Marprelate,' thus:

> Pen., with Pan, hath contended with Appollo, and you, lyke Midasses, haue ouerprised his musick. Good God, ẏ a Welch harpe should inchant so many English harts to their confusiõ, especially hauing nere a string belonging to it but a treble. Had a syren sung, & I drownd in attending her descante, I would haue bequeathed my bane to her beautie, but when Cerberus shall barke & I turne back to listen, thẽ let me perish without pittie in the delight of my liuing destruction (2).

The contemporaries, so Nashe contends, value Penry's eloquence too highly, for the enchanting powers of a Welsh harp are likely to lead them to their confusion. The idea that Penry's satirical vein produces an enchantment quite naturally suggests to Nashe the myth of the sirens, who were believed to have the power of enchanting, by their music, any one who came near them (see Homer, *Odyssey*, XII, 19). A singing siren might have lured him to his destruction as well, says Nashe, and, in that case, the siren's enchanting powers would have entitled her to the inheritance of his bane. But Cerberus, whose barking apparently exercises a much more powerful charm, would have filled Nashe with delight at the thought of his 'liuing destruction.' Nashe's suggestive phrases are no doubt meta-

---

(1) HARVEY, *A New Letter of Notable Contents* (1593), sig. D₁.
(2) NASHE, *Works*, III, 367.

phorical, and we get the impression that he is using the elements of the Cerberus-myth merely to heighten the effect of his style. It seems to me that Nashe, unwilling to bequeathe his 'bane' to a siren, wants Cerberus to inherit this, while '*liuing* destruction' reads like a sponsoring of the hellhound's cause. We must, I think, allow for a certain intentional looseness in Nashe's language, and this is why we can hardly expect the author to establish the equation with Cerberus directly. It is unfortunate that all the relevant evidence cannot but be presented step by step. As the argument proceeds, however, readers will yet more distinctly recognize the profoundly significant function of the symbolism inherent in the Cerberus-myth, as well as that of comparisons drawn from the sphere of music.

Two corroborative quotations from writings published between the publication-dates of *An Almond for a Parrat* and *Pierce Penilesse* yet remain for discussion; the first derives from Abraham Fraunce and the second from John Florio (1553-1625), the famous translator of Montaigne's *Essais*. It will be remembered that Fraunce's *Phillis Funerall* was a republication of an earlier work, to which had been added a newly written eclogue, the so-called 'eleuenth day.' *Phillis Funerall* was entered in the Stationers' Register on February 9, 1591, a date which, if the 'eleuenth day' can be shown to bear on Nashe, links up well with that of *An Almond for a Parrat*, which was published in February-March 1590. In Fraunce's work the following lines are to be found:

> Goe poore louing dogg, ould Light-foote, seeke thee a master.
> Get thee a new master, since thyne ould master *Amyntas*
> Gets him another dogg, fowle *Cerberus* horrible helhounde.
> Now shal I neuer more geue Light-foote bones to be gnawing,
> Now shal I neuer more cause Light-foote, glooues to be fetching (1):
>
> (*The eleuenth day*, ll. 49-53.)

Fraunce was no doubt the poorest of versifiers and it is difficult to believe that he ever took this kind of doggerel, let alone its 'allegory,' seriously. The interest of these verses indeed resides solely in their topical import. I do not know who is meant by 'ould Light-foote' (2), but it seems to me very likely that lines

---

(1) FRAUNCE, *The Countesse of Pembrokes Yuychurch* (1591), sig. K$_3$ v⁰.

(2) It may not be superfluous to mention that there is a writer of the name WILLIAM LIGHTFOOT, author of *The Complaint of England*, which was entered in the Register to JOHN WOLFE on March 4, 1587, and published in the same year. LIGHTFOOT is a name not listed by the *Dictionary of National Biography*.

2-3 have to be interpreted as an allusion to Nashe and his patron Ferdinando Stanley, Lord Strange. Unfortunately very little is known of Nashe's life in the years 1589-1592. His *Anatomie of Absurditie* (1589) was dedicated to Sir Charles Blount, whose acquaintance he had perhaps made through Greene, as McKerrow (1) conjectures; but this attempt to secure active support was apparently unsuccessful because no other work was dedicated to that nobleman. Through Greene's introduction, however, Nashe may also have become acquainted with Lord Strange, to whom Greene had dedicated his *Ciceronis Amor* (1589). If we assume the first contact to have been made in 1589, it has to be borne in mind that it was in the autumn of that year that Nashe became involved in the Marprelate Controversy, the very year in which the Earl of Derby, Ferdinando's father, is reported by Archbishop Whitgift to have arrested three printers while printing the Marprelate tract *More worke for the Cooper* in August 1589 (2). Nashe's anti-Martinist activity may therefore have brought him in contact with the Strange family. Why Fraunce found it necessary to allude to Nashe is a question that I shall try to answer more fully later. It may be that Fraunce had resented Nashe's publishing an edition of Sidney's *Astrophel and Stella* in 1591 with a preface from his hand. The preface contains a passage in praise of the Countess of Pembroke, but the edition was apparently unauthorized and replaced by another later in the year.

A few other contemporary passages also involving the use of canine imagery support the interpretation of the evidence before us. The author of them is John Florio, whose *Second Fruits* (1591), a language-manual for the study of Italian, must have caused a considerable stir at the time of its publication. The *Second Fruits* was dedicated to Nicholas Saunder of Ewell, who was related to Dr. Nicholas Sander, a well-known recusant. This dedication, which contains an allusion to one of Nashe's early works (to be referred to later), is followed by a preface to the reader with at the end the date 'The last of April. 1591.' In the second dialogue of the *Second Fruits* the following conversation is to be found:

---

(1) R. B. McKERROW, ed. *Nashe*, V, 16-17.
(2) See E. ARBER, *An Introductory Sketch to the Martin Marprelate Controversy. 1588-1590* (London, 1879), pp. 112, 117. Also J. DOVER WILSON, "The Marprelate Controversy," *CHEL*, III (1908), 382.

G. If any man wrong thee, wrong him againe, or else be sure to remember it.

T. With such people a man must needes doo so.

G. To wolfes flesh, a man must applie a doggs tooth (1).

Florio's manual is almost entirely made up of proverbial phrases, and it is therefore necessary first to verify whether 'To wolfes flesh, a man must applie a doggs tooth' is a real Elizabethan proverb. Apparently it is not, for, if it were more than ordinarily common, we would find it listed in the magnificent proverb-collection recently compiled by Professor Morris Palmer Tilley (2). That the 'proverbial' character of the phrase was already lost in the seventeenth century is further proved by the fact that Giovanni Torriano, whose great proverb-collection *Piazza Universale di Proverbi Italiani* (1666) was based on material mainly derived from Florio's writings, gives an explanation of the phrase which does not tally with the sense Florio attaches to it. To explain 'A *carne* di lupo, dente di cane' (translated as '*Woolfs* flesh *must have a dogs tooth*') Torriano says: 'Many revenge themselves on the wrong Partie, out of passion or over-sight' (3). The foregoing considerations strongly suggest that 'To wolfes flesh, a man must applie a doggs tooth' was not a merely 'proverbial' device to allow Londoners to brush up their Italian, but a statement once furnished with topical meaning. That a wolf-dog antagonism was clearly present to Florio's mind appears from his expressing the idea a second time in the sixth chapter of his work, where we read: 'If of the wolfe thou be in feare, Be sure to keepe a dog neare' (4). Florio's antipathy for the 'wolf' reappears in the next chapter where, in a different context, a Wolf's wolvish conscience is reviled. Bearing in mind that aconite, the poisonous plant originating from Cerberus's foam, means wolf's-bane, Florio's statements can be fittingly interpreted. They no doubt imply that there is a dog (= Cerberus-Nashe) who is at enmity with a wolf, and who could this 'wolf' be but John Wolfe, the printer who allied himself with Gabriel Harvey in the latter's quarrels with Nashe? It is therefore safe to infer from Florio's manual that there must have been some cause for hostility between Wolfe and Nashe.

---

(1) J. Florio, *Second Fruits* (London, 1591), pp. 19-21.

(2) M. P. Tilley, *A Dictionary of the Proverbs in England in the sixteenth and seventeenth centuries* (Ann Arbor, 1950).

(3) G. Torriano, *Piazza Universale* (London, 1666), I, 39, 58.

(4) Florio, *Second Fruits*, p. 97.

The reader now also recognizes, I hope, why Nashe in *An Almond for a Parrat* did not wish to bequeathe his 'bane' to a siren, and why he followed up this wish with an allusion to Cerberus, whose barking could cast such an ominous spell on him.

Before discussing a few minor points to help confirm the equation Nashe-Cerberus, a last suggestion remains to be put forward with respect to the possible origin of Nashe's nickname. Who was its inventor or initiator? It would of course be reassuring to find some golden thread to guide us through the vagaries of Elizabethan allusions, but it seems to me that Richard Harvey, Gabriel Harvey's brother, is to be credited with the invention of the label. As we shall soon see, there is reason for the belief that Nashe's enemies —or even friends—seized on a phrase in one of Richard Harvey's works, a phrase which, it is believed, suggested an apposite nickname to them. Students of the Harvey-Nashe quarrels know that the enmity between Gabriel Harvey and Nashe originated from a few lines in the Epistle to Richard Harvey's *A Theologicall Discourse of the Lamb of God and his Enemies*, a work entered at Stationers' Hall on October 23, 1589, and published in 1590. This Epistle, however, did not form part of the original work; this is evidenced by the interruption of the signatures and by the fact that the Epistle seems to occur in but a few copies of the *Lamb of God*. It has been printed in full in McKerrow's splendid edition of Nashe's works. McKerrow points out that the Epistle to the favourable and indifferent Reader contains an attack on Nashe which may be regarded as the origin of the famous Harvey-Nashe controversy, this being the only positive indication of enmity that McKerrow discovers. Two main reasons may be assigned for Richard Harvey's having had cause for grievance against Nashe: the arrogant tone Nashe assumed in his preface to Greene's *Menaphon* (1589), and his probable participation in the Martin Marprelate controversy. These reasons may have led Harvey to insert an attack on Nashe in the *Lamb of God*, although the attacker professes never to have heard of his victim before. It is, however, almost impossible to believe Richard Harvey, for Nashe had obviously thrust himself on the attention of the public through his anti-Martinist activity, while his satiric ability must naturally have aroused the curiosity of those who recognized his unmistakable talent.

Now in the *Lamb of God* Richard Harvey enumerates what he calls the 'wicked enemies of the lambe of God,' and observes that

Italy, formerly the true mirror of virtue, has now acquired notoriety for its atheists. He then names Pietro Pomponazzi, Machiavelli, and Pietro Aretino as 'three notable pernitious fellowes' among the atheists. Aretino, however, is described in a phrase which intimates Harvey's deliberate intention to associate the Italian with the Marprelate Controversy, for Harvey says that Aretino is 'a great courtier or rather courtisan, *the grandsire of all false and martinish courtiership.*' Then follows a long description of Aretino which requires full quotation.

Aretinus a man, or rather by morall metamorphose a beast of a most viperous & hellish spirit, in all kinde of diuelishe impiety *Vnicus,* and otherwise not so, in which respecte like enough neither *Gesner* nor *Simler* iudged him worthie to come into their libraries among other writers, although some Italians his vngracious disciples haue called him, diuine *Peter Aretine,* porter of *Plutoes* diuinitie, or much like *Tullies* diuine wit of *L. Lucullus,* or *Ouids, God is in vs, and Romish diuinity, which may euer haue a new stampe from his holines,* and other such Rhethoricall and poëticall lauish hyperbolees, he, I say of all other, was the arrogantest rakehell, and rankest villen, sauing your reuerence, that euer set penne to paper, like cursed Sodomites, iesting and sporting at that which good men in naturall modestie are ashamed to speake of *.Gen. cap.* 19. *vers.* 4, 5.
His horrible most damnable booke of three impostors, & his impudent famous Capricio, or Apologie of *Paedarastice* prooue him ἐπυχαι-ρεκακὸν, a very incarnat deuill you may call it, *and one Martin-marprelate of late hath done such a kinde of worke for very* ἐπυχαιρεκάκια, and nothing els (1).

If it is recalled that Nashe concludes his *Pierce Penilesse* with the wish that an Aretino among English writers might strip 'golden asses out of their gaie trappings,' and that he will write to Aretino's ghost to use his whip against 'our English Peacockes,' it is probable that Richard Harvey is the ultimate source of Nashe's being

---

(1) R. HARVEY, *The Lambe of God* (London, 1590), sig. N₁, pp. 95-6. In the 'Faults escaped' the above passage is corrected in two places : 'arrogantest read arrantst. pa. ead. for ἐπυχαιρεκακὸν read ἐπιχαιρεκακὸν.' With RICHARD's phrase that ARETINO is 'a great courtier or rather courtisan . . .' should be compared NASHE, *Works,* II, 264 : 'At that time was Monsieur *Petro Aretino,* searcher and chiefe Inquisiter to the college of curtizans,' and McKERROW's note, IV, 278 : 'Nashe's statement that he [Aretino] was 'Inquisiter to the colledge of curtizans' is, I believe, a fiction.' Compare also GABRIEL HARVEY, *Pierces Superogation,* sig. E₃ vᵒ : 'Na, Homer not such an author for Alexander : nor Xenophon for Scipio : nor Virgil for Augustus : nor Iustin for Marcus Aurelius : nor Liuy for Theodosius Magnus : nor Caesar for Selymus : nor Philip de Comines for Charles the fift : nor Macchiauell for some late princes : nor Aretin for some late Curtesans; as his Authour for him; the sole authour of renowned victorie.' See G. HARVEY, *Works,* ed. A. B. GROSART (London, 1884-5), II, 78.

associated with Aretino, the porter of Pluto's divinity, the hellhound Cerberus. The expression 'Pluto's porter' does not recur as such in Richard's treatise, but the 'hellhound' is attacked no less than four times elsewhere (1). A passage from *Pierce Penilesse* and one from Gabriel Harvey's answer to it are worth quoting for the purposes of comparison.

We want an *Aretine* here among vs, that might strip these golden asses out of their gaie trappings, and after he had ridden them to death with railing, leaue them on the dunghill for carion. But I will write to his ghost by my carrier, and I hope hele repaire his whip, and vse it against our English Peacockes, that painting themselues with church spoils, like mightie mens sepulchers, haue nothing but Atheisme, schisme, hypocrisie, & vainglory, like rotten bones lie lurking within them. O how my soule abhors these buckram giants, that hauing an outwarde face of honor set vppon them by flatterers and parasites, haue their inward thoughtes stuft with strawe and feathers, if they were narrowelie sifted (2).

Aretine, and the Diuels Oratour might very well bee spared in Christian, or Politicke Commonwealthes: which cannot want contagion inough, though they bee not poysened with the venemous potions of Inckhorne witches. . . . All the Inuectiue, and Satyricall Spirites, are their Familiars: scoffing, and girding is their daily bread: other professe other faculties: they professe the Arte of railing: Noble, Reuerend, or whatsoeuer, al pesants, and clownes; gowty Diuels, and buckram Giants: Midasses, and golden Asses (3).

It is clear that Harvey and Nashe entertain utterly different views: while for Harvey both Nashe and Aretino can be spared in England, Nashe erects the Italian into a model of excellence. The name of Aretino was of course a by-word for satirical power in the sixteenth century, and it is true, as McKerrow observes, that Nashe does not make clear in what respect he wished to follow him. But in Nashe's wish to see Aretino's like in England, it is clearly implied that he fancies himself a 'true English Aretine,' as Thomas Lodge was to describe Nashe in *Wit's Misery* (1596) (4). Richard Harvey's phrase '*Peter Aretine*, porter of *Plutoes* diuinitie' clearly states it that Aretino is a kind of Cerberus, and, on the assumption that Nashe was an English Aretine, the equation Nashe-Cerberus readily suggests

---

(1) R. HARVEY, *The Lambe of God*, sigg. I$_1$ v^o (p. 60), K$_2$ v^o (p. 68), M$_4$ r^o (p. 87), and Aa$_1$ v^o (p. 178).
(2) NASHE, *Works*, I, 242.
(3) G. HARVEY, *Foure Letters*, pp. 53-4.
(4) THOMAS LODGE, *Wit's Misery* (London, 1596). sig. I$_1$.

itself. A minor remark in connexion with the quotation from Richard Harvey remains to be made. The writer declares that 'neither *Gesner* nor *Simler*' judged Aretino worthy to come into their libraries. Among Gabriel Harvey's books was the *Epitome Bibliothecae Conradi Gesneri... per Iosiam Simlerum* Zurich, 1555), which contains several marginalia in Gabriel's hand, one of which is dated 1584 (1). The combination of Gesner, Simler and 'library' in the quotation from the *Lamb of God*, also combined in the title of a book belonging to Gabriel Harvey, suggests that Richard was at the time of writing thinking of the *Epitome*, and that it was thus that the reference to the two sixteenth century authors found its way into the theological discourse.

For want of an earlier allusion, then, 'porter of *Plutoes* diuinitie' is probably the phrase from which Nashe's nickname arose. Of course, the idea of associating Nashe with Cerberus may have had its origin in circumstances or literary sources quite other than those put forward in the foregoing paragraphs. But I confess that I have been unable to discover any relevant material.

Finally it is necessary to call attention to what Thomas Dekker had to say about Nashe. In the course of Dekker's *News from Hell* (1606), a pamphlet full of reminiscences of *Pierce Penilesse*, occurs the following address to him:

> And thou, into whose soule (if euer there were a *Pithagorean Metempsuchosis*) the raptures of that fierie and inconfinable *Italian* spirit were bounteously and boundlesly infused, thou sometimes Secretary to *Pierce Pennylesse*, and Master of his requests, ingenious, ingenuous, fluent, facetious, *T. Nash*: from whose aboundant pen, hony flow'd to thy friends, and mortall Aconite to thy enemies (2).

It is surely remarkable that Dekker uses the word aconite to describe the pungency of Nashe's satire, the poison which according to mythology originated from a plant that sprang from Cerberus's foam. In a later passage Dekker speaks of Pluto's porter, Cerberus, who 'executes his bawling office meerely for victuals,' and though Nashe is not identified with Pluto's dog, it is nevertheless telling that Dekker's 'allegorical' interpretation does not agree with that given by Fraunce in *The Third part of the Countesse of Pembrokes*

---

(1) G. HARVEY, *Marginalia*, ed. G. C. MOORE SMITH (Stratford-upon-Avon, 1913), pp. 125-7.

(2) DEKKER, *News from Hell* (London, 1606), sig. C$_2$.

Yuychurch. Indeed, Dekker's Cerberus does not wait to take money of those who enter hell, and the pamphleteer contrasts this type of porter with another who is greedy of his fees (1). The inference seems to be that Dekker is aware of a kind of allegorical interpretation different from the traditional one, and this hints Dekker's intention to praise his friend's attitude.

The frequent recurrence of allusions to aspects of the Cerberus-myth in works related to, or bearing on, Nashe establishes quite definitely, I think, that several Elizabethans currently assumed that Nashe embodied the attributes of the hellhound. It belongs to the nature of allusions, however, not to be sufficiently explicit, and Elizabethan authors, to be sure, deliberately avoided committing themselves too clearly. One could wish no better illustration of this non-committal attitude than Nashe's own *Pierce Penilesse*. Those who will take the trouble to read this extraordinary tract carefully, will notice that the passages in which the author deals with a 'dog' are elusive to the point of unintelligibility (2). Yet an attentive reading has convinced me that 'Cerberus' is a porter with a very useful key to Nashe's meaning. And this mythological figure does much more than elucidate Nashe's works, it clarifies the origins of the Harvey-Nashe quarrels which aroused such an enormous interest among the Elizabethan reading public in the years 1592-1593. But these origins cannot be properly investigated until the figures of Gabriel Harvey and Thomas Nashe have been dealt with separately.

---

(1) DEKKER, *News from Hell*, sig. E₃ vᵘ and sig. E₄.
(2) See NASHE, *Works*, I, 169, 171, 182, 183, 185, 191. One may further note the following anti-puritan statement : 'In Rome the Papal Chayre is washt, euery fiue yeare at the furthest, with this oyle of Aconitum' (I, 186), in which the demonstrative pronoun 'this' is used with emotional connotation.

CHAPTER V

GABRIEL HARVEY

It is not easy to appraise Gabriel Harvey. The disparity of his views, the obscurity of his language, the variety of his interests, and the learning displayed in his writings repel readers merely seeking delight in literature; and only when a writer becomes more widely appreciated is it possible for a general critical opinion to be formed (1). The uncharitable criticism which Harvey received at the hands of his nineteenth century editor, A. B. Grosart, was in a way typical of an approach which regarded Harvey as the very incarnation of pedantry. There was some justification in such an attitude, first because Harvey made continuous attempts to introduce the classical metres into English poetry, an experiment which looks ridiculous to modern judgment; and second because of the fierce attack on the dead Robert Greene, launched with a seemingly unwarranted violence at a most inopportune moment. In recent years, however, Gabriel Harvey has come into his own. If an editor like Grosart did not even try to arrive at a proper understanding of Harvey's character, McKerrow was to be one of the first great critics to defend Harvey from the easy contempt which had befallen his writings. Quite apart from the fact that the influence he exerted may have given Harvey undue prominence in general histories of literature, it is now recognized that his work, from a purely literary viewpoint, does possess an independent interest. Harvey's style is vigorous, and, when the peculiar rhythm of his phrases has been mastered, one may even begin to realize that Harvey is not a second-rate artist who deserves the neglect of both editors and critics.

---

(1) The fullest study of HARVEY's life is G. C. MOORE SMITH's introduction to his edition of *Gabriel Harvey's Marginalia*, pp. 1-76, from which the facts of my own account are taken. Some additional information is to be found in H. S. WILSON's introduction to an edition of HARVEY's *Ciceronianus*, in *University of Nebraska Studies in the Humanities*, No. 4 (Nebraska, 1945). See also H. S. WILSON, "The Humanism of Gabriel Harvey," in *J. Q. Adams Memorial Studies* (1948), pp. 707-721; N. ORSINI, "Gabriel Harvey, uomo del Rinascimento," in *Studii sul Rinascimento Italiano in Inghilterra* (Florence, 1937), pp. 101-120; H. OPPEL, "Gabriel Harvey," *Shakespeare-Jahrbuch*, LXXXII/LXXXIII (1946-47), 34-51; P. A. DUHAMEL, "The Ciceronianism of Gabriel Harvey," *SP*, XLIX (1952), 155-170.

Before proceeding to a more detailed argument, the chief facts of Harvey's life may be briefly set forth. Gabriel Harvey was born in 1550 or 1551, the son of John Harvey, ropemaker at Saffron Walden, a town some fifteen miles from Cambridge. He attended the Grammar School of Saffron Walden, and proceeded to Cambridge, where he matriculated from Christ's College on June 28, 1566. After four years he was elected a Fellow of Pembroke Hall through the influence of the statesman Sir Thomas Smith, probably a distant kinsman of his and also a native of Saffron Walden. When at Pembroke Harvey struck up a friendship with Edmund Spenser, a friendship which was to extend over many years. From the very beginning of his career in society Gabriel Harvey seems to have been unpopular with all those whom he had to encounter. When in the spring of 1573 he was ready to take his M. A. degree he had to face the refusal of certain other Fellows of Pembroke. He was charged with arrogance, was regarded as unsociable, and was reproached for defending paradoxes. These charges are comprehensible when we bear in mind that Harvey, in his youthful ardour for the new achievements of humanism, was apparently unable to bear his learning as easily as his fellow-students, for he was continually reminded of his humble origin. From Harvey's *Letter-Book* (1) we learn that the upshot of the matter was that the Master of Pembroke, Dr. John Young, intervened in his behalf and that the degree was granted.

On April 23, 1574, Harvey obtained the post of University Praelector or Professor of Rhetoric, a post to which he seems to have been re-elected in 1575 and 1576. In this capacity he delivered two Latin lectures, which were published in 1577, the one under the title *Ciceronianus* and the other (divided over two days) under the title *Rhetor* (2). The *Ciceronianus* discusses the burning question of the century: was Cicero's style the *only* possible model for Latin prose eloquence, and if so, how could prospective orators use that model to full advantage? An oration like the *Ciceronianus* offered Harvey the opportunity to define his attitude towards Ciceronianism, the craze of the age among students of rhetoric. As Professor H. S. Wilson has pointed out, Harvey is trying to outdo Erasmus

---

(1) E. J. L. Scott, ed. *The Letter-Book of Gabriel Harvey. A. D. 1573-1580*, Camden Society Publ., XXXIII (1884). See G. C. Moore-Smith, ed. *Marginalia*, pp. 12-13.

(2) Analysed by H. S. Wilson, in "Gabriel Harvey's Orations on Rhetoric," *JELH*, XII (1945), 167-182 and in his edition of *Ciceronianus*.

in his picture of Ciceronian affectation, and yet Harvey's style itself is interlarded with the familiar Ciceronian tags. Harvey's lectures give us an interesting picture of the intellectual atmosphere at Cambridge, not only because they inform us of the prevalent views on prose style, but also because they reveal that Cambridge had given a warm welcome to the educational reforms of the notorious Petrus Ramus. They also testify to the wide range of Harvey's reading, to his open-mindedness and to his clear insight into the humanist position.

In August 1577 occurred the death of Sir Thomas Smith and Harvey attended the funeral, on which occasion he fell foul of an insinuation from Dr. Andrew Perne, Master of Peterhouse; Perne had called Harvey a fox for having induced Sir Thomas' widow to present him with some rare manuscripts, an incident which Harvey was to recall in *Pierces Supererogation* (1593). Harvey's grief at his patron's death was recorded in a series of Latin elegies, published in 1578 as *Smithus, vel Musarum Lachrymae*. In 1578 he was chosen to dispute before the Court on the occasion of Queen Elizabeth's visit to Audley End, a great house close to Saffron Walden, on July 26, 1578. This event was celebrated in four books of Latin verses entitled *Gratulationes Valdinenses*, published in September 1578. The separate books were presented to the Queen, to Lord Leicester, to Lord Burghley, and to Sir Christopher Hatton. The disputation before the Court, next to enabling Harvey to make the acquaintance of several illustrious persons, probably brought him into contact with Philip Sidney also. Such was the significance of this experience for Gabriel Harvey that Thomas Nashe, almost twenty years later, could not but exploit it to the full in pouring ridicule on his opponent. Two incidents provided meat for Nashe's Cerberus: that Harvey had made love to and danced with the ladies of the Court, and, thus having attracted the Queen's attention, that he had been allowed to kiss the Queen's hand, while the Queen had remarked that he looked like an Italian. These are the relevant extracts from Nashe's account of the matter:

There did this our *Talatamtana* or Doctour *Hum* thrust himselfe into the thickest rankes of the Noblemen and Gallants, and whatsoeuer they were arguing of, he would not misse to catch hold of, or strike in at the one end, and take the theame out of their mouths, or it should goe hard. In selfe same order was hee at his pretie toyes and amorous glaunces and purposes with the Damsells, & putting baudy riddles vnto them.

And the oration Harvey made before the Queen's Maids of Honour is thus described:

> The proces of that Oration was of the same woofe and thrid with the beginning: demurely and maidenly scoffing, and blushingly wantoning & making loue to those soft skind soules & sweete Nymphes of *Helicon*, betwixt a kinde of carelesse rude ruffianisme and curious finicall complement; both which hee more exprest by his countenance than anie good iests that hee vttered. This finished, (though not for the finishing or pronouncing of this,) by some better frends than hee was worthie of, and that afterward found him vnworthie of the graces they had bestowed vpon him, he was brought to kisse the Queenes hand, and it pleased her Highnes to say (as in my former Booke I haue cyted) that he lookt something like an Italian (1).

About 1578 Harvey's fellowship at Pembroke was apparently expiring, and attempts were made to have him re-elected. This is what we learn from a letter (dated August 22, 1578) from Dr. W. Fulke, the new master of Pembroke College (2). Soon after, however, Harvey was elected to a fellowship at Trinity Hall with the object of studying Civil Law. Harvey had surely taken up this new subject because his former patron, Sir Thomas Smith, had frequently advised him to devote his time to legal studies. In the years 1579-1580 there is much evidence as to Harvey's intimate intercourse with Edmund Spenser. The two friends exchanged letters which got into print as *Three proper, and wittie, familiar Letters* and *Two other, very commendable Letters* (1580), while Spenser himself introduced Harvey in the famous *Shepheardes Calender* (1579) under the pastoral name 'Hobbinol.' This collection of eclogues was edited by one E. K., initials generally identified as Edward Kirke, a friend of Spenser's at Pembroke Hall. From a letter addressed by Edward Kirke to Harvey we learn that the latter had written many excellent poems, while in a note to the September Eclogue in the *Shepheardes Calender*, Kirke, first mentioning Harvey's two books of Latin verses, also enumerates other works by the Cambridge scholar.

> Beside other his sundrye most rare and very notable writings, partly vnder vnknown Tytles, and partly vnder counterfayt names, as hys Tyrannomastix, his Ode Natalitia, his Rameidos, and especially that parte of Philomusus, his diuine Anticosmopolita, and diuers other of lyke importance.

---

(1) NASHE, *Works*, III, 75, 76.
(2) E. J. L. SCOTT, ed. *Letter-Book*, p. 88.

The works here mentioned are all lost exept the *Ode Natalitia* (1); the *Rameidos* was perhaps a poem in praise of Ramus, and a work entitled *Anticosmopolita* is referred to in the Stationers' Register, though it must be pointed out that the Register does not mention an author (2).

A discussion of the significance of the letters exchanged between Harvey and Spenser need not detain us, as it is a subject that has often been gone into before (3). It is well-known that this correspondence constitutes the chief evidence for the widely held belief that Harvey, Spenser, Sidney, Sir Edward Dyer, and several others formed a so-called 'Areopagus' at Leicester House, a literary society on the model of the French *cénacles* (4). What needs mention here is that the publication of some of these letters gave offence, for in Harvey's last letter the University had been criticized; furthermore, Harvey had introduced a poem in it, entitled *Speculum Tuscanismi*, in which Harvey had satirized an Italianate Englishman. Through the offices of John Lyly, Lord Oxford seems to have been made aware of material offensive to him in this poem. In his *Foure Letters* (written and published in 1592) Harvey, referring to this indiscretion, denied that the satire was directed against Lord Oxford, and also explained that his irritation at conditions in the University had been caused only by his being thwarted by Dr. Andrew Perne in his candidature for the Public Oratorship at the University. This episode in Harvey's life found its reflection in *Pedantius*, a Latin play, performed about or in 1581. As the text of this play is a significant document in various respects, we had best reserve an account of it for a subsequent section that is devoted specially to that play.

In 1584, having completed his study of Civil Law, Harvey

---

(1) The *Ode Natalitia* (no entry in the Stationers' Register) has recently been discovered; see W. B. AUSTIN, "Gabriel Harvey's 'Lost' *Ode* on Ramus," *MLN*, LXI (1946), 242-7. This ode was printed anonymously in 1575, but the initials A. P. S. (= Aulae Pembrochianae Socius), signed to the formula by which the author takes leave of the reader, point to HARVEY as the writer. The ode stamps HARVEY as a very early enthusiastic disciple of Ramism in England.

(2) ARBER, *Transcript*, II, 354. The entry, made on June 30, 1579, refers to *Anticosmopolita. or Britanniae Apologia.*

(3) For this see R. M. SARGENT, *At the Court of Queen Elizabeth. The Life and Lyrics of Sir Edward Dyer* (Oxford, 1935), pp. 59-64.

(4) FULKE GREVILLE, SAMUEL DANIEL, ABRAHAM FRAUNCE, the COUNTESS OF PEMBROKE, and NICHOLAS BRETON have sometimes been included. G. C. MOORE SMITH, ed. *Marginalia*, p. 30, however, says : 'I see nothing in these letters to support the common statement that Harvey was a regular visitor at Leicester House at the meetings of Sidney's and Dyer's 'Areopagus'.'

was ready to receive his Doctor's degree, but for some reason or other the degree was not granted at his own University. In 1585, then, obtaining leave of absence from his college, Harvey went to Oxford and was admitted a Doctor of Civil Law of that University on 13th July (1). About this time Harvey probably succeeded Lancelot Browne in a medical fellowship at Pembroke, at least this is what we learn from a marginal note made by him in his copy of H. Braunschweig's *A most excellent and perfecte homish apothecarye* (Imprinted at Collen, 1561).

Hinc probabiliter potest iudicari, quantus fuerit medicus, chirurgus, pharmacopoeus, destillandi etiam artifex, Hieronymus iste Brunsuig. Nec temere hic mihi practicus liber commendatus a sagacissimo Medicinae doctore, Lanceloto Brouno fuit: cui iamtum aulae Pembrochianae medico succedebam in proprio illius professionis sodalitio (2).

That about 1584 Harvey took up the study of medicine is confirmed by a letter written by one 'I. W.' about 1586, a letter apparently addressed to Harvey and which seems to have been overlooked by the students of Harvey's works.

Of Harvey's subsequent literary career a few well-known facts remain to be mentioned; his quarrels with Nashe and their origins will be treated in the next chapters. Spenser's sonnet to him, included by Harvey in his *Foure Letters*, may be given first attention. It is dated from Dublin, July 18, 1586.

> Haruey, the happy aboue happiest men
> I read: that sitting like a Looker-on
> Of this worldes Stage, doest note with critique pen
> The sharpe dislikes of each condition:
> And as one careless of suspition,
> Ne fawnest for the fauour of the great:
> Ne fearest foolish reprehension
> Of faulty men, which daunger to thee threat.
> But freely doest, of what thee list, entreat,
> Like a great Lord of peerelesse liberty:
> Lifting the good vp to high Honours seat,

---

(1) See G. C. Moore Smith, ed. *Marginalia*, p. 49.
(2) Harvey, *Marginalia*, pp. 131-32. Lancelot Browne, Fellow of the College of Physicians, was chief physician to Queen Elizabeth and James I, and died in 1605. On Harvey's note Moore Smith comments (p. 262) : 'It would appear from the present passage that Harvey succeeded Browne at Pembroke in a fellowship set apart for medicine when Browne left Cambridge for London.' The College records, however, reveal no trace of anything of the sort.

And the Euill damning euermore to dy;
  For Life, and Death is in thy doomefull writing:
  So thy renowme liues euer by endighting.

Professor Moore Smith remarks (1) that Spenser is not mistaken in
praising his friend's critical ability, but that Harvey was far from
being happy above happiest men. This appears clearly from the
many difficulties that he experienced during a long life filled with
ambitious dreams. W. B. Austin has pointed out (2) that the sonnet
is an appropriate commendatory poem for a book of satires, and he
therefore believes that Harvey had a volume of satires in preparation
as early as 1580, for Harvey himself, in a passage in the *Three proper,
and wittie, familiar Letters*, seems to refer to his writing satirical
poetry.

After the quarrels with Nashe, so far as we know, Harvey
published nothing more. But the ropemaker's son remained ambitious to the end. This appears, for example, from a letter to Sir
Robert Cecil, dated May 8, 1598, which contains a request to obtain
the post of Master of Trinity Hall, a situation that had become
vacant through Dr. Preston's death. Harvey's hopes were again
disappointed. He lived on for another thirty-three years, and died
in 1630. We find his name entered in the Walden Burial Register as
'Mr. Doctor Gabriell Harvey,' an entry that occurs under the date
February 11, 1630. Nothing is known of the last twenty years of
Harvey's existence, except that there is a note by Thomas Baker
(1656-1740), the Cambridge antiquary, which runs: 'I have seen
an elegy on Dr. Harvey of Safron Walden composed by William
Pearson dated an: 1630. By that it would seem he practised physic
and was a pretender to astrology' (3).

It would be an injustice to Harvey not to mention the fact
that among his marginalia is to be found the famous note written
in a copy of Speght's Chaucer (1598), which contains a remarkable
tribute to Shakespeare. Our gratitude is the greater in that Harvey
has provided us with clear contemporary evidence as to Shakespeare's
existence as a poet and playwright.

The different sections which follow will deal with such aspects

---

(1) G. C. Moore Smith, ed. *Marginalia*, p. 57.
(2) W. B. Austin, "Spenser's Sonnet to Harvey," *MLN*, LXII (1947), 20-3.
(3) Quoted by G. C. Moore Smith, ed. *Marginalia*, pp. 75-76, from Baker MSS.,
Cambridge Un. Libr., xxxvi, 107. The elegy is now lost.

of Harvey's character, thought and intellectual attitude as have never yet received proper attention.

I

In the spring of 1579 the resignation of the Public Orator of King's College, Cambridge, Richard Bridgewater was expected; Bridgewater finally announced his resignation to Lord Burghley, the Chancellor, in a Latin letter dated October 25, 1579 (Lansdowne MS., 28, 88), but his decision only became known the following April. Gabriel Harvey felt it incumbent upon him to stand for the post and he accordingly wrote to Burghley and was able to secure the latter's support. Owing to the influence of Dr. Perne, however, Harvey's candidature was rejected and a rival, Anthony Wingfield, was chosen on March 18, 1580. These were the events which led to the composition of the Latin comedy *Pedantius* (1). According to Professor Moore Smith the play was probably brought out between the winter of 1580 and July 1581, and perhaps produced on February 6, 1581.

Pedantius was first printed anonymously in 1631, but it was also preserved in two manuscripts, one of the Library of Caius College, Cambridge, MS. 62, and the other in that of Trinity College, MS. R 17 (6). For purposes of textual comparison the latter manuscript may be disregarded, for it was apparently copied from the Caius College MS. Professor Moore Smith, the distinguished editor of the play, names the printed version P, while the Caius College MS. is called C. He bases his text on the printed version, and corrects only obvious errors, in which case even the corrections are seldom made without the authority of C. To conclude his provisional comparison between the two versions, Moore Smith states that P certainly, and C with much probability differs from the original form of the comedy and that neither is a certain authority for correcting the other (2). In the Caius College MS. *Pedantius* appears with two other plays, Thomas Legge's *Richardus III*, and

---

(1) It was edited by G. C. MOORE SMITH in the *Materialien zur Kunde des älteren Englischen Dramas*, VIII (1905). My quotations from the play are all taken from this edition. For Latin drama generally see G. R. CHURCHILL and W. KELLER, "Die lateinischen Universitäts-Dramen Englands in der Zeit der Königin Elisabeth," *Shakespeare-Jahrbuch*, XXXIV (1898), 221-323. The authors also give a useful summary of *Pedantius*. See also F. S. BOAS, *University Drama in the Tudor Age* (Oxford, 1914).

(2) MOORE SMITH, ed. *Pedantius*, p. viii.

Hymenaeus. Its full title, as this appears in the MS., runs: *Pedantius comoedia acta in collegio Sanctae et individuae Trinitatis authore M^ro Forcet*, and we are therefore informed that Forcet, i. e. Edward Forsett, wrote it, a scholar whose career has become known thanks to the investigations of Moore Smith. But the ascription to Forsett seems to conflict with what Nashe says in his *Foure Letters Confuted* (published about December 1592).

> Though I haue beene pinched with want (as who is not at one time or another *Pierce Penilesse*) yet my muse neuer wept for want of maintenance as thine did in *Musarum lachrimae*, that was miserably flouted at in M. *Winkfields* Comoedie of *Pedantius* in Trinitie Colledge (1).

This passage made Moore Smith in 1905 and R. B. McKerrow in 1910 still hesitate to ascribe the play definitely to Forsett, but other evidence has since confirmed the ascription of C (2). Nashe's statement must therefore mean that Forsett wrote the comedy at the instigation of Anthony Wingfield, which is accounted for by what we know of Harvey's difficulties in the years 1580-81. Nashe's hint that Harvey's collection of Latin verses had been mocked at in *Pedantius* is fully borne out by the contents of the play itself. These have been carefully examined by Moore Smith, whose conclusion is that it was certainly Harvey who was made fun of in the person of the 'pedant,' the mercilessly ridiculed central character of the play. It is therefore unnecessary, with regard to this feature of *Pedantius*, to go into the relevant textual evidence afresh.

The allusions to *Pedantius* to be found in Sir John Harington and in Nashe's second attack on Harvey yet remain to be quoted. A passage in Sir John Harington's Ariosto translation *Orlando Furioso* (1591) shows clearly that the performance left a lasting impression on Elizabethan minds. It occurs in the fourteenth book of the translation and reveals the fact that the 'noble Earle of Essex that now is' attended the production of the play.

> In the description of Discord and Fraud, and finding Silence in the house of sleepe, being long since banished from philosophers and diuines; the allegorie is so plaine, as it were time lost to spend time to expound it, because it expounds it selfe so plainly: only I will obserue one thing, in which mine Author is thought to keepe an excellent decorum. For,

(1) Nashe, *Works*, I, 303.
(2) See G. C. Moore Smith, "The Authorship of 'Pedantius'," *NQ*, CLIII (1927), 427, and the same writer's letter to *TLS*, Oct. 10, 1918.

making Discord and Fraud of the feminine gender, he still makes silence of the masculine; as the like pretie conceit is in our Cambridge Comedie *Pedantius*, (at which I remember the noble Earle of Essex that now is, was present) where the *Pedantius* himselfe, examining the Gramaticall instruction of his verse. *Cedant arma togae, concedat laurea linguae.* vpon speciall consideration of the two last words, taught his scholler *Parillus*, that *laurea, lingua sunt utraque foeminae generis, sed lingua potissimum*, and so consequently silence might not by any meanes haue bene of the feminine gender (1).

Finally, Nashe's *Have with you to Saffron Walden* (1596) also contains a long passage in which *Pedantius* is referred to and in which the author gives a wonderful display of his vituperative skill. Nashe's words, made up of many of Harvey's favourite tags and referring as they do to his victim's Latin verses, render the identification of Harvey with 'pedantius' incontrovertible.

Readers, be merry; for in me there shall want nothing I can doo to make you merry. You see I haue brought the Doctor out of request at Court, & it shall cost me a fall but I will get him howted out of the Vniuersitie too, ere I giue him ouer. What will you giue mee when I bring him vppon the Stage in one of the principallest Colledges in *Cambridge?* Lay anie wager with me, and I will; or, if you laye no wager at all, Ile fetch him aloft in *Pedantius*, that exquisite Comedie in *Trinitie Colledge;* where, vnder the cheife part, from which it tooke his name, as namely the concise and firking finicaldo fine School-master, hee was full drawen & delineated from the soale of the foote to the crowne of his head. The iust manner of his phrase in his Orations and Disputations they stufft his mouth with, & no Buffianisme throughout his whole bookes but they bolsterd out his part with; as those ragged remnaunts in his foure familiar Epistles twixt him and *Senior Immerito, Raptim scripta, Nosti manum & stylum*, with innumerable other of his rabble routs: and scoffing his *Musarum Lachrymae* with *Flebo amorem meum, etiam Musarum lachrymis;* which, to giue it his due, was a more collachrymate wretched Treatise than my *Piers Pennilesse*, being the pittifullest pangs that euer anie mans Muse breathd foorth. I leaue out halfe; not the carrying vp of his gowne, his nice gate on his pantoffles, or the affected accent of his speach, but they personated. And if I should reueale all, I thinke they borrowd his gowne to playe the Part in, the more to flout him (2).

The external evidence bearing on the pedant's identity is fully con-firmed by numerous textual features of the play itself, for *Pedantius*

---

(1) Sir JOHN HARINGTON, *Orlando Furioso* (1591), p. 111. MOORE SMITH, ed. *Pedantius*, p. viii, also gives this passage, but it is slightly misquoted, while a small sentence is also omitted.

(2) NASHE, *Works*, III, 79-80.

contains most of the characteristic tags with which Harvey 'stuffed' his early writings. *Pedantius* has therefore to be regarded as an important document when it comes to giving as complete a picture as possible of Harvey's mentality and intellectual interests.

To begin with, in connexion with the Harvey-Nashe quarrels it is worth noting that the pedant, at one time, is incensed by Juvenal's attack on Ciceronian eloquence (see Satire, X, 122 ff.), which makes the pedant exclaim: '*Serio* irascor *Iuvenali*, qui Poeticam Ciceronis facultatem non laudibus sed sannis persequitur' (*Pedantius*, 2427-8). Though this sally is quite natural in the mouth of an admirer of Cicero's, it may retain an added significance when it is borne in mind that around 1592 Nashe was considered the Juvenal of his age. Obviously such a view can count only if it is assumed that the play was produced in the early nineties. There are two small textual points which may well support the statement made in 1631 by the play's early editors that it had been performed forty years before. In I, iii the pedant and Dromodotus are discussing love; the latter sounds the note of warning with the words: 'Amor est ignis. Ergo cauendum est ab eo tanquam a *Scorpione* aut *Cane coelesti*, qui in diebus Canicularibus calore suo nocivo plus mordet quam ullus *Canis latrabilis*' (*Pedantius*, 458-461); the latter half of this quotation, from 'aut *Cane...*' onwards, is an insertion found in P only. It seems likely that the 'canis latrabilis' reference originated from Harvey's quarrels with Nashe, the latter being a 'bawling cur' indeed. A scene may also be quoted from V, ii between the pedant and his scholar Parillus; this is the very scene which contains an incident that Harington found worth recalling in 1591. The scholar having professed his admiration for the elegance of his master's language, Pedantius replies (ll. 2506-2519):

Ped. Optime, sic enim eris ingenij nostri partus aureus; *Cedant arma togae, concedat laurea linguae.* Quasi diceret, cedant Imperatores bellicis Paedagogis pacificis: cedant bombardae horrisonae fulminibus forensibus: cedant fures omnes & oppidani nobis literatis, qui sumus oculi reipublicae. Tum toga est prior *tempore:* nam nemo aptus est ad arma, antequam togam virilem sumpserit: & *natura,* nam arma sunt violenta: omne autem violentum est contra naturam: & *honore,* nam suscipiuntur arma, ut in pace vivatur: at pax & toga confunduntur: denique & *ordine,* nam ordo senatorius Togatorum est. Ergo (ut hoc Epiphonemate tanquam sigillo claudam omnia) *Cedant arma togae, concedat laurea linguae.*

The 'bombardae horrisonae' which have to yield to the lightnings of eloquence (1) apparently found a place in the imagery which both Nashe and Harvey used to attack each other. Nashe in *Pierce Penilesse* maintained that his terms were 'laid in steepe in *Aquafortis*, & Gunpowder, that shall rattle through the Skyes, and make an Earthquake in a Pesants eares' (2), while Harvey called his opponent 'Sir Bombarduccio,' and again a 'terrible bombarder of tearmes' in *Pierces Supererogation* (3), while Nashe further coined the word 'horrizonant' in the *Foure Letters Confuted*, his first pamphlet against Harvey. It will be granted that such correspondences as those just dealt with argue either a production date for *Pedantius* much nearer to the Harvey-Nashe war, say 1591, or that the imagery from the Cambridge comedy left ineffaceable memories in the imagination of those who were interested in Harvey. The whole matter seems somehow to have originated from Harvey's eccentric mind.

Pedantius also admirably illustrates Harvey's addiction to the fashion for emblems, devices, and imprese, which is in evidence on almost every page of the play. For instance at line 927 the pedant translates something 'emblematice' as *Aut uxor aut vexor*, while at line 1375 he mentions his beloved's ring on which the 'emblema' *Cor sagitta transfixum* is engraved; and hieroglyphs are referred to at line 2613. As early as 1578 Harvey commended Alciati's book of emblems to the attention of his undergraduate hearers, as is proved by a passage in G. H.'s *De Discenda Graeca Lingua Oratio*, to be found in Joannes Crispinus's *Lexicon Graecolatinum* (1581) (4); Alciati is again referred to in the *Musarum Lachrymae* (5), while in the same work Harvey also refers to the emblematist Paulus Jovius (6). In Elizabethan times the taste for emblems had become firmly established, but with Harvey the measure of his devotion is well brought out by his crowding the pages of *Pierces Supererogation* with devices, posies, imprese, and the like. Numerous examples might be cited from this extraordinary pamphlet; an interesting one is Harvey's 'devising' an epitaph for Dr. Perne,

---

(1) The latter comparison was a commonplace one in all of HARVEY's writings.
(2) NASHE, *Works*, I, 195. HARVEY repeats this passage almost verbatim in the *Foure Letters* (p. 54), and then styles NASHE a 'mightie Bombarder of termes.'
(3) HARVEY, *Works*, II, 18, 41.
(4) Discovered by T. W. BALDWIN, *William Shakspere's Small Latine & Lesse Greeke* (Univ. of Illinois Press, 1944), I, 436-7. As BALDWIN remarks, the orations ascribed to 'G. H.,' have GABRIEL HARVEY written all over them. The lectures belong to the period of the *Rhetor* and *Ciceronianus*.
(5) HARVEY, *Musarum Lachrymae* (London, 1578), sig. C$_3$.
(6) HARVEY, *Musarum Lachrymae*, sig. H$_1$ v⁰.

a practice which the author compares with the similar procedure of Archimedes who 'would haue the figure of a Cylinder, or roller engraued vpon his Toombe' (1). This latter device was already recorded in L. B. Alberti's *Architectura* (first printed in 1485) (2).

But *Pedantius*, next to informing us of Harvey's wide interests, perhaps also clarifies the mystery of the identity of one Torquato (or, Torquatus), a person who takes part in the dialogues written by Giordano Bruno under the title *Cena de le ceneri* (= the Ash Wednesday Supper), published in London in 1584. Torquatus is also one of the speakers in John Florio's *Second Fruits* (1591). It has already been recognized (3) that the interlocutors Nundinio and Torquato, introduced by Bruno under these coined names to conceal their identity, are related to those introduced by Florio in his language-manual, for Florio uses the same coinings and employs similar details in the portrayal of his characters, though, on comparison, Florio's satirical portraits are much less scathingly cast. Though it is possible that Nundinio stands for George Chapman (4), I see no serious evidence to establish Nundinio's identity. Before examining who Torquato was, it may first be mentioned that the 'Torquatus' attacked by John Marston in the satires of *The Scourge of Villainy* (1598) has been identified with Gabriel Harvey by H. C. Hart (5), an identification which no less an authority than Sir Edmund Chambers (6) finds more plausible than that which put forward Ben Jonson as the candidate for Torquatus. Evidently the sobriquet was of much longer standing if the contents and the wording of both the Cambridge *Pedantius* and Bruno's *Cena de le ceneri* also render it probable that 'Torquatus' was in Elizabethan times a descriptive name for Gabriel Harvey.

Giordano Bruno (?1548- ?1599), 'il Nolano,' as he preferred

(1) HARVEY, *Works*, II, 315-6.

(2) LEONBATTISTA ALBERTI, *L'Architettura* (Florence, 1550, transl. by C. BARTOLI), VIII, iv, p. 281, has : 'Cicerone Arpinate si vantaua di hauer' ritrouato a Siracusa il sepolcro di Archimede, albandonato per la antichità, come coperto da pruni, & non conosciuto da suoi Cittadini, presa coniettura da vno Cylindro, & da vna Sfera piccola, che ei vedde intagliata in vna certa colonna molto alta.'

(3) See Miss F. A. YATES, *John Florio* (Cambridge, 1934).

(4) 'Nundinio' means 'merchant' or 'chapman.' Miss D. W. SINGER, *Giordano Bruno* (New York, 1950), p. 35, however, thinks it reasonable that BRUNO may have known CHAPMAN. She suggests that Torquato stands for GEORGE TURNER (1569-1610), because of the pun on 'turner.'

(5) H. C. HART, "Gabriel Harvey and Marston," *NQ*, 9th Ser., XI (1903), 201. 281-2 and 343-5.

(6) E. K. CHAMBERS, *Eliz. Stage*, III, 428.

calling himself from his birth-place Nola near Naples, had abandoned his monk's habit and started to wander through Europe. In the spring of 1583 he arrived in London with a letter of introduction from the French king, Henri III, to the French ambassador, Michel de Castelnau de Mauvissière. It is likely that Bruno came across John Florio at the embassy where Florio was temporarily employed by de Mauvissière. Very little is known of Bruno's stay in England, but it is usually stated, on the authority of the account in the *Cena de le ceneri*, that Bruno went to Oxford where at that time the Palatine Prince Laski of Poland was being entertained. There is, however, no evidence in the Oxford records to support Bruno's visit. One of the features of Prince Laski's entertainment were public disputations in which Bruno probably took part, and it was reminiscences of these events which the Italian philosopher incorporated in the *Cena*.

This narrative in dialogue form was, however, not a precise account of what actually took place, as Bruno himself tells us in his preface, so that it looks as if the writer worked out a tissue of impressions gained during his stay in London. The *Cena* relates that the Ash Wednesday Supper party took place at Fulke Greville's house in London; among those present were probably John Florio and Philip Sidney, while the two messengers who came from Greville to invite Bruno were Florio and Matthew Gwinne (1). The Italian visitor was invited to expound his conception of the Copernican doctrine, one of the widely debated topics of the day. He was of an ardent and impetuous nature, an enthusiastic admirer of Copernicus, and his ardour must have clashed with the rigid dogmatism of certain English academic minds. Contemporaries obviously took a keen interest in the 'new philosophy,' and they must have taken an even much keener interest in the features of the *Cena* which bore an immediate relation to living persons. And the moment Bruno availed himself of the opportunity to attack two English doctors in particular, readers of the *Cena* probably knew who were being lashed under the thin disguise of Torquato and Nundinio. The former was especially singled out for his ridiculous pedantry as the leader of the academy. According to Bruno English doctors were

---

(1) G. GENTILE discovered a first draft of a few pages of the dialogues of the *Cena* in which these names occur. See his 1925-7 edition of BRUNO's works, an edition which I have been unable to consult.

. . . a constellation of most obstinate pedantry, ignorance and presumption mingled with a rustic incivility which would provoke the patience of Job. And if you do not believe this, go to Oxford, and inquire what happened to the Nolan when he disputed publicly with doctors in theology in the presence of the Polish prince Alasco and others of the English nobility. Learn how he replied to the arguments; how the miserable doctor, who came forward on that grave occasion as a leader of the Academy, stumbled fifteen times over fifteen syllogisms, like a hen amongst the stubble. Learn with what incivility and discourtesy that pig proceeded, and what patience and humility that other displayed, showing himself to be a Neapolitan, born and bred beneath a kindlier sky (1).

The violence of Bruno's satire leads one to suspect that Torquato and Nundinio were portraits of living characters. Knowing that certain jokes at Harvey's expense were given general currency in Elizabethan times, it is surely remarkable that Bruno uses some of these in order to ridicule 'Torquato.' Two passages in the *Cena* indeed refer to a few significant details of Harvey's personality, details also held up to ridicule in the Cambridge comedy. Just before the passage quoted above, Bruno portrays Torquato in a conversation between 'Smitho' and 'Teofilo,' the latter being probably John Florio. 'Smitho' there says that Torquato had better be decked out with the hangman's hempen rope (*un capestro al collo*) than with a gold chain, a slur which soon attracted all those who wanted to make fun of the ropemaker's son Gabriel Harvey.

Teo. Credo che profetasse (benchè non intendesse lui medesmo la sua profezia) che il Nolano andava a far provision d'elleboro, per risaldar il cervello a questi pazzi barbareschi.
Smi. Se quelli, che v'eran presenti, come erano civili, fussero stati civilissimi, gli arebbono attaccato, in loco della collana, un capestro al collo, e fattogli contar quaranta bastonate in commemorazione del primo giorno di quaresima.
Teo. Il Nolano gli disse, che il dottor Torquato lui non era pazzo, perchè porta la collana; la quale se non avesse a dosso, certamente il dottor Torquato non valerebe più che per suoi vestimenti; i quali però vagliono pochissimo, se a forza di bastonate non gli saran spolverati sopra (2).

And then, Torquato is also picked out for special reference to his

<hr>

(1) The translation is Miss YATES's, see her *John Florio*, p. 90. Miss YATES suggests on the authority of HARVEY's marginalia that Dr. J. UNDERHILL was one of the persons who fell foul of BRUNO at Oxford. See also her article, "Giordano Bruno's Conflict with Oxford," *Journal of the Warburg Institute*, II (1939), 227-242.
(2) GIORDANO BRUNO, *Opere Italiane*, ed. G. GENTILE (Bari, 1907), I, 96.

perfumed face (*profumato volto*) and his ridiculous moustaches, details which were also conspicuous in *Pedantius*. Florio, under the guise of Teofilo, describes Torquato as follows:

Ed a presso remirato al petto del Nolano, dove più tosto arrebe possuto mancar qualche bottone; dopo essersi rizzato, ritirate le braccia de la mensa, scrollatosi un poco il dorso, sbruffato co' la bocca alquanto, acconciatasi la beretta di velluto in testa, intorcigliatosi il mustaccio, posto in arnese il profumato volto, inarcate le ciglia, spalancate le narici, messosi in punto con un riguardo di rovescio, poggiatasi al sinistro fianco la sinistra mano per donar principio a la sua scrima, appuntò le tre prime dita della destra insieme, e cominciò a trar di mandritti, in questo modo parlando:—*Tunc ille philosophorum protoplastes?*— (1)

Compare *Pedantius*, III, v, 1460-1468, where the pedant says:

Tum non *Proteus* olim plures se in forma transtulit (de quo pene ubique legitur apud Poetas) quam ego vultum meum, & maxime quidem barbam, & potissimum superiorem eius hanc partem bicornem, quae barbare dicitur *Mustaches*. O barbariem, barba comptula & calamistrata indignem! Adde etiam, quod hunc habiturus sum puerum pedissequum, qui sandalia mea (*Pantofles* dicta ἀπὸ τοῦ παντα φέρειν) mecum vndique circumferet.

Moustaches were, of course, common in Elizabethan days, but it is striking and completely in line with the present argument that the detail of Harvey's ridiculous moustaches turns up in no less than four writers whose works display Harveyan connexions: Bruno (*Cena*), Edward Forsett (*Pedantius*), Greene (*A Quip for an Upstart Courtier*), and Nashe (*Foure Letters Confuted* and *Have With You to Saffron Walden*). Critics are unanimously of opinion that Nashe, Greene and Forsett directed their satire against Harvey, and, seeing that they employed the same stock jokes as Bruno, it is likely that the latter also had Harvey in mind in the *Cena*.

Though there is no evidence to show Harvey's presence in Oxford in 1583, we do know from Nashe's *Have With You to Saffron Walden* that Harvey was much enraptured over the 'Paradoxe as that of Nicholaus Copernicus' (2), a subject also touched on in *Pedantius* and debated by Bruno. Furthermore, in connexion with Torquato's

---

(1) Bruno, *Opere Italiane*, I, 92. The passage quoted above will be found translated in part by O. Elton, "Giordano Bruno in England," in *Modern Studies* (London, 1907), pp. 15-6.
(2) Nashe, *Works*, III, 94.

use of perfumes one may note that John Marston in the address 'To those that seems judicial perusers' in *The Scourge of Villainy* spoke of the 'late perfumed fist of judicial Torquatus,' while, on the other hand, the very first dialogue of Florio's *Second Fruits* works out the contrast between a Torquato addicted to fine clothing and a Nolano very simply dressed. And last but not least, 'Torquatus' is of course derived from 'torquere,' which verb in the expression 'funes torquere' can be applied to the trade of Harvey's father, the meaning being 'to make ropes.' The practice of choosing or coining Latin words to gird at persons was apparently not uncommon at Cambridge; for instance, the students coined a new Latin verb 'pernare' from the name of Dr. Andrew Perne, vice-chancellor of the University in 1574-75 and one of the earliest of Harvey's enemies. 'Pernare' is, of course, an example different from 'torquere' in that it is based on a person's name, not on a trade.

The contents of *Pedantius* also strengthen the probability that 'Torquatus' should have been a generally known nickname to make fun of the pedantry of Gabriel Harvey. That 'torquere' was really used with the implication of an allusion to the ropemaker's trade seems to be confirmed by the following four passages which all refer in some way or other to the twisting or rebutting of an argument, concurrently then with the veilèd reference to ropemaking. It should be noted that this verb, or some derivative, is used with special liking in the dialogues in which the pedant appears, while it hardly ever occurs in the other conversations. The extracts here quoted are preserved in both C and P (italics of the original).

Ped. Quae dixisti hactenus (etsi non fuerunt optima) tamen meliora quam quae deterrima. Ego elegantissime definirem amorem ex Terentio: esse nimirum *ignem femini generis.* Sic enim ille, *Accede ad ignem hanc.* Satin' hoc ex sententia?

Dro. Ego vero retorqueo hoc Argumentum tuum sic, Amor est ignis.

(I, iii, 452-8.)

Dro. . . . Vtinam ego hodie potius cum centum simul capitosis sophistis disputassem in scholis publicis nostris, modo vnius huius *strangulatorium argumentum* evitassem.

Ped. Quoniam mortale tum pectus coegit auri mei sacra fames (*Sacra* per antithesin, vel *Sacrum* est quod *Dijs inferis devotum*) opto, vt quicquid tetigeris, aurum statim fiat. Hoc tu fortasse praeclarum putares, sed eveniret tum tibi, quod *Midae* (cuius etiam obiter vtinam auriculas haberes) *Qui fame peribat, quod auro vesci nequibat.* Sed video jam campum in quo exultare possit oratio: te Mercurialem (non quoad linguam, sed

quoad manus) vexent saxum sitisque Tantali, Ixionis rota vaga vagum
torqueat, Charon remiger Orci Phlegetontis in undas deferat, qui falcem
tuam meam in messem immisisti. (I, iv, 676-690.)

(Gilbertus and the pedant in conversation:)
Gil. Potes ex codice meo conjicere, quid velim.
Ped. Non quaero, quid velis, mi Gilberte, sed cur tu in his regionibus
tam insolens adsis? Perstrinxi hominem hoc vocabulo facete. Nam *insolens*
non solum peregrinum significat, sed superbum etiam: & hoc ego volui,
siquidem me aggressus est imperiose admodum.
Gil. Quoniam extorquere vis, scias me saepius huc advenisse, tecum
ut agerem de gravissimis rationibus: semperque lusa opera est: itaque
certe mirifice gaudeo, praesentem hic te tandem contueri.
(V, iii, 2546-2555.)
Ped. *Simonides* in ardua illa questione *Hieronis*, deliberandi causa,
unum sibi diem postulavit, postridie vero biduum petijt, & deinceps
duplicavit numerum dierum. Haud aliter ego in hoc nodosa interrogatione
jam die perplexibiliter contortus cogor a te (qui es alter *Tyrannus Hiero*)
aliquot dies ad cogitandum postulare: quia quanto diutius considero,
tanto mihi res videtur obscurior. (V, iii, 2654-2661.)

Harvey is here pelted with a whole collection of words which
all display some connexion with the ropemaker's trade (strangulatorium, perstrinxi, nodosa, and the recurring variations of 'torquere'),
expressions which support the suggestion that Torquatus may be
a fitting nickname for the ropemaker's son Gabriel Harvey. That the
'torquere' element is not merely incidentally used, but really ob-
trusively present throughout the play is evident from *Pedantius*,
214-5, 1155-6, 1402, 1805.

I agree that the Torquato of the *Cena* cannot be as conclusively
identified as the pedant in the Cambridge comedy, but the allusions
Bruno makes and the insertion of characteristic details in the depiction
of Torquato plead strongly in favour of the identification, and one
may well declare with Professor Moore Smith that Torquato's
physical features given by the *Cena*—Moore Smith's conclusion,
of course, only refers to the data supplied by *Pedantius*—are most
apposite to Harvey.

It is true that, with the exception of a reference in one of the
Marginalia, Harvey never refers to Bruno in his published
writings (1), but it is also true that the Italian philosopher is hardly

(1) HARVEY's reference is worth quoting: 'Jordanus Neopolitanus, (Oxonij disputans
cum Doctore Vnderhil) tam in Theologia, quam in philosophia, omnia reuocabat ad Locos
Topicos, et axiomata Aristotelis; atque inde de quauis materia promptissime arguebat.
Hopperi principia multo efficaciora in quouis Argumento forensi.' (See *Marginalia*,
p. 156.)

ever mentioned elsewhere in Elizabethan literature (1). The best evidence for Bruno's connexion with the Elizabethan literary world is the account of the *Cena*, and the fact that his *Spaccio de la bestia trionfante* (1584) and *De gli eroici furori* (1585) were both dedicated to Sidney. The identification Torquato-Harvey, if correct, again bears out Harvey's intellectual arrogance, and stamps him as a man impervious to the spread of Italian culture in Elizabethan times. As such he was presumably a ready butt of the Italophils in the years 1580-1590.

II

Harvey's personality, as any other Elizabethan's, stood in close relation to the psychological theories of the age. As the text of *Pedantius* is of value in the interpretation of Harvey's character as this is revealed alike by his own writings and by other authors, it is worth while to discuss Elizabethan psychology in some detail. The most salient feature of this psychology was that its practisers applied the theory of the four humours. The theory was extremely popular and discussed in numerous learned treatises. It furnished the Elizabethan dramatists with a set of attractive 'scientific' categories which could serve as a basis for character portrayal. It was therefore quite natural for the author of *Pedantius* not to deviate from the generally accepted practice, and Forsett accordingly brought the theory of the four humours into his play.

Renaissance writers were notoriously fond of establishing correspondences (2) between the physical world and man, for example as the universe was composed of four elements, so man's constitution was made up of the four humours. The most current correspondences, with the seats of the humours and the planets which govern them, are best set out in a table.

Humour	Element	Qualities	Seat	Constellation
Melancholy	Earth	Cold and dry	Spleen	Saturn
Phlegm	Water	Cold and moist	Kidney, lungs	(Moon)
Blood	Air	Hot and moist	Liver	Jupiter
Choler	Fire	Hot and dry	Gall	Mars

---

(1) The only known passage seems to be N. W.'s reference to BRUNO in his preface to SAMUEL DANIEL's *Worthy Tract of Paulus Jovius* (1585). N. W. wrote: 'You cannot forget that which *Nolanus* (that man of infinite titles among other phantasticall toyes) truely noted by chaunce in our Schooles, that by the helpe of translations, al Sciences had their ofspring,' (see DANIEL, *Works*, ed. A. B. GROSART (London, 1885-96), IV, 7.

(2) See E. M. W. TILLYARD, *The Elizabethan World Picture* (London, 1943).

At birth man's body was believed to be furnished with 'radical heat' and 'radical moisture,' the latter being produced in the liver by the four humours. The radical moisture was continually consumed by the radical heat. As man grew older he became drier and colder, and finally death occurred through the failure of heat and moisture. The four humours produced by the liver had to be properly mixed to ensure man's normal growth and health. The abundance or deficiency of a particular humour was therefore regarded as the chief cause of illness. To restore the perfect balance of the humours Renaissance physicians chiefly employed two methods of treatment, bloodletting and purgations. It was also of great importance that a man should observe a proper diet because food, passing through the stomach to the liver, was transformed into the four humours, and the nature of that food obviously determined the harmonious composition of man's radical moisture.

As every student of Elizabethan literature knows, it was the melancholy complexion that proved most attractive to the artists of the age (1). Evidently melancholy was a mood largely consonant with the Renaissance temper, for it was generally believed that scholars were more than others apt to fall a prey to pensive sadness. The learned Dromodotus in *Pedantius* is an embodiment of such a melancholy type. If *Pedantius* was produced in 1580-81 Edward Forsett was apparently one of the first to present a particularly important aspect of Renaissance physiology and psychology to a Cambridge audience, for he anticipated Dr. Timothy Bright's *Treatise of Melancholy* (1586) by six years. The depiction of melancholy was not unknown in the earlier English Renaissance, but, as Professor Lawrence Babb points out (2), it became first conspicuous in the works of John Lyly, whose *Sapho and Phao* (1582) put the melancholy scholar on the scene in the person of Pandion. Here again *Pedantius* was two years ahead of Lyly's play. Professor Babb never mentions *Pedantius* or Harvey in his work, but in spite of this, as I hope to show, Harvey's intellectual attitude may be regarded as an important motive force in the propagation of the melancholy vogue.

---

(1) The subject of melancholy in general has of course been treated at length before. A recent study is that by LAWRENCE BABB, *The Elizabethan Malady. A Study of Melancholia in English Literature from 1580 to 1642* (East Lansing, Michigan State College Press, 1951).

(2) L. BABB, *The Elizabethan Malady*, p. 73.

The conception of the melancholy scholar, according to Professors Erwin Panofsky and Fritz Saxl (1), owed its popularity mainly to Marsilio Ficino. In the *De Vita* Ficino was concerned with the description of the Saturnine melancholic, a type to which Ficino believed that he himself belonged. He was also a staunch believer in the theory of Aristotle that melancholy is eminently characteristic of all great minds. Originated in the Florentine Academy by Ficino, the interest in melancholy theories was disseminated in other countries but their diffusion has not yet been fully studied. In France, for example, we find the subject of melancholy treated in *L'Univers, ou Discours des parties et de la nature du monde* (1557) by Pontus de Tyard, a work republished in 1578 as the *Premier Curieux* and *Second Curieux*. This is, of course, only an instance among many. The cure for the dangerous forms of melancholy as advised by Ficino is, as might be expected, dieting. A good diet is obtained by the avoidance of all excess and by a considered mapping out of the day, by the taking of proper food, etc. Ficino also speaks higly of music as a powerful agent to combat the cold and dry nature of the black bile (2), a method of treatment one finds very frequently advised in Renaissance medical works.

Traditionally there are two main types of melancholy people. Some persons are so much overwhelmed by their grief that their reasoning powers get dulled; their habitual sadness is such as to reduce them to the level of mere brutes and with such people melancholy therefore acts as a paralysing influence on their intellectual power. This is the conception of melancholy prevalent in medical works in the tradition of Galen. But in treatises of the time one also encounters descriptions of a second type of melancholy, a type very different from the one just mentioned. The philosopher who first described this type was Aristotle. In his *Problemata* Aristotle had discussed a 'problem' in which Renaissance thinkers were greatly interested. Aristotle's problem (3) was: 'Why is it that all those who have become eminent in philosophy or politics or the arts are clearly of an atrabilious temperament, and some of them to such an extent as to be affected by diseases caused by black

(1) E. PANOFSKY and F. SAXL, *Dürers 'Melencolia. I.' Eine Quellen- und Typengeschichtliche Untersuchung* (Leipzig, 1923).

(2) See E. PANOFSKY and F. SAXL, *Dürers 'Melencolia. I'*, pp. 21, 41.

(3) ARISTOTLE, *Problemata*, translated by E. S. FORSTER (Oxford, 1927), 953[a]. ARISTOTLE discusses the above mentioned problem in Book XXX, I. The translator points out that this problem is cited as Aristotelian by CICERO, *Tusc. Disp.*, I, 33.

bile, as is said to have happened to Heracles among the heroes ?'
Here, surely, was a conception of melancholy capable of exercising
a strong appeal on Renaissance minds, for the artists of the time,
in their awareness of belonging to the chosen few, were not slow
to subscribe wholeheartedly to Aristotle's proposition that melancholy was a distinctive feature of all those who had achieved
eminence in the arts. In the course of his discussion Aristotle also
mentions, next to Hercules, Ajax and Bellerophon among the Greek
heroes who were subject to melancholy. Finally, though sixteenth
century treatises could invoke the authority of Galen and Aristotle
for their views, it must be mentioned that, especially in matters of
detail, there was often a considerable amount of disagreement among
authors dealing with the psychology of melancholy (1). They often
admitted that, so far from being uniformly sad, people whose
complexion was predominantly atrabilious were often of a cheerful
frame of mind, indeed, were able to get much pleasure out of life.
Let us now examine the bearing of all this on Gabriel Harvey.

Pedantius, as we know, gives us a full-length portrait of Harvey.
The comedy frequently dwells on the choleric nature of the pedant's
temperament, but his sanguine or melancholy leanings are also
dragged in occasionally. In the first act the philosopher Dromodotus,
in conversation with the pedant, discusses the pestilential nature
of women and love generally in order to trick him out of Lydia's
love. Dromodotus advises an antidote against the infirmity caused
by love.

Dro. Nunc antidotum ministrabo contra pestem hanc. Primum,
ieiunandum est saepius, vt evacuatio siue evaporatio fiat humoris sensitivi
superflui : tum piscibus vescaris potius quam carnibus quae generant
sanguinem calidum & concupiscibilem ; vino abstineas & saccharo, in
quibus inest venereum provocamentum, tum otia vites, siquidem negotia
condensant hanc cerebri fluiditatem, quae gignit ex se turpissimum id
excrementum voluptatis.

(I, iii, 505-513.)

A similar subject is also debated elsewhere, in a passage where the
pedant states that a wife is a medicine against melancholy, the very

---

(1) See L. T. FOREST, "A Caveat for the Critics against invoking Elizabethan
Psychology," *PMLA*, LXI (1946), 651-672, and F. R. JOHNSON, "Elizabethan Drama
and the Elizabethan Science of Psychology," in *English Studies Today*, ed. C. L. WRENN
and G. BULLOUGH (Oxford, 1951), pp. 111-119.

malady to which studious and contemplative minds are particularly liable. Note further that Dromodotus saddles the pedant with a 'sanguine plethora.'

> *Dro.* Pestilentissima haec febris est, quae foeminam sitit.
> *Ped.* Quarto, nobis studiosis vxor medicamen est contra melancholiam & phrenesim, quae nobis imminet contemplationi deditis.
> *Dro.* Etiam vt contra plethoram sanguinis interdum, si saeviat. Sed haec esset impropria praedicatio, si inferius sic praedicaretur de suo superiori.
>
> (II, ii, 894-901.)

Another interesting passage is the one in which the contemplative Dromodotus recommends that the pedant should avoid the company of ordinary women and ladies of the court, while he advises a purgation for the pedant that his complexion may be changed.

> *Dro.* Deinde consortium fugias istarum aulicarum, quae valde agunt in haec inferiora corpora: Praeter haec, potio aliqua purgatiua sumenda est, qua complexionem istam immutes tuam. Nam vos cholerici propter ignei humoris copiam feroces ruitis, cum nos melancholici (praeterquam quod ingeniosiores sumus, teste Aristotele in problematis), tum quoque ob terrei sanguinis pigritiam, multo sumus ad hosce brutales motus minus proni. Haec quae praescripsi si ne quicquam prosint, veniendum est ad illud vltimum; nosti, quid sibi fecerit *Xenocrates* Platonicus.
>
> (I, iii, 520-530.)

Dromodotus maintains that choler predominates in the pedant's constitution. This typically choleric nature also appears from the pedant's exclaiming in Lydia's presence (line 1108): 'Ah! jam mitesco rursus. Nos cholerici & cito succensemus, & cito placamur.' Furthermore, it will be noted that Dromodotus quotes the authority of Aristotle's *Problemata* for his proposition, an Aristotelian 'problem' being the source, already referred to, whence most Renaissance writers, directly or indirectly, derived the idea that with great minds melancholy has become a second nature.

This whole question of the humours once surely formed a conspicuous feature of *Pedantius*, and if the pedant was intended to represent Gabriel Harvey one may reasonably expect Harvey's temperament to be made fun of by other writers in other contexts. Evidently choleric petulance was something Harvey suffered very much from in his quarrels with his contemporaries, while melancholy, as we shall soon see, was Harvey's *bête noire*, a temper he wanted to disclaim at all costs, without ever discrediting his claim to competence in the study of philosophy. And as to Harvey's sanguine complexion, Nashe, for example, distinctly referred to it when he used the word 'sanguine' to scoff at Harvey. In the *Foure Letters Confuted*, the reply to Harvey's *Foure Letters*, he wrote (original italics): 'Forgot hee the *pure sanguine of his Fairy Queene*, sayst thou? A *pure sanguine* sot art thou, ...' (1). Nashe is here of course referring to Harvey's association with Edmund Spenser.

The inference from what precedes seems to be that Harvey pretended or supposed that his complexion was characterized by the predominance of either blood or choler over the other two humours, so that he was either 'hot and moist' or 'hot and dry,' while on the other hand he seems to have been in constant fear of having the proper mixture of his humours disturbed by some sudden invasion of black bile to the detriment of his sanguine, 'Jovial' temper.

Harvey's marginalia, which provide a personal record of his ideas on matters of current interest, afford further evidence that the author of *Pedantius* did not misrepresent the peculiar temper of his comedy's central figure. The marginalia show that the theory of the humours had become a regular feature of Harvey's thinking, so much so that, at times, he let the terminology of the humours determine the pattern of his thoughts. Furthermore, from a cursory reading of Harvey's personal notes one indeed gains the impression that he had come to conceive an intense dislike for melancholy, while one has only to look at the number of entries under 'melancholy' and 'diet' (a subject also treated in *Pedantius*) in Professor Moore Smith's index to the *Marginalia* to be convinced of Harvey's preoccupation in these matters. Here are three typical marginalia:

An jmployed man, hath no leysure to be acowld jn wynter, to thinke uppon heate in sommer, to be heauy-hartid, or drowsely and swaddishly affectid, to be syck. but euer goith cheerefully, and lustely thorowgh with all his enterprizes, & affayres. He is A very swadd, & sott, that, dullith, or bluntith ether witt, or boddy with any lumpish, or Melancholy buzzing abowt this, or that. The right pragmaticall karrieth euermore liuely and quyck spirites, and takith continually the nymbliest, and speediest way. for the dispatch of his busines: wch he neuer attemptith withowt cause, nor euer slackith, or forslowith withowt effect.

---

(1) NASHE, *Works*, I, 281. That readers interested in the HARVEY-NASHE quarrels must have been prepared for satirical allusion to a detail of phrase such as 'sanguine' has already been noticed by A. DAVENPORT, ed. *The Collected Poems of Joseph Hall* (Liverpool, 1949). p. xlvii, footnote.

Nunquam ullo momento Melancholicus, aut abiectus: (uiltá) sed semper alacris, et iocundissimus.

Liuely, & floorishing actiuity, is durable: all pensiuenes, & slowth, deseased and deadly.

Ignaua, frigida et turpis Melancholia.

The neatest, finest, sweetest & brauest Theurgia: my platforme.

Sharp, & fine Witt: pure Sanguin, or braue Choller: Melancholy an Asse in Witt, & Memory: Saturne A Beast in Behauiour, & Action —no baser, or viler wretch, then Melancholy. The longer ye Melancholy man liueth, ye lesse he knoweth: quoth Doctor Phillip, in ye 6 Discourse of his Counsellour (1).

For the last statement in the third quotation Harvey gives his authority 'Doctor Phillip, in ye 6 Discourse of his Counsellour.' This refers to Bartolome Felippe's *Tractado de Conseio y de los Conseieres de los Principes* (Turin, 1589), a work translated by Harvey's friend John Thorius as *The Counseller*. The translation was printed by John Wolfe and entered in the Stationers' Register in 1589 (entry on April 4, 1589). Harvey's marginal note with the reference to Felippe therefore belongs to a period subsequent to 1589. The context in which Felippe states that 'the longer ye Melancholy man liueth, ye lesse he knoweth' is worth quoting. Having enlarged on the fact that 'the Counseller of a Prince, ought to be of a chollericke or sanguine complexion' (2), Felippe goes on:

They that are Melancholicke, as they are by nature sorrowfull, and of the selfe same complexion as the earth: so they be rusticall, base, and heauie, scarce able to lift themselues one handfull aboue the ground, vaine, and delighting in trifles, enemies to noble thoughts, malicious, superstitious: in so much that men of this complexion, haue wasted and vtterly spoyled all the Regions of ye world, with their dreames, foolish imaginations, and vaine visions. They are wonderfull superstitious, and the more they grow in age, the lesse they knowe: they are very hatred it selfe, and when they are angred, straight without any occasion, either they fall to blowes, or rattle out a thousand cursses, vsing all the iniurious and slaunderous words that euer were heard among men. Finallie, it is a strange thing to see, howe wonderfully all Philosophers, and such as

---

(1) HARVEY, *Marginalia*, pp. 87, 143, 154. At page 186 we find a diet for the melancholy in which 'tristes' are said to be relieved by music (*et musicae aliquo genere permulceantur*).

(2) B. FELIPPE, *The Counsellor* (London, 1589), sig. G_1, p. 49. FELIPPE invokes the authority of FEDERICO FURIO CERIOL for the above proposition. FURIO's work had appeared in translation by T. BLUNDEVILLE as *A very briefe treatise declaring howe many counsells, a prince ought to have* (1570).

study speculations of Astronomie, detest and flie from those that be borne vnder the Planet of *Saturne*. In so much that it is thought to be most certain, that the great *Appolonius Tyaneus*, founde a melancholicke person in the Cittie of *Ephesus*, who with his presence onely, had corrupted the whole Cittie, and infected it with a great plague. To conclude, they that are of a melancholicke complexion, be dull and drowsie, heauie, vnskilfull, vnlearned, and they haue no one vertue in them that excelleth, and all theyr qualities are lesse then meane.

Although the Mellancholicke complexion, be not so good as the Chollericke and sanguine, yet it is by many called the heroicall complexion, because they that are of that complexion, refuse not to tell the truth, making no account of any danger at all : and after the same manner, as wine causeth them that be drunke, to vtter all what euer they thinke, euen so melancholie, maketh them that are fulle of blacke choller, to speake the truth, and often-times they diuine & tell of thinges to come. There haue beene many excellent men (as *Aristotle* saith) that were melancholicke (1).

Aristotle's views about melancholy enjoyed such a considerable vogue in the sixteenth century that it is a little surprising to find Felippe challenging these so vehemently. Having decried melancholy people, Felippe drags in the authority of Aristotle merely to show, one may suppose, that he is conversant with the ideas propounded in the *Problemata*. His conception of melancholy, in thus running counter to that of a philosopher whose authority was still formidable, is therefore all the more remarkable. The sanguine and choleric complexions only are referred to in laudatory terms. Similarly Harvey praises 'Sharp, & fine Witt : pure Sanguin, or braue Choller,' while, on the other hand, he disparages 'Melancholy an Asse in Witt' just as his informant does. Such a coincidence strongly suggests that Harvey's marginal note is in its entirety indebted to Felippe. Evidently Harvey could be in full sympathy with one who maintained that philosophers and astronomers hold melancholy people in abhorrence, for philosophy and especially astronomy were subjects in which Gabriel Harvey and his brothers, Richard and John, were greatly interested. That Saturn in Harvey's note is regarded as a 'Beast in Behauiour, & Action' is another link with Felippe's dispraise of the melancholy.

Note now that the combination of 'sanguine' and 'choller' occurs rather frequently in Harvey's writings and that 'sanguine' was the very word mocked at by Nashe in his *Foure Letters Confuted.*

---

(1) FELIPPE, *The Counseller*, sig. G$_1$, pp. 49-50.

Nashe had jested at the following phrase in Harvey's *Foure Letters*: '. . . I must need say, Mother Hubbard, in heat of choller, forgetting the pure sanguine of her sweete Feary Queene' (1), which phrase combines 'choler' and 'sanguine' as Harvey's marginal note did. One more example may be quoted to illustrate this combination. Among the Sonnets which close Harvey's *Foure Letters* is one which reveals strikingly which humours proved most congenial to his temper.

> Let them forgett their cancred peeuishnes;
> And say to Choller fell: Thou wert our fall:
> Hadst thou not boilde in fretting waywardnes,
> We might haue laught at Fortunes tossing Ball.
> Choler, content thy malecontented selfe:
> And cleerest Humour, of right Sanguine pure,
> Neately refin'd from that felonious Elfe,
> With Iouiall graciousnes thy selfe enure.
> If euer siluer conduictes were abroche
> Of streaming Witt, and flowing Eloquence:
> Yee fludds of milke, and hoony reapproche,
> And bounteously poure-out your Quintessence.
>   Gently assemble Delicacies all,
>   And sweetely nectarize this bitter gall.

(Sonnet VIII.)

The phrase 'Mother Hubbard, in heat of choller, forgetting the pure sanguine of her sweete Feary Queene, wilfully ouer-shott her malcontented selfe' will be seen to be skilfully worked up into this sonnet (note the echo in 'Choler, content thy maleconted selfe'). Both the phrase and the sonnet just quoted express Harvey's regret that choler should have got the better of him and his enemies, while the sonnet in addition puts in a strong plea for a cessation of hostilities, a feature of Harvey's pamphlets that has not been sufficiently recognized by his commentators. Obviously, it is important to recognize that numerous phrases and tags were commonplaces in Elizabethan literature, and that the theory of the humours could effectually serve an artist's purposes. But it will be granted, I believe, that Harvey's phraseology is peculiar, while, to my knowledge, the coincidences just dealt with are not discoverable elsewhere in the literature of the time.

A last echo of the terminology of Harvey's important marginal note remains to be pointed out. In this note Harvey held that his

---

(1) HARVEY, *Foure Letters*, p. 15.

'platforme' was 'sweetest & brauest Theurgia.' Now Harvey, again girding at Nashe in *Pierces Supererogation*, maintains in this pamphlet that he has adopted the rule of Platonists and Pythagoreans as his own Theurgy, whereas this regimen (or diet) is too meagre a doctrine for the Devil's Orator, Nashe.

I will not offend your stomacke with the nice and queint regiment of the dainty Platonistes, or pure Pythagoreans: fine Theurgy, too-gant and meager a doctrine for the Diuels Oratour: if the Arte Notory, cannot be gotten without fasting, and praying muchgoditch-them that haue it: let phantasticall, or superstitious Abstinence, daunce in the aier, like Aristophanes clowdes, or Apuleius witches: your owne method of those deadly sinnes, be your Castell of Health (1).

Equipped with the evidence hitherto presented it is possible to shed fresh light on a lesser known Elizabethan play, namely *The Three Parnassus Plays*, a trilogy in which a curious reference to the diet observed by Platonists and Pythagoreans is to be found. This trilogy, which consists of *The Pilgrimage to Parnassus, The First Part of the Returne from Parnassus* and *The Second Part of the Returne from Parnassus*, contains a mass of topical material which critics have tried to interpret within the framework of Elizabethan literary history. In his recent edition of the three plays, Professor J. B. Leishman (2) dates the performance of the several parts as follows: the *Pilgrimage*, 1598/99; the *First Returne*, 1599/1600; and the *Second Returne*, 1601/1602. The trilogy was produced by the students of St. John's College, Cambridge, as appears from an entry in the Stationers' Register under the date October 16, 1605, recording the printing of the *Second Returne*. In this *Second Returne* the character of Luxurio was perhaps intended to represent Gabriel Harvey, as others have already recognized (3). Significantly, in the *Parnassus Plays* another character is introduced, one Ingenioso, who, according to the considered opinion of Professor Leishman, can 'almost certainly' be identified with Thomas Nashe. It is not surprising, then, that Ingenioso and Luxurio employ many of the tags which the disputants in the Harvey-Nashe quarrels hurled at

---

(1) HARVEY, *Pierces Supererogation* (1593), sig. F₃ vᵒ (*Works*, II, 90).
(2) J. B. LEISHMAN, ed. *The Three Parnassus Plays (1598-1601)* (London, 1949), p. 26. All references will be to that edition; the line-numeration will be given together with the page numbers between brackets.
(3) The first to suggest this was W. LÜHR in *Die drei Cambridger Spiele vom Parnass (1598-1601) in ihren litterarischen Beziehungen* (Kiel, 1900), pp. 39-43. Cf. J. B. LEISHMAN, ed. *Parnassus Plays*, pp. 79-80.

each other. Summarizing the various details relevant to the identification Luxurio-Harvey, Professor Leishman concludes by saying that it is 'very probable that the author intended Luxurio to be, at any rate in part, a caricature of Gabriel Harvey; but it must be admitted that, from the text alone, which is all we have, the portrait that emerges is not, like that of Pedantius, unmistakable' (1). I shall now endeavour to show that the equation Luxurio-Harvey is almost as much justified as the theory which regards Ingenioso 'almost certainly' as a portrait of Nashe.

Together with T. L. Summersgill, an American scholar, the present writer has independently discovered (2) a definite parallel between Harvey's works and the dialogue of Luxurio; and though the question of melancholy was also touched upon in the two articles mentioned in the footnote below, the subject was not argued in the light of the evidence that has just been discussed, since neither I myself nor T. L. Summersgill paid any regard to the data supplied by *Pedantius* and Harvey's *Foure Letters*. A very significant passage from the *Parnassus Plays* may therefore be discussed afresh.

Luxurio. Is it not time thinkest thou? I haue serued here an apprentishood of some seauen yeares, and haue liued with the Pythagorean and Platonicall Δίαιτα as they call it. Why, a good horse woulde not haue endured it. Adew single beare and three qus of breade, if I conuerse with you anie longer, some Sexton must toll the bell for the Death of my witt. Here is nothing but leuelinge of colons, squaringe of periods, by the monthe. My sanguin scorns all such base premeditation, Ile haue my pen run like a spigot & my inuention answerr it as quick as a drawer. Melancholick art, put downe thy hose, here is a suddaine wit, that will lashe thee in the time to come. *(First Returne, 417-428) (pp. 156-7).*

The one unquestionably clear parallel to the latter part of this quotation is as follows:

It is for Cheeke, or Ascham, to stand leuelling of Colons, or squaring of Periods, by measure, and number: his penne is like a spigot; and the Wine-presse a dullard to his Ink-presse (3).

The correspondence between the two texts no doubt considerably

(1) J. B. LEISHMAN, ed. *Parnassus Plays*, p. 80.
(2) See T. L. SUMMERSGILL, "Harvey, Nashe, and the Three Parnassus Plays," *PQ*, XXXI (1952), 94-5, and W. SCHRICKX, "The Portraiture of Gabriel Harvey in the Parnassus Plays and John Marston," *Neophilologus*, XXXVI (1952), 225-234.
(3) HARVEY, *Pierces Supererogation*, sig. Z$_4$ (*Works*, II, 278).

enhances the probability that the anonymous author of the *Parnassus Plays* had Harvey in mind when he put together Luxurio's speech. The nature of Harvey's diet tallies completely with that of Luxurio, for both Harvey and Luxurio mention the diet observed by Pythagoreans, a coincidence hitherto overlooked by the critics.

But it is Luxurio's 'Melancholick art' rather than his diet that gives occasion for the discussion of what was apparently a vitally significant problem in the early nineties. Miss F. A. Yates has pointed out that one of the issues in the Harvey-Nashe controversy was the question of the relative superiority of native over learned wit. Evidently Harvey's classical leanings led him to champion a classically inspired style of writing, full of learned allusion and characterized by the use of rhetorical amplification (which Harvey practised so much as to obscure his meaning), whereas Nashe's view was that one should use the resources of one's own wit (1). Though Nashe's style lacks distinction it is full of striking and vivid imagery drawn from the fullness of Elizabethan life.

There is a conspicuous passage in Harvey's *Pierces Supererogation* which conveys the controversy regarding 'art' with great circumlocution. It is a speech Harvey has put into the mouth of an anonymous friend, whose identity has been conclusively disclosed by Miss Yates. This friend was one John Eliot, author of a language manual entitled *Ortho-epia Gallica* (1593), a man who presumably took an active part in the literary wars of the day. His significance will be more fully discussed later on. In the Eliot speech in Harvey's *Pierces Supererogation* we find the following: 'Try, when you meane to be disgraced: & neuer giue me credit, if Sanguine witt putt not Melancholy Arte to bedd' (2). At first sight 'if Sanguine witt putt not Melancholy Arte to bedd' does not seem to be specifically related to Harvey's temperament and the phrase would appear to be of no more than quite general import. As the whole Eliot speech sets forth the view that bookish learning ('art') is much inferior to intellectual pleasure arising from native wit and as the 'sanguine' temper was one specially congenial to Harvey, it is likely, however, that the phrase implies that it is this temper which saves people in general, and Harvey in particular, from melancholy fits.

---

(1) See F. A. YATES, *John Florio*, pp. 179-184.
(2) The ELIOT speech is fully quoted by Miss F. A. YATES, *John Florio*, pp. 179-181; see HARVEY, *Works*, II, 62-65. The reader will find the speech in the present work on pp. 228-9.

Before returning to Luxurio's speech it is necessary to call attention to a stanza in Harvey's *New Letter of Notable Contents*, which supports the view just advanced that Harvey's curious terminology of the humours was not inadvertently employed. This stanza occurs in 'The Writers Postscript: or a frendly *Caueat* to the *Second Shakerley* of Powles' appended to the utterly unintelligible poem *Gorgon* which concludes the *New Letter*.

SONET.

Slumbring I lay in melancholy bed,
Before the dawning of the sanguin light:
When Eccho *shrill, or some* Familiar Spright
Buzzed an Epitaph *into my hed* (1).

Note now that Luxurio talks of 'Melancholick art,' just like Harvey does in the Eliot speech, and that a somewhat analogous imagery is used in the two Harvey quotations; but instead of being stirred by a sanguine humour (or wit), Luxurio is urged by a 'suddaine' wit. For his terminology the anonymous author of the *Parnassus Plays* is probably much indebted to that employed by Nashe, and therefore 'suddaine wit' may well apply to Nashe. Consider first in what terms Nashe is inveighing against Richard Harvey and his brother John in *Pierce Penilesse*. The passage is one which surely attracted Gabriel Harvey's notice and which probably prompted him to come to the rescue of his brothers. Nashe there cries to Richard: 'off with thy gowne and vntrusse, for I meane to lash thee mightily' (2), which combines the putting down of a hose and the lashing just like Luxurio's phrase. In the second place, Thomas Heywood's comedy *The Fair Maid of the Exchange*, presumably written about 1592, contains, according to the best Heywood authority (3), an unquestionably certain allusion to Nashe. Cripple, a character who at one time in the action apparently wishes to rival 'young Juvenal,' replies to Frank that he will become famous for a 'sodaine wit,' because Frank has maintained that Cripple was not in a position to write good poetry.

Yes sirra, I could conny-catch the world,
Make my selfe famous for a sodaine wit,

---

(1) HARVEY, *A New Letter of Notable Contents* (1593), sig. D₃ vº, *Works*, I, 296.
(2) NASHE, *Works*, I, 196.
(3) See A. M. CLARK, *Thomas Heywood, Playwright and Miscellanist* (Oxford, 1931), pp. 19-20.

And be admir'd for my dexterity,
Were I so dispos'd (1).

The rashness of Nashe's procedure seems, indeed, to have become proverbial thanks to Harvey's tedious harping on this in his *Pierces Supererogation*, while the fact that Nashe purged his antagonist's melancholy is confirmed by Harvey himself: 'Such an Antagonist hath Fortune allotted me, to purge melancholy, and to thrust me vpon the Stage' (2), while Nashe is elsewhere said to turn 'choler into sanguine, vineger into wine, vexation into sport' (3).

That the possibility of Luxurio's falling a prey to melancholy was not merely casually treated in the *Parnassus Plays* may appear from the following dialogue.

> *Boy* Why M^r, are you growne Melancholicke?
> *Luxurio* I faith noe boy, I haue a iollie soule, that scorns sorow; but I am in some choller with this assheaded age, where the honorable trade of ballet makinge is of such base reckoninge.
> (*First Returne*, 1481-6) (p. 207).

Note that Luxurio rejects the boy's imputation of being melancholy and that he has grown 'choleric,' or hot-tempered for that matter, about his age's degeneracy.

When we review the facts as a whole it may be concluded that the important extract from the *First Returne* quoted above, save for a few sentences of lesser significance, completely coincides with the tenour of the expressions unearthed from Harvey's works: the Pythagorean and Platonical diet (4), a sanguine temperament characterized by melancholy symptoms, while the parallelism in the imagery and the definite parallel would seem to clinch the matter regarding the question of Luxurio's identity. At this point it is best to quote the passage in which Professor Leishman summarizes the various details relevant to the identification Harvey-Luxurio: 'Luxurio . . . mocks at Ingenioso's poverty just as Harvey had mocked at Nashe's. He is represented, as Nashe had represented Harvey, as being chronically in debt. Like Harvey, he composes 'poetrie that hath a foot of the twelues,' and he is represented,

---

(1) THOMAS HEYWOOD, *The Dramatic Works* (London, 1874), II, 46.
(2) HARVEY, *Pierces Supererogation*, sig. Z$_2$ v° (*Works*, II, 273).
(3) HARVEY, *Pierces Supererogation*, sig. B$_2$ r° (*Works*, II, 42).
(4) Also NASHE harped on diet when taunting HARVEY, see *Works*, I, 256 and III, 96, 98, 101.

as Nashe had represented Harvey, both as a lover of popular ballads, and as an admirer of Elderton, the ballad-maker, to whom Harvey, in order to abuse him, had compared Greene, and to whom, in revenge, Nashe had represented Harvey as a rival. And like Nashe's Harvey, Luxurio is the Homer of his age' (1).

Yet there is one aspect of Harvey's personality which this summing up does not comprise. It will appear from the next section of this chapter that Harvey took a keen interest in alchemy, a 'science' which in his day had not yet completely fallen into disrepute. Alchemists may be said to be the founders of modern chemistry and, to a certain extent, medicine. Though the interest in alchemy was common to the age, the appearance of the following conversation in the *Parnassus Plays* was probably due to Harvey's participation in the pursuit of the philosopher's stone. One may note in passing that Ingenioso ridicules Luxurio's 'watery wit,' a concept perhaps connected with 'humidum radicale.'

Ingenioso Spirit calest thou ? It shoulde seeme by the fier thers a diuell. But I pray thee Luxurio, how meanest thou to bestowe thy waterie witt ?

Luxurio My waterie wit shall dwell in a waterie region. And yet thou doest abuse my witt to call it waterie: much haue I spente in rare Alcumie, in brewinge of wine and burninge sackes, to make my witt a philosophers stone, when I shoulde make vse of it; and now the time is come I hope what ere I make will beare marmelett and sukket in the mouthe, and sauore of wittes that haue bene familiar with the other quart & a reckoninge.

(*First Returne*, 399-409) (p. 155).

To conclude this section two important Harvey passages remain for quotation (2). They afford a striking illustration of his pre-occupation to wave aside any imputation of melancholy, while the fact that he did so indicates how great were the difficulties that he experienced in resisting that temper. An alternation between mirth and sadness is, indeed, a general psychological characteristic of the melancholy frame of mind.

Right magnanimitie neuer droupeth, sweet Musike requickneth the heauiest spirites of dumpish Melancholy: fine Poetry abhorreth the

---

(1) J. B. LEISHMAN, ed. *Parnassus Plays*, p. 80.
(2) The two extracts to be quoted are of fundamental importance to an adequate understanding of the controversy regarding 'art.' At a later stage of the argument fuller reference will be made to it, in the light of evidence yet to be presented.

loathsome, and vgly shape of forlorne pensiueness: what gentle minde detesteth not cursed, and damnable desperation? All abiect dolefulness, is woefully base, and baselie woefull. The die, the ball, the sponge, the siue, the wheele of Fortune, Fortune hirselfe, a trifle, a iest, a toy in Philosophy, & diuine resolution. Be a Musitian, & Poet vnto thy self, that art both, and a Ringleader of both, vnto other, be a Man, be a Gentleman, be a Philosopher, be a Diuine, be thy resolute selfe; not the Slaue of Fortune, that for euery fleabiting crieth out-alas & for a few hungry meales, like a Greeke Parasite, misuseth the Tragedy of Hecuba: but the friend of Vertue, that is richest in pouerty, freest in bondage, brauest in ieopordie, cheerefullest in calamitie, be rather wise, and vn-fortunate, with the siluer Swanne, then fortunate & vnwise, with the golden Asse: remember thine owne marginal Embleme, *Fortuna fauet fatuis.* Oh, solace thy miraculous selfe, and cheere the Muses in cheering thy daintie soule, sweetelie drunken with their delitious Helicon, and the restoratiue Nectar of the Gods. What can I say more? That cordial liquor, and that heauenly restoratiue, bee thy soueraigne comfort: and scorne the basenes of euerie crased, or fainting thought, that may argue a degenerate minde. And so much briefly touching thy deere selfe: whome I hope neuer to finde so pathetically distressed, or so Tragically disguised againe. Now a word, or two concerning him, who in charitie kisseth thy hand, and in pitie wisheth thee better lucke (1).

A melancholy boddy, is not the kindest nurse for a chearely minde: (the Iouiall complexion is souerainly beholding to Nature): but I know not a finer transformation in Ouid, then the Metamorphosis of dudgen earnest into sport; of harsh sower into sweet; of losse into gaine; of reproch into credit; of whatsoeuer badd occurrence into some good. I was neuer so splenetique, when I was most dumpish, but I could smile at a frise iest, when the good man would be pleasurable; and laugh at fustion earnest, when the merry man would be surly (2).

The first passage has been given at such length, first because it might possibly be misinterpreted as if the writer should have Nashe in mind. But note that Harvey is all the time addressing himself in the second person, and turns to the third when he touches upon Nashe: 'Now a word, or two concerning *him*, who in charitie kisseth *thy* hand, . . .' And second because Harvey extols music as the supreme restorative medicine for melancholy, a view which widely prevailed thanks to Marsilio Ficino's theories of melancholy dating as far back as the end of the fifteenth century.

---

(1) HARVEY, *Foure Letters*, pp. 47-8.
(2) HARVEY, *Pierces Supererogation*, sig. V$_4$ (*Works*, II, 245).

The short pamphlet written by one I. W., already referred to in passing, offers us an interesting insight into Harvey's medical interests in the years during which he probably succeeded Lancelot Browne in a medical fellowship at Pembroke. It only consists of thirty-two pages. Its title well describes the contents: *The copie of a letter sent by a learned Physician to his friend, wherein are detected the manifold errors vsed hitherto of the Apothecaries, in preparing their compositions, as Sirropes, Condites, Conserues, Pilles, Potions, Electuaries, Losinges, & c.* The pamphlet bears neither date nor imprint, but since its writer states at the end that the 'letter' was written 'From my house at S. the 21. of the present March. 1586,' it is reasonable to put its printing in 1586 (1). The letter concludes with the words 'Your louing Coosin and frend, student in Physicke. I. W.', which phrase seems to be inconsistent with the wording of the title of the pamphlet, wherein it is stated that it was sent by a 'learned Physician.'

The only critic who, as far as I know, seems to have taken notice of this *Copie of a letter* is Professor Paul H. Kocher (2), who points out that I. W.'s pamphlet deserves a place among works which were attacking Galenic medicine in the sixteenth century. Shortly after 1570 the surgical and chemical principles of Paracelsus were penetrating into Engeland, and, though opposed by the physicians John Jones and George Baker, there were others such as John Banister and William Clowes who made the first faint attempts to change the atmosphere in favour of Paracelsism. Paracelsus had mainly emphasized the need for experimental treatment and the application of inorganic compounds in medicine, whereas the followers of Galen were mostly theorists, who, amongst others, made much of the theory of the four humours. The scientist who played a prominent part in the assaults against Galenic pharmacology was John Hester, 'Paracelsan.' His first contribution was to write a translation of Lionardo Fioravanti's *Regimento della peste* (1565), which he published in 1579 as *A Ioyfull Iewel.* As Professor Kocher points out,

---

(1) I shall quote from the British Museum copy of this pamphlet. For convenience' sake the signature references will be added after each quotation.

(2) P. H. KOCHER, "John Hester, Paracelsan (fl. 1576-93)," in *J. Q. Adams Memorial Studies* (1948), pp. 621-638.

the only other Englishmen venturing to publish general assaults on Galenic medicine were R. B., whose book, *The difference betwene the auncient Phisicke and the latter Phisicke*, appeared in 1585, and I. W., with whose *Copie of a letter* we will here be concerned. Professor Kocher gives no more than passing mention to the *Copie*, as was fully justified by the nature of his contribution. I. W., however, has afforded us a valuable document regarding Gabriel Harvey and his letter therefore belongs to the present argument.

Who was I. W.'s addressee? I think I can give a probable answer to this question. Seeing that there are several important, hitherto unnoted, parallels in I. W.'s epistle to passages in Harvey's published writings, and that, furthermore, the drift of such expressions as deal with medical treatment and alchemy in *Pierces Supererogation* or the *New Letter of Notable Contents* is closely connected with that of the *Copie of a letter*, one may reasonably assume that Gabriel Harvey was one of those to whom the contents of the *Copie of letter* were specially directed. From a comparison between the statements made by Harvey and I. W. one gathers the impression that the latter's intention was to alter Harvey's medical opinions, and especially his attitude towards Paracelsus.

From the very beginning of his epistle I. W. charges ignorance of Paracelsus's works upon his addressee, for the letter-writer's advice runs: 'Iudge him [Paracelsus] not then good Coosin by the mouth of his enemies (who speake of enuie) no more then you would by the verdict of his friendes, but trie him by his owne wordes' (sig. A₂ rº). Having mentioned the three ways in which Paracelsus prepared mercury, and having attacked 'these woodden Physicians' who cry out 'the diet, the diet, and nothing but the diet, to the diet, to the diet' (sig. A₄ vº)—a method of treatment advocated by Harvey, as we already know, and also advised by Galen— I. W. proceeds to answer his correspondent 'concerning such medicines as you obiected in your letters against vs.' I. W. next examines his correspondent's medicines and then specially objects to the latter's purgations. It will be recognized that all this fits in remarkably well with what we already know about Gabriel Harvey, but it is the parallels which make the identity of I. W.'s 'Coosin' satisfactorily clear. I shall now quote the most striking parallels between Harvey and I. W. in the order of their appearance in the *Copie of a letter*. A first parallel has the merit of partly elucidating Harvey's jumble of phrases. Commenting on the saying *Omnis commoditas sua fert incommoda secum* (1) I. W. continues:

As for example, *Sena* did breed winde, *Rubarb* did drie the body ouermuch, *Agarick* ouerthrew the stomack, *Scammonie* weakened the liuer and intrailes, *Cassia* feebled the raines, *Colocinthus* bred the bloodie flixe, *Euforbium* inflamed the whole body, & c there is not one of them without fault. What order tooke you then, did you purge any of these from their euill qualities? not one, but by al meanes went about to hide and beguile nature, as for ilsample, to beguile the nose (for many of them haue a very ill sauour) you went to the perfumers & bought Muske, yee went also to the Cookes for hony and sugar, that you might betray the tast therof: and least the sight and ouglines thereof should bewray it, you ran to the goldsmithes to buy gold leaues to couer it (*Copie*, sig. A₈r°).

A happy *Truce*, if a happy truce: and an honorable *Triumph*, if durable. I say, *If*, and *If*, bicause I haue knowne many a *Truce*, like Scammony, that weakeneth the liuer; or Cassia, that enfeebleth the raines; or Agarick, that ouerthroweth the stomacke; the stomacke, that must worke the feate. And who hath not either by Experience, or by heare-say, or by reading, knowne many a *Triumph*, like Sena, that breedeth winde; or Rubarbe, that dryeth ouer-much; or Euforbium, that inflameth the whole body; the body, that must strike the stroake? Take-away that ouerthrowing, or weakening property from *Truce*: and *Truce* may be a diuine Scammony, Cassia, or Agaricke, to purge noysome and rebellious humours. Oh that it might be such a Purge in Fraunce. Correct that ventositie, or inflammation, that accompanieth Triumph: and Lo the gallantest Phisique, that nature hath affourded, witt deuised, or magnanimity practised, to abate the pride of the enemy, and to redouble the courage of the frende. No Tobacco, or Panacea so mightily vertuous, as that Physique. Oh that it might be such a Physique in Croatia, in Hungary, in Almany, in the whole Christian world. *Immensum calcar Gloria:* the golden spurre of the braue Grecian, & the worthy Romane. *Pollicy* is Politique: & will not easely be coosened with the muske of the Perfumer, though muske be a sweet Curtesan; or allured with the sugar, & hony of the Cooke, though sugar, & hony be dainty hypocrites; or enueigled with the goldleaues of the Goldsmith, though gold-leaues be eloquent & bewitching Oratours; or deluded, that is, betrayed with any coolerable counterfesance, howsoeuer smoothly enticing, or gloriously pretending (2).

And here is a passage from I. W.'s letter which Harvey used in two different works.

Alas good Cosin, why are you then displeased & out of charitie with such persons as do aduise, and of good will exhort you, not to couer the venome

---

(1) The saying was a commonplace, but compare HARVEY, *Pierces Supererogation*, sig. Aa₄ (*Works*, II, 288): 'what commodity of the world without discommodity.'
(2) HARVEY, *A New Letter*, sig. A₂ v° (*Works*, I, 260 ff.).

of *Scammonie* with Quinces, the windines of *Sene* with ginger, the drinesse of *Rubarbe* with succorie, the fretting of *Colocinthis* with gum *Tragaganth*, the burning and firie qualities of *Euforbium* with the iuice of lillies, the stinking sauour of *Sagapenum* with muske, the bitternes of *Aloes* with sugar ? but haue brought to light the manner how to take quite away these incommodities: that whether they worke or worke not there can no hurt come to the party. Which that you may bring to passe, you shall not need to send vnto *Atticum* for fine hony, nor into the East for *Saunders*, nor into *Spain* for sugar, nor into *Italy* for Anniseeds, but only bestow a litle mony with the poore Collier, & as much at the Glashouse, & with these two things of small cost you may draw the pure spirit of wine, which in few daies will seperate the good from the bad, the vertue from the venome, the pure from the vnpure, without any hinderance at all to the operation of the good (*Copie*, sig. B₁ v⁰).

Compare:

Much good may that aduauncement doe them; and many daintie webbs may I see of those fine Spiders: but although I dote vpon curious workemanship, yet I looue not artificiall poyson; and am almost angrie with the trimmest Spinners, when they extort venom out-of flowers, and will needes defile their friends Libraries with those encroching cob-webbs. Iwis it were purer Euphuisme, to winne hoony out-of the thistle; to sweeten Alöe with sugar; to perfume the stinking Sagapenum with muske; and to mitigate the heat of Euforbium with the iuice of the lilly (1).

All is well, that endeth effectually well: & so in some hast he endeth, that wisheth you entirely well: and for your instruction can assure you, he needeth not send to Athens for hony, or to Spaine for sugar, or to Italy for Anniseedes, or to the Orient for saunders, or pearles; that may finde as fine, and dainty choice, neerer hand (2).

The real gist of I. W.'s advice to his correspondent is already disclosed in the two long quotations just given. He remonstrates against his correspondent's purging the evil, poisonous, or impure qualities of drugs by the *addition* of 'musk, honey, or sugar,' whereas his own argument is that the right procedure to prepare drugs is *separation* or *extraction* ('seperate the good from the bad, the vertue from the venome, the pure from the vnpure'). Elsewhere I. W. says that his addressee's procedure is contrary to nature's rules because the latter (apparently Harvey) does not seek to separate substances from their impurities, while he again insists that Harvey

---

(1) HARVEY, *Pierces Supererogation*, sig. T₁ v⁰ (*Works*, II, 227).
(2) HARVEY, *A New Letter*, sig. D₂ v⁰. For a third parallel, not of much importance to the argument, see *Copie*, sig. B₂ v⁰ and *A New Letter*, sig. A₄ v⁰.

adds sugar and honey 'for to preserue those and other things from putrifaction' (*Copie*, sig. A₅ vᵒ). Further on he maintains that the sweetest balms are to be obtained from strong poisons rather than from roses.

> . . . each creature had an euill ioyned to his good, but like vnto like, vnto strong life was added strong death or venome, for the death of Roses is not so strong as the death of Arsenicke, which may be perceaued hereby, in that the balme of Arsenick is far stronger then the balme of roses, as the life or balme of roses is inferiour to the balme of Arsenick, which is of such force that he is able to preserue from death & dissolution many yeares, that most strong poison which is ioyned with him, whereby wee may perceiue that in the strongest poysons are the most pure & sweetest balmes to be found (*Copie*, sig. B₆ vᵒ).

Compare with this the following extract from Harvey's *Pierces Supererogation*, and the connexion between I. W. and Harvey will become clear.

> The *abiectest naturalls* haue their specificall properties, and some wondrous vertues: and Philosophy will not flatter the *noblest, or worthiest naturals* in their venoms, or impurities. True Alchimy can alledge much for her Extractions, and quintessences: & true Phisique more for her corrections, and purgations. In the best, I cannot commende the badd; and in the baddest, I reiect not the good: but precisely play the Alchimist, in seeking pure and sweet balmes in the rankest poisons. A pithy, or filed sentence is to be embraced, whosoeuer is the Autor: and for the lest benefit receuied, a good minde will render dutifull thankes, euen to his greatest enemy. ô Humanity, my Lullius, or ô Diuinitie, my Paracelsus, how should a man become that peece of Alchimy, that can turne the Rattes-bane of Villany into the Balme of honestry; or correct the Mandrake of scurrility with the myrrhe of curtesie, or the saffron of temperance (1).

The quotations from I. W.'s letter as well as those from Harvey's works bristle with terms borrowed from botany and alchemy, sciences which attracted a countless number of practisers in Harvey's day. Persons interested in these sciences could find information on their respective subjects in the many, mostly bulky, treatises compiled by professional botanists and alchemists. This is why it is not beyond possibility that both Harvey and I. W. might be indebted to some common source. I can only say that I have examined several botanical and alchemical works of the time and

---

(1) HARVEY, *Pierces Supererogation*, sig. Bb₁ vᵒ and Bb₂ rᵒ (*Works*, II, 292 ff.).

that I have failed to discover anything that resembles the passages of either writer. The very fact that Harvey borrows so extensively and with such curious alterations indicates clearly, I hope, that there is little need to search for a common source.

The various Harvey extracts given here produce the impression that Harvey had come to some kind of reconciliation with I. W.'s views. True alchemy deserves nothing but praise for its 'extractions,' Harvey writes, but 'true Phisique' deserves even higher praise for its 'corrections' and 'purgations', and Harvey even acclaims Paracelsus as the man who might help him to turn Nashe's bane into balm. About 1585, however, he apparently entertained views which were at variance with I. W.'s, while at a later date he seems to have adopted a middle course between the Galenic and the Paracelsan 'alchemy.' But whichever method Harvey adopted, it is pretty clear that the author of the second play of the *Parnassus* trilogy was fully justified in depicting Luxurio as an alchemist if he was designing that character as a stage-portrait of Gabriel Harvey.

I. W. has also taken occasion to make mention of Harvey's 'temperament,' and, characteristically enough, at the very beginning of his epistle I. W. is indignant at the 'scandalous and slanderous termes, which from the corrupt coller of your angrie mind you haue giuen forth against him [Paracelsus]' (*Copie*, sig. A_2 v°). Furthermore, a few pages further down we find I. W. stating that his correspondent's friends disparaged 'oil of vitriol,' unless it were prepared according to I. W.'s prescriptions, and even then those friends would not give it a '*Paracelsian* name,' but 'they haue giuen it a new name, and termed it their artificiall *Melancholie*' (sig. A_3 v°). Through its references to melancholy and especially to 'choler,' the *Copie of a letter* is entirely consistent with the Cambridge comedy *Pedantius* and the *Parnassus Plays*, in which plays the humours were treated with a view to pouring ridicule on Harvey.

Yet another passage—it again states in a condensed form what the letter-writer is insisting on in so many words—is worth our notice, because it sheds light on a few lines in the John Eliot speech to be found in *Pierces Supererogation*.

Thus you may perceaue that your indeuour is and alwaies hath beene, to preserue that which nature abhorreth: to pound and pouder that which she by al meanes expelleth: for you see that your preparation is cleane contrary to her: for she worketh by subtraction and diuision, but you labour to adde & multiply: you are very expert in addition and multiplication, *Natura paucis contenta*, Nature is content with a little or a few things, haue you forgotten this rule? (*Copie*, sig. A$_6$).

This apparently explains why Harvey puts into John Eliot's mouth that it is 'the Multiplying spirit, not of the Alchimist, but of the villanist, that knocketh the naile one the head, and spurreth cutt farther in a day, then the quickest Artist in a weeke.' Harvey's, or the alchemist's, multiplying spirit proves ineffectual when compared to Nashe's, or the villanist's, there being no possibility of mistaking the sense here. Moreover, the whole John Eliot speech, as I have already suggested before, praises the 'villanist' to the detriment of the 'artist,' so that the whole speech indeed reads like a kind of surrender on Harvey's part. Miss Yates (1) has traced the terminology of the multiplying spirit of the alchimist in John Eliot's *Ortho-epia Gallica*, a terminology that figures as one of five proofs to identify the anonymous speaker in *Pierces Supererogation*. Curiously enough, Miss Yates' third argument that Harvey makes some attempt to suggest Eliot's style in the speech in question also finds a parallel in I. W.'s letter. Just after the 'Alchemist' reference Harvey puts the following words into Eliot's mouth: 'Whiles other are reading, wryting, conferring, arguing, discoursing, experimenting, platforminge, musing, buzzing, or I know not what: that is the spirrit, that with a woondrous dexterity shapeth exquisite workes, and atchieueth puissant exploites of Supererogation.' This indeed recalls the list of words to be found in Eliot's preface to the *Ortho-epia Gallica*: '... I haue bene busie, labourd, sweat, dropt, studied, deuised, sought, bought, borrowed, turnd, translated, mined, fined, refined enterlined, glosed, composed ...' But one may as well regard I. W. as the originator of this stylistic trick, though the context to be quoted is confined merely to alchemical terms.

Can you giue the Dier leaue to quaffe, & the Smith to carrowse, and will you grudge *Paracelsus* to drinke measurably and with reason? remember with your selues (for I speake to you and all your companie and fauorites) that *Paracelsus* sate not all day on a cushion with a pen in his hand, but was occupied both night and day in distilling, subliming, calcining, melting, fixing, resoluing, coagulating, reuerberating, digesting, & cementing, which things could not be be performed without great horrible and strong fires, which must needes cause a man to haue a iust quarrell to the cuppe (*Copie*, sig. A$_2$).

---

(1) F. A. YATES, *John Florio*, pp. 181-2.

The stylistic device and the reference to 'muitipiying' (in an earlier quotation from I. W.'s letter), occurring as they do in three different works, suggest a textual interdependence of some sort. It must be pointed out, however, that John Lyly's comedy *Gallathea*, first published in 1592 but probably written earlier, contains similar lists of words, a device already to be found in Reginald Scot's *Discovery of Witchcraft* (1584), a work used by Lyly when composing the *Gallathea*.

I. W.'s intention to lend topical colour to his epistle also appears from his introducing 'Dier' and 'Smith' into the above extract. The former name probably refers to Sir Edward Dyer, a friend of Sidney's, and one of those with whom John Florio had failed to ingratiate himself about 1578 (1). And if Sir Edward Dyer was of Harvey's 'companie and fauorites', as the letter states, this may indirectly support the contention before advanced that Harvey had about 1584 excited the ridicule of the Italophils John Florio and Giordano Bruno. Who the 'Smith' was I. W. refers to there is no way of telling.

The foregoing discussion of the *Copie of a letter* has not exhausted all the possible points of contact with Harvey's works, but those that remain offer little occasion for interesting remarks. I believe that it has become abundantly clear, however, that the *Copie of a letter* must be regarded as a document of importance to any student who wishes to determine Harvey's position in the Elizabethan world of letters.

Reviewing all the aspects of Harvey's personality as a whole it is difficult to find an expression sufficiently comprehensive to label it, but Harvey may perhaps lay claim to Coleridge's famous epithet 'myriad-minded,' so diverse were his interests and so engrossed was his attention by all contemporary currents of thought. Alchemy, medicine, emblems, astronomy and astrology, botany, rhetoric, education, mathematics, philosophy, all these were Harvey's province. Of course 'myriad-minded' does not apply to Harvey's achievement as an artist, which should, in point of fact, be his sole title to the epithet. But Harvey did possess and display the characteristics of the *uomo universale* of the Renaissance.

---

(1) See F. A. YATES, *John Florio*, pp. 45-7.

CHAPTER VI

THOMAS NASHE

A description of Nashe's early literary career is now needed, in the first place, to enable the reader to become acquainted with something of the background of the most famous literary quarrel of the age, that between Harvey and Nashe; and, in the second place, to gain a fuller understanding of Nashe's work itself in its relation to the contemporary output.

Thomas Nashe was born in November 1567, the son of a Lowestoft minister. In his youth he was probably educated by his father until in 1581 or 1582 he was sent to St. John's College, Cambridge, where he graduated B. A. in March, 1585-86. In the latter half of 1588 he probably left Cambridge for London. Nashe's presence in the capital may be inferred from the fact that it was possible for Thomas Hacket, a publisher, to enter Nashe's earliest work, *The Anatomie of Absurditie*, in the Stationers' Register. It is reasonable to assume that this entry, made on September 19, 1588, was only possible owing to Hacket's having had some personal knowledge of Nashe's existence; for else it becomes difficult to explain how a writer entirely unknown at the time was able to have his work entered for publication. R. B. McKerrow puts the composition of the *Anatomie* in the summer of 1587 or the spring of 1588. It is probable, however, that it was not published until August 1589, for Nashe announces the publication of the *Anatomie* in his preface to Greene's *Menaphon*, a work entered in the Stationers' Register on August 23, 1589, and published in the same year. Nashe's announcement of the publication of his first work lends support to the view that Greene knew his friend's work personally, a circumstance relevant to an interpretation of the trend of Nashe's thought; for, the one person pre-eminently in a position to be cognizant of Nashe's purpose in writing would no doubt have been Greene and, significantly, it is Greene who is believed to tell us that Nashe was a young Juvenal. As very little is known of the circumstances of Nashe's life itself, such information as there is (and as far as we need it) will be sketched in as we proceed with the discussion of his works.

The style of the *Anatomie* is in the tradition of euphuism. Euphuistic mannerisms are much in evidence: arrays of balanced sentences, antitheses, assonance and alliteration, with the addition of the usual quota of puns. Since Lyly had well-nigh exhausted the possibilities of his style, nothing was left to his successors but to follow the beaten track. Nashe could therefore hardly hope to attain novelty in the field of euphuistic experiment. The pamphleteer apparently expected to achieve success by treating a question that was of absorbing interest to many contemporaries: the question whether love is a wasteful or an ennobling emotion. Obviously the whole matter is one of perennial interest (1). About 1590, however, the controversy about love seems to have been raised with renewed insistence. Elizabethan scholars generally trace the misogynist tendency in literature to Antonio de Guevara's *Libro Aureo* (1528-9), which, as translated by Sir Thomas North under the title *The Diall of Princes* (1557), enjoyed a wide popularity. The language-manuals *First Fruits* and *Second Fruits*, published by John Florio respectively in 1578 and 1591, were representative of the two sides of the controversy: the earlier manual offered its readers a selection of moralizing sentences from Guevara, but the later, abandoning the dismissal of love, exalted womanhood to the skies.

There is a likelihood that, in the late eighties, it was Greene who posed the problem of love in a most conspicuous manner, so much so that writers like Nashe, Florio, and even Shakespeare, may be said to reveal traces of his influence. In the initial stages of his literary career Greene had in the main espoused the cause of womanhood, but from 1588 onwards his views seem to have undergone a kind of metamorphosis, a drastic change, in that he had come to the recognition that feminine 'beauty is seldom without pride, and wit without inconstancy' (2). From about the end of 1588, as the tone of the pamphlets composed between that date and his death shows, Greene was possessed by a penitent mood for his earlier dissolute life, and this state of mind no doubt led Greene to abjure the claims of love. The first work of Greene to set forth distinctly misogynist views was *Alcida, Greenes Metamorphosis*, a work now only known in a printed version of 1617, but already in existence

---

(1) As further evidence to the parallel development of certain currents of thought in France and England, the *querelle des femmes* may be cited. The best-known volume of poems to owe much to this *querelle* is ANTOINE HÉROET's *La Parfaicte Amye* (1542), a defence of womanhood. Historically the controversy is traceable to Ficinian Platonism, a system of thought which had assigned a large place to the discussion of amorous psychology.

(2) GREENE, *Works*, IX, 8. See also IX, 25 and XII, 252.

as early as 1588, as appears from its entry in the Stationers' Register on December 9, 1588. Professor René Pruvost (1) suggests that Greene may have been inspired by his anxiety to protect his reputation from the discredit that might be thrown upon him by the publication of Nashe's *Anatomie of Absurditie,* a pamphlet conceived in a decidedly anti-feminist spirit. The licensing of the *Anatomie* preceded that of Greene's *Alcida* by nearly four months. For some reason the publication of both works was delayed, and *Alcida* did not even see the light of print until twenty-nine years later.

I agree with Professor Pruvost that Nashe had apparently forestalled his friend in the disparaging of women, and that he especially directed his criticism against Greene by referring to a certain 'Homer of women,' and this in a passage which Pruvost demonstrates to be connected with one in Greene's *Mamillia.* This latter work consists of two parts, respectively entered in the Register on October 3, 1580, and on September 6, 1583 (the only editions known bear the dates 1583 for the first and 1593 for the second part). Nashe's allusion to *Mamillia* would lead one to suppose that Greene had ventured to defend the cause of women, a defence which need not necessarily be confined to literature, and that for some reason or other Nashe wanted to admonish Greene on that score. Nashe, a few pages further in the *Anatomie,* again alluded to Greene when he censured the idolaters of women for adorning their Gorgonean shapes with 'Greene colours.' Here, too, I subscribe to Pruvost's view that this phrase refers to Greene the writer.

For crueltie they [women] seeme more terrible then Tygers: was not *Orpheus* the excellentest Musition in any memory, torne in peeces by Women, because for sorrow of his wife *Euridice,* he did not onelie himselfe refuse the loue of many women, and liued a sole life, but also disswaded frõ their company? Did not mercilesse *Minerua,* turne the hayres of *Medusa,* whom shee hated, into hyssing Adders? Therefore see how farre they swerue from theyr purpose, who with Greene colours, seeke to garnish such Gorgonlike shapes (2).

Both Nashe's *Anatomie* and Greene's *Alcida* were dedicated to Sir Charles Blount, the later Earl of Devonshire, the nobleman who had succeeded Sidney as the secret lover of Penelope Devereux. The similarity of topic in both works, seen in conjunction with their

(3) R. Pruvost, *Greene et ses romans,* pp. 320-3.
(4) Nashe, *Works,* I, 16.

being dedicated to the same patron, argues a certain amount of purposefulness on the part of Greene and his young friend. Of the two dedications that in the *Anatomie* stands out for its implications as the more interesting piece of evidence, and to consider this is to embark upon a fairly detailed discussion of Nashe's supposed identity with 'young Juvenal.'

The dedication to Blount opens with a curious mistake in that certain statements are wrongly attributed to 'the olde Poet *Persaeus.*' This should be Juvenal, as appears from following references to Juvenal's Satire II, 24-7.

If (right Worshipfull) the olde Poet *Persaeus*, thought it most pre-iudiciall to attention, for *Verres* to declaime against theft, *Gracchus* against sedition, *Catiline* against treason: what such *supplosus pedum* may suffi-ciently entertaine my presumption, who beeing an accessarie to Absurditie, haue tooke vppon me to draw her Anatomie. But that little alliance which I haue vnto Arte, will authorize my follie in defacing her enemie: and the circumstaunce of my infancie, that brought forth this *Embrion*, somewhat tollerate their censures, that would deriue infamie from my vnexperienst infirmities. What I haue written, proceeded not from the penne of vain-glory but from the processe of that pensiuenes, which two Summers since ouertooke mee: whose obscured cause, best knowne to euerie name of curse, hath compelled my wit to wander abroad vnregarded in this *satyricall* disguise, & counsaild my content to dislodge his delight from traytors eyes (1).

The general topic of Juvenal's Second Satire is that there are many moralists who are without morals themselves, and Nashe consequently hints that he belongs to their class. I am, Nashe writes, 'an accessarie to Absurditie' and yet 'haue tooke vppon me to draw her Anatomie.' But the above passage also yields other information. The author holds that he has been compelled to walk abroad in '*satyricall* disguise' (Nashe's own italics), and, furthermore, he insists that he is very young and inexperienced. 'Infancie,' 'Embrion,' 'vnexperienst infirmities' are so many words that indicate the writer's concern to impress his audience with his youthfulness. A young writer who walks abroad in a satirical disguise might quite naturally have been regarded as a 'young Juvenal' by the Elizabethan reading public. Greene, for that matter, does not seem to have invented this expression on the spur of the moment at the time when he addressed his fellow-writers from his death-bed in September

---

(1) NASHE. *Works*, I, 5.

1592. One small point remains to be made: the expression 'the olde Poet *Persaeus*' looks like a deliberate mistake on Nashe's part, for Persius (A. D. 34-62) only reached the age of twenty-eight (Juvenal lived to be seventy or thereabouts). 'Olde,' it is true, may merely imply that Persius is a poet 'of antiquity.' But the double mistake Nashe commits in the very first phrases of his dedication, and the attractiveness of the combination 'juvenile Juvenal'—antithesis and pun rolled into one—argue that there was perhaps something behind Nashe's 'old Persius' as well.

A few relevant allusions may now be adduced in support of the generally accepted theory that Nashe was the young Juvenal of his age, merely another of Nashe's satirical disguises. As far as Nashe's other disguises are concerned, Cerberus was apparently one of them, while, at times, Nashe also made the impression of an English Aretino. Passages from three writers can be quoted in support of the Nashe-Juvenal theory: Shakespeare, Francis Meres, and the anonymous author of the *Three Parnassus Plays*.

The second scene of the first act of *Love's Labour's Lost* is one that many scholars, since the investigations of F. G. Fleay (1), have come to regard as highly significant for its topical content. Shakespeare introduces only two characters into this scene, the witty, sprightly Moth and the rather pompous Armado. Professor J. Dover Wilson, in his valuable edition of *Love's Labour's Lost* (Cambridge, 1923), has pointed out that Moth was probably designed as a stage-portrait of Nashe, and it is therefore little to be wondered at that Shakespeare employs the juvenile-Juvenal pun with evident relish in the course of his description of Moth and Armado. In the following quotations the speech-prefix 'Boy' stands for 'Moth.'

Arm. How canst thou part sadnes and melancholy, my tender Iu-uenall?
Boy. By a familier demonstration of the working, my tough signeor.
Arma. Why tough signeor? Why tough signeor?
Boy. Why tender iuuenall? Why tender iuuenall?
Arm. I spoke it tender iuuenal, as a congruent apethaton apperteining to thy young dayes, which we may nominate tender.
Boy. And I tough signeor, as an appertinent title to your olde time, which we may name tough.
(I, ii, 7-18.)

I now quote Professor Dover Wilson: 'Apart from the obvious

---

(1) See F. G. FLEAY, "Shakespeare and Puritanism." *Anglia*, VII (1884), 221-231.

punning—'Juvenal,' 'juvenile,' 'signior,' 'senior'—here would seem
to be a hit and a back-hit underscored for the audience... 'Young
(juvenile) Juvenal' is indeed the sort of nickname no Elizabethan
could resist for a youthful-looking satirist who lacked a beard in 1596,
and was calling himself 'stripling' so late as 1599. The epithet
'tender,' moreover, is not to be overlooked. Neshe was a recognized
variant of the surname Nashe, and 'nesh' or 'nash' at that time
= 'soft, delicate, pitiful, tender' ' (1).

Corroborative evidence for the topicality of the whole conversation between Moth and Armado is furnished by another part
of this scene.

> *Arm.* . . . Who was *Sampsons* loue my deare Moth?
> *Boy.* A Woman, Maister.
> *Arm.* Of what complexion?
> *Boy.* Of all the foure, or the three, or the two, or one of the foure.
> *Arm.* Tell me precisely of what complexion?
> *Boy.* Of the sea-water Greene sir.
> *Arm.* Is that one of the foure complexions?
> *Boy.* As is haue read sir, and the best of them too.
> *Arm.* Greene in deede is the colour of Louers: but to haue a loue
> of that colour, mee thinkes *Sampson* had small reason for it. He surely
> affected her for her wit.
> *Boy.* It was so sir, for she had a greene wit.

(I, ii, 80-93.)

'Melancholy' and the theory of the complexions, though admittedly
a widely discussed subject at the time, certainly reminds us of
Harvey. But it would also seem that Shakespeare permits us to catch
glimpses of Nashe's phrase 'Greene colours.' Nashe used this, it
will be recalled, with the implication that certain persons swerved
from their purpose in using green colours to adorn the female sex.
It is in this very connexion that Shakespeare has Armado and Moth
talk of 'Greene' and 'colours.' The above passage was probably
written in the latter half of 1592, when the quarrels between Nashe
and Harvey reached their high-water mark.

That Nashe's satirical vein continued to be associated with
Juvenal appears from Francis Meres' *Palladis Tamia* (1598) and
from a passage in the *Three Parnassus Plays*. After suggesting in
his *Palladis Tamia* that Nashe's satiric gift was his undoing, in the
expression 'As *Actaeon* was wooried of his owne hounds: so is *Tom*

---

(1) J. Dover Wilson, ed. *Love's Labour's Lost*, p. xxii.

Nash of his *Ile of Dogs,*' Meres went on 'but bee not disconsolate gallant young *Iuuenall*' (1).

In the beginning of the *Second Part of the Return from Parnassus* Ingenioso—who, as we know, is 'almost certainly' a portrait of Nashe—appears alone on the stage with a copy of Juvenal in his hand. He starts his soliloquy with a quotation from that satirist, and winds it up by referring to 'truth telling *Aretine.*' Here are the initial lines of this soliloquy:

> *Difficile est, Satyram non scribere, nam quis iniquae*
> *Tam patiens vrbis, tam ferreus vt teneat se?*
> I, Iuuenall: thy ierking hand is good,
> Not gently laying on, but fetching bloud;
> So, surgean-like, thou dost with cutting heale,
> Where nought but lanching can the wound auayle.
> O suffer me, among so many men,
> To tread aright the traces of thy pen,
> And light my linke at thy eternall flame,
> Till with it I brand euerlasting shame
> On the world's forhead, and with thine owne spirit
> Pay home the world according to his merit.
>
> (*Second Returne,* 84-95) (p. 225).

After having completed the *Anatomie of Absurditie,* Nashe's next literary effort was to write a preface to Greene's romance *Menaphon.* This preface was Nashe's decisive step towards literary renown, because of the very fact that Greene, one of the most influential writers of the day, had been willing to associate with a young man just down from the University. The preface, addressed 'To the Gentlemen Students of both Universities,' next to giving the satirist a chance to insert an advertisement for the forthcoming publication of his *Anatomie,* is primarily an exposition of his critical principles and of his stylistic aims. As such the preface to *Menaphon* deserves a place in the history of English Renaissance criticism. Professor J. W. H. Atkins (2) has already given a critical evaluation of Nashe's contribution to criticism, but this does not render a fresh examination superfluous. Some of the points Nashe makes have yet to be related to the general trend of his thought and to several statements made by Nashe's immediate contemporaries.

---

(1) F. Meres, *Palladis Tamia* (London, 1598), sig. Oo$_6$.
(2) See J. W. H. Atkins, *English Literary Criticism: The Renascence* (London, 1947, 2nd ed., 1951), pp. 181-187.

The prefatory material to *Menaphon* is an attack on all forms of pedantry. Nashe censures schoolmen, grammarians and translators for their too slavish adherence to the inflated style of classical or foreign writers. He denounces bombastic eloquence as *sublime dicendi genus*, and, applying what he calls the 'remedie of contraries,' holds that his contemporaries should practise *temperatum dicendi genus*. This type of remedy is illustrated by the example of the Sabeans, whose senses, according to Strabo, were so much cloyed with odoriferous savours that they wanted to refresh their nostrils 'with the vnsauourie sent of the pitchy slime that *Euphrates* casts vp.' Such a simile suggests that Nashe, in his quest for a homelier style, would seek to enliven it by realistic and vivid imagery, a procedure which, when pushed to an extreme, would lend a violent and even vulgar tone to his language. It is no matter for surprise, then, to find Nashe criticizing the contemporary output as 'mediocre.' 'Mediocre' and 'mediocritie' were apparently terms to which Nashe took a particular fancy (1); and they were also expressions to which many of his readers seem to have been highly sensitive.

Nashe's views on poetry are not original but they are the natural outcome of his advocating an informal, direct and natural style. He regrets that cowardice should have prevented English writers from imitating certain Romans and attributes this lack of daring partly to the large number of 'louers of mediocritie,' and partly to the influence of the Puritans, 'who account wit vanitie and poetry impiety.' Nashe's strong aversion to Puritanism appears also from his enthusiastic praise of Bacchus (the deity itself is not named in the preface to *Menaphon*), whose wine is of such an inspiring force that the influence of '*Pallas* with the nine Muses on *Pernassus* top' is trifling in comparison. '*Qui bene vult* poiein, *debet ante* pinein,' says Nashe, and though he allows for views opposite to his, the poetry inspired by Bacchus is in his opinion second to none. To conclude his preface Nashe claims that Chaucer, Gower and Lydgate are in no way inferior to the Italian poets Petrarch,

---

(1) In his glossary to NASHE's works R. B. McKERROW lists 'mediocrity' once only, in the meaning of 'mediocre person'; it occurs as such in the dedication to the *Anatomie* (NASHE, *Works*, I, 7). Compare also NASHE, *Works*, I, 192; III, 152; III, 316; III, 320. The passage at III, 152, in the epistle 'To his Readers, hee cares not what they be' in *Nashes Lenten Stuffe* (1599) deserves quotation : 'Know it is my true vaine to be *tragicus Orator*, and of all stiles I most affect & striue to imitate *Aretines*, not caring for this demure soft *mediocre genus*, that is like water and wine mixt togither; but giue me pure wine of it self, & that begets good bloud, and heates the brain thorowly. . . .'

Tasso and Ariosto. And after having saluted Matthew Roydon, George Peele and a few others as poets of promise, Nashe takes leave of the reader by intimating that he will go on persecuting those who 'haue made Art bankerout of her ornaments, and sent Poetry a begging vp and downe the Countrey.'

For a youthful writer to assume so arrogant and dogmatic an attitude towards literary production prior to 1589 was by no means common, and it cannot be denied that Nashe's pronouncements would inevitably call forth the irritation of some who held the conviction that they were much better qualified than Nashe. Richard Harvey was apparently among them, for into his work *A Theologicall Discourse of the Lamb of God*, entered in the Stationers' Register exactly two months after Greene's *Menaphon*, Richard inserted an epistle in which Nashe was openly attacked. The passage in which this attack occurs shows, I believe, that Richard Harvey had read Nashe's preface, as weu as the latter's anti-Martinist tract *An Almond for a Parrat* (1).

Nashe's anti-Puritan feelings are, in *An Almond for a Parrat*, displayed in an abundance of satirical sallies. The tract was no doubt the work upon which he was engaged after having completed his insolent preface to Greene's romance. In 1904, McKerrow still classed the tract among the doubtful works, but it has since been convincingly attributed to Nashe (2). The most likely date for its publication is February-March 1590. The *Almond* furnishes important clues to a proper comprehension of Nashe's position in Elizabethan literature. To begin with, it contains an allusion to 'my L. of *Darbies* men,' who, it will be remembered, had arrested printers of Marprelate tracts in 1589. Henry Stanley, Earl of Derby, had been Lord-Lieutenant of Lancashire since 1572, his son Ferdinando acting as his deputy since 1585. Nashe, as defender of the episcopal cause, may thus have come into contact with Ferdinando Stanley, that nobleman who, as a presumable member of the School of Night and as an actors' patron, probably played a prominent role in the artistic life of the time.

Nor is this all. A passage in this tract goes to explain why John Florio, in his *Second Fruits*, could refer to Nashe as one who, in the shape of a dog, should attack a wolf. Here is Nashe's allusion

---

(1) For the evidence see Chapter VII.
(2) See DONALD J. McGINN, "Nashe's Share in the Marprelate Controversy," *PMLA*, LIX (1944), 952-984.

to John Wolfe, at whose printing-house is said to reside an M. A. who may well have been Gabriel Harvey.

> Stand to it, *Mar-martin Iunior*, and thou art good inough for ten thousand of them; tickle me my *Phil.* a litle more in the flanke, and make him winche like a resty iade, whereto a dreaming deuine of Cambridge, in a certain priuate Sermon of his, compared the wicked. Saist thou me so, good heart, then haue at you, Maister Compositor, with the constructiõ of *Sunt oculos clari qui cernis sydera tanquam*. If you be remembred you were once put to your trumpes about it in *Wolfes* Printing-house, when as you would needes haue *clari* the infinitiue moode of a verbe passiue, which determined, you went forward after this order. *Sunt* there are, *oculos* eies, *qui* the which, *cernis* thou doest see, *clari* to be cleare, *tanquam sydera* as the Stars. Excellent well done of an old Maister of Arte, yet why may not hee by authority challenge to himselfe for this one peece of worke the degrees he neuer tooke? (1)

'Mar-martin Iunior' refers to Nashe himself, and it is one more expression destined to remind us that the author is 'juvenile.'

I fully agree with F. G. Fleay who says: 'The Cambridge M. A. who challenged the degrees he never took for making *clari* a passive at Wolf's printing-house, is, of course, Gabriel Harvey' (2). In order to understand why Nashe's tract can be regarded as intentionally provoking Harvey's anger, it is necessary to throw light on the relations between Harvey, Nashe, and Wolfe in 1589-91. What little we know of the relations between these three Elizabethans must now be set forth in an attempt to explain why Nashe got at loggerheads, first with Wolfe and then with the Harvey brothers.

Bearing in mind that three of Harvey's books, all concerned in the notorious controversy with Nashe, were printed by Wolfe, it is not inherently improbable that Harvey knew Wolfe in the years 1589-91. Besides, from references in his work it appears clearly that Harvey displayed much interest in the books printed by Wolfe immediately after they were sold to the public. For example, B. Felippe's *The Counseller*, a book translated by John Thorius and printed by Wolfe in 1589 (entered to Wolfe on April 4, 1589), must have been in Harvey's hands very soon after it was entered, for Harvey took occasion to refer to the book and its author in *An Aduertisement for*

---

(1) NASHE, *Works*, III, 357-8.
(2) F. G. FLEAY, *A Biographical Chronicle of the English Drama, 1559-1642* (London, 1891), II, 126. FLEAY's suggestion is rejected as 'extremely doubtful' by McKERROW, ed. *Nashe*, IV, 468.

Pap-hatchet, and Martin Mar-prelate, dated at the end November 5, 1589, but not published until 1593, when the *Aduertisement* was included in *Pierces Supererogation* (1). Another book, Antonio de Corro's *Spanish Grammer* (1590), also translated by Thorius and of Wolfe's printing, now in the Huntington Library, contains MS notes in Harvey's hand, one of which is dated 1590 (2).

Though a background figure, John Wolfe (3) was, under certain circumstances, a man to be counted with in Elizabethan letters. After terminating his apprenticeship with the printer John Day, he left England to study the trade in Florence. On his return he probably made the acquaintance of Philip Sidney for in the imprint to *Una essortatione al timor di Dio,* a book ascribed in the preface to Jacobus Acontius and conjecturally dated 1580 by the *Short-Title Catalogue,* Wolfe called himself 'seruitore de l'illustrissimo Filippo Sidnei,' a further reason for believing that Harvey had known Wolfe for a very long time. Perhaps because of Wolfe's own experience as a pirate in the printing trade, the Stationers' Company appointed him Beadle of the Company (July 23, 1587), and he went to reside in rooms at the Stationers' Hall, where he lived until after February 1, 1591. His official duties were to attend the Master and the Wardens and to summon the Assistants to Courts, but in reality he was much more concerned in tracking down illegal Marprelate printers. His first object was to carry out the seizure of Robert Waldegrave's press. In his capacity of printer he entered two anti-Martinist tracts, *A Myrror for Martinists* by one T. T., and *A Friendly Admonition to Martin Marprelate* by Leonard Wright, entered in the Register respectively on December 29, 1589, and January 19, 1590. The entry for the *Myrror* has some bearing upon Nashe, because in the margin of the entry there is a note running 'Nashe yt is saide' (4). On the strength of the marginal note the *Myrror* has been several times ascribed to Nashe, but Edward Arber doubts the authenticity of the handwriting which looks like 'an indifferent imitation of the original,' while R. B. McKerrow definitely rejects Nashe's authorship, the tract being a 'sermon rather than a

---

(1) HARVEY, *Pierces Supererogation,* sig. P$_2$ v°.
(2) G. C. M. SMITH did not reprint any marginalia from CORRO's *Spanish Grammer.* I consulted this book in microfilm at the Shakespeare Institute in 1952.
(3) See an important article by Professor H. R. HOPPE, "John Wolfe, Printer and Publisher," *The Library,* 4th Ser., XIV (1933), 241-288, from which the above information is largely derived.
(4) ARBER, *Transcript,* II, 537.

polemical discourse.' Moreover, the tract itself names T. T. as the writer. So far from being conclusive one may further note that, contrary to the *Myrror*, *An Almond for a Parrat* was not at all entered in the Register, which leads us to surmise that Wolfe may have been instrumental in preventing Nashe's tract being entered. It was, indeed, being printed while Wolfe was still residing at the Stationers' Hall.

There is yet another feature of the *Almond* that demands underlining in this connexion. It will be remembered that this tract contained Nashe's first allusion to Cerberus, the hell-hound whose attributes were peculiarly apposite to the satirist. The implications of this mythological reference have been studied before, and it will be recognized that they are in keeping with the circumstance that Nashe, in the long passage from the *Almond* quoted above, refers slightingly to Wolfe's printing-house. On the whole the tract suggests that its author was already at variance with Harvey and Wolfe as early as February-March 1590. John Florio was no doubt one of those who sided with Nashe. Florio's wolf-dog proverb, however slight its bearing on the Wolfe-Nashe situation may at first sight appear, hints the Italian writer's concern to support his friend. Furthermore, he was ill-disposed towards Wolfe himself, for, as Miss F. A. Yates observes, 'Florio had an enemy who was a traveller and who was engaged about 1591 in translating French news-letters for Wolfe, the publisher. This enemy's name was John Eliot' (1). We thus see that we may suspect Florio of having approved of Nashe's unwillingness to collaborate with Wolfe, the 'dog' being enjoined to attack the 'wolf.'

Finally, the title-page motto of the *Almond* calls for comment. The tract bears on its title-page the motto *Rimarum sum plenus* (2). As a matter of fact, for an author to inform his readers that he is full of cracks and crevices is quite exceptional. One wonders why Nashe used the phrase at all and what he may have had in mind. On the face of it 'I am full of cracks and crevices' seems hardly relevant to any author, though it certainly accords with the slap-in-the-face nature of many of Nashe's similes. The phrase *rimarum sum*

---

(1) See F. A. YATES, *John Florio*, p. 135.
(2) It has been recently recognized that Latin title-page mottoes were by no means just casually noticed by Elizabethan readers and in this connexion the reader is referred to an article by J. G. McMANAWAY, "Latin Title-page Mottoes as a Clue to Dramatic Authorship," *The Library*, Ser. 4, XXVI (1945), 28-36.

plenus is of course traceable to Terence, *Eunuchus*, I, ii, 25, and was no doubt widely known. Terence himself uses it in the meaning of 'I am indiscreet.' But it is bound to acquire increased significance when we notice that Abraham Fraunce uses part of this very phrase in his *Third part of the Countesse of Pembrokes Yuychurch*, in a passage which looks to me like a second unmistakable allusion to Nashe in that work. Giving several 'allegorical' interpretations of the tale of the Danaides, who were condemned to try for ever to fill a sieve with water, Fraunce also gives this one:

> It may also note the exchecquer or treasury of a prince, which like the sea, still receaueth, and is neuer full: or lastly, the nature of a blab, that is like a broken tub, *plenus rimarum*, full of sliftes, flowing out here and there, keeping nothing secret, that is imparted vnto him (1).

Plenus rimarum and 'full of sliftes' and Fraunce's allegorization apparently hold the key to Nashe's motto, for, as we shall soon see, Nashe, at one time of his literary career, committed an indiscretion which was such that it caused a considerable sensation in London as well as worrying its perpetrator for the rest of his life. Of this indiscretion we are informed by various Elizabethan authors, and even by Nashe himself. Gabriel Harvey, for instance, after calling his opponent 'a youngman of the greenest springe, as beardles in iudgement, as in face; and as Penniles in witt, as in Purse' in his *Pierces Supererogation*, suggests that Nashe would accomplish a work of supererogation only if he published 'Nashes *Penniworth of Discretion*' (2). 'Discretion' and the imagery just discussed also occur in *Love's Labour's Lost*, and elsewhere in *Pierces Supererogation*, but it seems best to return to these features in the argument concerned with Shakespeare's play. But it may now be noted that at least one other writer employs imagery consistent with Fraunce's allegorization of the broken tub: Barnabe Barnes, author of sonnets published in 1593 under the title *Parthenophil and Parthenophe*, girds at Nashe as a 'Base broaching tapster of reports vntrue,' a line which occurs in the sonnet 'Nash, or the Confuting Gentleman' to be found in the prefatory matter to *Pierces Supererogation*.

---

(1) FRAUNCE, *Third part*, sig. H$_4$ v⁰. The earliest example of 'slift' recorded in the *Oxford English Dictionary* belongs to 1657. As FRAUNCE uses the word in the meaning of 'crevice,' it may be an error for 'slifter' (plural 'slifters'), of which the *OED* quotes an example of 1607.

(2) HARVEY, *Pierces Supererogation*, sig. E$_2$ r⁰ (*Works*, II, 75).

The inference from all this would seem to be that Nashe was indeed, as McKerrow suggests, employed to gather information and to direct the pursuivants rather than to write anti-Martinist tracts, and it was such information, apparently, which Nashe may have been apt to divulge. Several reasons have already been advanced why Fraunce felt inclined to speak unfavourably of Nashe, but I may here add that he was at one with Harvey and the Sidney circle generally in admiring Ramus's new logical principles, his *Arcadian Rhetorike* and his *Lawiers Logike* being largely inspired by Ramus and Talaeus, and Fraunce surely felt the sting of Nashe's insistent scorn for Ramist logic.

That Nashe was strongly determined to continue indulging in his invective vein is apparent from his next pamphlet, entitled *A Wonderfull Strange and Miraculous Astrologicall Prognostication*. It presumably appeared early in 1591. This pamphlet was, like *An Almond for a Parrat*, placed by McKerrow among the doubtful works. In his discussion of the tract's authorship he flatly stated: 'So far, then, as I can discover there is not the slightest reason for connecting it in any way with Nashe' (1). In spite of this sweeping assertion, this distinguished critic was apparently reluctant to remove the tract from his edition, and so far from there not being the slightest reason for attributing it to Nashe, the evidence for his authorship is sufficiently convincing. It will be as well to set the prognostication in its proper perspective (2).

A *Wonderfull . . . Prognostication* states on its title-page that it was written by 'Adam Fouleweather, Student in Asse-tronomy.' Two other prognostications were published about the same time as Foulweather's: one was Simon Smellknave's *Fearefull and lamentable effects of two dangerous Comets, which shall appeare in the yeere of our Lord, 1591. the 25. of March*, while the other, only known from its entry in the Stationers' Register, was 'A booke entituled Ffrauncis Fayre Weather,' entered to William Wright on February 25, 1591 (3). Simon Smellknave was perhaps the ballad-writer Anthony Munday. In his Epistle to the Reader he refers to Foulweather as

---

(1) R. B. McKerrow, ed. *Nashe*, V, 139.
(2) See especially F. P. Wilson, "Some English Mock-Prognostications," *The Library*, Ser. 4, XIX (1939), 6-43; and D. C. Allen, *The Star-Crossed Renaissance* (Durham-North Carolina, 1941), *passim*.
(3) Arber, *Transcript*, II, 576.

his familiar friend. Foulweather's book no doubt took with London readers for a reprint was needed in 1591 itself (1).

The tracts under consideration are all comic parodies of astrological prediction. Professor F. P. Wilson has pointed out, in the article mentioned in footnote 2. p. 149, that, to his knowledge, the earliest English comic prognostication was published in 1544, while between that date and 1591 there are no extant examples of this kind of parody. On the Continent, however, the literary genre was not uncommon and one may mention the *Pantagruélines pronostications* (1533 and 1535) of Rabelais, and Johann Fischart's *Aller Praktik Grossmutter* (1572), while other well-known satirical prognosticators were Heinrich Bebel and J. Henrichmann von Sindelfingen. In Italy the most famous writer in the genre was Aretino, whose *Pronostico satirico* for 1534 has come down to us in a late sixteenth-century manuscript and whose *Judicio over pronostico de maestro Pasquino, quinto evangelista* gave offence to the Pope and the papal court. Both Rabelais and Aretino were writers to Nashe's taste and temperament, though it must be admitted that traces of their direct influence are practically non-existent. Nashe's writings, however, do show a certain resemblance to those of Rabelais (2) and Aretino: like them, he favoured a language interlarded with colloquialisms and enlivened by striking and out-of-the-way imagery; and like them, he was a satirist seeking wit in questionable places. It stands to reason that this spiritual affinity need not have induced Nashe to imitate them in writing a prognostication, and it is therefore necessary to inquire into the reasons that can be advanced in proof of Nashe's authorship of *A Wonderfull... Prognostication*.

To begin with, most modern readers will recognize, I believe, that, on the whole, the very vocabulary of this tract is entirely consistent with that of Nashe's genuine writings. We are, however, fortunate in possessing more compelling evidence than this. The first of three main reasons for ascribing the prognostication to Nashe is that a passage in its initial part strongly suggests that Nashe has written his own signature into it.

   ... Cancer being a watrie signe and cheefe gouernour of flouds and

---

(1) This second edition was discovered by F. P. WILSON, " 'A Wonderfull Prognostication' (1591)," *MLR*, XIII (1918), 84-85.

(2) For Foulweather's indebtedness to RABELAIS, see HUNTINGTON BROWN, *Rabelais in English Literature* (Cambridge, Mass., 1933), pp. 37-41; but Professor F. P. WILSON, *art. cit.*, p. 23, is not convinced by BROWN's arguments.

streams, it foresheweth that Fishmongers, if they be not well lookt to, shall goe downe as farre as Graues end in Wherries and forestall the market, to the great preiudice of the poore, that, all Lent, ground their fare on the benefit of Salte fishe and red herring: besides it signifieth that Brewers shal make hauocke of Theames water, and put more liquour then they were accustomed amongst their Maulte; to the ouerthrowe of certaine crased Ale knights, whose morning draughtes of strong Beere is a great staye to their stomacks: a lamentable case if it be not lookt into and preuented by some speedye supplication to the woorshipfull order of ale cunners. But in this we haue great hope that, because the effects cannot surprise the cause, diuers Tapsters shall trust out more then they can get in; and altough they fill their Pots but halfe full, yet for want of true dealing die in the Brewers debt (1).

The latter half of the quotation just given certainly harmonises with Fraunce's notion that one 'plenus rimarum' may be likened to a broken tub full of cracks (the nature of a blab) and with Barnes' attack on Nashe as a base broaching tapster of untrue reports. 'Tapsters shall trust out more then they can get in,' says Foulweather, with a pun on thrust-trust; and, for want of true dealing, he adds, they shall die in the brewers' debt, and lose their 'credit,' a suggestion of 'pennilessness' he elaborates more fully in the course of his tract. The middle passage of the above quotation is evidently connected with one in Smellknave's mock-prognostication.

Auicen saith, that hote complexions in this yeere are very dangerous, and they that drinke too much Spanish sack, shall about Julie be serued with a *Fierie facies*. But oh you Aleknights, you that deuoure the marrow of the Mault, & driue whole Aletubs into consumptions, that sing *In Creete when Dedalus*, ouer a cup, and tell Spanish newes ouer an Ale-pot, howe vnfortunate are you, who shall pisse out that which you haue swallowed downe so sweetlie, and singing *Druncke demittis* ouer night, had neede of *Absterge Domine* in the morning: the rotte shall infect your purses, and eate out the bottome, wast shall consume your bodies, and make you sicklie, and if you eate not more then you are accustomed, alas, alas, you will loose your stomacks (2).

The second reason for attributing *A Wonderfull . . . Pro-*

---

(1) NASHE, *Works*, III, 382-3.

(2) SIMON SMELLKNAVE, *Fearefull and lamentable effects of two dangerous Comets* (London, 1591), pp. 10-11, sig. B₁ v⁰ and sig. B₂ r⁰. Smellknave's statement (and, in consequence, Foulweather's as well) hints an allusion to GABRIEL HARVEY. *In Creete when Dedalus* is the ballad referred to by NASHE when ridiculing HARVEY in *Have with you to Saffron-Walden* (*Works*, III, 67); on the other hand, Luxurio (who, as we have seen, was probably HARVEY) also refers to this ballad in *The Three Parnassus Plays, First Returne*, 414-5, p. 156. One may further note that Torquato (HARVEY?) in FLORIO's *Second Fruits*. p. 3, tells BRUNO that 'It is good to drinke in a morning to charm the mist.'

gnostication to Nashe is that it strongly anticipates the complaints of pennilessness which Nashe was to raise so emphatically in his *Pierce Penilesse his Supplication to the Diuell*. The title-page of the prognostication already informs us, again with a pun, that if there be found one lie in it 'the Author will loose his credit for euer.' And the text itself continues in the same vein: 'many fooles shall haue full cofers, and wise men walke vp and downe with empty pursses' (III, 381); 'diuerse fluxes, and especiallie in poore mens purses, for they shall bee so laxatiue, that money shall runne out faster then they can get it' (III, 394); and to wind up the tract, 'good fellowes this yeere for want of money shall oft times be contented to part companie' (III, 395). The following passage would seem to place the attribution in question beyond reasonable doubt: 'yong men that haue Vsurers to their father shal this yeer haue great cause to laugh, for the Deuill hath made a decree that, after they are once in hell, they shall neuer rise again to trouble their executors' (III, 383). The idea that 'yong' men shall be offered hospitality by the 'devil' in order to prevent them from troubling their executors, was to be so clearly elaborated by the 'young' Nashe in his 'supplication' to the 'devil,' that the analogy in the expressions could hardly have proceeded from the imagination of two different authors.

Thirdly, Foulweather may have had the serious prophecies of Richard Harvey in mind when he set about poking fun at serious astrological prediction, and who could be better fitted for the job than Nashe, whose overt attacks on Richard caused such a great sensation in 1592? It is therefore quite conceivable that the following extract may have a bearing on Richard Harvey.

Some curious Astronomers of late dayes, that are more Propheticall then Iuditiall, affirme that Martin the kill-hog (for his deuout drincking by the Pope canonized a Saint) shall rise againe in the apparell of a Minister, and tickle some of the baser sorte with such lusty humors in their braines that diuers selfe conceited fooles shal become his disciples, and grounding their witlesse opinion on an heriticall foundation, shall seeke to ruinate authoritie and peruert all good orders established in the Church, to the great preiudice of vnity and religion, tituling thẽselues by the names of Martinistes, as the Donatists grew from Donatus: were it not that the Moone being in Taurus, which gouernes the neck and throat, shewes that the Squinancie shall raigne amongst them, and diuers for want of breath dye of the strangling (1).

---

(1) NASHE, *Works*, III, 387.

The initial sentence echoes a passage from Richard Harvey's *Astrological Discourse* (1583) in which the author asserts that the recent eclipse 'betokeneth, according to the Iudicials of Astrologie that great abundaunce of rayne is like to ensue' (1). And *if* Foulweather-Nashe is thinking of Richard, allusions to hanging or 'strangling' are bound to crop up. The moon being in Taurus shows that the Squinancie (a less common word for quinsy: inflammation of the throat) shall reign. 'Squinancie' is derived from medieval Latin *quinancia*, in its turn derived from Greek κυνάγχη, a compound in which the words 'dog' and 'throttle' are combined, and as such this fits in remarkably well with what we already know about Nashe and the Harveys.

It is legitimate, it seems to me, to infer from the reasons so far advanced that Nashe is to be regarded as the most likely candidate for the authorship of Foulweather's prognostication. To credit others with it would present well-nigh insuperable difficulties, and, to my knowledge, no critic has ever argued for another author.

The jocular prognostications of Foulweather, Smellknave, and Fairweather are all three alluded to in the dedication of Florio's *Second Fruits* to Nicholas Saunder of Ewell. Florio probably sided with Nashe in the early nineties, and it is therefore likely that this dedication may shed further valuable light on the literary events of the time. In Florio's two language-manuals *First Fruits* (1578) and *Second Fruits* (1591) there runs an undercurrent of criticism of the contemporary literature which stamps Florio as a figure to be reckoned with in Elizabethan letters after 1578. To give only one example of his concern in matters of current interest: in his epistle to the reader, printed after the dedication to Saunder, Florio makes a cursory allusion to his aversion for the Puritans in the statement that 'exact examination' is the 'puritane scale of a criticall censor.' This epistle is dated at the end, 'The last of April. 1591. Resolute I. F.,' which is an important piece of information with regard to the matter in hand.

The *Second Fruits* is pervaded with reminiscences of Giordano Bruno, and its dialogues seem to be intentionally conceived so as

---

(1) Quoted from R. W. BOND's edition of *The Complete Works of John Lyly* (Oxford, 1902), II, 422. Professor BOND points out that the phrase is also echoed in LYLY's *Gallathea*, III, iii, 73 ('our Iudicials Astronomicall'), a play entered in the Stationers' Register on October 4, 1591, and published in 1592.

to remind the reader that in 1591 Bruno's visit was still dwelling in the memories of many people. The most obvious link with Bruno is 'Nolano's' introduction in the very first dialogue with one 'Torquato.' Florio's choice of the sobriquet Torquato no doubt harks back to the account of Bruno's dispute with Torquato in the *Cena de le ceneri*, and so there is a likelihood that this character was introduced to remind Elizabethan readers of Gabriel Harvey. Florio also finds Bruno's second opponent worth resuscitating, for 'Nundinio' appears in one of the other dialogues of the *Second Fruits*. The manual as a whole reflects the author's new attitude towards life and letters: he has moved with the times and no longer thinks love-making an idle pastime, while the general drift of the dialogues harmonises remarkably well with the spirit of the sonneteering fashion then in full swing.

The opening lines of the dedication of the *Second Fruits* must now be quoted.

Sir in this stirring time, and pregnant prime of inuention when euerie bramble is fruitefull, when euerie mol-hill hath cast of the winters mourning garment, and when euerie man is busilie woorking to feede his owne fancie; some by deliuering to the presse the occurences & accidents of the world, newes from the marte, or from the mint, and newes are the credite of a trauailer, and first question of an Englishman. Some like Alchimists distilling quintessences of wit, that melt golde to nothing, & yet would make golde of nothing; that make men in the moon, and catch the moone shine in the water. Some putting on pyed coates lyke calendars, and hammering vpon dialls, taking the eleuation of *Pancridge* Church (their quotidian walkes) pronosticate of faire, of foule, and of smelling weather; men weather-wise, that wil by aches foretell of change and alteration of wether. Some more actiue gallants made of a finer molde, by deuising how to win their Mistrises fauours, and how to blaze and blanche their passions, with aeglogues, songs, and sonnets, in pitifull verse or miserable prose, and most for a fashion: is not Loue then a wagg, that makes men so wanton? yet loue is a pretie thing to giue vnto my Ladie. Other some with new caracterisings bepasting al the posts in *London* to the proofe, and fouling of paper, in twelue howres thinke to effect *Calabrian* wonders: is not the number of twelue wonderfull? Some with Amadysing & Martinising a multitude of our libertine yonkers with triuiall, friuolous, and vaine vaine droleries, set manie mindes a gadding; could a foole with a feather make men better sport? I could not chuse but apply my self in some sort to the season, and either prooue a weede in my encrease without profit, or a wholesome pothearbe in profit without pleasure. If I prooue more than I promise, I will impute it to the bountie of the gracious Soile where my endeuours are planted, whose soueraigne

vertue diuided with such worthles seedes, hath transformed my vnregarded slips to medcinable simples (1).

Miss Frances A. Yates (2) has observed that this passage
is a remarkably comprehensive review of the contemporary production
in the different departments of journalism, lyric poetry, and the
drama. The chief points of her paraphrase of Florio's words may
now be summarized. There is first a hint at Greene's *Mourning
Garment* (1590), then the passion for 'news' is mentioned, and next
comes an allusion to Lyly's recent play, *Endimion, The Man in the
Moone*. Then Florio combines the three prognostications that had
recently appeared in the phrase 'of faire, of foule, and of smelling
weather.' Of these productions Miss Yates says: 'These jocular
prognostications were perhaps connected with the amusement caused
by the serious predictions of Gabriel Harvey's brother Richard,' a
conclusion the foregoing argument has no doubt corroborated. Then
Florio notices with some contempt the aeglogues, songs, and sonnets
which were much in vogue at the time. The allusion to 'new
caracterisings bepasting al the posts in *London*' whose authors think
'in twelue howres to effect *Calabrian* wonders' is interpreted as
referring to the popular plays, advertised on posts in London.
Florio, in Miss Yates's opinion, is suggesting that Elizabethan
dramatists and audiences violate the unity of time, which would
tally with Florio's disapproval of the violation of the decorum
principle, a principle often advocated by Renaissance theoreticians
of literature. Miss Yates further notes that there may be, as well,
an allusion to some particular play in the title of which the number
twelve had a place, and she instances Greene's *Orlando Furioso one
of the twelue Pieres of France*. I do not think that this last interpretation is justified. A first reason is that Greene's play was written
in the autumn of 1591, while Florio was apparently writing in the
spring of that same year. But there are other reasons as well.

Professor Chauncey Sanders (3) has remarked that several
passages in Nashe's work suggest that he may have had the Harvey
brothers in mind when referring to 'Calabria.' John Doleta, in
Straunge Newes out of Calabria, had foretold in 1586 that the following year the world would be threatened by floods, earthquakes and

(1) FLORIO, *Second Fruits*, sig. A₂ r⁰ and sig. A₂ v⁰.
(2) F. A. YATES, *John Florio*, pp. 127-9.
(3) C. SANDERS, *Robert Greene and the Harveys* (*Indiana University Studies*, XVIII,
Sept. 1931), pp. 35-40.

all sorts of strange events. In his own *Strange Newes* Nashe attributed Doleta's work to one of the Harveys, though the reader is of course at liberty to doubt the writer's seriousness. Professor Sanders instances a 'Calabria' reference in the *Anatomie of Absurditie*, and expresses his belief that the '*Calabrian* floode,' mentioned in that work, is directed against the Harveys as astrologers. But there are similar references in Nashe's other works, for instance in *An Almond for a Parrat*, which, as I will try to demonstrate in the next chapter, bears on Richard Harvey. It looks therefore as if Florio's '*Calabrian* wonders' suggests an allusion to the Harveys, and to Richard in particular. Furthermore, Florio is dwelling on 'twelve' because he wishes to refer to the twelve houses of heaven, the signs of the zodiac which Richard boasted to be so well acquainted with; and one of the targets in Gabriel's *Foure Letters* is Nashe's ignorance of what Foulweather so humorously calls 'Asse-tronomy,' while it is noticeable that Nashe's amusing prognostication bristles with references to the zodiacal signs. There is little doubt in my mind that Florio is actually thinking of Nashe and the Harveys, and especially of Richard, because he lives in the expectation that Nashe's satirical digs will finally rouse the Harveys' anger. A passage in Richard Harvey's *Philadelphus* (1593), not hitherto drawn on for purposes of comparison, makes great play with 'twelve'; and, be it noted, Richard's statement could hardly refer to anything else than to the 'paper-wars' of the time.

Arthur slew in one day an hundred and fortie Saxons with his owne hand. *Cadwallader* slew *Lothary* Prince of Kent, and *Athelwald* king of *Southsex*, and possessed those landes. *Cadwallin* droue the Saxons all along to Middlesex and made *Penda* pay him tribute. Now armies stay in Saxony, and papermen flye from those coastes: these do more harme in many places then those old armies did: these will be sauced as they were, and hunted out of the land by order of discipline: none so busie as they, and yet more slight then they: there is an *Arthur* in paperworke against their inuasions, which may in all right and equitie giue them twelue disgraces at the least, and perhaps twelue times twelue: let the triall proue all, or let that labour be lost, if they can recouer there 12 losses of this newe *Arthur* (1).

Let us now return to Florio's survey of the contemporary output. Last on his list he mentions 'Amadysing & Martinising,'

_____
(1) R. HARVEY, *Philadelphus* (London, 1593), sig. M₃ vº and sig. M₁ rº, pp. 90-91. This work will be more fully noticed later.

which refers to Anthony Munday's translation of the romance of *Amadis de Gaule*, probably published in 1590, and to the Martin Marprelate controversy. The Martin Marprelate controversy proper, however, had come to an end towards the close of 1589, but it had apparently given rise to other disputes in which, as we will see later, Nashe and Munday were mixed up. In connexion with Florio's allusion, then, it is worth noting that Munday, with John Eliot and others, worked for John Wolfe's printing-house as translators. In the very year of Florio's *Second Fruits* John Wolfe entered Munday's translation of L. T. A.'s *The Masque of the League and the Spanyard discouered* (entry on June 5, 1591). A few months later, on February 22, 1592, it was entered to John Charlewood and printed by that printer in the same year. One may note in passing that Smellknave's prognostication was also printed by Charlewood, but for John Busby, the year before; and that Nashe, in *Pierce Penilesse*, makes a cursory allusion to 'the exployts of *Vntrusse*,' a ballad of Munday's, as the product of a 'grosse braind Idiot' (1).

In 1591, the year of his prognostication, Nashe also wrote a preface to an edition of Sidney's *Astrophel and Stella* (printed early in 1591 by Thomas Newman). Though the preface, characteristically headed 'Somewhat to reade for them that list,' contained a passage in praise of Sidney's sister Mary, Countess of Pembroke, the Countess probably did not approve of the venture, for Newman issued another version later in the year. Another publishing venture bearing indirectly on the relations between Nashe and the Countess of Pembroke is the publication of Sidney's *Arcadia*, apparently a matter of grave concern to the Countess in the years 1590-1593.

The chief facts of the textual history of the *Arcadia* are these (2). Sidney probably wrote his romance between 1580 and 1585. It was brought into circulation among his friends in numerous manuscript copies highly valued by their owners and one of these manuscripts was in the possession of Fulke Greville, Lord Brooke, Sidney's most intimate friend. From a letter Greville wrote to Sir Francis Walsingham, Sidney's father-in-law (letter endorsed November, 1586, *State Papers Domestic*, CXCV), we learn that William Ponsonby, publisher, had given Greville to understand that an unauthorized

---

(1) Nashe, *Works*, I, 159; see also V, 195, footnote 15.
(2) The facts have often been stated. See especially R. W. Zandvoort, *Sidney's Arcadia* (Amsterdam, 1929), pp. 1-7, and Miss Mona Wilson, *Sir Philip Sidney* (London, 1950), pp. 135-155. Compare also Miss F. A. Yates, *John Florio*, pp. 188-212.

edition of the *Arcadia* was being planned. Greville then confided an edition of the manuscript in his possession to Ponsonby, who accordingly issued the romance in a quarto edition in 1590. It was preceded by a dedication to Mary, Countess of Pembroke, and contained two books, and a large part of a third, its incompleteness being due to Greville having thought fit to publish only those books that had been revised by Sidney himself, a circumstance which explains why the narrative breaks off where the author's revision ended. But even Greville did not remain completely faithful to the manuscript for an 'overseer of the print' divided the work into chapters and prefixed descriptive headings to each chapter 'for the more ease of the reader.' We cannot definitely say who this overseer was; he may have been Greville himself or, and this is Miss Yates's hypothesis, John Florio.

The Countess of Pembroke, however, was not pleased with the publication of her brother's romance for she soon had the publisher Ponsonby issue a second edition of the *Arcadia* in 1593. This 1593 Folio edition was prefaced by an address 'To the Reader,' signed H. S., initials which have been shown to stand for Hugh Sanford, secretary to Henry Herbert, Earl of Pembroke, and tutor to the Earl's son, William. The 1593 *Arcadia* is a reprint, with corrections, of the 1590 edition. In his address to the reader Sanford complains that the first edition had been given to the public with a 'disfigured face,' and this is why the 'end' is now supplied, namely three books from an unrevised so-called *Old Arcadia*. Though modern critics have generally discounted the editorial efforts of Sanford and the Countess of Pembroke, Sanford's edition remained the only version in which it was transmitted from generation to generation. It was not until the years 1907-1909 that several manuscripts of the *Old Arcadia* came to light, manuscripts from which it appeared that the version they contained must have been that with which Sidney's contemporaries were most familiar. Most students of Sidney's romance have regarded this more recently discovered version as artistically superior to the later revision.

But how is all this connected with Nashe's writings? McKerrow has observed that Nashe in the dedication to Humphrey King of his *Lenten Stuffe* (1599) attacked the editor of the 1593 *Arcadia* as follows:

Most courteous vnlearned louer of Poetry, and yet a Poet thy selfe, of no lesse price then H. S., that in honour of Maid-marrian giues sweete Margerã for his Empresse, and puttes the Sowe most sawcily vppon some great personage, what euer she bee, bidding her (as it runnes in the old song) *Go from my Garden go, for there no flowers for thee dooth grow.* . . . . (1)

McKerrow points out that Nashe discloses that the H. S. he is attacking is the editor of the 1593 *Arcadia* through his allusion to the title-page of that edition, with its pig smelling at a bush (= marjoram) round which is the motto 'non tibi spiro.' As we have already had occasion to observe, the significance of the import of devices and mottoes for the interpretation of allusions in Elizabethan literature can hardly be overrated. The use of the pig-and-marjoram device and the ridicule it entailed show that the 'science' of devices, emblems and the like could serve various purposes.

A few minor points regarding the *Astrophel and Stella* edition bearing Nashe's preface are worth brief notice. In the first place, twenty-eight sonnets by Samuel Daniel were appended to those of Sidney. Daniel seems to have been not a little disturbed by seeing his poems published in a form other than he himself had contemplated, for he decided to issue an authorized version of his poetry by entrusting it to the care of Simon Waterson, a publisher who constantly enjoyed Daniel's full confidence. In this way the sonnet-cycle *Delia* (1592) appeared, and again we find the Countess of Pembroke associated with the publication. In his dedication Daniel complained of having been 'betraide by the indiscretion of a greedie Printer' and of having some of his secrets 'bewraide to the world, vncorrected.' Secondly, Nashe's preface also contained a hostile allusion to Nicholas Breton, another poet who belonged to the Countess of Pembroke's circle. The phrase 'Gentlemen . . . that haue seene *Pan* sitting in his bower of delights, & a number of *Midasses* to admire his miserable hornpipes' in the preface, is an unmistakable allusion to Breton's *Bowre of Delights*, printed in 1591 and entered in the Stationers' Register on May 3, 1591, by the printer Richard Jones. Though Breton's relations with Jones were no doubt friendly, the author none the less found it necessary to voice his displeasure with the printer's interference, for in *The Pilgrimage to Paradise, Ioyned with the Countesse of Penbrookes loue* (1592) he

---

(1) Nashe, *Works*, III, 147, and R. B. McKerrow, ed. *Nashe*, IV, 375. The imagery of the device in question also occurs in the epistle prefixed to John Florio's dictionary *Worlde of Wordes* (1598) for the purpose of attacking a certain H. S.; it is therefore clear that both Nashe and Florio are speaking of the same man.

added a protesting note to his preface 'To the Gentlemen students and Scholars of Oxforde' (1).

In what precedes I have tried to show that Nashe, in two of his publications, hinted clearly that he had committed an indiscretion. To give further support to this view it is necessary to explain the significance of an allegorical tale in his *Pierce Penilesse* and to describe in some detail the extraordinary events of the year 1592. As Gabriel Harvey's *Foure Letters* is closely connected with Nashe's pamphlet I shall also provide an account of the former work.

Pierce Penilesse was evidently an astonishing performance on the part of its author, for it was in constant demand in the latter half of 1592, no less than three editions being needed in that year to satisfy popular curiosity. A fourth followed in 1593 and a fifth in 1595. The pamphlet was entered in the Stationer's Register on August 8, 1592, and licensed to the printer Richard Jones, who seems to have taken advantage of Nashe's absence to print it. Though it has long been assumed that the first edition printed by Jones was a surreptitious one, Sir Walter W. Greg (2) has now shown that such a view is incorrect. It is true that the second edition was printed by Abel Jeffes for the publisher John Busby, but this fact is not in itself evidence that Nashe was dissatisfied with Jones' printing and that he had decided to transfer the publishing rights to another publisher. To the second edition, published after the death of Greene, Nashe prefixed 'A priuate Epistle of the Author to the Printer,' which Greg shows to be addressed to Richard Jones. Nashe's use of such expressions as 'you write to me my book is hasting to the second impression' and 'it was abroad a fortnight ere I knewe of it' argues that Jones obtained the manuscript in a perfectly regular way.

In his epistle Nashe advises Jones to 'cut off that long-tayld Title,' a long sub-title being a feature of the first edition title-page. *Pierce Penilesse his Supplication to the Diuell*, the full title of Nashe's pamphlet, is followed in edition A by the words 'Describing the

<hr>

(1) See H. E. ROLLINS, ed. *Brittons Bowre of Delights* (*1591*) (Cambridge, Harvard University Press, 1933), p. xv. Professor ROLLINS notes that WOLFE registered *The Pilgrimage to Paradise*, with no author's name, on January 23, 1591; that is, more than three months before *The Bower* was licensed—a confusing series of events. He further observes that BRETON's disclaimer appears to be an afterthought to his formal preface.
(2) W. W. GREG, "Was the First Edition of *Pierce Penniless* a Piracy," *The Library*, 5th Series, XXXIII (1952), 122-124.

ouer-spreading of *Vice*, and suppression of *Vertue*. Pleasantly interlac'd with variable delights: and pathetically intermixt *with conceited reproofes*,' whereas in B they are replaced by the motto 'Barbaria grandis habere nihil,' a motto derived from Ovid's *Amores*. As the use of this motto calls for some comment we must needs place it in its context.

> Et quisquam ingenuas etiamnunc suspicit artes,
> Aut tenerum dotes carmen habere putat ?
> Ingenium quondam fuerat pretiosius auro;
> At nunc barbaria est grandis, habere nihil.
>
> (*Amores*, III, viii, 1-4.)

In Marlowe's translation these lines run as follows:

> What men will now take liberal arts in hand,
> Or think soft verse in any stead to stand?
> Wit was sometimes more precious than gold;
> Now poverty great barbarism we hold.

The phrase 'Barbaria grandis habere nihil' was no doubt a ready device to bring Nashe's pennilessness home to his readers. When examined in its context the motto carries with it a strong suggestion of the alleged worthlessness of Nashe's 'wit.' It is therefore illuminating to note that the four opening lines of Ovid's elegy seem to have been present to the satirist's mind when he wrote the marginal note 'Ingenio perij qui miser ipse meo' (borrowed from Ovid, *Tristia*, ii, 2, and to be found in A only) to accompany the lines

> Ah worthlesse Wit, to traine me to this woe,
> Deceitfull Artes, that nourish Discontent:

which occur in his complaint on the very first page of *Pierce Penilesse*. It is sometimes contended that a motto on a title-page was chosen by printers for advertising purposes, but in the case of the *Pierce Penilesse* title-page there is little doubt that it was of Nashe's own devising. The term 'ingenium,' then, was one eminently apposite to Nashe, interesting evidence to this effect being furnished by the fact that much later it turned up in the form 'Ingenioso,' the character who stands for Nashe in the *Three Parnassus Plays*. And an ingenious man Nashe certainly was.

The second edition of *Pierce Penilesse* probably did not become available until October 1592: first, one may note that Gabriel Harvey alludes to the A title-page only (1), and, second, Nashe himself, through his reference to Greene's *Groatsworth of Wit* in his epistle to Jones, has enabled us to date the publication of his pamphlet a few weeks after Greene's death. From this reference we learn that it had been rumoured that the *Groatsworth of Wit* was of Nashe's doing, while Nashe's description of it as 'a scald triuial lying pamphlet' strongly suggests that he was far from flattered by contemporaries' having laid its authorship at his door. Nashe, to quote Harvey's words, 'would not, or happily could not performe the duty of an affectionate, and faithfull frend' after Harvey's violent assault on Greene; the motives, however, which withheld Nashe from striking out without delay still remain obscure. Harvey, on the contrary, seems to have been playing a waiting game only until the moment that Greene's decease enabled him to attack his victim with impunity. It has recently come to light that there were two issues of Harvey's letters in 1592, one before the end of September under the title *Three Letters, and certaine Sonnets*, and the other printed by Wolfe before the end of October and now commonly known as the *Foure Letters* (2). The latter issue, however, was not entered in the Stationers' Register until December 4, 1592, but was widely known by that time. A copy of the *Three Letters* is at present in the Berg collection in the New York Public Library. The significance of the existence of a first issue lies in the fact that the sonnets, which in modern reprints follow the fourth letter, originally followed the third. This is of interest because some of these appended sonnets contain a few details relevant to things treated in the third letter. A brief survey of the contents of the four letters will put the reader in possession of the main facts.

The *Foure Letters* opens with an epistle, dated September 16, 'To all Courteous Mindes that will voutchsafe the readinge.' From its date this appears to have been written last; and, though clarity is not Harvey's forte, one gathers from it that it was probably

---

(1) Compare HARVEY, *Foure Letters*, p. 45: 'Surely it must needes be current in matter, and autentical in forme, that had first such a learned president : and is now pleasantly interlaced with diuers new-founde phrases of the Tauerne : and patheticallie intermixt with sundry dolefull pageantes of his own ruinous & beggerlie experience.'

(2) See F. R. JOHNSON, "Gabriel Harvey's *Three Letters*: A First Issue of his *Foure Letters*," *The Library*, 5th Series, XXVII (1946), 134-136, and the same writer's article, "The First Edition of Gabriel Harvey's *Foure Letters*," *The Library*, 4th Series, XV (1934), 212-223.

designed to give vent to his feelings of regret that the quarrel had ever been started. Then comes the first letter; it consists of an introductory epistle from Christopher Bird to Emmanuel Demetrius and concludes with a mock-commendatory sonnet addressed to Greene. The second letter, then, is in the main an attack on Robert Greene. It refers to Nashe, but without naming him, as a fellow-writer of Greene's who was a 'principal guest at that fatall banquet of pickle herring' which was the cause of Greene's illness. The expression 'I spare his name, and in some respectes wish him well' suggests that Harvey's animosity against Nashe was not particularly deepseated in the initial stages of the quarrel. The third letter, addressed 'To euery Reader, fauourablie, or indifferentlie affected' and dated September 8 and 9, falls into two parts; the first part is a general defence of himself and the second is a reply to *Pierce Penilesse*. In connexion with my contention that Nashe had about 1590 committed an indiscretion it is certainly worth notice that Harvey twice intimates something to that effect in the course of his third letter. Having advised overweening 'youthes' to remember themselves and 'the good auncient oracle of sage *Apollo*,' Harvey goes on: 'There is a certaine thing, called Modestie, if they coulde light vpon it: and by my younge Masters leaue, some pritty smacke or discretion would relish well.' What is more, the passage in which Nashe is alluded to as the narrator of 'parlous Tales of Beares and Foxes'—the very tale in *Pierce Penilesse* which carries a suggestion of 'indiscretion'— concludes as follows: 'Would Christ, they had more discretion in them, and lesse rancour against other, that neuer wished them the least euill, but still beseech GOD to encrease the best, and to pardon the worst in them' (3). Finally, the fourth letter, addressed 'To the same fauourable, or indifferent Reader' and dated September 11 and 12, does not contain any fresh attacks but mainly serves the purpose of justifying Harvey's course of action to his readers. The letter also possesses some value for the light it throws upon the personality, the opinions and artistic tenets of Harvey himself: e. g. 'one perfect Mechanician' being worth 'ten vnperfect Philosophers' and 'an ignorant man' less injurious to the 'Common-wealth, then a putatiue Artiste.' From a passage near the end of the fourth letter, then, we learn that the letter against Greene 'was in a manner voluntary,' that against Nashe 'in sort necessary,' and the last

---

(3) HARVEY, *Foure Letters*, pp. 50, 55. See also p. 80.

'wholy superfluous, but violently extorted after the rest.' The last statement no doubt explains why a second issue of Harvey's epistles was needed, that the fourth might be included. We now turn to the interesting information yielded by the tale of the Bear and the Fox in Nashe's *Pierce Penilesse* (1).

In *Pierce Penilesse*, a series of disconnected attacks on all manner of vice rather than a homogeneous narrative, the pamphleteer also introduces a long allegorical tale to satirize hypocrisy. It describes how a Bear, 'chiefe Burgomaster of all the Beasts vnder the Lyon,' having at first pursued his prey among ordinary beasts, became satiated with these 'ordinary vyands,' and began to long for 'Horse-flesh.' He therefore went to a meadow where a Horse was grazing, but realizing that the Horse was a 'huge beast and well shod,' he decided to exact homage from the Horse so as to 'stifle him before he should be able to recouer himselfe from his false embrace.' The Horse, however, repulsed the Bear, who thereat 'enrag'd, that he should be so dishonoured by his inferiour,' 'consulted with the Ape how he might be reuenged.' At the Ape's suggestion, the Bear trapped and devoured the Horse. The Bear then pursued his malpractices by poisoning a Deer, tearing out the heart of a Unicorn, and sowing discord among the lesser beasts. Then the Bear resolved upon a milder diet and fixed upon honey to satisfy his appetite. Persuading 'the Husbandmen of the soyle' that the Bees they kept were most of them Drones, he tried to rob the Bees of their honey, and for this purpose he engaged two deceivers, a Fox and a Chameleon, who, 'vnder the habite of Simplicity,' went up and down the countrey to persuade 'poore silly Swaines' that the honey 'their Bees brought foorth was poysonous and corrupt.' In turn they made their 'popular Patients' believe that they were 'cunning Phisitions' and 'cunning Philosophers.' The Fox and the Chameleon therefore studied Galen anew in order to 'seeke out splenatiue simples to purge their popular Patients of the opinion of their olde Traditions and Customes.' Their theories found general favour with 'the light vnconstant multitude, that will daunce after euerie mans pipe; and sooner prefer a blind harper that can squeake out a new horne-pipe, than *Alcinous* or *Apolloes* varietie, that imitates the right straines of the *Doryan* melodie.' The plotting of these two 'Deuisers' went on until one day a Fly

---

(1) Nashe, *Works*, I, 221-226.

overheard their talk and buzzed in Lynceus's ears 'the whole purport of their malice.' As a result they were 'apprehended and imprisoned, and all their whole counsaile detected.' Meanwhile the Bear, consumed with grief because a fat Hind had outwitted him, went into the woods 'all melancholie, and there died for pure anger: leauing the Foxe and the Camelion to the destinie of their desert, and mercie of their Iudges.' Nashe concludes his tale: 'How they scapte I know not, but some saie they were hanged, and so weele leaue them.'

For a full and clear-sighted analysis of the beast fable just summarized we are indebted to Professor Donald J. McGinn (1), who has tracked down the identity of most of the beasts in Nashe's tale. Earlier investigators such as J. P. Collier and R. B. McKerrow already pointed out that the Bear might stand for Robert, Earl of Leicester, for the Earl's cognizance was the bear and ragged staff. McKerrow further observed that 'a passage about bringing the husbandmen into opinion that the bees which they kept were really drones evidently alludes to the Puritan attacks on the ministry for their neglect of their duties' (2). Professor McGinn has worked out these suggestions in detail by using evidence yielded by an anonymous tract entitled *Leycesters Common-wealth* (printed on the Continent first in English in 1584, then in French and in Latin in 1585), as well as by relying on evidence derivable from Nashe's anti-Martinist pamphlet *An Almond for a Parrat*.

Leycesters Common-wealth became very popular in England, and, though not printed there until 1641, was widely circulated in numerous manuscript copies. It is therefore understandable that Nashe did not disdain to take suggestions from the *Commonwealth* if, like the anonymous writer of this tract, he wished to satirize Leicester's intrigues. Following in the wake of the *Common-wealth* Nashe's success was assured; and as Leicester had died in 1588 Nashe hardly needed to trouble his head about being persecuted for disclosing secrets to London readers, though he did take advantage of the still existing interest in Leicester's affairs. Incidentally, it is likely that John Eliot's mock-dedication in the *Ortho-epia Gallica* (1593) is in part to be set down to the author's desire thus to rouse

---

(1) DONALD J. McGINN, "The Allegory of the 'Beare' and the 'Foxe' in Nashe's *Pierce Penilesse*," *PMLA*, LXI (1946), 431-453.
(2) R. B. McKERROW, ed. *Nashe*, IV, 139.

interest in his work and to curry favour with the public. The identifications proposed for the second part of Nashe's allegorical tale must now be referred to.

Professor McGinn interprets Nashe's allegory as follows: the Bees are the Bishops; the Fox is Thomas Cartwright, master of the Earl of Leicester's hospital at Warwick and one of those who enjoyed the Earl's patronage as the chief exponent of Puritanism; the Chameleon is Martin Marprelate, *i. e.* John Penry; the passage in which the Fly is said to report the activities of the Fox and the Chameleon to Lynceus figures the capture of the Marprelate press, the Fly being a pursuivant who discovers the whereabouts of the press and reports it to Lynceus, the High Commission with its hundred eyes. In a footnote Professor McGinn (1) says that the allusions to the Fly in Harvey's *Foure Letters* and Nashe's *Strange Newes* (late 1592), the reply to Gabriel Harvey, strongly suggests that the Fly in the satire on the Puritans is Nashe himself.

Since the identity of the Fox and the Chameleon, as argued by Professor McGinn, is largely dependent on his interpretation of Nashe's pamphlet *An Almond for a Parrat* as an attack on Penry alone, it is evident that McGinn's theory needs qualification if one makes allowance for the view that *An Almond* has some bearing on Richard Harvey, a point to be argued in the next chapter. It has to be borne in mind in this connexion that Lyly had also aimed at the Harveys in his attack on Penry, and this is why there is a likelihood that Nashe, too, would combine an attack on Martin with slighting remarks on one of the Harvey brothers. Here are some of the traces the 'Fly' left in some of the works following in the wake of *Pierce Penilesse*.

In the epistle 'To the Gentlemen Readers,' prefixed to *Strange Newes*, Nashe, evidently conscious of having offended many persons by his *Pierce Penilesse*, bitterly complains that 'vpstart Interpreters, haue extorted & rakte that vnreuerent meaning out of my lines, which a thousand deaths cannot make mee ere grant that I dreamd off.' After some reflexions on Dr. Andrew Perne, Nashe goes on to discuss the nature of his beast fable:

Who but a Foppe wil labour to anatomize a Flye? Fables were free for any bondman to speake in old time, as *Aesope* for an instance; their

(1) D. J. McGINN, *PMLA*, LXI, 452.

allusion was not restrained to any particular humor of spite, but generally applyed to a generall vice (1).

Even in one his later works, *Lenten Stuffe* (1599), Nashe could not refrain from easing his conscience by referring to 'a number of Gods fooles' who

out of some discourses of mine, which were a mingle mangle cum purre, and I knew not what to make of my selfe, haue fisht out such a deepe politique state meaning as if I had al the secrets of court or common-wealth at my fingers endes. Talke I of a beare, O, it is such a man that emblazons him in his armes, or of a woolfe, a fox, or a camelion, any lording whom they do not affect it is meant by (2).

That insect similes formed an integral part in the constructive design of Nashe's and Harvey's attacks can be demonstrated with singular cogency from Harvey's fourth letter. Before turning to this matter, however, it is entertaining to notice that the fourth of the sonnets appended to the *Foure Letters* contains a few lines about a jolly and a doughty Fly, obviously an allusion to Nashe, for who else could Harvey have in view in the sonnet superscribed 'The miserable end of wilful desperatnesse'?

> The iolly Fly dispatch'd his silly selfe;
> What Storyes quaint of many a douty Fly,
> That read a Lecture to the ventrous Elfe?
> Yet he will haue his lusty swing, to dy.

And on the assumption that Nashe had represented himself as a Fly in his allegory, it is comprehensible that Gabriel Harvey should have yielded to the temptation to insert allusions to other insects when he came to attack Nashe and Greene in his fourth letter.

For in many cases, I take it a better Pollicy, to vse the flying Legge, then the cumbersome Horne: and at this instant, I should much more haue pleased my selfe, if I had still practised my former resolution, to scorne the stinginge of a pieuish waspe: or the biting of an eleuish gnat: or the quipp of a mad companion: and rather to pocket-vp a pelting iniury, then to entangle my selfe with trifling businesse: or any-way to accrew to the most-contemptible fellowship of the scribblinge crew, that annoyeth this Age, and neuer more accloyed the world. Alas, he is piti-

---

(1) NASHE, *Works*, I, 260-1.
(2) NASHE, *Works*, III, 214.

fully bestead, that in an Age of Pollicy, and in a world of Industry, (wherein the greatest matters of Gouernement, and Valour, seeme small to aspiring capacities) is constrained to make woeful *Greene*, and beggarly *Pierce Pennylesse*, (as it were a Grashopper, and a Cricket, two pretty musitians, but silly creatures) the argumente of his stile: and enforced to encounter them, who onely in vanity are something: in effect, nothing: in account, lesse then nothing: howsoeuer the Grashopper enraged, would bee no lesse then a greene Dragon: and the Cricket male-contented, not so little as a Blacke Bellwether: but the only Vnicorne of the Muses (1).

Attacking both Greene and Nashe, Harvey has evidently striven to introduce such allusions and puns as are necessary to point to the identity of his adversaries: Greene, with the usual pun on 'green,' is a grasshopper and a green dragon, Nashe an elvish gnat, a cricket and a black bell-wether.

To modern eyes such imagery seems ridiculous and so little appropriate to an acrimonious quarrel that one wonders in what spirit Harvey wanted his contemporaries to read passages like the one just quoted. It looks as though the writer merely indulges in his taste for the humorous grotesque and nothing more. However that may be, he had decided to continue in the same vein in his two next pamphlets, *Pierces Supererogation* and *A New Letter of Notable Contents*. Though there are several passages in these two works in which 'flies' occur, I do not wish to argue their relevance to Nashe, lest 'flies' might make one lose one's sense of discrimination (2). There is little doubt, however, that these insect similes could hardly fail to appeal to Elizabethan readers.

Nor can it reasonably be doubted that the Fly's indiscretion, as this is depicted in Nashe's allegorical satire on the Puritans, is identical with the one that had compromised Nashe's reputation ever since he published *An Almond for a Parrat*. This was the very pamphlet whose evidence pointed to his participation in the Martin Marprelate controversy and to his indiscretion. Terence's expression *rimarum sum plenus*, displayed on the *Almond* title-page, is a proverbial phrase for 'I am indiscreet;' with which one may also compare Horace, *Satires*, II, 6, 46: *quae rimosa deponuntur in aure* (remarks which are trusted to a leaky ear). The contents of both the *Almond* and the allegorical tale in *Pierce Penilesse* strongly suggest

---

(1) HARVEY, *Foure Letters*, pp. 71-2.
(2) Compare HARVEY, *Pierces Supererogation*, sigg. B_2 v°, T_1 r°, X_2 v° (*Works*, II, 44, 225-6, 252); and *A New Letter of Notable Contents*, sig. B_3 v°.

that Nashe's indiscretion consisted in disclosing the identity of Martin Marprelate. None of the other anti-Martinist writers had even covertly hinted at Martin's identity, but the phraseology of the *Almond*, with its frequent punning on 'Pen' and 'rye,' could not but remove any doubt on this head. From the moment the *Almond* was published it must have become widely known that Martin was none other than John Penry.

Except for *Strange Newes* and the comedy *Summers Last Will and Testament*, all of Nashe's other works fall outside my range of dates and therefore do not require as full a discussion in the present study. *Summers Last Will*, it will be recalled, bore some relation to the Marprelate controversy. Other features of this interesting play, as we will see, are related to Shakespeare's *Love's Labour's Lost*. As far as *Strange Newes* is concerned, suffice it to say that it was printed prior to its entry (January 12, 1593), and that it mainly consists of a running commentary on Harvey's *Foure Letters*. Its printer was John Danter, whose irregular printing activities had been the concern of the Stationers' Company in the years 1586-1591. For Nashe Danter printed *Strange Newes*, *The Terrors of the Night* (1593), and *Have With You to Saffron-Walden* (1596). It is likely that Nashe had some kind of business relationship with Danter, at whose office he may have been a press corrector. It was apparently in that capacity that Nashe may have had a hand in the press correction of Greene's *Orlando Furioso* (1).

Considering his literary undertakings prior to 1592, Nashe stands out clearly as one of the most conspicuous writers of his time. Here was a new planet that had swum into the ken of the Elizabethan literary public. Even a rapid survey of his output throws his conspicuity into relief. He first thrust himself upon the attention of the public both by his fierce denunciation of women in the *Anatomie of Absurditie* and by his association with Greene's *Menaphon*, a tale written by one of the most famous writers of the day. He then stopped the mouth of Martin by the publication of *An Almond for a Parrat* and by disclosing Martin's identity. These satirical pieces were followed by a humorous prognostication and *Pierce Penilesse*, in which Nashe's satirical power was displayed

---

(1) For DANTER's printing career see H. R. HOPPE, *The Bad Quarto of Romeo and Juliet* (Cornell University Press, 1949), pp. 18-38.

SEGMENT

to full advantage. Nashe had achieved his end: he had decided to appear in a 'satyrical disguise,' and he soon did in the person of 'young Juvenal' and 'true English Aretino.' But his ingenuity led him to exploit the efficacy of other disguises as well: Mar-Martin-Junior, Adam Foulweather, Cerberus, and a Fly were so many shapes or metamorphoses that proved to his taste. Nashe was no doubt the most versatile of Elizabethan authors in contriving satirical disguises and it was these which did as much as anything else to establish his reputation for ingenuity.

CHAPTER VII

NASHE, GREENE AND THE HARVEYS

As the literary quarrel between Nashe and the Harveys is directly traceable to the Marprelate controversy, a controversy merely religious in intention, it is desirable to give an account of how professional men of letters came to take up the gauntlet against Martin. This will enable us to understand why Gabriel Harvey was so angered by the attacks of Lyly, Greene and Nashe that they finally succeeded in pushing him into the literary arena. For an outline of the later stages of the Harvey-Nashe dispute — after the publication of the *Foure Letters* — readers are referred to the admirable treatment by McKerrow (1). An investigation of the earlier stages has already been undertaken in a pamphlet, *Robert Greene and the Harveys* (1931), by Professor Chauncey Sanders. In the light of the foregoing pages, however, it is evident that the whole matter deserves to be gone into afresh.

It is not my intention to delineate the Marprelate controversy in detail (2); suffice it to say that there were seven Martinist tracts, known as *The Epistle* (issued early in November, 1588), *The Epitome* (in readers' hands before December 6, 1588), *The Minerall Conclusions* (issued at the end of February, 1589), *Hay any worke for Cooper* (issued about March 25, 1589), *Theses Martinianae* (about July 22, 1589), *Martin Senior* (about July 29, 1589) and *The Protestation* (September, 1589). The fifth tract was professedly written by 'Martin Junior' and the sixth by 'Martin Senior.' Soon after the publication of *The Epistle* it became evident that the bishops ought to take energetic measures with a view to stemming the wave of sympathy with Martin which swept over the country. The episcopalians had two works issued in defence of their cause: *An Admonition to the People of England*, published in January, 1589, by Thomas Cooper, Bishop of Winchester, and Richard Bancroft's sermon preached at Paul's Cross on February 9, 1589, which was published next March. The *Admonition* was not originally composed with

---

(1) R. B. McKerrow, ed. *Nashe*, I, 65-110.
(2) As yet there is no thoroughly satisfactory account of the controversy. The reader may be referred to E. Arber, *An Introductory Sketch to the Martin Marprelate Controversy* (London, 1879); J. Dover Wilson, "The Marprelate Controversy," *CHEL*, III, 374-398; W. Pierce, *An Historical Introduction to the Marprelate Tracts* (London, 1908); and R. B. McKerrow, ed. *Nashe*, I, 34-65 and 184-192.

the object of answering Martin's *Epistle*, for only a single section in it is devoted to an attack on Martin.

Among Martin's immediate forerunners his personal friend John Udall calls for special mention. In 1588 Udall (?1559-1592), at that time parish priest of Kingston-on-Thames, wrote a dialogue entitled *The state of the Church of Englande, laide open in a conference betweene Diotrephes a Byshopp, Tertullus a Papiste, Demetrius an vsurer, Pandochus an Inne-keeper, and Paule a preacher of the worde of God*. This work, generally known as *Diotrephes*, was printed in April, 1588, by Robert Waldegrave, a printer already noted for printing writings of puritan tendency. *Diotrephes* is a clever piece of work. Udall's manner is different from Martin's; he has no recourse to banter or raillery but deals with his subject in a spirit of seriousness and even serenity. But Udall's denunciation of the Episcopate was no doubt as effective as was Martin's, for the Star Chamber decreed that Waldegrave's press, type and stock of *Diotrephes* should be seized and taken to Stationers' Hall. On April 16, 1588, John Wolfe and a few others executed this task, but Waldegrave managed to escape with a box of type under his cloak, and sought refuge with Mrs. Crane, widow of Nicholas Crane, a presbyterian. On the very day of the capture of Waldegrave's press John Wolfe went to Archbishop Whitgift at Croydon to get further instructions.

As time went on Waldegrave realized that he would no longer be allowed to print in London and he probably set up a secret press at Kingston-on-Thames, which allowed him to work in closer association with John Penry and Udall. On June 10, 1588, 'the Pursuyvant with John wolf, Thomas Strange and Thomas Draper wente to Kingston' (1), probably going in search of Waldegrave. Since they did not find him, it is reasonable to suppose that by that time he had moved to the country house of Mrs. Crane at East Molesey, a village three miles north-west from Kingston. It was here that the *Epistle*, the first Marprelate tract, was printed. It appeared simultaneously with Udall's *Demonstration of Discipline*. In writing the *Epistle* Martin was largely inspired by his indignation at Udall's being deprived of his benefice, and Martin being Penry (2),

---

(1) See ARBER, *Transcript*, I, 528.
(2) It must be admitted that Professor McGINN's arguments regarding MARTIN's identity have failed to convince A. PEEL, who maintains that 'it hardly seems likely that the secret will be revealed at this time of day'; see A. PEEL, ed. *The Notebook of John Penry 1593* (Camden Third Series, LXVII, 1944), p. xiii.

the *Epistle* is a human document of Penry's devotion to the cause of Udall. Among the depositions made at Richmond in November, 1588, on the first appearance of the *Epistle*, there is one which contains the statement that it was written 'for and in the behalf of Master Vdall of Kingston' (1), while it was generally rumoured that many of Udall's personal notes were worked up into Martin's first tract. Martin's main object was to attack the enemies of Udall and Waldegrave. He was loud in his abuse of Wolfe, who is dubbed 'Iohn Woolfe alias Machiuill Beadle of the Stationers and most tormenting executioner of Walde-graues goods' (2), which is one more indication of the important role played by Wolfe in the whole controversy.

Both the *Epistle* and *Diotrephes* denounce the bishops for two main reasons: their policy of repression in matters of religious belief and their leniency towards all forms of popery. There is, however, one small point of contact between these two tracts which is of some importance to the following survey of the Marprelate controversy. Udall had censured the practice of lending money at interest in the character of the usurer Demetrius in *Diotrephes*, a practice to which the bishops seem to have given countenance. Now Martin's *Epistle* takes several Anglican churchmen to task for applying for financial assistance to a Kingston usurer, one Harvey, who is called 'a professed aduersary to M. Vdall.' The ecclesiastics who took advantage of the usurer's enmity towards Udall were James Cottington, Archdeacon of Surrey, Stephen Chatfield, vicar of Kingston, and one Dr. Hone. All three are said to have gone to Kingston because they knew that 'Harvey' wanted to stop Udall's mouth, 'Harvey' being a man who held that Udall railed in his sermons. Martin goes on to attack 'Harvey' thus:

Doth he [Udall] rail / when he reproueth thee (and such notorious varlets as thou art) for thy vsery / for thy oppressing of the poore / for buying the houses ouer their heads that loue the gospell / and the Lord his faythfull minister ? (M. Vdall) And art not thou a monstrous atheist / a belly God / a carnall wicked wretch / and what not (3).

Curiously enough, in his *Almond for a Parrat* Nashe shows intimate acquaintance with Martin's passage containing the attack on the

(1) E. Arber, *Introductory Sketch*, p. 82.
(2) Martin Marprelate, *The Epistle*, ed. E. Arber (London, 1895), p. 22.
(3) Martin Marprelate, *The Epistle*, p. 32.

three ecclesiastics just mentioned. Nashe quotes several phrases almost verbatim from Martin's tract, mentions Cottington, Hone, and Chatfield, but does not refer to 'Harvey.'

I thought you [Udall] such another, when I first sawe you emblazoned in *Martins* bookes. Tis you that are so holy that you wil not forsooth be seene to handle anie monie, nor take golde though it shoulde filch it selfe into your purse, but if God moued the heartes of anie of your brethren or sistren in the Lord, to bring in pots, beds, or houshold stuffe into your house, you would go out of doores of purpose whiles it was brought in; and then if anie man aske you how you come so well storde, your answere is that you know not how, but only by the prouidence of God. I must belabour you, when all is done, for your backbiting & slandering of your honest neighbours, and open inueighing against the established gouernment in your sermons. Helpe him, *Martin*, or else his vpbraided absurdities will make thee repent that euer thou belyedst or disgracedst *Hone, Cottington*, or *Chatfield* in his cause (1).

It is a little odd and a measure of the sinuosity of his satire that Nashe should turn the tables upon Udall for the very sin lashed by Udall himself. Martin's censure of Hone, Cottington, Chatfield, and 'Harvey' caused much offence for it was an important item in the examination of John Udall on January 13, 1589 (2). Let us now resume the thread of our chronological account of the puritan controversy in its later stages.

It was the publication and the success of the Marprelate tracts that finally resulted in the undoing of those best known to have been engaged in their production. On May 29, 1593, Penry was executed at St. Thomas a Watering in Surrey, and John Udall died in the Marshalsea prison about the end of the year 1592. Nor were the printers and bookbinders of their tracts left unmolested. One of those who assisted Penry throughout the controversy was Henry Sharpe, bookbinder of Northampton, the man whose depositions unveiled to the Lord Chancellor, Sir Christopher Hatton, the whole story of the Marprelate press. Sharpe, no doubt the most valuable of Martinist suspects in the hands of the High Commission, was examined on October 15, 1589. His judges tried to worm the secret of Martin's identity out of him, and though in his depositions he did not state categorically that Martin was Penry, it was Sharpe

---

(1) NASHE, *Works*, III, 364-5.
(2) See E. ARBER, *Introductory Sketch*, pp. 91-2. It is tempting to suppose that the Kingston usurer 'HARVEY' had something to do with one of the Saffron Walden brothers.

who communicated the greater part of the Marprelate secret to the Government. He also told his examiners he suspected Penry of being Martin and 'that Penry was thought generally at London to be the Author of these Bookes' (1). After his examination he is no more heard of in connexion with the controversy and he probably gained his liberty by his partial disclosure.

What impresses us most is that the High Commission had not yet been able to get definitely behind Martin's identity, despite the fact that its most cunning officers used their best endeavours to discover it. A year had elapsed since the *Epistle* had thrown the bishops into confusion and yet the authorities had not been able to bring its author to book. Archbishop Whitgift, it would seem, entertained strong suspicions that Penry was the chief motive force in the whole controversy. It is important to bear in mind that the authorship of the Marprelate tracts had not yet been ascertained at the moment the bishops began to realize that the theological argument of Bishop Cooper and of Richard Bancroft, at that time canon of Westminster, was no match for Martin's satirical sallies. An attempt had already been made to ridicule Martin on the stage, but the plays in which he was held up to scorn have not come down to us. Probably at the suggestion of Bancroft, it was decided that Martin should be attacked by professional writers so that he might be answered in a style similar to his own. It is impossible to determine to what extent the new policy was officially supported by the Church, because it is 'improbable that the [anti-Martinist] tracts were given any open support by the authorities, otherwise we should hardly have expected to find members of the clergy, such as Richard Harvey and the author of the *Mirror for Martinists*, using such contemptuous language about them' (2).

Three writers are now known to have participated in the attack on Martin: Munday, Lyly, and Nashe; as far as Greene's share is concerned this is as yet an open question. The first literary man to open the campaign was Anthony Munday (1553-1633), whose meagre pamphlet *A Countercuff to Martin Junior* appeared in London in August, 1589. The *Countercuff* is the first of a series of three tracts purporting to be written by one Pasquil of England (3).

---

(1) For SHARPE's depositions see E. ARBER, *Introductory Sketch*, pp. 94-104.
(2) R. B. McKERROW, ed. *Nashe*, V, 44.
(3) For the evidence that Pasquil is MUNDAY see CELESTE TURNER, *Anthony Mundy, an Elizabethan Man of Letters* (University of California Publ. in Engl., No. II, 1928),

Munday's second contribution was *The Return of Pasquil*, which was probably issued at the end of October or the beginning of November, 1589; third in the series was *The First Part of Pasquil's Apology*, a belated publication for it was published after July 2, 1590. All of Munday's tracts were the work of the same printing-house for the printer's device and the type are identical in all three. Their printer was probably John Charlewood, the man also responsible for printing Smellknave's prognostication. During his journey on the Continent in 1578 Munday had distinguished himself by spying on English Catholics and had thus gained some experience for his future job of pursuivant. Even before Munday had contributed any pamphlet to the controversy, he was already attacked by Martin Senior.

Or, haue you diligently soght mee out Walde-graue the Printer, Newman the Cobler, Sharpe the bookebinder of Northampton, and that seditious Welch man Penry, who you shall see will prooue the Author of all these libelles? I thanke you Maister Munday, you are a good Gentleman of your worde. Ah thou Iudas, thou that hast alreadie betrayed the Papistes, I thinke meanest to betray vs also. Diddest thou not assure me, without all doubt, that thou wouldest bring mee in, Penry, Newman, Walde-graue, presse, letters, and all, before Saint Andrewes day last (1).

The Return of Pasquil is written in the form of a dialogue between Pasquil and Marforius. In it Marforius is depicted as one who is Pasquil's junior, as a kind of pupil eager to be instructed in the trade of anti-Martinist pamphleteering. Marforius was apparently not merely fancifully invented by Munday for Pasquil informs us at the end of his conversation that Marforius has been busy writing about the death of Martin, 'and though he [Martin] liue yet, it may be you [Marforius] prophecie of his end' (2). 'Marforius' performed this task for he published *Martin's Month's Mind*, probably early in November, 1589. The tract was introduced

pp. 83-87. See also J. DOVER WILSON, "Anthony Munday, Pamphleteer and Pursuivant," *MLR*, IV (1908), 484-490. In his article DOVER WILSON attributes *An Almond for a Parrat* to MUNDAY, an attribution with which I cannot agree.—As to 'Pasquil' : Pasquino or Pasquillo was the name given to a mutilated statue disinterred at Rome in 1506, to which it became the custom to affix libels on St. Mark's day. These 'pasquinades' tended to become satirical and the term began to be applied to all sorts of satirical compositions.
(1) MARTIN SENIOR, *Just Censure and Reproof* (Wolston, 1589), sig. A₂ v⁰.
(2) A. MUNDAY in NASHE, *Works*, I, 101. MUNDAY's three tracts are all reprinted in MCKERROW's NASHE edition. Pasquil's identity was not established until CELESTE TURNER in 1928 produced convincing evidence that Pasquil must have been MUNDAY.

by an 'Epistle dedicatorie to Pasquine of England,' a dedication indicating clearly that Pasquil and Marforius were two different writers. The authorship of *Martin's Month's Mind* has not yet been ascertained but critics have generally tended to ascribe it to Nashe. Personally I do not feel inclined to express an opinion on this question as I see no evidence for a serious ascription.

After Munday and Marforius it was John Lyly's turn to be engaged in defending the episcopal cause. Though the tract *Pappe with an Hatchet* was published anonymously (in October or in the first days of November, 1589), it cannot be seriously questioned that it is Lyly's. Gabriel Harvey's allusions to Lyly and his work in *An Aduertisement for Pap-hatchet, and Martin Mar-prelate*, an essay to be presently noticed, put the attribution in question beyond all doubt. *Pappe with an Hatchet* was an occasion for Lyly to revive his old feud with the Harveys. It will be remembered that Gabriel Harvey's displeasure with Lyly arose from the fact that the latter had drawn the attention of the Earl of Oxford to a poem in Gabriel Harvey's *Three proper, and wittie, familiar letters* (1580), a poem which might be read as an attack on that nobleman. It is not clear why Lyly was again at variance with the Harveys in 1589 but so he was, for he attacked his enemies in unmistakable terms.

And one will we coniure vp, that writing a familiar Epistle about the naturall causes of an Earthquake, fell into the bowells of libelling, which made his eares quake for feare of clipping; he shall tickle you with taunts; all his works bound close, are at least six sheetes in quarto, & he calls them the first tome of his familiar Epistle: he is full of latin endes, and worth tenne of those that crie in London, *haie ye anie gold ends to sell.* If he giue you a bob, though he drawe no blood, yet you are sure of a rap with a bable. If he ioyne with vs, *perijsti Martin*, thy wit wil be massacred: if the toy take him to close with thee, then haue I my wish, for this tenne yeres haue I lookt to lambacke him. Nay he is a mad lad, and such a one as cares as little for writing without wit, as *Martin* doth for writing without honestie; a notable coach companion for *Martin*, to drawe Diuinitie from the Colledges of *Oxford* and *Cambridge*, to Shoomakers hall in Sainct *Martins*. But we neither feare *Martin*, nor the foot-cloth, nor the beast that weares it, be he horse or asse; nor whose sonne he is, be he *Martins*, sonne, *Iohns*, sonne, or *Richards*, sonne; nor of what occupation hee be, be a ship-wright, cart-wright, or tiburn-wright (1).

The allusions to John and Richard Harvey and to the trade of the

---

(1) LYLY, *Works*, III, 400.

Harveys' father in the word 'tiburn-wright' are clearly recognizable, while 'familiar Epistle' refers to Gabriel's *Three Letters*. It would seem that Lyly expresses some regret for Harvey's unwillingness to participate in the Marprelate controversy, but on the other hand, he rather prefers to see Harvey enter the lists on the side of Martin, for then has Lyly his 'wish.' The phrase 'for this tenne yeres haue I lookt to lambacke him' is a further indication that Lyly may have attacked his enemy in other pieces as well. Lyly's opinion that Gabriel is a notable companion for Martin to draw divinity from the Colleges of Oxford and Cambridge to 'Shoomakers hall in Sainct *Martins*' is almost certainly connected with the Harveys' attempt to 'patch' matters up, they being like 'cobblers' in shoemakers' hall in Saint Martin's.

I should like to make a small remark here. The reference to 'ends' in 'haie ye anie gold ends to sell' is related to the expression *respice finem* with which Nashe familiarized the Elizabethans in the pun *respice funem*, of course with the intention of referring to ropemaking, the trade of the Harveys' father. Shakespeare himself gives evidence of this familiarity in *The Comedy of Errors*, IV, iv, 44-6 : 'Mistres *respice finem*, respect your end, or rather like the Parrat, beware the ropes end,' which explains the pun finis-funis, end-rope. Both Professor McGinn and Professor E. I. Fripp believe that Shakespeare is alluding to Nashe in the just quoted passage (1). Note now that *Pappe with an Hatchet*, the first direct challenge to Gabriel and his brothers, contains the phrase 'Here I was writing *Finis* and *Funis*, and determined to lay it by, till I might see more knauerie fild in' (2). Professor T. W. Baldwin (3) has placed the saying *respice finem* in its proper Renaissance perspective, and pointed out that the pun with *funem* existed as early as 1570, when Buchanan originated the Latin quibble. But Professor Baldwin does not cite any example of it in use between 1572 and 1592 when Nashe came to avail himself of the pun; and though he does refer to Lyly's *Mother Bombie* and *Midas* in this connexion, he does not point out that the Latin expression as such occurs in a kind of disguise in *Pappe with an Hatchet*. One can, indeed, never be sure of having retrieved all the puns in Elizabethan literature.

---

(1) See D. J. McGinn, *PMLA*, LIX (1944), 957, and E. I. Fripp, *Shakespeare Man and Artist* (London, 1938), I, 320-321.
(2) Lyly, *Works*, III, 410.
(3) T. W. Baldwin, "Respice Finem : Respice Funem," in *J. Q. Adams Memorial Studies*, pp. 141-155.

There is one outstanding feature of *Pappe*, specially relevant to Martin's identity, which sharply distinguishes this pamphlet from those of Munday or from any other publication connected with the Marprelate controversy: Lyly's tedious harping on the anonymity of Martin. Lyly dwells on Martin's anonymity and his impending apprehension so emphatically that *Pappe with an Hatchet* must have piqued contemporary curiosity to the quick. It is necessary to quote the passages dealing with the secret of Martin's identity because of the nature of their imagery (1):

I doo but yet angle with a silken flye, to see whether *Martins* will nibble; and if I see that, why then I haue wormes for the nonce, and will giue them line enough like a trowte, till they swallow both hooke and line, and then *Martin* beware your gilles, for Ile make you daunce at the poles end (394, 31-35).

Such dydoppers must be taken vp, els theile not stick to check the king (395, 7-8).

I am ignorant of *Martin* and his maintainer, but my conscience is my warrant, to care for neither (397, 10-11).

Nay gesse olde knaue and odd knaue: for Ile neuer leaue pulling, til I haue thee out of thy bed into the streete; and then all shall see who thou art, and thou know what I am (398, 3-5).

Doost think *Martin*, thou canst not be discouered? (401, 39-40).

Scratch not thy head *Martin*, for be thou *Martin* the bird, or *Martin* the beast; a bird with the longest bill, or a beast with the longest eares, theres a net spread for your necke (402, 8-10).

Would those Comedies might be allowed to be plaiù that are pend, and then I am sure he would be decyphered, and so perhaps discouraged (408, 18-20).

The hogshead was euen come to the hauncing, and nothing could be drawne from him but dregs: yet the emptie caske sounds lowder than when it was ful; and protests more in his waining, than he could performe in his waxing. I drew neere the sillie soule, whom I found quiuering in two sheetes of protestation paper (410, 25-29).

Thou seest *Martin* Moldwarpe, that hetherto I haue named none,

---

(1) For convenience' sake the page and line references to the third volume of Professor Bond's Lyly edition will be quoted between brackets after each quotation.

but markt them readie for the next market: if thou proceed in naming, be as sure as thy shirt to thy knaues skinne, that Ile name such, as though thou canst not blush, because thou art past shame, yet they shall bee sorie, because they are not all without grace (413, 9-13).

I haue manie sequences of Saints; if naming be the aduantage, & ripping vp of liues make sport, haue with thee knuckle deepe, it shall neuer bee said that I dare not venter mine eares, where *Martin* hazards his necke (413, 15-18).

The first quotation compares 'Martins' to fishes, the second calls them dabchicks ('dydoppers'), waterbirds known for hiding their heads in the water, while two others hint that 'Martins' will be caught in a net. Munday in *The Return of Pasquil* uses related imagery in connexion with 'Martins,' but without any hint as to their capture: 'They are the very Spawnes of the fish *Saepia*, where the streame is cleere, and the Scriptures euidentlie dyscouer them, they vomit vp yncke to trouble the waters' (1). 'Martins' resemble cuttle-fishes and these are said to be discovered by the Scriptures, a discovery which causes them to 'vomit vp yncke to trouble the waters' of religion. There is a certain generic resemblance between the metaphorical language of Munday and Lyly, but Lyly's state-ment is different from Munday's in that it implies that 'Martins' are in imminent danger of being apprehended. Furthermore, when Lyly reaches the conclusion of his pamphlet he states in un-ambiguous terms that he avoids 'naming' who Martin is, even though advantage is to be gained from doing so. The significance of all this will be recognized at a later stage of the argument.

Pappe with an Hatchet was no sooner published than Gabriel Harvey set himself to write a reply to Lyly's attack and he composed a long essay entitled *An Aduertisement for Pap-hatchet, and Martin Mar-prelate*. This work did not appear in print until the publication of *Pierces Supererogation* (1593), of which diatribe it forms the middle portion. The *Aduertisement*, dated at the end 'At Trinitie hall: this fift of Nouember: 1589,' is made up of three distinct parts. The initial pages up to sig. K_2 v° contain a reply to Lyly's *Pappe*, and next comes a long section which, except for a few incidental references to Lyly, is devoted to a very serious treatment of the Marprelate controversy. As Harvey reached the

---

(1) A. MUNDAY in NASHE, *Works*, 1, 87.

end of his *Aduertisement*, however, he seems to have realized that his invective against Lyly was much too short for it to be very effective, and he therefore decided to wind up his argument by declaiming against Lyly once more.

It is the central part of the *Aduertisement* which is by far the most interesting. Harvey maintains that theological questions should be debated in a spirit of high seriousness and not in the railing tone of Martin and his opponents: 'it is sound Argumentes, and grounded Authorities, that must strike the definitiue stroke, and decide the controuersy, with mutuall satisfaction' (1). Harvey assumes an attitude of impartiality in the quarrel and advises a reconciliation between the parties involved. As he proceeds in his argument he seems to have become increasingly aware that there existed a striking analogy between the religious situation in his own day and that of the Primitive Church during the reign of Constantine the Great. It is well-known that the emperor Constantine regarded the Catholic Church as an excellent means of preserving the unity of his vast empire and that he summoned the first general or oecumenical council, that of Nicaea, in 325. The main object of this council was to settle the religious questions of the hour and to induce the representatives of the churches of the empire to agree upon a definition of their faith. The Council of Nicaea also repudiated the so-called Arian heresy, a creed defended by Arius, a learned presbyter in the church of Alexandria. Arius's chief contention was that God the Son was subordinate or inferior to God the Father. Harvey, when writing his *Aduertisement*, apparently discovers a striking resemblance between this Arian controversy and that caused by Marprelate. When he discusses the validity of the episcopal office and the unbroken Apostolic succession, vital points in the development of the history of the early church, Harvey points out that the title of bishop 'hath successiuely continued to this age, without any empeachment of value, or contradiction of note; sauing that of the angrie Malcontent, and prowd heretique Aërius, scarsely worth the naming' (2). The root of the Marprelate controversy was precisely that the puritans questioned the divine right of bishops; that they refused to recognize the episcopal office as established by the Anglican church settlement; and that they objected to the civil

---

(1) G. HARVEY, *Pierces Supererogation*, sig. K₃ rᵒ.
(2) G. HARVEY, *Pierces Supererogation*, sig. M₃ rᵒ. HARVEY mentions CONSTANTINE three times (sigg. K₃ vᵒ. L₁ rᵒ. N₃ rᵒ). and ARIUS twice (sigg. M₃ rᵒ and M₄ rᵒ).

magistrate interfering with church matters. Harvey repudiates these puritan claims and supports the episcopalian partly, at least in the passage just quoted. He specifically names Arius as one who, like Martin Marprelate, rejected both episcopal and secular authority. In his line of reasoning he appears to have followed—or to have been followed by—his brother Richard, who, in his *Lambe of God*, developed similar ideas, insisting, for example, that he 'might well name our reformers a sort of new Arrians, that inuent lies against our spirituall lords' (1).

An extract from the *Aduertisement* may now be quoted to show that Harvey wants the authorities to imitate the ecclesiastical policy of the early church in summoning 'some Generall, and some Prouinciall Councels.'

The auncient Fathers, and Doctors of the Church, wanted neither learning, nor iudgement, nor conscience, nor zeale: as some of their Greeke, and Latine woorkes very notably declare: (if they were blinde, happy men that see:) and what wiser Senates, or hollyer Congregations, or any way more reuerend assemblies, then some Generall, and some Prouinciall Councels? (2)

Towards the end of his essay Harvey again holds up the Primitive Church as an example to his contemporaries and points out that 'Primitiue founders of churches were no railers' and that 'their Doctrine was full of power.' He then exhorts his readers to 'read the sweet Ecclesiastical Hystories, replenished with many cordiall narrations of their souerain Vertues' and also refers to 'the most vigorous Censures of their professed enemies' (3). He then mentions Porphyrius, Hierocles, Flavius Philostratus, and a few others, as opponents of early Christianity. All this makes it abundantly clear that, throughout his essay, Harvey was continually intent on drawing a parallel between the Primitive and the Elizabethan Church. About 1589 he had no doubt been studying Eusebius of Caesarea's *Ecclesiastical History*, a work he may have read either in the original or in the English translation made by M. Hammer and published in 1577 and re-issued in 1585. Eusebius, moreover, is also referred to in the *Marginalia* as 'ye Ecclesiastical historiographer, & bishop of Caesaria' (4). The marginal note in

(1) R. HARVEY, *The Lambe of God*, sig. S₃ vᵒ, p. 134. See also sig. Aa₃ vᵒ, p. 182.
(2) HARVEY, *Pierces Supererogation*, sig. L₁ vᵒ.
(3) HARVEY, *Pierces Supererogation*, sig. Q₄ rᵒ.
(4) HARVEY, *Marginalia*, p. 153, and compare G. C. M. SMITH's note, p. 272; see also RICHARD HARVEY, *The Lambe of God*, sig. M₃ vᵒ, p. 86 and sig. M₄ rᵒ, p. 87.

question deals with Eusebius because of his having written a tract against Hierocles, governor of Bithynia, who had compared the miracles of Christ with those of Apollonius Tyanaeus in a pamphlet written against the Christians. Harvey probably derived his knowledge of Apollonius from the biography of him by Flavius Philostratus. Harvey's thorough acquaintance with Eusebius's *Ecclesiastical History* explains why the *Aduertisement* displays so much learning connected with early church history. Eusebius, as is well known, led the large middle party of the Moderates at the Council of Nicaea, a position even more explicitly maintained by his namesake Eusebius of Nicomedia. Eusebius of Caesarea's conciliatory disposition was much appreciated by the emperor Constantine.

There are two passages in the *Aduertisement* in which Harvey mentions one 'Eusebius'.

Some Stoiques, and melancholie persons haue a spice of ambition by themselues: and euen *Iunius Brutus* the first, was somway a kinde of *Tarquinius Superbus:* and *Iunius Brutus* the second, is not altogither a mortified Creature, but bewrayeth as it were some reliques of fleshe, and bloud, aswell as his inwardest frend *Eusebius Philadelphus.*

Were it possible, that this age should affoord a diuine and miraculous Elias: yet, when Elias himselfe deemed himselfe most desolate, and complained hee was left all-alone; there remained thousandes liuing, that neuer bowed their knees vnto Baal. But Faction, is as sure a Keeper of Counsell, as a siue: Spite, as close a Secretary, as a skummer: Innouation, at the least a bright Angell from heauen: & the foresaid abstractes of pure diuinity, will needes know, why Iunius Brutus, or Eusebius Philadelphus should rather be Pasquils incarnate, then they.

Considering that Harvey associates 'Eusebius' with 'Philadelphus' and with 'Iunius Brutus' it is necessary to quote a third passage in which only 'Eusebius' is missing.

Oh a thousand times, that Melancton could traine Iunius Brutus; Sturmius, Philadelphus; Ramus, Beza; Iewell, Cartwright; Deering, Martin; Baro, Barrow; to embrace the heauenly Graces of Christ, and to kisse the hand of that diuine Creature, that passeth all Vnderstanding. What a felicitie were it, to see such heades as pregnant, as Hydras heades; or Hydras heades as rare, as such heades? (1)

---

(1) HARVEY, *Pierces Supererogation*, sig. L$_4$ r⁰; sig. N$_3$ v⁰; sig. O$_1$ v⁰ (*Works*, II, 146; 167-8; 172).

Who are 'Iunius Brutus' and 'Eusebius Philadelphus'? Probably Eusebius Philadelphus is one of the pseudonyms adopted by the Huguenot writer Nicolas Barnaud, whose *Réveille-matin des François* created a considerable stir in religious circles in France. The *Réveille-matin* was published in Basle in 1573, and in Lausanne in 1574; the latter edition, however, bore 'Edimbourg' on its title-page. Junius Brutus, on the other hand, was the author of the *Vindiciae contra tyrannos*, a celebrated Huguenot treatise defending the right of rebellion against unworthy and tyrannical monarchs. This book was published at Basle in 1579, and a translation in French appeared in 1581. Like Barnaud's work, the *Vindiciae* bore Edinburgh on its title-page. The identity of Junius Brutus is a vexed question. Though many Huguenot thinkers have been proposed as the author of the *Vindiciae*, most critics have argued that either Philippe du Plessis-Mornay (1549-1623) or Hubert Languet (1518-1581) is to be credited with its authorship. A third theory is that the treatise was written in collaboration. A recent student of the problem (1), however, is inclined to attribute the *Vindiciae* exclusively to Languet. It is remarkable that this attribution receives some support from Harvey's third statement on Junius Brutus. Harvey there says 'Oh a thousand times, that Melancton could traine Iunius Brutus'. This is consonant with what we know of Languet whose conversion to Protestantism in 1549 was largely due to his reading Melanchthon's *Loci communes*. Such was Languet's admiration for Melanchthon that he stayed in Wittenberg for a considerable time and became friends with the great reformer. Apparently, then, Harvey offers us additional evidence to the identity of Junius Brutus. Harvey probably possessed considerable first-hand knowledge about Languet, for the latter had been in correspondence with Sidney from about 1572 onwards and it is unlikely that Harvey was ignorant of the Languet-Sidney friendship. The probability is, however, that reference was made to Junius Brutus in the *Aduertisement* because Harvey had recently read Brutus' tract *A Short Apologie for Christian Souldiours*, which was entered to Wolfe on April 26, 1588. It was a translation of book IV of the *Vindiciae* by one H. P. We are here

---

(1) See CLÉMY VAUTIER, *Les théories relatives à la souveraineté et à la résistance chez l'auteur des Vindiciae contra tyrannos (1579)* (Lausanne, 1947); for an argument in favour of double authorship see G. T. VAN YSSELSTEYN, "L'auteur de l'ouvrage Vindiciae contra tyrannos publié sous le nom de Stephanus Junius Brutus," *Revue historique*, CLXVII (1931), 46-59.

provided with one more indication that Harvey may have been a kind of publisher's reader to Wolfe.

It would be erroneous to suppose that Harvey's suggestion that a general council should be summoned is very original. In a Europe divided by fierce religious feuds, politicians and religious thinkers (such as du Plessis-Mornay) kept on advocating the necessity of convening representatives of the different religious sects to agree upon a religious peace, and the general council of Nicaea was frequently invoked as a good example of how political unity was maintained in spite of religious 'nonconformity'. Precisely in the year 1589, a few months before Harvey wrote the *Aduertisement*, the new king of France, Henry IV, had issued a declaration in which he announced his intention to seek the advice of a 'general council' with a view to avoiding the break-up of France's unity. As Harvey's interest in continental affairs can hardly be questioned, it is likely that he is indebted for some of his ideas to contemporary French political thinkers.

There is just a possibility that Harvey, when including the names of Junius Brutus and Eusebius Philadelphus in his account of the Marprelate controversy, is also thinking of the conciliatory policy adopted by his brother Richard and himself. Note, for example, that the first quotation, given above, emphasizes the friendly relations between Brutus and Philadelphus ('*Iunius Brutus...* aswell as his inwardest frend *Eusebius Philadelphus*), while the second plainly states that these two people would make much fitter 'Pasquils' to take up the cudgels against Martin Marprelate than would 'Faction' and 'Spite.' 'Philadelphus' of course means 'one who loves his brother' and would fit the relationship between Richard and Gabriel. In this connexion the title of Richard Harvey's would-be historical treatise *Philadelphus* (1593) seems to be relevant. It was a work that seems to have been designed to defend the cause of the two notorious brothers against their opponents. Richard himself, moreover, was soon to follow in Gabriel's track and published *Plaine Percevall*, a short, undated and anonymous pamphlet. It is to Nashe that we owe the information of the tract's authorship and of its approximate date, for in *Strange Newes* (1) he tells us that *Plaine Percevall* preceded Richard Harvey's *Lamb of God*, which latter work was published in the early months of 1590.

---

(1) NASHE, *Works*, I, 270.

On the title-page of *Plaine Percevall* Richard Harvey professes to be a 'peace-maker of England' and to intend, by 'blunt persuasions,' to 'botch vp a Reconciliation between Mar-ton and Mar-tother.' The book contains a mock-dedication, headed 'To the new vpstart Martin, and the misbegotten heires of his body,' in which two anti-Martinist writers are specifically named, namely Pasquil and Marforius; while a third, Lyly, is covertly hinted at in the expression 'all Cutting Huffsnufs, Roisters, and the residew of light fingred younkers.' In the course of the pamphlet itself these three writers are always mentioned together. It may here be added that Lyly's words '*Martin*, wee are now following after thee with hue and crie, & are hard at thy heeles; if thou turne backe to blade it, wee doubt not but three honest men shall bee able to beate sixe theeues' (1) also imply that there are actually *three* notable anti-Martinist authors. In his note on this passage Professor Bond suggests that Lyly means Nashe, Greene, and himself. Since Munday should be included in this group of three, either Nashe or Greene must be eliminated. It is certainly safer to reject Greene and to keep Nashe in this list, a circumstance which seems to point to Marforius being Nashe (2).

The tone of Richard's pamphlet is radically different from that of Gabriel's essay. Gabriel's case is seriously, at times even pompously and ponderously, argued, whereas Richard's is facetiously set forth. Like the literary free-lances Munday and Lyly, Richard Harvey is little concerned with the scriptural aspects of the Marprelate controversy, and the significance of his work lies entirely in its topical import. Immediately after the dedication Richard Harvey enters upon his task of reconciliation. Though his attitude towards Martin cannot be said to be in any way favourable, it is nevertheless clear that he wants to spare the famous controversialist. What strikes us most about his conciliatory policy is that he not only advises Martin's adversaries to refrain from any further attacks, but recognizes that his intervention will not at all be appreciated. He even goes so far as to express his fears that his intervention will discredit him. From *Plaine Percevall* we often get the impression that its author would gladly experience what the result of his being

---

(1) LYLY, *Works*, III, 406-7.
(2) Note that A. FEUILLERAT, *John Lyly* (Cambridge, 1910), p. 546, believes that GABRIEL HARVEY has NASHE in mind in one passage in the *Aduertisement* (*Works*, II, 213; *Pierces Sup.*, sig. R₄ vº).

crushed between the two contending parties would be; and he also recognizes that railing of any sort is to extremely little purpose. The uselessness of the strife is well brought out in the following suggestive passage:

Martin is the man and the marke you shoot your forked arrowes at: if you strike his face, you can raise no skin, for his forhead is brasse: nor fetch vp hisblood, bicause he is giuen to blush no more then my black dog at home: welfare a faire face vpon an ill paire of shoulders yet: if you pearce his hart, you can doo him little harme, for he is liude like a Cat: strike his toong, the biternes of the same, will trace out the Author of the wound, like the fish *Torpedo*, which being towchd, sends her venime alongst line and angle rod, till it cease on the finger, and so mar a fisher for euer. Fie, fie, will you vpon a spleen, run vpon a Christen body, with full cry and open mouth? Though indeed I cannot blame you, sith his proceedings were so vnchristianlike, if you tooke him for a Monster, or a Maddog: and so went about to worme him: but I am afraide such a carelesse curre, is cureles: wormeseede and reasons will doo him no good: and for other remedies that might come by insicion, his worm-eaten Conscience refuseth, (as *Dionysius* did the hands of his Barbar, for feare lest mistaking his beard, he would haue cut his throat) and there-fore keeps him out of your Clutches. Yt were good to keepe such a Cur in awe, but alas hurt him not, for a dogs mouth is medicineable, (they say:) *Verum est*, if he bite not where he should licke, I am answered (1).

Martin Marprelate is likened to the fish torpedo, the electric eel, which was believed to have a benumbing force, or, to put it in Harvey's words, 'to mar a fisher for euer.' Certainly Martin 'mars' more than he mends, and yet Harvey feels compelled to insert a few remarks in extenuation. The imagery he uses is partly in keeping with that employed by Lyly in the initial pages of *Pappe with an Hatchet*. Lyly, it will be recalled, speaks of angling for Martin 'with a silken flye, to see whether *Martins* will nibble; and if I see that, why then I haue wormes for the nonce, and will giue them line enough like a trowte, till they swallow both hooke and line, and then *Martin* beware your gilles, for Ile make you dance at the poles end.' Richard Harvey's warning is addressed to the anti-Martinist writers and runs that the capture of Martin will 'mar' the fisherman, whereas in Lyly's view it is Martin himself upon whom injury will be inflicted. Leave off attacking Martin, Richard Harvey says in effect, for his fury will not abate and may well wreck the fiercest opponent. By treating the anti-Martinist writers in this

---

(1) R. HARVEY, *Plaine Percevall* (London, (?) 1590). sig. B₁ vᵒ.

off-handed way Richard could not but hurt their susceptibilities; so that, instead of making for peace, *Plaine Percevall* must have intensified the strife to a considerable extent.

Other points of contact between the pamphlets of Lyly and Harvey likewise suggest that authors did not write independently of one another. There is in *Plaine Percevall* the same tendency to make allusions to Martin's anonymity; a striking example is that where Harvey, again borrowing his imagery from the sphere of the art of fishing, writes: 'Go to *Martin*, go to: I know a man is a man, though he haue but a hose on his head (& thou hast a close house on thine) but the greatest quarrellers meet often with their ouer-match' (1). By 'hose' the author presumably means the bag at the lower end of a trawl-net or other fishing-net (see *Oxf. Engl. Dict.*), and it would therefore seem as if the expression 'to have a hose on one's head' links up with Lyly's idea that there was a net spread for Martin's neck. It is noticeable that several other expressions concerning Martin's anonymity are scattered over the few pages of *Plaine Percevall*.

We do not know why both Gabriel and Richard Harvey wished to assume an independent attitude in the Marprelate controversy, nor is it clear why they endeavoured to reconcile Martin with his adversaries. Gabriel, to paraphrase Lyly's words, was a notable coach champion for Martin to draw divinity from the colleges to shoemaker's hall; in Lyly's view Gabriel was no doubt one eminently suited to 'patch' matters up. But one thing is certain: the conciliatory attempts of the two brothers proved utterly ineffectual. On the one hand the publication of Gabriel's *Aduertisement* was for some reason postponed; it may, of course, have circulated in manuscript, but even then there is little evidence to show that anything was known of its existence prior to 1593. Richard's pamphlet, on the other hand, could hardly assist in mitigating controversial ardour: its tone was anything but serious, while its remarks on Lyly, Munday, and Marforius, were far too slighting for them to be really pacificatory. Moreover, it became soon apparent that Richard did not feel inclined to fight shy of his enemies, for in the prefatory letter to his *Lamb of God* he openly attacked another writer, namely Nashe.

No sooner was *Plaine Percevall* published than Nashe came

(1) R. Harvey, *Plaine Percevall*, sig. A₃ r⁰.

along with his *Almond for a Parrat*. To have got this bulky pamphlet
ready for publication so soon after *Plaine Percevall* Nashe must
have been working in feverish haste, for it appeared in the early
months of 1590. *An Almond* was in many respects a timely publication,
for it gathered up and developed many of the suggestions contained
in the controversial tracts hitherto discussed. In the first place,
we find Nashe boasting on the *Almond* title-page that he is
'indiscreet,' informing his readers by his motto *rimarum sum plenus*,
a widely known phrase from Terence (1), that they will find
Martin's identity disclosed in the body of his pamphlet. This indiscretion is so clearly anticipated by the hints thrown out by Lyly
and Richard Harvey that no Elizabethan, following the pamphlet-war
of the time, could be left untouched by Nashe's declaration. To
learn who Martin was contemporary readers must have turned over
the leaves of the *Almond* with ever growing curiosity, especially
since they now watched a professional writer forestall the High
Commission's attempts to get behind the Marprelate secret. Nashe
was the first author to write with the avowed intention of disclosing
that Martin was none other than the Welshman John Penry.

The *Almond* is also remarkable in other respects. I have
already pointed out that it contains an allusion to John Wolfe, at
whose printing-house is said to reside an M. A. who is presumably
Gabriel Harvey. It is therefore no wonder that the *Almond* also
contains other material connected with the Harveys, the only wonder
is that it should be there without having ever attracted the attention
of Elizabethan scholars. Several passages in the *Almond* give
evidence that Nashe made his work serve more than one purpose.
On the face of it his tract leaves the impression of being exclusively
concerned to attack Martin, but a careful reading soon reveals that
it is Nashe's evident intention to drag in passages referring to
the notorious brothers. Even so much so that the more one studies
the *Almond* the more one becomes aware that its author was not
primarily aiming at Martin. It is of course impossible, within the
compass of the present study, to devote a detailed analysis to the
whole text of this remarkable tract. But when due allowance is made
for the conditions amid which Nashe wrote his *Almond*, it will be

---

(1) R. B. McKerrow, ed. *Nashe*, V, 60, points out that W. Pierce, *Historical
Introduction*, p. 238, seems to misunderstand *rimarum sum plenus* as 'I am full of rimes';
McKerrow's comment runs : 'The phrase was so well known that I doubt whether it
would have occurred to anybody at the date so to misunderstand or mistranslate it.'

recognized that the following two or three extracts prove convincingly that the idea of the Harvey brothers' conciliatory policy often engrossed Nashe's attention. Here is a first passage, which, though inordinately long, requires full quotation.

Authority best knows how to diet these bedlamites, altough *Segnior Penry* in his last waste paper hath subscribed our magistrats infants. Repent, repent, thou runnagate lozill, and play not the Seminary any longer in corners, least thy chiefest benefactors forsake thee, and recouer the pouerty of their fines by bringing the pursiuants to thy forme. I heare some vnderhande whisperers and greeneheaded nouices exclaime against our Bishops for not granting thee disputation. Alas, alas, brother *Martin*, it may not be: for thou art known to be such a stale hackster with thy welch hooke, that no honest man wil debase himselfe in buckling with such a braggar. But suppose we should send some Crepundio forth our schools to beat thee about the eares with *ergo*. Where should this *sillogistica concertatio* be solemnized? what, in our Vniuersity schooles at Oxford, or in *puluere Philosophico* at Cambridge? No, they were erected in time of Popery, and must be new built againe before they can giue any accesse to his arguments. Truly I am afraide ẙ this Generall counsaile must be holden at Geneua, when al is done, for I know no place in England holy inough for their turne, except it be some barne or out-house about Bury, or some odde blind cottage in the hart of Warwicke shire; and thither, peraduenture, these good honest opponents would repaire without grudging: Prouided alwaies that they haue ther horse-hire and other charges allowed them out of the poor mans box, or els it is no bargain. All this fadges wel yet, if we had once determined who shold be father of the act. Why, what a question is that, when we haue so many persecuted elders abroad. The blinde, the halt, or the lame, or any serues the turn with them, so he hath not on a cloak with sleues, or a cap of the vniuersity cut. Imagin that place to be furnished; where shall we finde moderators, that may deale indifferently twixt both parts (1).

We are informed that 'whisperers and greeneheaded nouices' (2) reprove the bishops for their unwillingness to enter into a public disputation with Martin. As no honest man will so debase himself, some empty talker or 'crepundio' should be entrusted with the task of beating Martin about the ears with 'ergo' (3). Nashe first suggests Oxford or Cambridge, and then Geneva, as the place where this

---

(1) NASHE, *Works*, III, 369-370.
(2) Compare R. HARVEY, *Plaine Percevall*, sig. C₁ r⁰ : 'Backe with that leg *Perceuall*: Nouice as thou art, dost thou thinke that we are some, all mad?'
(3) D. J. McGINN, *PMLA*, LIX (1944), 974, points out that the *OED* gives only one example of 'crepundio' in a passage from NASHE'S preface to GREENE'S *Menaphon*, and that 'ergo' and 'puluere philosophico' are expressions used by NASHE to attack GABRIEL HARVEY.

disputation or 'Generall counsaile' should be held. Then he argues that 'good honest opponents' prefer some barn or out-house about Bury to the university schools and concludes his argument with the question whether 'moderators, that may deale indifferently (1) twixt both parts' will be found.

When the events immediately preceding the publication of the *Almond* are borne in mind, this question almost certainly bears on the existence of a middle party in the Marprelate controversy, a middle party made up, as we know, of the Harvey brothers. A few verbal echoes, pointed out in the footnotes below, similarly indicate Nashe's awareness of the existence of Richard Harvey's recent pamphlet. It is even more remarkable that the suggestions Nashe is advancing in the above extract seem to run parallel to those recently put forward by Gabriel Harvey. The whole train of Nashe's thought, touching as it does on a 'Generall counsaile' or a public disputation, was no doubt inspired by certain ideas in Gabriel's treatment of the Marprelate controversy. The latter's *Aduertisement* was an essay in which the authorities were advised to imitate the example of the Primitive Church in settling religious disputes. In Gabriel's view the general council of Nicaea provided a notable instance of how religious controversies were peaceably settled by mediators or 'moderators,' and this is why Harvey suggested in his *Aduertisement* that the authorities should imitate this example and that they should likewise summon a general council. The figure of Eusebius of Caesarea, the leader of the middle party at Nicaea, greatly attracted Harvey, seemingly because he saw his own ideal of conciliating opponents exemplified in the attitude and the achievement of Eusebius. This distinctive feature of the *Aduertisement* may be held responsible, I believe, for such passages in the *Almond* as deal, either briefly or at greater length, with aspects of early church history. The passage, for example, in which Nashe speaks of 'the Nycen Creede, Athanasius Creede, and the Apostles Creede' (2) seems to be indirectly traceable to Gabriel Harvey's having drawn an elaborate parallel between the Marprelate and the Arian controversy. It is true that the *Aduertisement* was not published until 1593 and could not therefore have reached Nashe in print in 1590, but it is highly probable that public attention was directed to the activity

---

(1) Compare R. HARVEY, *Plaine Percevall*, sig. B₃ rᵒ : 'If I vse indifferency, call me not *Iohn Indifferent* now, for my good will . . .'

(2) NASHE, *Works*, III, 372.

of both Gabriel and Richard Harvey by the latter's *Plaine Percevall*, a tract which contains several characteristic 'brother' references ('Co-brother,' 'the fall of a brother,' 'the blemish of a brother'), apparently all of them relating to Gabriel.

When the *Almond* is read through from end to end the impression is further strengthened that Nashe often tended to deviate from what was supposedly his main purpose. The following more or less veiled allusion to the 'intermediary' position occupied by one of the parties involved seems to be relevant in this connexion:

All England must bee vp together by the eares, before his penne rest in peace, nor shall his rebellious mutinies, which he shrouds vnder the age of *Martinisme*, haue any *intermedium*, till religious prosperity and our Christian libertye, mis-termed of him by the last yeare of Lambethisme, doe perishe from amongst vs and depart to our enemies (1).

Like Lyly in *Pappe with an Hatchet*, Nashe in his *Almond* also uses imagery drawn from the shoemaker's trade and the question arises if it refers to the Harveys, as it did in Lyly's tract.

But how euer his crazed cause goes on crutches, that was earst so brauely encountered by *Pasquin* and *Marphoreus*, and not many moneths since most wittily scofte at by the extemporall endeuour of the pleasant author of Pap with a hatchet; yet is not the good old creeple vtterly discouraged, or driuen cleane from his dounghill, but he meanes to make the persecuted Coblers once more merrie (2).

One of Richard Harvey's stylistic tricks in *Plaine Percevall* is to enumerate all the 'professional' or 'literary' anti-Martinist writers by their coined names, a procedure not usually resorted to by Nashe, except in the above quotation. Martin Marprelate is a cripple, attacked in turn by Munday, Marforius, and Lyly; even so the controversy has not subsided and makes the 'cobblers' once more merry. It is often hazardous to attribute deliberate motives to seemingly significant features of Nashe's text, but on the assumption that these cobblers were participants in the controversy with Martin, one may confidently regard the Harvey brothers as fitting candidates for this profession. Furthermore, those who take the trouble to read the initial page of the *Almond* with great care will note, I believe, that Nashe hints clearly that Martin has been satisfactorily disposed of:

(1) NASHE, *Works*, III, 356.
(2) NASHE, *Works*, III, 347.

his funeral service has been celebrated and he is even likened to a carrion visited by crows which have to be scared away by 'that long tongd doctresse, Dame *Law.*' who now employs her 'Parrats tong in stead of a winde-clapper' (1).

In the light of the data hitherto presented, Richard Harvey's epistle 'To the fauourable or indifferent Reader' from the *Lamb of God* now takes on fresh significance. The gist of the three initial paragraphs of this epistle is that Martin has got what he deserved: scurrility was answered with scurrility and invective was rampant, but the author of the *Lamb of God* holds such procedure in abhorrence. In the fourth paragraph Richard takes up the train of thought developed by his brother Gabriel: 'the primitiue Church did not flourish by iybing or railing: we know or should knowe the Ecclesiasticall hystories, before we vndertake the reformation of Ecclesiasticall causes and persons.' What Richard says a few lines further is exceptionally revealing:

It were hard with Diuines, if we knewe no more of the Scriptures, the Ecclesiasticall Hystories, and the generall Councels, besides our auncient Doctors, learned Schoolemen, and later Writers, then this *Pseudomartin* doth; yet, forsooth, must we needes be schooled and re-formed by his ruffianly tearmes: *Medice cura teipsum: Gascoigne* may see himselfe in his owne Steele Glasse: *Martin* is no Angell, no Saint, no mortifyed man (2).

There can be little doubt that the author is here thinking of Eusebius of Caesarea's *Ecclesiastical History,* the general council of Nicaea, and the settlement of religious disputes in the Primitive Church, as Gabriel Harvey had done in his *Aduertisement;* Richard, it is true, avoids committing himself to any specific allusion. In a later passage in Richard's epistle to the *Lamb of God* Nashe is explicitly described as a 'iolly man . . . playing the douty *Martin* in his kinde' and this is why the term 'Pseudomartin' seems to cover Nashe as well. That 'Pseudomartin' was not a term merely inadvertently used appears from a passage in the sixth paragraph:

If *Martin* were right *Martin* indeede, I should fynde him by his singular example of vpright and entire conuersation, though not discerne

---

(1) NASHE, *Works*, III, 344. 'The ecclesiastical cobler' who breaks up 'his brotherly loue-meeting abruptly,' mentioned on the same page, again suggests one of the HARVEY brothers.

(2) The epistle is reprinted in full in McKERROW's *Nashe*, V, 176-183. The quotation above is on page 178.

him by his counterfaite and fantasticall stile. Nowe I must bee fayne to descry him otherwise, and I beleeue, I can goe as neere the left-handed Ape, either Senior, or Iunior, as any one in England, that cannot assuredly saye, This is he. A black Sheepe is a perilous beast: and we little men are shrewde fellowes: *Habet & musca splenem:* courage is a iolly matter; and a little pragmaticall conceite is ready to mount aloft: I am a blinde Asse, and you are a blinde Asse, but who so bould as blind bayard? (1)

For purposes of comparison it is now necessary to quote in full the paragraph from Richard's epistle in which Nashe is explicitly named:

I was loth to enter this discourse, but vppon request where I might be commaunded: I prouoke not any but *Martin* who prouoketh all men: I was desired to giue like iudgement of certaine other, but it becummeth me not to play that part in Diuinitie, that one *Thomas Nash* hath lately done in humanitie, who taketh vppon him in ciuill learning, as *Martin* doth in religion, peremptorily censuring his betters at pleasure, Poets, Orators, Polihistors, Layers, and whome not? and making as much and as little of euery man as himselfe listeth. Many a man talketh of *Robin Hood*, that neuer shot in his bowe; and that is the rash presumption of this age, that euery man of whatsoeuer qualitie and perfection, is with euery man of whatsoeuer mediocrity, but as euery man pleaseth in the aboundance of his owne swelling sense. Iwis this *Thomas Nash*, one whome I neuer heard of before (for I cannot imagin him to be *Thomas Nash* our Butler of *Pembrooke Hall*, albeit peraduenture not much better learned) sheweth himselfe none of the meetest men, to censure Sir *Thomas Moore*, Sir *John Cheeke*, Doctor *Watson*, Doctor *Haddon*, Maister *Ascham*, Doctor *Car*, my brother Doctor *Haruey*, and such like; yet the iolly man will needes be playing the douty *Martin* in his kinde, and limit euery mans commendation according to his fancy, profound no doubt and exceeding learned, as the world nowe goeth in such worthy workes (2).

In the last quotation but one Richard Harvey says that he should descry the 'right' or true Martin by 'his example of vpright and entire conuersation,' were it not that he is now compelled to descry him otherwise, for, we are told in effect, the identity of Martin the Ape, Martin Senior as well as Martin Junior, has already been disclosed; it is apparently implied that Martin's identity has got widely known. We already know that the only author who is to be held responsible for accomplishing this disclosure is Nashe. Harvey then maintains that, had there been need, he too would have had enough daring to say 'This is he,' but he now realizes that all

---

(1) See ed. *Nashe,* V, 179.
(2) See ed. *Nashe,* V, 179-180.

need for calling Martin by his real name has passed away. As things stand, Harvey has no alternative but to descry 'Pseudomartin,' and not the 'right' one it would seem, as a black sheep and a Fly whose courage is a 'iolly matter.' If it is remembered that Nashe probably represented himself as a Fly in his allegorical tale in *Pierce Penilesse* and that Gabriel Harvey wrote a sonnet in his *Foure Letters* about a jolly and a doughty Fly (1), there is little doubt that the expression 'Habet & musca splenem' refers to Nashe as a Fly venting its spite or 'spleen.' Note that the paragraph in which Richard Harvey attacks Nashe explicitly winds up with the phrase 'yet the iolly man will needes be playing the douty *Martin* in his kinde,' the very terms of which are particularly close to those used by both Gabriel and Richard Harvey, and there is ample justification for regarding Richard as the real inventor of the Fly as a descriptive name for Nashe. Furthermore, Richard's defence of 'euery man of whatsoeuer mediocrity' against 'euery man of what-soeuer qualitie and perfection' who is but 'as euery man pleaseth in the aboundance of his owne swelling sense' is an adherence to the cause of 'mediocrity' which can only be accounted for by Richard's 'medi-ating' policy. To confirm this interpretation there is an interesting statement in the dedicatory epistle to the Earl of Essex occurring in *Philadelphus*.

Yet I take the defence of mediocritie for a matter of some weight, both in this historie of *Brute*, which is made litigious, and in any other position of much lesse importance, euen of haire it selfe; insomuch as mediocritie cannot be disalowed (2).

To judge from its contents generally, the epistle from the *Lamb of God* may be said to contain clear indications that Richard Harvey knew perfectly well what kind of message Nashe's *Almond for a Parrat* kept in reserve for its readers. There can be little doubt that this epistle was not written until Nashe's tract had been published, an inference confirmed by the fact that it did not form part of Harvey's original work.

A chronological conspectus of the chief works discussed in the foregoing pages may be of service here and conveniently summarize the chief points made in the course of the argument.

---

(1) See p. 167 of this study.
(2) R. HARVEY, *Philadelphus*, sig. A₂ r⁰.

Author	Title of work	Date	Significant Allusions
Munday	*Return of Pasq.*	Oct. 20, '89	To Marforius
Marforius	*Month's Mind*	Oct.-Nov. '89	
Lyly	*Pap*	Oct.-Nov. '89	The Harveys attacked, hints as to Martin's anonymity
G. Harvey	*Aduertisement*	Nov. 5, '89	Lyly gets a reply
R. Harvey	*Plain Perceval*	Nov.-Dec. '89 early 1590	The anti-Martinists provoked; was Nashe one of them? was Nashe Marforius?
R. Harvey	*Lamb of God*	Ent. S. R. on Oct. 23, '89 publ. early 1590	Aretino, a porter of Pluto's divinity, the grandsire of all false and martinish courtiership, probably an allusion to Nashe
Nashe	*Almond*	Feb.-March 1590	Mediators and moderators slighted; John Wolfe provoked and Cerberus' cause sponsored; Nashe indiscreet
R. Harvey	*Epistle to Lamb of God*	March '90	Nashe a Pseudomartin and a Fly; mediocrity defended
Nashe	*Prognostication*	Early '91	Ridicule of R. Harvey's serious prognostications
Florio	*Second Fruits*	April '91	The dog enjoined to attack the 'wolf'; prognostications referred to

The present conspectus makes no mention of two of Nashe's works belonging to a period slightly earlier than, or more or less contemporary with, Richard Harvey's *Plaine Percevall*, namely the preface to Greene's *Menaphon* and the *Anatomie of Absurditie*. In both works Nashe voices his scorn for Ramus, and for 'mediocrity' as well, while in the dedication of the *Anatomie* he declares his intention to appear in satirical disguises. This dedication was apparently written in August, 1589, at the very time when Nashe is believed to have taken part in the Marprelate controversy for the first time. Nashe's rejection of Ramist logic, a quite natural thing for an old student of St. John's College, Cambridge, could not fail to displease the Harveys, and it is noticeable in this connexion that

Plaine Percevall contained a characteristic statement concerning the controversy between Ramus and his Aristotelean opponents, a statement in which 'yoong maisters' and 'children' were taken to task for their inability to debate matters of logic (1).

Finally it remains to describe Greene's share in contemporary controversies, which is by no means an easy matter. As far as the Harveys are concerned Professor Pruvost (2) has observed that Greene's *Planetomachia* (1585) is very likely to have caused their anger. The *Planetomachia* may be regarded as Greene's contribution to the astrological disputes in which Richard Harvey was at loggerheads with the mathematician Thomas Heth, who, himself an astrologer, had dared to question the mathematical conclusions of Richard's *Astrological Discourse*. The *Planetomachia*, making fun of astronomy, probably irritated Gabriel Harvey, a man who resented any encroachment on what he considered the province of those who took such things seriously. Another cause for divergence of opinion was, of course, the Marprelate controversy, which was obviously an occasion for writers to prove their mettle. The extent of Greene's share in it is difficult to determine, for, so far, none of the genuine anti-Martinist tracts has been attributed to him by the students of the controversy, even though Nashe described his friend as the chief agent for the company (3).

Greene's *Spanish Masquerado*, entered in the Stationers' Register on February 1, 1589, is perhaps the only work of his which may be said, through its date and its topic, to belong to the period of anti-Martinist pamphleteering. On the face of it this work is merely another set of tales to celebrate the defeat of the Armada. In it Greene also takes occasion to denounce the Catholics and, to

---

(1) R. HARVEY, *Plaine Percevall*, sig. D₂ vº : 'I haue seene them, which haue seene such hurly burlies about a couple, (that were no Fathers of the Church neither) *Aristotle* and *Ramus*, or els aske the Vniuersities, such a quoile with *pro* and *con*, such vrging of *Ergoes*, til they haue gone from Art togither by the eares, & made their conclusions end with Clunchfist, right like the old description of Logicke. My yoong maisters could not be content to whet their wits with such a contention: but fel to whetting their Tuskes at one another : like those children which sitting in the Chimney corner, some at one side, some at another, with the fire in the middle; fell to it with firebrands, when they should haue but warmde themselues and away.'

(2) R. PRUVOST, *Greene et ses romans*, pp. 216-8.

(3) NASHE in his *Strange Newes* (*Works*, I, 271) says : 'Hence *Greene*, beeing chiefe agent for the companie.' The meaning of 'companie' is still in dispute. I think that R. PRUVOST, *Greene et ses romans*, p. 417, is right in his belief that 'companie' refers to an actors' company.

paraphrase his own words in his short epistle 'To the Gentlemen Readers,' adventures to discover his conscience in religion. The *Spanish Masquerado* ends with an address to the reader which points the moral: Greene is convinced that his narrative has shown clearly that God has ordained that the Queen be his Minister on earth in order to protect the religion of her subjects. This admonishing conclusion may in its day have been regarded as a timely warning to the Martinists to stop their activity.

When the Marprelate controversy was a thing of the past, however, Greene set about attacking the Harveys in *A Quip for an upstart Courtier*, a pamphlet whose satirical remarks finally succeeded in overcoming Gabriel Harvey's reluctance to take up the gauntlet himself. The *Quip* was entered in the Stationers' Register on July 20, 1592, and printed and published by John Wolfe. It was dedicated to Thomas Burnaby. There were apparently two editions: one, an edition represented by the Bodleian Library copy (1) in which an attack on the Harveys occurred, an attack subsequently removed; and the other, an edition from which a few other offensive references were withdrawn, represented by the copy in the British Museum.

Greene borrowed the framework for his narrative from a didactic poem by F. T. entitled the *Debate between Pride and Lowliness*, conjecturally assigned to 1570 and attributed to Francis Thynne by the *Short-Title Catalogue*. Edwin H. Miller (2) has determined the extent of Greene's indebtedness to F. T. and pointed out that the *Quip* owes much to a great many other sources as well: Thomas Harman's *A Caveat for Cummon Cursetors* (1560- ?), Lodge's *An Alarum against Usurers* (1584), and especially Philip Stubbes' *The Anatomy of Abuses* (1583); furthermore, Greene also borrows extensively from his own writings.

Greene's purpose in the *Quip* was to present a dispute between a courtier (velvet breeches), symbolic of the upstart's pride, and a tradesman (cloth breeches), representative of ancient gentility and true English citizenship. The dispute as to who merits the greater respect will be settled by a selected jury. On the whole the *Quip* has been well described by E. H. Miller as an 'elaborate commentary

---

(1) My references will be to the Bodleian Library copy.
(2) E. H. MILLER, "The Sources of Robert Greene's 'A Quip for an Upstart Courtier' (1592)," *NQ*, 198 (1953), 148-152 and 187-191. See also E. H. MILLER, "Deletions in Robert Greene's *A Quip for an Upstart Courtier* (1592)," *HLQ*, XV (1952), 277-282.

on practically all trades and professions of the Elizabethan era.'

At the beginning Greene gives an allegorical turn to his story. The author imagines he is in a valley strewed with all kinds of flowers, which wayfarers gather in accordance with their different tastes. When these people disappear the narrator notices an 'vncouth headlesse thing come pacing downe the hil' which proves to be Velvet Breeches. Then Cloth Breeches arrives 'more soberlye marching, and with a softer pace,' and the author soon recognizes that 'their meeting would grow to some dangerous conflict.' He intervenes to offer his services in assembling a jury who will pass final judgment. People representing all kinds of classes and occupations approach and it is from these that a jury is selected. Most of these tradesmen, however, are challenged either by Cloth Breeches or by Velvet Breeches; but in the end they agree to empanel twenty-four people of different callings; the case is presented and, of course, determined in favour of Cloth Breeches. So far for the bare story. Among the members of the jury, however, there is a ropemaker and this gives Greene an opportunity of attacking the Harveys.

And whether are you a going qd. I? Marry sir qd he, first to absolue your question, I dwel in Saffron Waldon, and am going to Cambridge to three sons that I keep there at schoole, such apt children sir as few women haue groned for, and yet they haue ill lucke. The one sir is a Deuine to comfort my soule, & he indeed though he be a vaine glorious asse, as diuers youths of his age bee, is well giuen to the shew of the world, and writte a late the lambe of God, and yet his parishioners say he is the limb of the deuill, and kisseth their wiues with holy kisses, but they had rather he should keep his lips for madge his mare. The second sir is a physitian or a foole, but indeed a physitian, & had proued a proper man if he had not spoiled himself with his Astrological discourse of the terrible coniunction of Saturne and Iupiter. For the eldest he is a Ciuilian, a wondrous witted fellow, sir reuerence sir, he is a Doctor, and as Tubalcain was the first inuentor of Musick, so he Gods benison light vpon him, was the first that inuented Englishe Hexamiter: but see how in these daies learning is little esteemed, for that and other familiar letters and proper treatises he was orderly clapt in the Fleet, but sir a Hawk and a Kite may bring forth a coystrell, and honest parents may haue bad children (1).

_____

(1) This extract is taken from an article by G. W. COLE, who discovered and printed GREENE's attack on the HARVEYS in "Bibliography—A Forecast," *Papers of the Bibliographical Society of America*, XIV (1920) (off-print in the British Museum). The Bodleian Library copy of the *Quip* contains two cancel leaves, E_8 and E_4, replacing the original ones, in which the attack occurred; see R. B. McKERROW, ed. *Nashe*, V, 77.

Greene's allusions to each of the Harveys, Richard and Gabriel, need to be discussed separately. Richard and his *Lamb of God* are first referred to, after which Richard is accused of taking liberties with his parishioners' wives, who are kissed with holy kisses. On the assumption that the rumour went that Richard was a lusty, worldly and somewhat indecent vicar, it is interesting to note that the only plays in which Shakespeare mentions 'parishioners' are the very plays containing echoes connected with the Marprelate controversy: *Love's Labour's Lost* (V, ii, 76) and *As You Like It* (III, ii, 164). We have already indicated in what respect the latter comedy links up with Greene's *Orlando Furioso*, a play belonging to 1592. Professor Dover Wilson and Sir Arthur Quiller-Couch (1) have argued that several other pieces of internal evidence 'suggest a date round about 1593 for Shakespeare's first handling' of *As You Like It*. One of these is the appearance of Sir Oliver Martext, a Puritan preacher whose name could possess great topical interest only at the time when the name of Martin was on the lips of everybody. It would seem that this feature of the play may explain Shakespeare's 'parishioners' as well.

But Greene's denigration of Richard Harvey acquires increased significance when it is noted that Nashe, attacking Richard in *Strange Newes*, levels the same reproaches at Richard as Greene does.

It was not for nothing, brother Richard, that *Greene* told you you kist your Parishioners wiues with holy kisses, for you that wil talk *of opening the senses by carnal mixture* (the very act of lecherie) in a Theological Treatise, and in the Pulpit, I am afraide, in a priuater place you will practise as much as you speake (2).

In *Love's Labour's Lost*, IV, ii, 76, it is noteworthy that Shakespeare hints at a similar indecency when he has Holofernes say that parishioners' daughters 'profite very greatly vnder' Nathaniel the curate. The dramatist was apparently destined to remember Greene's phrase in *As You Like It* as well (3). Compare III, iv, 12:

> *Ros.* And his kissing is as ful of sanctitie,
> As the touch of holy bread.

---

(1) J. Dover Wilson and A. Quiller-Couch, ed. *As You Like It*, pp. 103-8. The argument is Dover Wilson's.
(2) Nashe, *Works*, I, 273.
(3) Compare Chapman, *An Humorous Day's Mirth* (a comedy performed in 1597), sc. viii, 281 : 'Why, you swore but by a kiss, and kisses are no holy things, you know that'; see Chapman, *The Plays and Poems*, ed. T. M. Parrott (London, 1910-14), II, 80.

It need not, of course, be assumed that Shakespeare is here thinking of Richard Harvey, but the references discussed do seem to point back to the early stages of the Harvey-Nashe controversy. Nor are these clues the only ones in the play suggesting some connexion with the writings of Harvey and Nashe, and a few more will later be dealt with. But let us return to Greene's attack on the Harveys itself.

The next member of the Harvey family to be subjected to Greene's ridicule is John Harvey, the youngest of the three brothers, who was in 1587 licensed by the University of Cambridge to practise physic. This is why Greene refers to John Harvey's medical profession. After that he briefly alludes to the fact that John Harvey also wrote a supplement to his brother's *Astrological Discourse*. John Harvey died young, in July, 1592, and the paucity of his works as well as his early death make it quite understandable that his share in contemporary disputes is negligible.

Greene's charge against Gabriel Harvey, however, stands out for its bearing on other matters as the most important part of the whole attack. Harvey's poetic raptures are ridiculed by comparing him to Tubal-cain who, Greene says, was 'the first inuentor of Musick.' Tubal-cain was the brother of Jabal and Jubal, sons of Lamech (see *Genesis*, IV, 21-22); Tubal-cain was the originator of several industries and arts, chiefly of the production of vessels and instruments. *Genesis*, IV, 21-22, however, makes no mention of Tubal-cain's inventing music; in fact he is only mentioned in the Bible as an 'instructor of every artificer in brass and iron,' whereas it is his brother Jubal who is called 'the father of all such as handle the harp and the organ.' Whatever the origin of Greene's mistake may have been (1), both Harvey and Nashe seem to have felt the power of this comparison (2), and its special point was no doubt that Harvey was so arrogant as to regard himself as the most musical of poets. The mythological significance of this part of Greene's allusion remains to be studied in the next chapter.

A few other features of Greene's *Quip* may also have caused offence to the Harveys. For example, by Greene's satirical remarks

---

(1) Note, however, that the *Quip* also contains the following comparison (sig. C$_4$ v^0) : 'But leauing this by-talke, methought I heard you say *Signior* veluetbreeche, that you were the father of mechanical Artes and handiecrafts were found out to foster your brauery.'

(2) Compare HARVEY. *Foure Letters*. p. 32. and NASHE. *Works*. I. 298.

on Velvet Breeches' running to the apothecary's shop on the slightest pretext we are reminded of Harvey's interest in pharmacology, as this was evidenced by a confrontation of the pamphlet by I. W. and Harvey's own writings (1). Furthermore, the only passage in the *Quip* containing clear references to Martin and a few other religious writers is a speech put into the mouth of a worldly and licentious vicar, who spends his living with his parishioners (2). This speech may have reminded Elizabethan readers of Richard Harvey.

The foregoing account has shed light on how the Harvey-Nashe polemic originated in the controversial atmosphere created by the appearance of Martin and his opponents. All the participants involved, even the small party of mediators, were loath to give up their anonymity. It is difficult to penetrate to the hidden springs of human action, and to determine precisely why only the 'literary' men participating in the Marprelate controversy endeavoured to preserve their anonymity, while, in general, the non-professional writers did not. The textual links between the tracts in their chronological sequence, as well as other pieces of evidence, indicate, however, that those who wrote them were perfectly aware of one another's identity. But evidence is not lacking that Martin's ability to conceal his intrigued the anti-Martinists considerably. It was not until Nashe had disclosed who Martin was that Richard Harvey, in his *Lamb of God* and its prefatory epistle, came forward with the claim that a 'Pseudomartin,' a porter of Pluto's divinity, and a grandsire of 'false' and martinish courtiership, had stepped into the shoes of Martin. *Philadelphus*, as we shall soon see, was the work in which Richard Harvey criticized 'Pseudomartin' further on his own account.

(1) GREENE, *Quip*, sig. D$_4$.
(2) GREENE, *Quip*, sig. G$_4$ v^o.

CHAPTER VIII

THE USES AND IMPLICATIONS OF MYTHOLOGY

CERBERUS

Before examining more closely how mythology influenced literary composition in the period with which we are concerned, it may not be amiss to survey a few salient points bearing on Cerberus, that 'allegorical' name for Nashe that had passed into currency in the years 1590-92. Nashe professed his allegiance to Cerberus in his *Almond for a Parrat* (published in February-March, 1590). Cerberus's barking, he maintained, exercised such a powerful fascination over him that he would gladly perish 'in the delight of [his] liuing destruction.' A year later, a probable allusion to Nashe in the shape of a dog cropped up in Florio's *Second Fruits* (date of its dedicatory epistle: April 30, 1591). About the same time, Abraham Fraunce in *Phillis Funerall* (entered in the Stationers' Register on February 9, 1591, and published together with *Amyntas Pastorall* under the title *The Countesse of Pembrokes Yuychurch* in 1591), is found contrasting 'fowle Cerberus horrible helhounde' with a 'poore louing dogg, ould Light-foote.' Since the poem in which these references occur was an addition to eclogues originally issued in 1587, I have suggested that some special reason could have induced Fraunce to introduce them. Though there was no evidence to identify 'Lightfoot,' what little we know of Nashe's position in Elizabethan letters justifies my contention that Fraunce's unflattering Cerberus allusion was directed against the well-known satirist. And finally, if I am right, Fraunce twice referred to him in *The Third part of the Countesse of Pembrokes Yuychurch* (entered in the Register on October 2, 1592). On the one hand, Fraunce confirmed the generally current rumours about Nashe's alleged untrustworthiness when he gave an allegorical interpretation of the Danaids' vessel as being symbolical of the nature of a blab; and on the other, interpreting the Cerberus myth with the help of Natalis Comes' *Mythologiae* he consciously altered a few phrases in his rendering that they might properly describe the satirist's predicament.

Though Gabriel Harvey's *New Letter of Notable Contents* was explicit in stating that Nashe was a hellhound incarnate, it was a passage from Nashe's play *Summers Last Will and Testament* (probably written in September or October, 1592) that contained the most striking allusion to Cerberus in his capacity of producer of aconitum, that poison from which, so Nashe maintained, ink was made.

The foregoing outline, for all its succinctness, demonstrates clearly the very significant part played by mythological allusion in the period of Elizabethan literature we are dealing with, and it shows above all that such allusions were hardly ever inadvertently made, certain readers being keenly alive to the vivid impression any myth might produce through its implied associations. The connotative power of classic myth was to be efficiently exploited by Richard Harvey in his *Philadelphus*.

Philadelphus, or A Defence of Brutes, and the Brutans History, apparently Harvey's last book, appeared in 1593. Its imprint runs 'Imprinted at London by Iohn Wolfe. 1593.' It was entered to Wolfe on February 23, 1593 (1), consequently some six weeks after the entry of Nashe's *Strange Newes*. The book was dedicated to the Earl of Essex and in the dedication, as we know, the author was concerned to defend 'mediocrity.' To quote his own words again: 'Yet I take the defence of mediocritie for a matter of some weight, both in this historie of *Brute*, which is made litigious, and in any other position of much lesse importance, euen of haire it selfe; insomuch as mediocritie cannot be disalowed.' In connexion with Harvey's defending mediocrity 'in any other position . . ., euen of haire it selfe' it may be noted that Wolfe entered *A defence of shorte haire* in the Stationers' Register on February 3, 1593 (2). Harvey's words may or may not be related to this *Defence of shorte haire*, a work which, so far as I know, has not come down to us, and whose author is unknown.

Philadelphus purports to give an account of early English history, mainly based on Geoffrey of Monmouth's *Historia Regum Britanniae*. It is a defence of the legend of Brutus against the discredit thrown on it by Buchanan and others. Richard Harvey makes no attempt to write a connected account, so much that he often deviates from the stories told of legendary British kings by Geoffrey of Monmouth, and frequently takes occasion to exalt the moral

---

(1) ARBER, *Transcript*, II, 627.
(2) ARBER. *Transcript*. II. 626.

virtues of his beloved 'Brutans.' Some of these deviations will presently receive attention. An epistle which is inserted between two sections of *Philadelphus* requires to be discussed first. Richard inscribes it 'To his most loving brother, Master Gabriell Haruey, Doctor of Lawes' and writes:

When I saw, both how *iestingly*, and *seriously* our Historie of *Brute* was reiected of some auncient and newe bookmen, I tried their maruellous *iestes* and *reasons*, and felt them too weake to moue me. Now my Answere is on foot with their Reply, I may iustly hold mine owne, and stand on *Brutes* side against all challengers that are or will come. I saye, Puissant *Brute* is no *fabulous Prince*, but a true example, no counterfeit man, but a corporall possessor of this Iland; let them saye what they can. With this minde I haue here taken *one Essay* of our Chronicles in the best historicall Methode that I could make out of the best Historiognomers. I am sure, any Historie is easier for memorie, and readier for vse this way, then any other way, which I haue hitherto seene in other mens Collections, Tables, Directories, or any other such inuentions: yet as it is in proofe, so approue it, or reproue it; I am not wedded to myselfe, nor tyed to any sect in the world, but heartily wish euery man to take euery thing as it is, not as it is made of this and that scribler or pratler, which can tell better, howe to play the mocking Ape, then the iust controller. Almightie God defend you dayly, and amend them one day: you know my minde in all my matters, and that I would those petite Momes had better manners: the schollers head without moderation is like the merchantes purse pennilesse without all credite: I desire that euerie student may smell as the Lillies of *Salomon*, and that euerie wilde Lilly may be set in his Gardens. I saye, out Hemlocke, out Bramble, out Weedes, and let the bloud of furious *Aiax* himselfe, saith *Ouid*, be turned into a pleasant herbe. I write not this, to flatter any that should seeke after me, but to follow you, good Brother, in your *last Letters*, in whose Example I euer yet dwelt, and am like to dwell, euen till my Soule shall dwell in the Commonwealth of Heauen. I cannot bid you farewell in a better minde, and in this respect I set me rest here, I remember your counsell, and beginne my *Essaye*. 1592. the 14. of Iune (1).

Sidney Thomas (2) has recently examined the contents of this epistle and has pointed out that the phrase 'Almightie God defend you dayly, and amend them one day,' written as it was in June, 1592, almost certainly indicates that the Harvey-Nashe quarrel was very much alive in the early part of 1592. Mr. Thomas further observes

(1) R. HARVEY, *Philadelphus*, sig. C₁, pp. 13-4.
(2) SIDNEY THOMAS, "New Light on the Nashe-Harvey Quarrel," *MLN*, LXIII (1948), 481-83.

that both Richard and Gabriel Harvey were determined to persevere in a conciliatory policy, as appears from the expression 'the schollers head without moderation is like the merchantes purse pennilesse without all credite' and from the end of the Harvey epistle. He then points out that 'purse pennilesse' is obviously a reference to Nashe's *Pierce Penilesse* and that Richard had therefore seen Nashe's attack on him before *Pierce Penilesse* got printed. I may point out that 'without all credite' is probably relevant to Nashe's lack of reticence, and reminds us of an expression on the title-page of Fouleweather-Nashe's prognostication suggesting that Fouleweather would 'loose his credit for euer.'

The last item of evidence adduced by Mr. Thomas is the following passage from *Philadelphus*:

An Ape must not come among Churchmen, Serpentes must not dwell in chambers of Counsell, makebates are not in case to conuerse in the dwellings of peaceable Lords, who can abide, to haue a deformed mocker with hys distorted mouthes, a venimous hisser with his noysom breath, a rayling stageplayer with his trifling actions for his companion? (1)

Mr. Thomas argues that 'this is probably, from the nature of its language, a reference to Nashe, though it may be a curiously belated attack on the anti-Marprelate writers as a group. If we accept McKerrow's cogently reasoned argument that Nashe was with Archbishop Whitgift at Croydon during the late summer and autumn of 1592, and was then engaged in the composition of *Summers Last Will and Testament*, then the probability that this passage is directed at Nashe becomes a very strong one' (2). It is not difficult to agree with these views; and it only remains to add that other reasons have been indicated in the foregoing chapters why Nashe's comedy is connected with the Marprelate controversy.

We come now to those portions of *Philadelphus* in which the author's controversial purpose declares itself in expressions and imagery interpretable with the help of that which we know about Gabriel Harvey and Nashe. In his work Richard Harvey does not evolve an historical method of his own, except that he arranges his material in tabular form and departs from his main source in putting much stress upon the 'arts' and 'acts' of the legendary British kings, which are 'set downe in their Vertues and Vices.'

---

(1) R. HARVEY, *Philadelphus*, sig. N₃ r⁰, p. 97.
(2) S. THOMAS, *MLN*, LXIII, 483.

In book IV, chapter xx of Geoffrey of Monmouth's *Historia Regum Britanniae* is mentioned one king Bledgabred, whose skill in playing upon musical instruments was so remarkable that he was regarded as the king of jesters. Here are Geoffrey's own words: 'bledgabred. hic omnes cantares quos retro etas habuerat. & in modulis & in omnibus musicis instrumentis. ita ut deus ioculatorum diceretur' (1). Richard Harvey sees fit to expand this simple statement considerably, and says that the virtue and prudence of British kings was shown

In the art of Musicke: Bledgabrede both studied and practised musicke: hee was very famous: and I thinke, in respect of his charge and gouernment, very wonderfull. A monasticall liuer, and much more an oeconomicall hath no partes of time for such young childish studies, if he looke wel about him: and how can a king that is the keeper of all other men haue any time for such vaine insignificant voices: Yet the circular wisdome of this king had such a capacitie by some myraculous infusion from heauen, that hee was fit both for the grauest and the lightest studies, either to learne them by contemplation, or to vse and teach them by action. He saw by his instrumentes, how to tune and string his kingdome: he could preuent and pacifie tumultes with his musick: he might perhaps allay the waues of the Sea, and breake the thunders aloft with his diuine melodie: he coulde keepe himselfe from wearinesse by his musicke: he could mitigate the violence of diseases with his sweete voices: musicke was his prosody, his pronunciation, his disposition, his instrument of instrument, and the life of his life (2).

It is probable that this elaborate praise of music has something to do with the ideas developed by Gabriel Harvey, whose pretence to the title of 'Musitian, & Poet vnto [himself]' (3) was much in evidence in the third of his *Foure Letters*. It will also be remembered that in Greene's *Quip* Harvey was derided as a new Tubal-cain, 'the first inuentor of Musick,' who 'inuented Englishe hexamiter.' Significantly, the very passage in the third letter containing Gabriel's address to himself as a poet, a musician, and a minion of the Muses, reads like an anticipation of his brother's idea that music is the supreme antidote against weariness. Like his brother, Gabriel believes that 'sweet Musike requickneth the heauiest spirites of dumpish Melancholy.' Despite the commonness of such views,

---

(1) GEOFFREY OF MONMOUTH, *Historia Regum Britanniae*, ed. ACTON GRISCOM (London, 1929), p. 300.
(2) R. HARVEY, *Philadelphus*, sig. G₄ r⁰, p. 51.
(3) For a full quotation of the passage referred to above see pp. 126-7.

there can be little doubt that it was the very peculiarity of Harvey's way of putting his case which is accountable for the fact that many contemporaries were greatly interested in it. Fuller reference will be made to this interest in the next section, where the mythological aspects of his imagery will be more fully dealt with. But let us come back to *Philadelphus*.

Immediately after his statement on the beneficial influence of music Richard Harvey praises the temperance of certain kings and declares:

A contented mind is not contentious. *Porrex* the 2. behaued himselfe, either fatherly toward his youngers, or brotherly toward his equals, or gently toward all men. By this meane he was more happie with the help of the Graces, then the first *Porrex*, whome the Furies destroied. The Graces are moderate Vertues, the Furies are immoderate Vices (1).

The first Porrex (2) quarrelled with his brother Ferrex over the division of the kingdom; he killed his brother but was in his turn murdered by his mother. This explains why the first Porrex was, according to Harvey, destroyed by the Furies. The second Porrex gets no more than passing mention in Geoffrey of Monmouth's *Historia Regum* but Harvey eulogizes him for behaving 'fatherly towards his youngers, or brotherly toward his equals, or gently toward all men.' It is hard to escape the impression that this phrase was in 1592-93 a topical one, and that it was designed to point to the Harvey brothers, particularly to Gabriel, inspired by the Graces to preserve his equanimity. Later quotations will lend additional support to a topical interpretation of 'Graces' and 'Furies.'

In another part of his would-be historical treatise Richard Harvey, having referred to the fact that the music of Bledgabred 'and the actions of the rest were, belike, in no place of great account,' deplores that the studies and actions of British kings were far from effective and explains why:

Now I diuine modestly, heere were actors without recorders of their actions, patrons of learning, but no learned men: or, they were of both sortes, but their studies came to no effect, by some force: or, they were

---

(1) R. HARVEY, *Philadelphus*, sig. G$_4$ r⁰, p. 51.

(2) Compare NASHE who, in the dedicatory epistle of the *Anatomie of Absurditie*, declares: 'For my part, as I haue no portion in any mans opinion, so am I the *Prorex* of my priuate thought : . . .' (*Works*, I, 5). 'Prorex' is not uncommon in Elizabethan literature for 'viceroy,' but McKERROW, not usually nonplussed by NASHE's diction, calls the expression 'somewhat peculiar.'

very old when they came to the Crown, and could do nothing: or, the furies and helhoundes raged so extreamely, that the Muses and Graces could not bee quiet for them (1).

It hardly needs saying that this expatiation is entirely of the author's own invention and that Geoffrey does not write anything about Graces and the like. What Harvey says here is no doubt related to the previous quotation in which he writes that the Furies destroy one king, whereas the Graces distribute gentleness to the other. In the extract just quoted, however, the Furies are associated with hellhounds and they both prevent the Muses and the Graces from keeping their temper. It requires little consideration to recognize that Harvey's expressions can hardly be merely metaphorical and that they are connected with the most famous controversy of the time, that between Harvey's learned brother and Nashe. The final lines of the fifth sonnet in Gabriel's *Foure Letters* may bear out the views advanced here that, for certain circles of readers, mythological symbolism and allusion were around 1592 charged with accretive meanings.

> Would Alciats Embleme, or sum scarlet whood,
> Could teach the Pregnant sonnes of shiny Light,
> To interbrace each other with delight.
> Fine Mercury conducts a dainty band
> Of Charites, and Muses, hand in hand.

The fifth sonnet bears the significant title 'The learned should louingly affect the learned'; it voices Gabriel's concern to conciliate his opponents. Compare also the poet's 22nd sonnet, lines 7-8:

> But he the Diuell, and she his Dam display:
> And Furies fell annoy sweete Muses cheere.

It is now all the more comprehensible that Richard's 'furies and helhoundes [that] raged so extreamely, that the Muses and Graces could not be quiet for them' contains a veiled reference to Nashe in his capacity of Cerberus, the hellhound, an allusion once perfectly clear to many of his original readers. The use of decorative reference to 'Graces' (or 'Charites') and 'Muses' brought in its train other classical imagery, a short account of which I shall include

---

(1) R. Harvey, *Philadelphus*, sig. H₂ vᵒ, p. 56.

in the next section (1). Illuminatingly enough, *Summers Last Will*, the very comedy containing Nashe's most important Cerberus reference, also sounds the praises of 'dogs' generally, a purpose achieved in the speeches of Orion (ll. 663 ff.).

Whatever Harvey's intention was when he arranged his material for *Philadelphus*, it is clear that his book stands in closer relation to the Harvey-Nashe controversy than has hitherto been suspected. The date of its inserted epistle, Nashe's prognostication and the suggestions contained in Florio's *Second Fruits* warrant the conclusion that the quarrel between Nashe and Richard Harvey did not remain dormant during the period between the publication of the offensive epistle in the *Lamb of God* and *Pierce Penilesse*.

There are a few more expressions in *Philadelphus* which seem to reveal the author's controversial purpose, but I abstain from discussing them, because I fail to see what can be brought up in support of an acceptable interpretation.

In conclusion attention may be drawn to the fact that Shakespeare uses the word 'aconitum' (the poison produced by Cerberus) only once in his accepted writings. Every student of the two *Henry IV* plays knows that they contain a large number of parallels with the works of Nashe. Most of them are indicated by R. P. Cowl and A. E. Morgan, the Arden editors of the plays; and they have again been collected by Dover Wilson in his recent edition of 1 *Henry IV* (2). Now in 2 *Henry IV* at IV, iv, 48, aconitum is associated with gunpowder in the phrase 'though it doe worke as strong as *Aconitum*, or rash Gunpowder.' Such an association stamps this phrase as a reminiscence of the Harvey-Nashe controversy. Because of their

---

(1) It is a point of incidental interest that Chapman's *Hymnus in Cynthiam* contains the following lines (ll. 453-455):
> And no Herostratus shall euer race,
> Those holy monuments : but pillers stand,
> Where euery Grace, and Muse shall hang her garland.

and that Harvey mentions the story of Herostratus in the introductory epistle to the *Foure Letters*, an epistle written after the completion of his work. Chapman devotes a long passage to this story of which the quoted lines are the final ones. Except these final lines, most of Chapman's material derives from Comes' mythological treatise. Allusions to the story of Herostratus are, of course, common enough in Elizabethan literature. Considering, however, that Chapman's epistle to Roydon contains the phrase 'Now what a supererogation in wit this is, to thinke skil so mightilie pierst with their loues,' a phrase probably connected with Harvey's *Pierces Supererogation* (see F. A. Yates, *A Study of LLL*, p. 83), there is good reason to assume that there may be other points of contact as well.

(2) See J. Dover Wilson, ed. *I Henry IV* (Cambridge, 1949), pp. 191-196; and Dover Wilson's article "The Origins and Development of Shakespeare's *Henry IV*," *The Library*, 4th Ser., XXVI (1945), 2-16.

number it is needless to enumerate such passages as associate 'aquafortis and gunpowder' in the writings of Harvey and Nashe, that expression being used to describe the effect of Nashe's satire. Of course, aquafortis is not identical with aconite, but Shakespeare's substitution of the latter for the former would seem to be accounted for by the equation Nashe-Cerberus. It is likely therefore that 'though it doe worke as strong as *Aconitum*, or rash Gunpowder' in 2 *Henry IV* has to be regarded as one more reminiscence of Nashe.

PEGASUS AND BELLEROPHON

As one examines the works of Gabriel Harvey with care one encounters instance after instance of his being fascinated by mythology. Most Renaissance poets and artists ransacked classical lore in search of material which might give new lustre to their art. There were many poets of inferior talent, however, who were often merely humanists with a gift for arranging such material metrically; and Harvey was no exception in this respect. But he did differ from his contemporaries in that he indulged in using highly rhetorical and inflated language. About Harvey's whole literary output there hangs such an atmosphere of pomposity verging, one might perhaps say, upon tomfoolery, that it becomes almost impossible to know whether he is at all serious and that there is no wonder that he excited the ridicule of his contemporary readers. His chief desire seems to have been to impress his audience with his ability to accumulate simile upon simile, hyperbole upon hyperbole. From the point of view of interpretation generally a study of these figures of style would not be devoid of importance, but we must now turn to those involving the use of mythology.

Harvey's interest in mythology can be traced back to his Cambridge days. In his Latin oration *Ciceronianus*, delivered in 1575 and printed in a revised form in 1577, he is found extolling Cicero, using comparisons we are already familiar with.

All the others uttered conversation that I thought delightful, and indeed nothing less than pure delight; but Cicero alone (my heart leaps at the recollection) had the sweetest voice to invite me, the clearest to entertain me, and far the pleasantest to dismiss me. On the tongues of the others I thought there dwelt the Muses, and the Graces, and that 'Marrow of Persuasion' so celebrated by the ancients; but in his utterance there was an indiscribable distinction, more perfect and divine than Apollo himself and Minerva (1).

But his Latin elegies written on the occasion of Sir Thomas Smith's death and published under the title *Smithus, vel Musarum Lachrymae* (1578) contain passages which are exceptionally revealing. *Musarum Lachrymae* is a book divided into nine 'cantica,' each of which is called by the names of the nine Muses. At the end of this collection comes an epilogue 'Alter Epilogus, ad Ricardum Harueium, fratrem ac pupillum,' and, finally, a poem purporting to be by Richard himself entitled 'Ricardi Harueij Mercurius, siue Lachrymae, a fratre, ac tutore extortae.' In the epilogue Richard is urgently requested by his brother to compose verses in celebration of Smith's death, and this explains why a poem by Richard closes the volume. The epilogue contains the following high-flown lines :

> Tantum ô, quis tantum popularem [Smith] non super astra
> Efferat, atque adeo super ipsum mobile primum?
> Vnicus ille omnes sic est praedatus honores
> Atque hominum, atque Deum, quorum est ascriptus in album.
> Crede mihi, meritum est Manes placasse canendo.
> Ergo age, & impositis capiti, manibusque corollis,
> Mente super nubes fixa, raptaque per altum,
> Pierides, Phoebum, Charites, iuga summa bicollis
> Parnassi, delubra Deum, delubra Dearum
> Sedulus implora : totumque Helicona duobus
> Haustibus epotans, ingentem imitare furorem,
> Atque altum quiddam spira, dignumque cothurno;
> Ad fingendum audax : sic nostri ex tempore facti
> Grandiloqui Vates, Ioue dignum carmen anhelant.
> Protinus & sic tu fies, plaudente popello,
> Egregius vates, magnusque, Ricarde, Poeta (2).

Richard apparently complied with the ardent wishes expressed here. In what purports to be his own poem—it rather looks like Gabriel's— he describes his arrival at Jove's theatre, which resounds with the heavenly music produced by the Muses and the Graces.

> Jntonuit laeuum Joue discedente : sed ipse
> Adpropero, celerique gradu per sydera voluor.

---

(1) HARVEY, *Ciceronianus*, ed. by H. S. WILSON and transl. by C. FORBES, p. 47. 'Marrow of Persuasion' (Suadae medullam) was a favourite phrase with the admirers of RAMUS.
(2) G. HARVEY, *Musarum Lachrymae* (London, 1578), sig. H₁ vᵒ and sig. H_{ij} rᵒ.

Post varios coeli anfractus, reditusque viarum,
Ad Jouis aeternum venio, celsumque theatrum,
Musarum plectris resonans, Charitumque Camoenis.

On the same page, a few lines further on, he goes on:

Plura etiam dictura fuit: sed protinus illi
Assensere omnes Musae, Charitesque: statimque
Juppiter, Anglorum iubet exornare coronam;
Magnificosque viros sacris decorare Camoenis (1).

Having such specimens of the Harveys' versification at his disposal,
the author of the Cambridge comedy *Pedantius*, in 1580, was perfectly
justified in making fun of Gabriel's notorious fondness for allusion
to the Graces and the Muses. Edward Forsett aimed at giving a
full-length portrait of his victim and so he also made the 'pedant'
address his beloved Lydia in these terms (IV, iv, lines 2151-2157):

Eleganter, ut omnia; tres Gratiae sunt in labellis, & videor mihi
ore tuo non *Mussas*, sed *Musas* loquentes audire: anhelitus tuus est aurum
potabile: Te dum fruor, in campis sum Elysijs: Caro tua remedium est
contra morsus aspidis (videlicet amoris mei:) Denique (ut contraham
omnia in compendium, seu epitomen) tu es accumulatissima quaedam
Cornucopia mea.

No better illustration of the appeal made by Harvey's decorative
imagery could be asked.

A long time was to elapse before Harvey was to claim the
assistance of the Muses again; in fact, it was only in 1592, as
we have seen, that they were invoked with renewed fervour as the
protectors of concord and equanimity. By 1589, the time of his
participation in the Marprelate controversy, he had apparently come
to realize that a more sparing use of mythology would render him
less liable to the criticism and ridicule of his more fastidious readers.
Prose, moreover, was not the proper vehicle for invoking the Muses
or for showing off one's knowledge of classic myth.

In his *Aduertisement for Pap-hatchet, and Martin Mar-prelate*
Harvey refers once only to the Graces and the Muses, his argument
being that Lyly, one of the 'freshe quaffers of Helicon,' should
no longer be permitted to drink from the waters flowing from the
fountains on the Helicon.

---

(1) G. HARVEY, *Musarum Lachrymae*, sig. Hiv r⁰.

The finest wittes preferre the loosest period in M. Ascham, or Sir Philip Sidney, before the tricksiest page in Euphues, or Pap-hatchet. The Muses, shame to remember some freshe quaffers of Helicon: and which of the Graces, or Vertues blusheth not, to name some lustie tospots of Rhetorique? (1)

In September 1592, then, the time had come when he much needed the inspiration issuing from the Helicon for he had to compose no less than twenty-two sonnets in commemoration of Greene's funeral, and these sonnets were all written in approximately a week's time. The *Foure Letters* does not abound in mythological allusions but the ones Harvey does introduce are all the more striking because they are all logically connected with those already quoted from his other works (for a fuller quotation see p. 127).

Oh, solace thy miraculous selfe, and cheere the Muses in cheering thy daintie soule, sweetelie drunken with their delitious Helicon, and the restoratiue Nectar of the Gods. What can I say more? That cordial liquor, and that heauenly restoratiue, bee thy soueraigne comfort: and scorne the basenes of euerie crased, or fainting thought, that may argue a degenerate minde.

One who delights in using such turgid and apparently mock-humorous language and who professes to be intoxicated with the spell of the Muses, may be expected to follow the bent of his own 'miraculous' nature and to cast himself for the part of a Pegasus rider as well; and Harvey's works lend support to his having done so. In the eleventh sonnet appended to the *Foure Letters* it is quite clearly intimated that Harvey is a kind of Pegasus rider.

> Or lend me Pegasus, thy mounting winges:
> And let me heare, how quire of Angels singes.

For a Renaissance poet to regard himself as a Pegasus rider, or Bellerophon, may seem the most natural thing to do. But Harvey seems to have lacked the sense of propriety and decorum to make his claim acceptable and to write really good poetry, not for an age, but for all time. As a matter of fact, many Elizabethan readers may have realized, like Coleridge's schoolmaster was to realize about 1790, that 'lute, harp, and lyre, Muse, Muses, and inspirations, Pegasu, Parnassus, and Hippocrene were all an abomination' to them.

---

(1) G. HARVEY. *Pierces Supererogation*, sig. S₂.

And one of these readers, Nashe, might certainly have exclaimed with our schoolmaster: 'Harp? Harp? Lyre? Pen and ink, boy, you mean! Muse, boy, Muse? Your nurse's daughter, you mean! Pierian spring? Oh aye! the cloister-pump, I suppose!' (1)

Before indicating in what respect the symbolism of the Bellerophon myth is worked up in *Pierces Supererogation*, it is first necessary to quote from Harvey's third letter a passage in which Bacchus is mentioned. In the course of his third letter the writer develops the idea that 'due circumspection' is advantageous to a 'soueraigne Empire' and goes on:

> Especially in a tumultuous age, and in a world of warre: wherein not Bacchus, but Mars: not Venus, but Mercury, not Ryot, but Valour, not Phansy, but Pollicy must strike the stroke (2).

Bacchus ('Ryot') and Venus ('Phansy') are disowned, whilst Mars ('Valour') and Mercury ('Pollicy') are praised. One wonders why Harvey stresses Bacchus's inability to strike the stroke. At first sight this reference seems to be of merely general import and unrelated to the contemporary output. It is not inconceivable, however, that Harvey's statement should have been prompted by Nashe's claim that one should take one's inspiration from drunken revels and not, by implication, from the Muses' well. In the preface to Greene's *Menaphon* Nashe enthusiastically praises 'a pot of blew burning ale' as an excellent means of getting inspired.

> Let frugall scholers and fine fingered nouices take their drinke by the ounce and their wine by the halfe penny worths, but it is for a Poet to examine the pottle pots, and gage the bottome of whole gallons; *qui bene vult poiein, debet ante pinein*. A pot of blew burning ale, with a fiery flaming toste, is as good as *Pallas* with the nine Muses on *Pernassus* top: without the which, in vaine they may crie, O thou my Muse, inspire me with some penne, when they want certaine liquid sacrifice to rouze her forth her denne (3).

It takes little consideration to recognize that this passage bears some relation to Harvey's ideas. In his *Aduertisement*, as we have seen, he maintains that the 'Muses, shame to remember some freshe quaffers of Helicon' and that the Graces blush 'to name some lustie

(1) COLERIDGE, *Biographia Literaria* (London, Everyman's Library ed., 1906), p. 4.
(2) HARVEY, *Foure Letters*, p. 42.
(3) NASHE, *Works*, III, 321-322.

tospots of Rhetorique.' And one has only to read the important passage in Harvey's third letter beginning 'Now, good sweete Muse, I beseech thee by thy delicate witte, and by all the queintest Inuentions of thy deuiseful braine' to become convinced that Harvey and Nashe were developing their ideas so as to suggest that there were actually two kinds of stimulating beverage, one cheering the followers of Bacchus, the other inspiring the visitors of Helicon. Furthermore, such hints as commended wine in Nashe's early works were elaborated more fully and more effectively in *Summers Last Will* where Nashe devoted a separate scene to a conversation between Bacchus, 'Autumne,' and Will Summer, the hero of the play. Nashe gave up more than two hundred lines to a portrayal of Bacchus, who comes before the audience dressed in vine leaves and a garland of grapes on his head. Bacchus's praise of wine is formulated in such a wealth of racy Elizabethan phrases that the scene in which this occurs could not have failed to strike home to its original spectators, especially since the subject was one of topical interest.

Of course, it is a far cry from pointing out contrasting uses of mythology to determining the circumstances which originated them. Two things one can be sure about are: first, that mythological symbolism played an important part in the literary game of Harvey and Nashe; and second, that their use of mythology stood in close relation to one of the main points at issue in their quarrel, namely the controversy concerning the superiority of native over learned (or 'artistic') wit. As John Eliot's *Ortho-epia Gallica* contains a few dialogues relevant to this controversy regarding 'art' and to the foregoing discussion generally, a short account of Eliot's life and personality deserves to be sketched in here.

John Eliot, like Shakespeare, was a Warwickshire man. He was born in 1562. He studied at Brasenose, Oxford, for some time, and spent much of his existence abroad. About 1588 we find Eliot in London as a language-teacher and translator of French political tracts for Wolfe, the printer and publisher. He no doubt got acquainted with several literary celebrities, for by 1588 he already knew Greene, for whose *Perimedes the Blacksmith* (printed by Wolfe for E. White in 1588) he wrote a commendatory sonnet in French which, through its lavish references to a number of foreign writers, augured well for the future of English letters. In 1593 he published *Ortho-epia Gallica*, a language-manual whose significance for a more adequate understanding of contemporary writers has already been recognized by Miss Yates (in her book on Florio) and, quite recently, by J. W. Lever (1). This manual affords the most striking example of the influence of Rabelais in English literature.

The *Ortho-epia Gallica* was entered in the Stationers' Register on December 18, 1592. The title-page of the book bears the imprint 'Printed by Iohn VVolfe,' but the ornament of a woman's head with cornucopias which figures on the title-page leaves no doubt that the book was actually printed by Richard Field (1579-1626) (2). This printer, son of Henry Field, tanner of Stratford-upon-Avon, had through his father some Shakespearean connexions. John Shakespeare, the poet's father, had valued Henry Field's goods on August 25, 1592. Richard Field himself left Stratford in 1579 and, coming up to London, apprenticed himself to two printers, first to George Bishop and then to Thomas Vautrollier. After the latter's death in 1587, Field set up his own business and consolidated his position by marrying his master's widow and thus inherited much of the stock; this explains why the ornament used in Eliot's book, once belonging to Vautrollier, had passed to Field. But the printer's device is not the only clue to the identification of the printer of the *Ortho-epia Gallica*, for the letter-type and the other ornaments bear witness to Field's printing as well. It is well known that Field also printed Shakespeare's *Venus and Adonis*.

Several features stamp the *Ortho-epia Gallica* as a remarkable Elizabethan document. It opens with a dedication in Italian to Robert Dudley, Earl of Leicester, but the striking fact about this dedication is that the Earl had been dead for five years. Miss Yates (3) argues that this feature has to be interpreted as a challenge to Florio, whose *First Fruits* contained a very pompous dedication to the same nobleman. In her study Miss Yates shows convincingly that the chief victim of Eliot's satire was Florio. This is proved by the parallelism in the development of certain dialogues in *Ortho-epia Gallica* and Florio's two language-manuals: Eliot had both the *First* and the *Second Fruits* on his desk when writing out part of his 'French Fruits.'

---

(1) J. W. LEVER, "Shakespeare's French Fruits," *Shakespeare Survey*, 6 (1953), 79-90.

(2) See R. B. McKERROW, *Printers' & Publishers' Devices in England and Scotland, 1485-1640* (London, Bibliographical Society, 1913), device number 179. In ELIOT's book the ornament appears without the initials T. V., and this form of the ornament therefore occurs nine years earlier than the one McKERROW gives from Sir THOMAS NORTH's *Lives of Epaminondas* (1602).

(3) F. A. YATES, *John Florio*. pp. 153-4.

Writing as Eliot was in the latter half of 1592 there was but one course open to him if he wished to score a success with his work: he had to develop in his own typically Rabelaisian way some of the topics debated not only by Florio, but also by Harvey and Nashe. It is noteworthy that two dialogues in Eliot's manual stand out more vividly than any others: one 'The Drunken Mens Banket' (to be sure, the very subject-matter suggests Bacchus here!) and the other 'The Bragger.' The latter dialogue, according to Professor Lever, left its mark in 2 *Henry IV*. There is yet further proof of Shakespeare's using literary reminiscences in the design of certain scenes in 2 *Henry IV*, where there is a marked resemblance in vocabulary to the *Ortho-epia Gallica*. Similarly, Eliot's work appears to have been the source of much of Shakespeare's knowledge of French displayed in *Henry V*. Seeing that the *Ortho-epia Gallica* followed in the wake of the Harvey-Nashe dispute, there is considerable justification for regarding Eliot as an intermediary agency in transmitting literary influence between Harvey and Nashe on the one hand, and Shakespeare on the other. An extract from Eliot's work now demands our attention in order to show how Eliot's mind was imbued with the controversial atmosphere of the time.

It has been pointed out by Huntington Brown (1) that both 'The Bragger' and 'The Drunken Mens Banket' are largely based on certain passages in Rabelais' *Vie de Gargantua et Pantagruel*. Now, there is one of Eliot's borrowings which seems to have been deliberately chosen so as to cover the two varieties of inspiration I have previously referred to.

Tarry a little that I deduce a dram out of this bottell: Lo here my very and sole Helicon. See here my Fountaine Caballine. This is mine onely Enthusiasmos. Here drinking, I deliberate, I discourse, I resolue and conclude. After the conclusion, I laugh, I vvrite, I compose, I drinke.

Ennius, the father of Latine Poets, drinking did write, writing did drinke.

Aeschylus (if you giue credit to Plutarchus in his bankets) did drinke composing, did compose drinking (2).

It is obvious that there is a quite definite generic resemblance in

(1) H. BROWN, *Rabelais in English Literature*, pp. 43-7 and 216-220.
(2) J. ELIOT, *Ortho-epia Gallica* (London, 1593), sigs. f₁ and f₁ v°. The quotation above is a very close translation from a passage in RABELAIS, *Gargantua*, Book III. Prologue de l'auteur. Miss F. A. YATES, *A Study of Love's Labour's Lost*. p. 46. also discusses this ELIOT passage. but not its mythological implications.

this Rabelaisian effusion to Harvey's exaltation in the *Foure Letters* of the 'restoratiue Nectar of the Gods' issuing from the Helicon.

Certain passages in Nashe's *Strange Newes* can now be read in a fresh light. One understands why the satirist praises 'bonauenture licour' as the only true source of wit and inspiration and why Harvey's friendship with Spenser is ridiculed in terms of the Pegasus myth. Spenser's *Faerie Queene*, says Nashe, should ride upon an 'vnspotted Pegasus . . . through all reports dominions' and, by implication, not on a spotted one in the company of Harvey.

Helter skelter, feare no colours, course him, trounce him, one cup of bonauenture licour will inspire you with more wit and Schollership than hee hath thrust into his whole packet of Letters.

Immortall *Spencer*, no frailtie hath thy fame, but the imputation of this Idiots friendship: vpon an vnspotted *Pegasus* should thy gorgeous attired *Fayrie Queene* ride triumphant through all reports dominions, but that this mud-born bubble, this bile on the browe of the Vniuersitie, this bladder of pride new blowne, challengeth some interest in her prosperitie (1).

Had we no other material relevant to the Pegasus myth, it would be dangerous to build any theory on it regarding Harvey's preference in this respect. An examination of his voluminous *Pierces Supererogation* may bring into clearer focus his tendency to interweave with his diatribe specific elements of the Pegasus story. The winged horse of the Muses, as the myth has it, was tamed by Neptune or Minerva and given to Bellerophon to enable him to conquer the Chimaera (literally 'goat'), a monster with a lion's head, a goat's body, and a dragon's tail. The head of the Chimaera continually vomited flame. According to some traditions Bellerophon attempted with Pegasus to rise into heaven, but Jupiter, incensed at Bellerophon's pride, made a gad-fly sting Pegasus with the consequence that the rider was thrown off his horse. Bellerophon's downfall was later interpreted allegorically as a warning against a too high-soaring ambition. If Harvey regarded himself as a Pegasus rider he was bound to cast himself for the part of Bellerophon, Nashe, by a process of natural inference, becoming a kind of Chimaera. A few quotations will bring this symbolism to light.

In the first half of his work Harvey says of himself: '. . . but

---

(1) NASHE. *Works*. I, 280, 282.

what a notable Asse indeede was I, that sought the winges of a mounting Pegasus, or a flying Phenix, where I found the head, & feete of a braying creature?' (1) And just after the Eliot speech Harvey sarcastically suggests that his enemy is still as miserable as the Chimaera: 'His other miraculous perfections are still in abeyance: and his monstrous excellencyes in the predicament of Chimera' (2). Many pages further Nashe's invective violence calls up in Harvey's mind the picture of one who threatens to surpass the flights of Bellerophon: 'He wil soone be ripe, that already giueth so lusty onsets; & threateneth such desperate maine carreers, as surpasse the fiercest Caualcads of *Bellerophon*, or *Don Alonso d'Aualos*' (3).

Near the end of *Pierces Supererogation* there occurs a more detailed reference to the Bellerophon story, whose relevance to Harvey I find it difficult to explain.

Did the flying Pegasus of the redoubted Bellerophon, before his aduanturous expedition against the hideous Lion-dragon Chimaera, that is, against the fierce sauages, which inhabited that fier-vomiting mountaine in Lycia, prouide to arme himselfe with a braue Posie; or boast of his horrible mother Medusa, or of his owne Gorgonean winges? (4)

For this passage, containing a specifically 'allegorical' interpretation, Harvey may be indebted to the various mythographical publications of the time, but the probability is that he was either inspired by Alciati's graphic account of the Bellerophon story in the *Emblematum Liber*, or owed something to Fraunce's *Third part of the Countesse of Pembrokes Yuychurch*, which also includes one. Alciati is, indeed, mentioned both in the *Foure Letters* and in *Pierces Supererogation*. Fraunce, who lays more stress on the purely allegorical interpretation of the Chimaera than Harvey does, also used Alciati for his allegorization of the myth (5).

A last feature of Harvey's text deserves special notice, since,

---

(1) Harvey, *Pierces Supererogation*, sig. B₁ vº (*Works*, II, 40-1); for other Pegasus allusions see *Works*, II, 279, 282, 307, 322.

(2) *Pierces Supererogation*, sig. D₂ vº (*Works*, II, 66).

(3) *Pierces Supererogation*, sig. V₃ rº (*Works*, II, 243). 'Alonso d'Avalos' is presumably Alfonso de Avalos, the marquis of Vasto (1502-1546), who fought in the armies of Charles V. Vasto had pronounced literary interests.

(4) *Pierces Supererogation*, sig. Cc₃ rº (*Works*, II, 307-8).

(5) A quotation of Fraunce's allegorization would needlessly overweight these pages; it occurs at sig. H₂ vº in his *Third part*. The only thing I wish to point out is that Fraunce partly used a portion of book 13 of Boccaccio's *Genealogia Deorum*; which adds one more item to the list of Fraunce's indebtednesses.

as we shall see, it is circuitously connected with the controversy in which the source of poetic inspiration was a major item of argument. Harvey frequently accuses Nashe of being 'capricious.' He does so for the first time in the *Foure Letters*, and repeats the charge in his two next pamphlets. Seemingly there is nothing special about being 'capricious,' but when it is realized that Harvey was apparently the first to introduce its use into English—a fact overlooked by the *Oxford English Dictionary* (1)—'capricious' takes on more than just an ordinary significance. A capricious man resembles a goat, an animal which leaps and skips fantastically, and which makes its 'caprioles' preferably on the hills. 'Goat' was also a byword for lechery, and 'goatish' is still nowadays used as a synonym for lustful. It so happens that Shakespeare also uses 'capricious'; he does so only once in his whole work, namely in *As You Like It*, III, iii, 8. It need not come as a surprise to find the term precisely in this play, for we have already seen that there are reasons for dating its first draft in 1593. Before turning our attention to III, iii, let us first re-examine III, ii.

The links existing between Greene's *Orlando Furioso* and *As You Like It* tended to show that Shakespeare may have handled his comedy soon after the period that Greene's play was on the boards (2). It will be remembered that certain similarities in the portrayal of Orlando suggest a textual interdependence of some sort between both plays. It is now perhaps possible to strengthen the ties connecting them. To begin with, it is already illuminating to note that the very scene in *As You Like It* (namely III, ii) connected with Greene's play is precisely a scene in which scholars have also detected links with the works of Nashe. These links are worth studying in detail.

---

(1) See also C. H. HERFORD, P. and E. SIMPSON, edd. *Ben Jonson*, IX (Oxford, 1950), 318. 'Capricious' raises a small lexicographical problem. The *OED* quotes it in use in RICHARD CAREW's translation of JUAN DE HUARTE's *Examen de Ingenios*, printed for the first time in 1594. CAREW did not translate directly from the Spanish original but from CAMILLO CAMILLI's Italian version. Note now that *The Examination of Mens Wits* was entered to WOLFE on Aug. 5, 1590 (see ARBER, *Transcript*, II, 557), that is, practically more than three years before its publication. The entry in the Register mentions that the book is 'to be printed in Italian and Englishe.' Though 'capricious' is certainly not beyond HARVEY's inventive power, it is worth remarking that he knew HUARTE's work (see *Marginalia*, p. 138), and may have got 'capricious' there, either by way of CAREW's MS. (or, perhaps, by way of a lost edition), or from his own reading.

(2) The theory that GREENE was perhaps thinking of HARVEY when portraying Orlando may now find further support from the fact that he twice applies the expression 'poet laureate' (in the Alleyn MS. only) to Orlando, an expression that would fit HARVEY around 1592.

The 'poet' Orlando in *As You Like It* has hung his rhymes upon the trees and has carved the name of Rosalind on their bark. Rosalind enters in the disguise of Ganymede and discovers Orlando's love-tokens; she plucks them down and starts to read them aloud. Then the clown Touchstone parodies Orlando's poetry and describes it as 'the right Butter-womens ranke to Market' (III, ii, 103-4). After that Touchstone offers a sample of his own versification and says that it is 'the verie false gallop of Verses' and asks Rosalind 'why doe you infect your selfe with them?' (III, ii, 119-20). It was long ago pointed out by Malone that 'the verie false gallop of Verses' could be paralleled in the following passage from *Strange Newes*:

I would trot a false gallop through the rest of his ragged Verses, but that if I should retort his rime dogrell aright, I must make my verses (as he doth his) run hobling like a Brewers Cart vpon the stones, and obserue no length in their feete; which were *absurdum per absurdius*, to infect my vaine with his imitation (1).

It is striking that Touchstone criticizes the poetic attainments of Orlando in terms showing some relation or other to Nashe's, and that Shakespeare's Orlando is related to that of Greene, who depicts his character as a 'poet laureate' in terms suggesting that he may have had Harvey in mind. Nashe himself, moreover, hints in *Strange Newes* that Harvey has had the laureateship conferred upon him, when he maintains that he would obstinately defend 'abhominable Atheistes . . . onely because *Laureate Gabriell* articles' against them (2).

Here is Dover Wilson's comment on Shakespeare's borrowing from Nashe: 'Here we have not merely the coincidence of 'false gallop of verses,' but also (as Furness noticed, though Malone did not) the peculiar use of the word 'infect' in both passages, while the most interesting link of all, which no one has hitherto observed, is that between 'hobling like a Brewers Cart vpon the stones' and 'the right butter-women's rank to market'—a parallel which shows that the borrowing so far from being deliberate on Shakespeare's part was probably unconscious' (3). The use of 'infect' calls for some comment. Nashe's baneful disposition—for he sometimes had a violent poison at his disposal—would seem to account for the

---

(1) NASHE, *Works*, I, 275.
(2) NASHE, *Works*, I, 285.
(3) J. D. WILSON, ed. *As You Like It*, pp. 106-107.

'peculiar use' of 'infect' in both passages. It would be absurd, Nashe holds, were I to infect my vein with imitating Harvey.

There are further signs that 1593 is a not improbable date for Shakespeare's first handling of *As You Like It*. In the very scene we are dealing with 'Gargantua's mouth' (III, ii, 238) is mentioned. This tends to show Shakespeare's knowledge of Rabelais, perhaps by the intermediary of Eliot; or, more probably, the expression found its way into his play because he remembered Harvey's words that Nashe was 'such a Gargantuist, as can deuoure [Harvey] quicke in a sallat' (1). Note also that there was a book 'Gargantua his prophesie,' now lost, which was entered to Wolfe on April 6, 1592. Its very title suggests a person behind 'Gargantua.' Professor F. P. Wilson (2) points out that it is unlikely that it was a translation of Rabelais' *Pantagruélines Pronostications*, for why was it called 'Gargantua his prophesie'? Wilson also says that it may be that the parody was transferred from Pantagruel to Gargantua because Gargantua was more familiar to the English public. Gargantua, originally the name of a giant in French folklore, was mentioned in English literature as early as 1547. Let us now leave the field of conjecture and turn to III, iii.

Shakespeare here introduces us to Sir Oliver Martext, a puritan hedge-priest. His name would be rather pointless about the turn of the century; only in the early nineties would 'Martext' make a much more marked impression. And what is more, evidence is not lacking that the Martext scene as a whole abounds in literary reminiscences traceable to the highly sensational pamphlets of Nashe and Harvey. At the very beginning of *As You Like It*, III, iii, there occurs the following conversation between Touchstone and Audrey, a country wench.

> *Clo.* Come apace good *Audrey*, I wil fetch vp your Goates, *Audrey:* and how *Audrey* am I the man yet? Doth my simple feature content you.
> *Aud.* Your features, Lord warrant vs: what features?
> *Clo.* I am heere with thee, and thy Goats, as the most capricious Poet honest *Ouid* was among the Gothes.

This introductory dialogue probably bears the imprint of Shakespeare's recent reading of Harvey. When applying the epithet 'capricious' to Ovid Shakespeare does not want his audience to miss his meaning

---

(1) HARVEY, *Pierces Supererogation*, sig. S₄ v⁰ (*Works*, II, 223.)
(2) F. P. WILSON, *The Library*, Ser. 4, XIX (1939), 25.

and so he explains the quibble concealed in the term by hinting that it has something to do with 'Goats,' and, indirectly, with 'Gothes.' Shakespeare introduces into Touchstone's language the very epithet wherewith Harvey ridicules Nashe no less than five times in *Pierces Supererogation* (1). In that same pamphlet Harvey also calls Nashe 'Signior Capricio,' while elsewhere 'Capricians, Inuentours of newe, or reuiuers of old leacheries' are attacked. Attention may further be drawn to the fact that Shakespeare also alludes to Ovid's exile from Rome when he has Touchstone say that Ovid was at one time among the Goths. Though the point is obvious enough, no one seems to have cared to notice it. In this connexion it is worth pointing out that both *Strange Newes* and *Pierces Supererogation* contain passages referring to Ovid's exile. Nashe (2) devotes to the cause of Ovid's exile a fairly long passage which, because of its imagery and its implications, is by no means devoid of interest. Harvey's statement is the more immediately relevant to this argument, because he also drags in Nashe, his ostensible point being that as Ovid was banished from Rome, so Nashe deserves to be exiled from London.

One Ouid was too-much for Roome; and one Greene too-much for London: but one Nashe more intollerable then both: not bicause his witt is anye thinge comparable, but bicause his will is more outrageous (3).

Harvey, moreover, pursues his train of thought and cites Pomponazzi, Aretino, and Machiavelli as typical examples of undesirable citizens.

But there is even more remarkable evidence of Shakespeare's well-nigh conscious intention to invest his play with topical meaning. Practically immediately after the 'capricious' passage Touchstone remarks to Audrey (III, iii, 12-16):

Clo. When a mans verses cannot be vnderstood, nor a mans good wit seconded with the forward childe, vnderstanding, it strikes a man more dead then a great reckoning in a little roome: truly, I would the Gods hadde made thee poeticall.

Dover Wilson (4), following O. W. F. Lodge's suggestion in the

---

(1) HARVEY, *Works*, II, 52, 53, 54, 95, 278. 'Capricians' occurs at II, 91 and 'Signior Capricio' at II, 109. See also the 'Capricio' allusion in RICHARD HARVEY's 'porter of Pluto's divinity' passage, quoted in this study on p. 90.
(2) NASHE, *Works*, I, 286.
(3) *Pierces Supererogation*, sig. G₁ rº (*Works*, II, 94).
(4) Ed. *As You Like It*, pp. 104-5.

Times Literary Supplement (May 14, 1925), observes that Touchstone's words probably refer to Marlowe's death on May 30, 1593. On that day Marlowe was killed by Ingram Frysar in the room of a house at Deptford Strand (1) and it is therefore likely that the 'great reckoning in a little roome' was the very reckoning over which Marlowe quarrelled with Frysar with the result that the dramatist was struck dead. Compare also Marlowe's line in *The Jew of Malta*, I, i, 37: 'Infinite riches in a little room,' a line Touchstone perhaps glances at.

In what follows the above quoted extract, Touchstone and Audrey enter upon a humorous discussion of the origin of poetic inspiration, a subject, as we know, that was part and parcel of the Harvey-Nashe controversy. In itself the occurrence of such a discussion would be of extremely little evidential value, were it not that the very setting wherein Shakespeare's humorously coloured conception of poetry appears, abundantly corroborates the view that Shakespeare had the Harvey-Nashe dispute in mind and that he therefore wrote his play very soon after Harvey had published *Pierces Supererogation*. On the page where Harvey denounces 'Capricians,' Nashe is charged with invoking a 'brothell Muse' to assist him in composing 'bawdye, and filthy Rymes.' The reader will understand why Harvey insists that his opponent is inspired by a vulgar Muse, and not by the nine Muses.

I will not heere decipher thy vnprinted packet of bawdye, and filthy Rymes, in the nastiest kind: there is a fitter place for that discouery of thy foulest shame, & the whole ruffianisme of thy brothell Muse, if she still prostitute her obscene ballatts, and will needes be a younge Curtisan of ould knauery (2).

And a few lines further we find this:

Such riotous, and incestuous humours would be launced, not feasted: the Diuell is eloquent enough, to play his owne Oratour: his Damme an old bawde, wanteth not the broccage of a young Poet (3).

The devil is eloquent enough and does not require the help of Nashe,

---

.(1) See L. Hotson, *The Death of Christopher Marlowe* (London, 1925).
(2) *Pierces Supererogation*, sig. F$_4$ r^0 (*Works*, II, 91).
(3) *Pierces Supererogation*, sig. F$_4$ r^0 (*Works*, II, 92). In support of the interpretation of 'devil's dam' and 'young Poet', compare Harvey, *Foure Letters*, p. 69: 'I desire not to be a blacke Swanne: or to leaue behind me any Period in the stile of the Diuels Oratour: or any verse in the vaine of his Dammes Poet.'

who is a typical devil's orator as he has carried things so far as to address a supplication to the devil. In the course of *Pierces Supererogation* Harvey frequently dubs his opponent a devil's orator. In his next comparison it is said that the devil's dam, an old bawd, is in no need of the brokage of a 'young Poet.' In other words, Harvey merely states in different terms his previous idea that Nashe, the 'young Poet,' is courting a decidedly immoral Muse. Significantly, it is in related terms that Nashe deplores—on the very first page of *Pierce Penilesse*—that his 'vulgar Muse was despised & neglected'.

By a lucky chance Harvey has also taken care to specify what the name of Nashe's Muse is, and she appears to be no less a person than 'Audrey.'

His mountaines of Imagination, are too-apparent: his designements of Vanitie, too-visible: his plots of Ribaldry, too-palpable: his formes of libelling, too-outragious: S. Fame, the goddesse of his deuotion: S. Blase, the idoll of his Zeale: S. Awdry, the lady of his loue: and the young Vicar of old S. Fooles, his ghostly Father (1).

St. Audrey is St. Etheldreda, the patron saint of Ely. This Audrey is the lady of Nashe's love and she is no doubt identical with his 'brothell Muse,' a kind of procuress needing the 'brokage,' or procuracy in immorality, of a 'young Poet.' It is very remarkable how closely Shakespeare models the dramatic situation between Touchstone and Audrey on the pattern of the abuse levelled at Nashe in *Pierces Supererogation*. Touchstone replies in the affirmative to Audrey's question whether he would have desired that the 'Gods had made [her] Poeticall' (III, iii, 23-4), and then suggests that, if she is a poet, he may well hope that she is really feigning when she maintains that she is 'honest' (= 'chaste' in its Elizabethan meaning); for, poets are notable dissemblers. And Touchstone ends with the satirical comment: 'Well, praised be the Gods, for thy foulness; sluttishnesse may come heereafter' (III, iii, 40-1).

One more link between Shakespeare and Harvey remains to be discussed. The Folio prints Touchstone's last words in *As You Like It*, III, iii, as follows (his words were headed 'Ol.' in error):

> *Ol.* Come sweete *Audrey*,
> We must be married, or we must liue in baudrey:
> Farewell good Mʳ *Oliuer*: Not O sweet *Oliuer*, O braue

---

(1) *Pierces Supererogation*, sig. T₂ rᵒ and vᵒ (*Works*, II, 234-5).

Oliuer leaue me not behind thee: But winde away, bee
gone I say, I wil not to wedding with thee.

The Folio, as Dover Wilson remarks in his note on the passage, prints
Touchstone's farewell to Oliver Martext in prose, whereas his words
to Audrey form a couplet. It therefore looks as if the prose may
have been added to the original scene. For his Audrey-bawdry pun
Shakespeare may have owed something to Harvey. In *Pierces Supererogation* it is said that asses' dung is good for the 'mouth of Bawdery
in ryme' (1), obviously a veiled allusion to Nashe. In the *New
Letter of Notable Contents* 'bawdry' is also combined with 'capricious' in Harvey's statement that Nashe 'discoursed the Capricious
Dialogues of rankest Bawdry' (2). There is little doubt that Nashe's
'bawdy Muse' Audrey gave rise to the Audrey-bawdry couplet in
As You Like It around 1593.

The coincidences pointed out between III, iii of *As You Like It*
and the tenour and vocabulary of several important statements in
Pierces Supererogation are far too numerous to be simply due to
blind chance. 'Capricious,' 'Ovid,' 'Audrey-bawdry,' the discussion
of the origin of poetic inspiration, offer distinctive traces of
Shakespeare's familiarity with Harvey's writings. And when these
are considered in conjunction with the coincidental treatment of the
character of Orlando by Greene and Shakespeare in the plays of
either writer, the theory seems justified that Shakespeare wrote
the first draft of *As You Like It* in the latter half of 1593.

As the works of Harvey are not easily accessible in Belgium and
—for the matter of that—on the Continent generally, it is desirable
to end this section by quoting the full Eliot speech from *Pierces
Supererogation*. In a few pregnant phrases it epitomizes most of the
items of argument encountered in the course of the foregoing pages.
'One smart Pamflet of knauery' is contrasted with 'ten blundring
volumes of the nine Muses,' the 'villanist' with the 'artist' or 'alchimist'
point of view, and 'Sanguine witt' with 'Melancholy Arte.' Eliot
is in full sympathy with Nashe whose 'climbinge reach of Inuention'
cannot be surpassed—to paraphrase Harvey's own words in his
Foure Letters (3)—by whatever stylistic gems of Invention or flowers
of Elocution Harvey can boast.

---

(1) *Pierces Supererogation*, sig. X$_2$ v⁰ (*Works*, II, 251).
(2) *New Letter*, sig. D$_1$ r⁰ (*Works*, I, 290).
(3) *Foure Letters*, p. 68.

Well, my maisters, you may talke your pleasures of Tom Nash; who yet sleepeth secure, not without preiudice to some, that might be more ielous of their name: but assure your selues, if M. Penniles had not bene deepely plunged in a profound exstasie of knauery, M. Pierce had neuer written that famous worke of Supererogation, that now stayneth all the bookes in Paules-churchyard, and setteth both the vniuersities to schoole. Till I see your finest humanitie bestow such a liberall exhibition of conceit, and courage, vpon your neatest wittes; pardon me though I prefer one smart Pamflet of knauery, before ten blundring volumes of the nine Muses. Dreaming, and smoke amount alike: Life is a gaming, a iugling, a scoulding, a lawing, a skirmishing, a warre; a Comedie, a Tragedy: the sturring witt, a quintessence of quicksilver; and there is noe deade fleshe in affection, or courage. You may discourse of Hermes ascending spirit; of Orpheus enchanting harpe; of Homers diuine furie; of Tyrtaeus enraging trumpet; of Pericles bounsinge thunderclaps; of Platos enthusiasticall rauishment; and I wott not what maruelous egges in mooneshine: but a flye for all your flying speculations, when one good fellow with his odd iestes, or one madd knaue with his awke hibber-gibber, is able to putt downe twentye of your smuggest artificiall men, that simper it so nicely, and coylie in their curious pointes. Try, when you meane to be disgraced: & neuer giue me credit, if Sanguine witt putt not Melancholy Arte to bedd. I had almost said, all the figures of Rhetorique must abate me an ace of Pierces Supererogation: and Penniles hath a certayne nimble and climbinge reach of Inuention, as good as a long pole, and a hooke, that neuer fayleth at a pinch. It were vnnaturall, as the sweete Emperour, Marcus Antoninus said, that the fig-tree should euer want iuice. You that purpose with great summes of studdy, & candles to purchase the worshipfull names of Dunses, & Dodipoles, may closely sitt, or sokingly ly at your bookes: but you that intende to be fine companionable gentlemen, smirkinge wittes, and whipsters in the world, betake yee timely to the liuely practis of the minion profession, and enure your Mercuriall fingers to frame semblable workes of Supererogation. Certes other rules are fopperies: and they that will seeke out the Archmistery of the busiest Modernistes, shall find it nether more, nor lesse, than a certayne pragmaticall secret, called Villany, the verie science of sciences, and the Familiar Spirit of Pierces Supererogation. Coosen not your selues with the gay-nothings of children, & schollers: no priuitie of learning, or inspiration of witt, or reuelation of misteryes, or Arte Notory, counteruayleable with Pierces Supererogation: which hauing none of them, hath them all, and can make them all Asses at his pleasure. The Book-woorme was neuer but a pick-goose; it is the Multiplying spirit, not of the Alchimist, but of the Villanist, that knocketh the naile one the head, and spurreth cutt farther in a day, then the quickest Artist in a weeke. Whiles other are reading, wryting, conferring, arguing, discoursing, experimenting, platforminge, musing, buzzing, or I know not what: that is the spirrit, that with a woondrous dexterity shapeth exquisite workes, and atchieueth puissant exploites of Super-erogation. O my good frends, as ye loue the sweete world, or tender your deare selues, be not vnmindfull what is good for the aduauncemente of your commendable partes. All is nothing without aduancement. Though my experience be a Cipher in these causes, yet hauing studiously perused the newe Arte-notory, that is, the foresaid Supererogation; and hauing shaken so manie learned asses by the eares, as it were by the hands; I could say no lesse, and might think more (1).

MERCURY

It is customary to interpret Mercury as the patron god of eloquence. I should like to set forth the proposition, however, that in the early nineties 'Mercury' acquired a somewhat different sense and that it covered 'learning' in its widest possible meaning. The sixteenth century had witnessed an unprecedented growth of the prestige of the sciences and learning generally, but especially in its last decade they seem to have been cultivated with new enthusiasm. The English nation had come into the inheritance of the literary and distinctly 'academic' achievements of France, though, as yet, there was no formal counterpart to the Académie du Palais of Henry III. Alone the so-called School of Night seems to have united a more or less coherent body of scientists, thinkers and artists. For the conveyance of their aims and philosophy the 'academicians' of France had recourse to a peculiar kind of symbolism which has been fully analysed by Miss Yates (2). Because of the paucity of material it is not possible to furnish a detailed account of the symbolism used by the School of Night. There is one writer, however, who presumably exercised a strong fascination on its adherents : Hermes Trismegistos. From the point of view of mythology Hermes is, of course, identical with Mercury, and this is a deity which often appears in the writings with which we are concerned. A short historical exposition of the main facts relating to Mercury and a discussion of his attributes may not be out place (3).

The most ancient god of wisdom and science was Thoth, a deity venerated by the Egyptians. From the time of Herodotus (c. 480-c. 425) Thoth was identified with Hermes by the Greeks.

---

(1) *Pierces Supererogation*, sig. D_1 v°-D_2 r° (*Works*, II, 62-4). For a full analysis of this remarkable passage see F. A. YATES, *John Florio*, pp. 181-4. Miss YATES was the first to recognize the paramount significance of it.

(2) F. A. YATES, *The French Academies of the Sixteenth Century* (London, The Warburg Institute, 1947).

(3) For this survey I am indebted to J. FESTUGIÈRE, *La Révélation d'Hermès Trismégiste* (Paris, 1944), chap. IV.

But not all Greek writers established such an identification and Plato, for example, did not do so. The honoric designation by which Hermes was generally addressed was 'Trismegistos,' the thrice greatest Hermes. In ancient times Thoth was already identified with the moon deity, and as such, perhaps, he came to be regarded as the inventor of chronography. He also fulfilled the function of scribe of the gods with the result that he was soon converted into an inventor of speech and letters; from this invention many other sciences dependent on speech and writing arose and it was but natural to ascribe these to him as well. Magic, alchemy, and astronomy were the sciences most currently associated with the cult of Hermes. Another science reputedly invented by him was mathematics, an achievement attached to his name from the end of the fourth century B. C. In later times Hermes was regarded as the author of a number of syncretistic treatises, usually assigned to the third century A. D. and now grouped together by modern scholars under the name *Corpus Hermeticum*.

The hermetic treatises that were most widely known in the sixteenth century were the *Poemander* and the *Asclepius*. Such was the popularity of these gnostic writings that there were no less than 22 editions of the *Poemander* between 1471 and 1641. It has already been pointed out that an important agent in diffusing the cult of Hermes was Marsilio Ficino.

In his purely mythological role Hermes, the son of Maia and Zeus, was the messenger of the gods, the god of wealth, the patron of travellers, merchants and thieves. He was equipped with the *caduceus*, a rod entwined by two serpents, the *petasus* or broad-brimmed hat, and the *talaria*, or winged sandals. Currently accepted etymological interpretations of 'Mercurius' are recorded in several sixteenth-century Latin dictionaries, of which the most widely used were those compiled by Ambrosius Calepinus, whose *Dictionarium* first appeared in 1502, and by Robertus Stephanus (or Estienne), whose *Thesaurus Linguae Latinae* was first printed in 1531. In these and in similar works we are told that 'Mercurius' means 'medius inter homines currens, quod sermo currat inter homines medius'; and 'sermo' can be 'literally' equated with ἑρμῆς. The interpretation of Mercury as one who acts as an intermediary in intercourse is also responsible for the view that he is a 'hermeneus' or 'interpreter' of sacred writings. Another explanation of Mercury as 'a mercibus est dictus' accounts for his being considered the patron of merchants ('merx' = ware). To put it plainly, Mercury is a merchant in words.

Regard being had to the fact that magic, alchemy, astronomy, and mathematics exercised a strong attraction on most members of the reputed School of Night, it is no wonder that its adherents claimed Hermes Trismegistos as their highest authority. We know already, for example, that one of its presumable members, George Chapman, knew the *Poemander*. Further contemporary evidence of some acquaintance with this treatise is provided by Simon Forman, the astrologer, who, in *The Groundes of the Longitude* (1591), mentioned '*Mercurie Trismegistus*' and 'his booke Intituled by the name of *Pymander*' (1). How hermetic doctrine was propagated has not yet been described. An early English translation of what is now known as treatise XVI was made by John Harvey under the title *Iatromathematica, that is, the Phisical Mathematiques, or Mathematical Phisickes, directed vnto Ammon the Aegyptian* (1583). It is the purpose of the following account to show that 'Mercury,' quite apart from its primary meaning, was often used in the early nineties to symbolize learning.

George Peele's *The Honour of the Garter*, written in 1593, is a poem introduced by a prologue in which Peele dedicates his work to the Earl of Northumberland, a man who was perhaps the most noted member of the School of Night. The poem dedicated to him states in terms too plain to be misunderstood that the Earl, having shaken off the trammels of scholasticism, has now been permitted to soar through the highest regions of wisdom. In it, too, the Earl's sympathy with the distinctly esoteric doctrines propounded by Hermes Trismegistus is clearly perceptible.

> Renowmèd lord, Northumberland's fair flower,
> The Muses' love, patron and favourite,
> That artisans and scholars dost embrace,
> And clothest Mathesis in rich ornaments;
> That admirable mathematic skill,
> Familiar with the stars and zodiac,
> To whom the heaven lies open as her book;
> By whose directions undeceivable,
> Leaving our schoolmen's vulgar trodden paths,
> And following the ancient reverend steps
> Of Trismegistus and Pythagoras,
> Through uncouth ways and unaccessible,

---

(1) S. FORMAN, *The Groundes of the Longitude* (London, 1591). sig. A₃ rᵒ.

Dost pass into the spacious pleasant fields
Of divine science and philosophy;
From whence beholding the deformities
Of common errors, and world's vanity,
Dost here enjoy that sacred sweet content
That baser souls, not knowing, not affect:
And so by Fate's and Fortune's good aspéct
Raised, in thy height, and these unhappy times,
Disfurnish'd wholly of heroical spirits
That learning should with glorious hands uphold,
(For who should learning underbear but he
That knows thereof the precious worthiness,
And seeks true science from base vanity?)
Hast in regard the true philosophy
That in pure wisdom seats her happiness (1).

A specific allusion to Mercury is wanting in Peele's poem. It is, however, evident from Nashe's *Summers Last Will* that Hermes-Mercury and Hermes Trismegistus could be interchangeably used at the time. In that comedy, ll. 1260-65, immediately after Nashe's allegorization of Cerberus as one whose ink 'seru'd men a while to make rude workes withall,' we find that

> *Hermes*, secretarie to the Gods,
> Or *Hermes Trismegistus*, as some will,
> Wearie with grauing in blind characters,
> And figures of familiar beasts and plants,
> Inuented letters to write lies withall.

These lines suggest that Nashe was far from being an admirer of Trismegistus, an impression which is certainly strengthened by the speeches that follow. These speeches, spoken by 'Winter,' are nothing but a sustained attack on branches of learning such as astronomy, alchemy, and mathematics, all, in fact, sciences sponsored by Hermes. Suppose for one moment that about 1590-92 certain artists and philosophers regarded Hermes-Mercury as a symbol of learning generally, then Nashe's view of the worshippers of that deity becomes pre-eminently clear from Winter's speeches in *Summers Last Will*. The speech in which astronomy is attacked is obviously related to and perhaps partly echoed by certain expressions in *Love's Labour's Lost*.

---

(1) PEELE, *Works*, II, 316-20.

Winter. Next them, a company of ragged knaues,
Sun-bathing beggers, lazie hedge-creepers,
Sleeping face vpwards in the fields all night,
Dream'd strange deuices of the Sunne and Moone;
And they, like Gipsies, wandring vp and downe,
Told fortunes, iuggled, nicknam'd all the starres,
And were of idiots term'd Philosophers:

(Ll. 1285-1291.)

However superficial the resemblance, one may compare Nashe's
'nicknam'd all the starres' with Shakespeare's 'These earthly God-
fathers of heauens lights, That giue a name to euery fixed Starre'
(*Love's Labour's Lost*, I, i, 88-9). McKerrow has pointed out that
Nashe, when he composed a good deal of the speeches of Winter,
leaned heavily upon the *De Incertitudine et Vanitate Scientiarum*
(1527) by Henry Cornelius Agrippa von Nettesheym (1486-1535).
Agrippa's work was a widely popular satirical denunciation of the
sciences, which Nashe seems to have been very fond of using, now
in the original and now in the translation made by James Sandford
(first edition in 1569). But the lines just quoted are entirely of
Nashe's invention. Nor are the ensuing speeches of Winter derived
from Agrippa's work, though, of course, Agrippa and Nashe are
dealing with the same theme. Nashe attacks 'word-warriors' and
'lazy star-gazers,' mathematicians and alchemists, his special target
being contemplation.

So those word-warriers, lazy star-gazers,
Vsde to no labour but to lowze themselues,
Had their heads fild with coosning fantasies,
They plotted how to make their pouertie
Better esteemde of then high Soueraignty:
They thought how they might plant a heaue on earth,
Whereof they would be principall lowe gods (1);
That heauen they called Contemplation, . . .

(Ll. 1326-1333.)

Skie measuring Mathematicians,
Golde-breathing Alcumists also we haue,
Both which are subtill witted humorists,
That get their meales by telling miracles,
Which they haue seene in trauailing the skies: . . .

(Ll. 1371-1375.)

---

(1) Compare *Love's Labour's Lost*, I, i, 191-196 :

Clowne. Sir the Contempls thereof are as touching me.
Fer. A letter from the magnificent *Armado.*
Bero. How low soeuer the matter, I hope in God for high words.
Lon. A high hope for a low heauen God grant vs patience.

— 233 —

Innumerable monstrous practises
Hath loytring contemplation brought forth more,
Which t'were too long particular to recite:
Suffice, they all conduce vnto this end,
To banish labour, nourish slotfulnesse,
Pamper vp lust, deuise newfangled sinnes.

(Ll. 1388-1393.)

The impression one gathers from this disparagement of the sciences
tallies with that conveyed by the Eliot speech in *Pierces Supererogation*, a speech specially designed to expose the vanity of book-
learning and containing a characteristic dismissal of 'flying speculations' and of 'Hermes ascending spirit.'

That Mercury was often associated with learning around 1592,
is brought out by a survey of the pronouncements of the authors
we have been chiefly concerned with. Fraunce, whose *Third part* has
already proved an enlightening book, affords a starting-point. There
are no less than three passages in his *Third part* which emphasize
that the figure of Mercury is a fitting symbol for 'mind,' 'reason,'
'understanding,' and especially 'mathematical knowledge.' For his
first allegorization Fraunce quotes Comes as his authority (1).

Natalis Comes maketh this ethicall moralization of it. The celestiall
and heauenly power in Man, called reason or vnderstanding, figured by
Mercurius, doth moderate, pacifie, and temper all those inordinate motions
and affections proceeding from that other facultie of the minde, prouoking
to wrath and anger.

Mercury, according to his diuers aspects, worketh diuers influences
in mens minds: if he be predominant, he afordeth eloquence, elegancy,
learning, and especially mathematicall knowledge.

A few pages further Fraunce gives an account of the tale of Salmacis
and Hermaphrodite and follows it up by the following remarkable
'allegorical' explanation.

Elpinus was as briefe, as *Ergastus* had beene tedious in his tale of
his two wantons. If qd he, at any mans birth, there be a coniunction
of *Venus* and *Mercurie*, it makes him neither man nor woman, both woman
and man, giuen to inordinate and vnnaturall lust, noted by *Salmacis*.
For these two planets are so repugnant, that they can neuer be well
conioyned; sith *Venus* is all for the body, and *Mercury* onely for the
minde (2).

(1) See Comes, *Mythologiae*, p. 241.
(2) Fraunce, *Third part*. sigg. D_3 v⁰, K_4 r⁰, N_4 r⁰.

In 1592, the year of the publication of the *Third part*, we learn from Harvey's *Foure Letters* that 'not Venus, but Mercury' should 'strike the stroke,' a phrase which pits Venus against Mercury, just as Fraunce's third explanation does. Considering that *Love's Labour's Lost* is a decidedly topical comedy on the theme 'love versus learning' and that the play was presumably written in the latter half of 1592, it looks as though the opposition Venus-Mercury had originally some topical relevance. It is enlightening to find that Florio, a writer whose participation in the literary disputes of the time cannot be questioned, can also be drawn on for purposes of comparison.

Florio had in 1591 been expending his talents on the praise of feminine charm in his *Second Fruits*. Turning the tables upon those who despised 'love' in favour of 'learning', he even went so far as to maintain that feminine beauty was *the* fountainhead of what was in his view the only true form of learning. Mercury is but once mentioned for his 'wiles' in the *Second Fruits*, but there is a relevant allusion in *The Italian Tutor*, a language-manual published in 1640 by Giovanni Torriano. Miss Yates (1) has shown why *The Italian Tutor* can be attributed to Florio. On Florio's death in 1619 his wife disposed of her deceased husband's manuscripts, and, eventually, some of these must have come into the hands of Torriano. The dialogues in *The Italian Tutor* are so different in character and scope from those published by Torriano at a later date, and they remind us so much of Florio's manner in the *First* and *Second Fruits*, that Miss Yates does not hesitate to claim that Torriano almost certainly used the manuscript of what may be called Florio's *Third Fruits* to publish it under his own name as *The Italian Tutor*. In this work Florio defends his former position that love is superior to knowledge, but, significantly, he contrasts these in mythological terms. In a dialogue entitled 'Concerning being learned and poore, ignorant and rich' we find this:

Heare me this one thing more. You know that men, the more they are given to *Mercury*, the lesse they doe pleasure *Venus*, so that for their Armes, full sore against their wills, they give the two celestiall signes *Taurus* and *Aries* (2).

---

(1) F. A. YATES, *John Florio*, pp. 327-8.
(2) G. TORRIANO, *The Italian Tutor* (London, 1640), sig. H$_4$. The interlocutors of the dialogues are not named but indicated by the successive letters of the alphabet.

It stands to reason that the preceding quotations do not exhaust the number of allusions to Mercury in Elizabethan literature (1). The selection offered here has been largely determined by chronological considerations. One more quotation may be adduced to show that many Elizabethans were aware of the fact that Mercury was ultimately identical with Thoth, the Egyptian god of wisdom. Here is what Harvey has to tell us of 'the Aegyptian Mercury':

> The Aegyptian Mercury would prouide to plant his foote vpon a square; and his Image in Athens was quadrangular, whatsoeuer was the figure of his hart: and although he were sometime a Ball of Fortune, (who can assure himselfe of Fortune?) yet was he neuer a wheele of folly, or an eele of Ely. The glibbest tungue must consult with his witt; & the roundest head with his feete: or peraduenture hee will not greatly thanke his tickle deuise (2).

Harvey is, of course, referring here to the *hermae*, posts on which Hermes' head was put. Mercury is associated with the idea of roundness and squareness, attributes that made him a suitable symbol for the transforming substance of alchemy. Though Harvey's source for the above passage cannot be pinned down with precision, it is likely that he got the notion of Mercury's planting his foot upon a square, and of his quadrangular image, from Cartari's *Imagines Deorum* (3). As Harvey asserts that Mercury's statue was set up in Athens—obviously, to ornate the 'Academy'—so Cartari tells us that it was erected quadrangularly to ornate the academies (4).

It is in the light of the 'hermetic' symbolism prevalent in the early nineties that I should like to suggest a new interpretation for the motto-like ending of *Love's Labour's Lost*, a play apparently permeated by ideas connected with the claims of the learned. The play has an abrupt ending, says Sir Edmund Chambers (5), running 'The vvordes of Mercurie, are harsh after the songes of Apollo.' Sir Edmund observes that Mercury has nothing to do with what

---

(1) A very important passage on TRISMEGISTOS occurs in the account of the Gray's Inn Revels (held in the Christmas season of 1594-95), preserved in the *Gesta Grayorum*, ed. W. W. GREG (London, 1914), pp. 34-5.

(2) HARVEY, *Pierces Supererogation*, sig. C₃ (*Works*, II, 56).

(3) See CARTARI, *Imagines Deorum* (Lyons), pp. 217-8.

(4) C. G. JUNG, *Psychology and Alchemy* (London, 1953), p. 127, points out that Thoth was associated with squareness and roundness in ancient Egypt. The only later authority he quotes for this association is CARTARI, but it was commonplace before CARTARI wrote his work.

(5) E. K. CHAMBERS, *Shakespeare*, I, 338.

precedes, and he is no doubt right with regard to the immediately preceding lines. But he is probably wrong should he think that the symbolism currently attached to Mercury is not bound up with the very texture of Shakespeare's play. It is generally assumed that Shakespeare, in the final line of his play, contrasts eloquence (prose) with inspired poetry, and this is surely an interpretation that cannot be disregarded. Granting the probable existence of a School of Night and the association Mercury-learning, however, it is more probable that the phrase expresses Shakespeare's disavowal of hermetic speculation. That a quite special significance must be attached to 'The vvordes of Mercurie, are harsh after the songes of Apollo' is borne out by the fact that the sentence is printed in larger type in the original Quarto text (1). In his analysis of the 'copy' for *Love's Labour's Lost*, 1598, Professor Dover Wilson (2) observes that the Quarto prints it without speech-heading and in larger type than the rest of the text, and remarks that the compositor would hardly have troubled to take out a fresh case of types unless he had a strong leading in his 'copy.' There are, therefore, bibliographical as well as textual reasons which stress the paramount importance of the contrast Mercury-Apollo. Did Shakespeare himself write the 'motto' in a large hand ? Or was it a comment on the play by someone to whom Shakespeare had lent his text for perusal, as Dover Wilson suggests ? These questions cannot be definitely answered and the two suppositions seem equally suitable.

The motto-like character of the sentence in question calls to mind the only other motto found in Shakespeare's writings. *Venus and Adonis* appeared in 1593 with the following lines from Ovid on the title-page:

Vilia miretur vulgus; mihi flavus Apollo
Pocula Castalia plena ministret aqua.

Professor Alexander (3) has emphasized that it would be wrong to dismiss this motto as a merely conventional assertion of Shakespeare's literary talents. As Alexander says, the motto is hardly intelligible if Shakespeare had not already given proof of his genius. It is

(1) The Folio gives the sentence to Armado and adds 'You that way; we this way.'
(2) Ed. *Love's Labour's Lost*, p. 185. The editorial comment runs : 'No one has explained the sentence hitherto; and we make no attempt . . .'
(3) P. Alexander, *Shakespeare's Life and Art*, p. 93.

therefore natural to regard the final line of *Love's Labour's Lost* as a new affirmation of Shakespeare's poetic consciousness. 'Harsh' words hardly fit eloquence, as whose patron Mercury is customarily viewed. But Mercury and Apollo do contrast the aspirations of a peculiarly esoteric type of learning with those of divinely inspired poetry.

CHAPTER IX

LOVE'S LABOUR'S LOST RE-STUDIED

INTRODUCTION (1)

In recent years *Love's Labour's Lost* has aroused considerable attention, partly because many scholars have come to recognize that this comedy is distinguishable from those of Shakespeare's so-called first period by an unmistakable maturity of style, and therefore worth their serious consideration; and partly because it deals with a theme in which many of Shakespeare's contemporaries seem to have been deeply interested: whether the pursuit of knowledge and truth is a loftier ideal of life than love. But the play has proved attractive to many students for quite different reasons. It bristles with puns and allusions which have taxed the ingenuity of a long line of critics and commentators, and this led many to cherish the hope that convincing solutions might one day be offered. It is therefore not just a passing whim of scholars to think of *Love's Labour's Lost* as a battling-ground for imaginative minds, a 'happy hunting-ground for the unbridled theorist and the crank' (2). After repeated readings the conviction grows upon the reader that the play is decidedly topical one, and yet, in spite of a growing number of efforts to determine the play's bearing on contemporary events, one often gathers the impression that it is unlikely that the mystery of *Love's Labour's Lost* will ever be cleared up satisfactorily.

Nor is the problem a merely topical one; scholars have been at pains to determine the date of Shakespeare's first handling of

---

(1) On *Love's Labour's Lost* the following studies have been consulted :

H. C. Hart, ed. *LLL* (London, Arden Shakespeare, 1906).

H. B. Charlton, "The Date of *Love's Labour's Lost*," *MLR*, XIII (1918), 257-266 and 387-400.

A. Quiller-Couch and J. D.Wilson, ed. *LLL*.

A. K. Gray, "The Secret of *Love's Labour's Lost*," *PMLA*, XXXIX (1924), 581-611.

O. J. Campbell, "*Love's Labour's Lost* Re-Studied," in *Studies in Shakespeare, Milton and Donne* (Univ. of Michigan, 1925), pp. 1-45.

R. Taylor, *The Date of Love's Labour's Lost* (New York, 1932).

F. A. Yates, *A Study of Love's Labours Lost*.

M. C. Bradbrook, *The School of Night*, esp. chapter VII.

F. P. Wilson, *Elizabethan and Jacobean* (Oxford, 1945).

T. W. Baldwin, *Shakspere's Five-Act Structure* (Urbana, Illinois, 1947), pp. 579-664.

R. David, ed. *LLL* (London, 'New' Arden Shakespeare, 1951).

(2) See Quiller-Couch and Dover Wilson, edd. *LLL*, p. xvi.

the play, but, this question being tied to the one of re-writing or revision, no confident solution has ever been offered. Early dates have been advanced by those who relied on metrical tests, while more recent students have grouped the play with *A Midsummer-Night's Dream*, *Romeo and Juliet* and the Sonnets, on the strength of stylistic similarities. *Love's Labour's Lost* is clearly set off from comedies such as *The Comedy of Errors* and *The Two Gentlemen of Verona* by a kind of engaging self-assurance, a peculiar dynamism and gusto which animate the play throughout. Though still a structurally weak play, Shakespeare makes us forget this deficiency by his definite awareness that he can put his hand to really 'fine' writing, that he can write brilliantly and persuasively, particularly when embarking upon what looks like a statement of his personal views.

Love's Labour's Lost was the earliest of Shakespeare's dramas to be published under his own name. The only quarto edition before the 1623 Folio bears the date 1598 and has the following title-page: A / Pleasant / Conceited Comedie / called, / Loues labors lost. / As it was presented before her Highness / this last Christmas. / Newly corrected and augmented / by W. Shakespeare. / Imprinted at London by W. W. / for Cutbert Burby. / 1598. Its printer was William White, a man who had just set up business. From the bibliographical analysis given by Professor Dover Wilson (1) it appears that the compositor working in White's office must have been a person with little professional experience. The compositor's shortcomings are, however, certainly made good in another respect: an inexperienced compositor is likely to examine and to follow a manuscript with care, and thus manuscript spellings may get into print. When there are reasons for supposing that the manuscript underlying a printed quarto is Shakespeare's autograph, it is even possible to study more closely how Shakespeare wrote his plays and what his original manuscript looked like. As far as the 1598 quarto of *Love's Labour's Lost* is concerned its text was probably based on a Shakespearean autograph.

The title-page itself also calls for comment. It states that the comedy was performed in the presence of Queen Elizabeth, and that it was 'newly corrected and augmented.' If this statement is correct it would seem to imply that the play was not published for the

---

(1) Ed. *LLL*, pp. 97-130.

first time in 1598, and Professor A. W. Pollard's conclusion (1) was that the 1598 quarto replaced a surreptitious or 'bad' quarto. Many subsequent commentators (2) have accepted this conclusion. But the questionable validity of 'newly corrected and augmented' was clearly demonstrated by Leo Kirschbaum, who argues that there is almost no 'probability that a bad quarto preceded Burby's Love's Labour's Lost, and there is little probability that the lost quarto was very different from Burby's edition' (3). I fully subscribe to Kirschbaum's argument, since he shows conclusively that almost nothing can be deduced from statements on title-pages asserting correction or augmentation. This does not mean, however, that Love's Labour's Lost does not show signs of revision or addition, but these signs do not furnish ground for the belief that any 'bad' quarto of the play ever existed (4).

Two pieces of external evidence testify to the existence of Shakespeare's comedy in 1598. Francis Meres mentions it in his famous list of plays in *Palladis Tamia* and groups it with another play *Love's Labour's Won*, which critics have tried to identify with almost any comedy in the Shakespearean canon. A second writer referring to the comedy is Robert Tofte, whose poem *Alba, or the Months Mind of a Melancholy Lover* (1598) contains the line

Loues Labour Lost, I once did see a Play.

Because of the double meaning of 'once' it is not possible to interpret Tofte's line definitely. It looks, however, as though Tofte means that he had seen the play long ago.

Love's Labour's Lost was to leave more distinct traces in the work of yet another poet, John Weever. Weever's *Faunus and Melliflora* (1600) is an interesting poem containing allusions to several

---

(1) A. W. POLLARD, *Shakespeare Folios and Quartos* (London, 1909), p. 71.

(2) J. D. WILSON, ed. *LLL*, p. 99.

W. W. GREG, "Principles of Emendation in Shakespeare," in *Aspects of Shakespeare* (Oxford, 1933), p. 163.

E. K. CHAMBERS, *William Shakespeare*, I, 162, 333.

F. P. WILSON, "Shakespeare and the New Bibliography," in *Studies in Retrospect* (London, Bibliographical Society, 1945), p. 120.

R. DAVID, ed. *LLL*, pp. xix-xx.

(3) L. KIRSCHBAUM, "Is *The Spanish Tragedy* a Leading Case? Did a bad quarto of *Love's Labour's Lost* ever exist?," *JEGP*, XXXVII (1938), 501-512.

(4) On KIRSCHBAUM's evidence Miss G. HJORT,"The Good and Bad Quartos of *Romeo and Juliet* and *Love's Labour's Lost*," *MLR*, XXI (1926), 140-146, cannot possibly argue that BURBY's quarto was printed from a corrected 'bad' quarto.

contemporary productions (1). It is in the main an erotic poem, but near the end it turns into a mythological account of the origin of satires, which leads A. Davenport, the editor of the poem, to conclude that Weever had no such ending in mind when he wrote the greater part of his work. Just before this mythological narrative there is a long passage in which Weever describes how Faunus tries to make Melliflora see that she cannot possibly keep her vow of chastity. The speech of Faunus contains distinct echoes from *Love's Labour's Lost* and Davenport observes that 'from the context in which they occur and from the echoes themselves it appears that, to Weever's mind, *Love's Labour's Lost* was a play about an *irreligiously* presumptuous vow of austerity' (2). It is lines 919-934 of *Faunus and Melliflora* that bear the clearest traces of the influence of Shakespeare's play.

> A Votaresse, a Secluse, and a Nunne,
> Nay you must be forsworne when all is done:
> For, can you study, fast, and pray among?
> No no, (faire nymph) your stomacke is too yong,
> Your beautie will dispense with this decree,
> You must be periurde of necessitie.
> If you but come your Orizons to say,
> *Dianaes* Hunts-men will forget to pray,
> Or rather leaue before they do beginne.
> Are you not then the Autresse of this sinne?
> Or if her priests such fairenesse do espie,
> They will be conquerd by your lookes, and die,
> Committing murder, what wil follow then?
> This odious name, The Murdresse of men,
> Which is flat treason gainst all Deitie:
> For murder is much worse than periurie.

As to the plot of *Love's Labour's Lost*, its ultimate origin has not been satisfactorily or convincingly traced. Divergent theories have been proposed but most scholars are now agreed that *Love's Labour's Lost* reflects certain events at the court of Henry, King of Navarre, at Nérac. The scene of the action of our play is Navarre itself, while the initial speech is put into the mouth of Ferdinand, 'K. of Nauar.' Abel Lefranc (3), following the suggestions of Sir

---

(1) They have all been discussed by A. DAVENPORT in his edition of *Faunus and Melliflora (1600)* (University Press of Liverpool, 1948).
(2) Ed. *Faunus and Melliflora*, pp. vii-viii.
(3) A. LEFRANC, *Sous le masque de 'William Shakespeare'* (Paris, 1919), II, 59 ff. The first to point out these correspondences was SIDNEY LEE in "A New Study of *Love's*

Sidney Lee, shows that there is a remarkable coincidence between the names of the characters in *Love's Labour's Lost* and those of the followers of the King of Navarre, the later Henry IV. The comedy's central figure Biron, or Berowne, is named after marshall Biron, a well-known leader in the French wars. He was accidentally killed about July 1592. The son, Charles de Gontaut, possessed even greater military genius than his father and the highest honours were showered upon him, but he later conspired against his master and was sentenced to death (beheaded in the Bastille, July 31, 1602). The latter's career became the subject of Chapman's Biron tragedies. The battles fought by Shakespeare's 'Biron' soon after Henry's accession to the throne were no doubt followed with great interest by most Elizabethans, for in 1591 and 1592 Biron often fought in concert with Essex. Another supporter of Henry of Navarre in his wars for the French crown was Henri d'Orléans, Duc de Longueville (died 1595), whose name appears in the play as Longaville. The Dumaine of the comedy, however, derives his name from Henry's great opponent Mayenne, Charles of Lorraine, Duc du Maine, the most prominent representative of the 'Ligue' after the death of Henri de Guise (Dec. 23, 1588). The nominal correspondences between the characters of the play and French leaders in the Wars of Religion suggest that Shakespeare was perfectly familiar with contemporary French history.

Another feature of *Love's Labour's Lost*, more closely connected with the plot, is the embassy of the Princess to Ferdinand, an embassy whose delegates succeed in thwarting the King and his companions in their purposes to set up an academy. This aspect of the plot seems to reflect the visit paid by Marguerite de Valois to her husband at Nérac in 1578. The object of this visit was to arrive at an agreement concerning the settlement of Marguerite's dowry of Aquitaine. The dowry is referred to at II, i, 7-8:

Matchles *Nauar*, the plea of no lesse weight,
Then *Aquitaine*, a Dowrie for a Queene.

Lefranc (1) further observes that expressions such as 'I saw him at the Duke *Alansoes* once' (II, i, 61) and 'Did not I dance with you

---

Labour's Lost," *Gentleman's Magazine* (1880), an article enlarged and corrected in his *A Life of William Shakespeare* (London, 1925).
(1) A. LEFRANC, *Sous le masque*, II, 70-71.

in *Brabant* once' (II, i, 114-5) are probably connected with the contemporary events immediately preceding Marguerite's visit. The correspondences just mentioned are so remarkable that they render it likely that Shakespeare got his fairly detailed knowledge of French history from some Englishman or other who had visited Henry of Navarre's fashionable court.

The social atmosphere of *Love's Labour's Lost* is also entirely consistent with that prevalent at the court of Nérac. Both in the play and at Nérac the object of Marguerite's visit recedes into the background and is soon lost sight of to leave time for love-making and conversational gaiety. Thus far the correspondences are striking, but the parallelism is not complete. The Marguerite of history, it is true, was accompanied by a bevy of ladies bent on making love-conquests, but she herself could not take part in them since she was already married. This historical fact is, of course, disregarded by Shakespeare and he makes the Queen participate in the pursuit of her ladies in waiting. Another element of divergence noted by Lefranc and O. J. Campbell (1), but discounted by the former for the weakest of reasons, is the fact that the court of the play is 'tinged with asceticism' and decidedly intellectual. The ascetic tendencies of the comedy's chief characters are most clearly pronounced in the initial part of the action. The King and his fellows wish to seek the light of truth, and resolve 'Not to see Ladyes, study, fast, not sleepe' (I, i, 48), in order to find out things hidden and barred from common sense (I, i, 57). The arrival of the French embassy soon defeats the serious pursuits of Navarre's court, and each of the 'philosophers' abandons his vow of chastity to court the lady of his predilection. This tinge of asceticism, setting the tune of what is to follow, appears to be entirely of Shakespeare's invention. Chapman, in *The Shadow of Night*, strikes the same note by emphasizing the cult of austerity and recommending 'inuocation, fasting, watching,' in terms echoing Shakespeare's.

The 'academic' atmosphere of *Love's Labour's Lost*, on the other hand, can be related to the academic movement that was so characteristic an achievement of sixteenth century intellectual life, as well as to the efforts of Henry of Navarre to rival Henry III's Académie du Palais. The Protestant poet Agrippa d'Aubigné tells us in an undated letter that the King of Navarre created a small

---

(1) O. J. CAMPBELL, in *Studies*, p. 8.

academy in imitation of the one at the court and also mentions some of its members. Among the most noted were d'Aubigné himself, Du Bartas and du Plessis-Mornay (1). The most important contemporary work that is to be regarded as the outcome of the French academic movement is Pierre de la Primaudaye's *L'Académie Françoise*, published in part in 1577 and finally as a collected whole in 1613. La Primaudaye dedicated his work to Henry III. It enjoyed a great reputation among all those interested in learning in the sixteenth century. The first part of the *Académie Françoise*, containing the section on moral philosophy, was translated into English by T. Bowes and published in 1586. Such was the vogue of *The French Academie* that it was reprinted four times within less than 30 years. La Primaudaye's work is linked through an extraordinary coincidence with *Love's Labour's Lost*. It relates how four young men of Anjou, after the interruption of their studies caused by the wars, found an academy, and Professor Theodore Spencer (2) has suggested that Shakespeare may well have got his philosophic King of Navarre and his three companions from La Primaudaye's work.

In one respect, however, the play deviates most markedly from historical fact. Acts IV and V are mostly concerned with the 'pageant of the nine worthies,' a progress wholly unrelated to Henry IV's acquisition of the French throne. It is generally agreed that this pageant has nothing to do with the play proper, so much so that some critics have claimed that it did not form part of the original version, and that it was 'thrust in from the outside' (3). Campbell, for example, holds that the play was not given any closely knit structure, but was planned as a chronicle of entertainments provided for Queen Elizabeth.

On the possibly topical nature of the pageant Sir Edmund Chambers (4) comments:

There may be other topical allusions in an obviously satirical play over which time has drawn a veil. Many attempts have been made to trace portraits in the exponents of the *Worthies*. Armado has been identified with the Monarcho, Antonio Perez, Lyly, Philip of Spain, and Sir Walter Raleigh; Holofernes with John Florio, Bishop Cooper, Thomas Harriot, Chapman, and one Richard Lloyd, who wrote lines on

---

(1) See F. A. YATES, *The French Academies*, p. 123.
(2) T. SPENCER, *Shakespeare and the Nature of Man* (New York, 1943), p. 87 ff.
(3) See the excellent summary of the various hypotheses in O. J. CAMPBELL's study.
(4) E. K. CHAMBERS, *Shakespeare*, I. 336.

the Worthies in 1584; Moth with La Mothe-Fénelon, a French ambassador, as far back as 1568-75, and with Nashe; and so forth. Most
of this is mere beating the air. As Campbell points out, this underworld
of *Love's Labour's Lost* represents the stock masks of Italian comedy,
the *capitano* and his *zanni*, the *pedante* or *dottore*, the parasite or *affamato*,
the clown, the magistrate. It does not follow that there may not be
personal touches in the reproduction of them.

Chambers is no doubt right in stressing the conventional nature of
the stock types of Italian comedy, but the 'personal touches in the
reproduction of them' which he allows for will bear further in-
vestigating. It hardly needs saying that Chambers is an arch-sceptic
in all matters connected with Shakespeare.

Whatever Chambers may maintain, the portrayal of Armado
and Moth has appeared peculiar to many investigators. Rupert Taylor
and Miss Yates have achieved great merit by clarifying much in
tracing the identity of these two characters: Taylor has suggested
that Armado owes much to the personality of Harvey, while Miss
Yates, following the 'New' Cambridge editors, has argued that Moth
represents Nashe. In what follows I shall try to substantiate these
claims further. *If* the latter half of 1592 appears as the most likely
date for Shakespeare to be engaged in writing out the first draft
of *Love's Labour's Lost*, the belief is justified that he may have
wished to incorporate in it certain aspects of the Harvey-Nashe
controversy. It is my aim, in the following pages, to make such a
date-ascription acceptable.

But before going any further, it cannot be too strongly
emphasized that Shakespeare, as contrasted with his immediate
contemporaries, is often enigmatically non-committal in his attitude.
His artistic creation, though indubitably rooted in his personal
experience, is more often than not separated by an almost unbridge-
able gap from the remote causes which first set his imagination in
motion. More frequently than in any other play of his, Shakespeare
is in *Love's Labour's Lost* speaking with his tongue in his cheek.
To any theorizer about the play this should be a warning for caution
in the extreme.

THE DATE OF *LOVE'S LABOUR'S LOST*

As the date advanced by Professor H. B. Charlton in his brilliant
article "The Date of *Love's Labour's Lost*," *MLR*, XIII (1918),

257-266 and 387-400, is the autumn of 1592, a date-ascription with which I find myself in full agreement, it may not be amiss to follow the chief points of his contribution and to pass a few criticisms on his argument. Indeed, it is comprehensible that most of the evidence he adduces comes almost necessarily under review here. But the contributions of other critics in the field will also be taken into account.

Charlton points out that the French names are irrelevant to the issue of the play, and that, therefore, Shakespeare used them to add topical interest to his drama. This 'French' aspect narrows down the period of composition between 1589 as the earlier time limit—accession of the Protestant King Henry IV—and 1593 as the later time limit, for after Henry's conversion to Catholicism—on July 25, 1593—the French names would no longer be palatable to an English public. It is difficult to believe Charlton, however, when he suggests that these names were a second and not a first choice. Ferdinand, as the King of Navarre is named in the initial part of the play, in the speech allocations up to II, i (1) as well as in the first stage-direction, was, so Charlton implies, Shakespeare's first choice. And as the poet proceeded with his work he changed his mind and put 'King' instead. Ferdinand, it is true, could not have suggested Henry to the audience, for every Englishman knew perfectly well what the name of the King of France and of Navarre was. But 'Ferdinand' was not explicitly suggested to the original audience, for during a performance that name was not at all heard on the stage. It is evident, it seems to me, that 'Ferdinand' was Shakespeare's completely personal choice, and apparently his first and only choice, for this name was what was left standing in the manuscript that was handed over to the printer in 1597-8. What is more, the view of a double choice is further rendered untenable by the fact that the very first stage-direction 'Enter Ferdinand K. of Nauar, Berovvne, *Longauill, and Dumaine*' shows clearly and unmistakably that Shakespeare wished to confer the royal dignity upon Ferdinand from the moment he began to write the play. It is sometimes argued that stage-directions were inserted after the speeches

---

(1) The last time 'Ferd.' appears is at II, i, 167 and this seems a little early for the christian name to drop out. But note that in Act III Berowne is the only courtier, while Navarre appears as 'King' only from IV, iii, 21 onwards. On the assumption that SHAKESPEARE wrote the play right through from beginning to end, a considerable time must have elapsed between the composition of II, i and IV, iii, and he may have found it easier to use 'King.'

had been written out, or that they were of playhouse origin. The latter view may be disregarded here for the source of the printed text was probably Shakespeare's own manuscript, while the one who prepared the prompt-book cannot be credited with the introduction of 'Ferdinand.' And if the initial stage-direction was supplied after the composition of I, i, Shakespeare's use of 'K. of Nauar' is all the more remarkable in that he associates the titular indication with 'Ferdinand,' an at first sight inexplicable error on his part, for no King of Navarre ever bore that christian name. A probable explanation is that this seeming error is attributable to Shakespeare's having Ferdinando Stanley, Lord Strange, in mind.

The choice of the Navarre background places the original composition date of *Love's Labour's Lost* between 1589-1593, but this space of time requires to be narrowed down further. In the autumn of 1592 the English interest in French affairs appears to have been greatest. From the moment of his accession Henry IV had appealed urgently to Queen Elizabeth for sending money and troops to help him, but it was only in January 1591 that Burghley was beginning to realize that English interests were at stake. Sir Roger Williams was sent with an expeditionary force to Dieppe, and in April this was followed by a contingent led by Sir John Norreys. The first expedition to create a really great sensation was that led by Essex, who was despatched to France in July 1591. Despite the combined efforts of the French and English troops the war turned into a failure and especially after the siege of Rouen, which lasted from December, 1591, to April, 1592, it dawned upon Elizabeth that Essex had better be recalled. And Essex returned to England.

Henry IV's great opponent was Alexander Farnese, Duke of Parma, the leader of the Spanish forces, who compelled him to raise the siege of Rouen. Essex's warlike enterprises were referred to in Nashe's *Pierce Penilesse*. Nashe mentioned 'a dapper Iacke, that hath been but ouer at *Deepe*,' and 'a Pioner before the walls of *Roan*' (1), and also referred to the siege of Guingamp in which Norreys, and not Essex, was concerned, in 1591.

In the summer of 1592 a new contingent was despatched to France under Norreys and this period marked, as Charlton says, the highest level of public interest in the French wars. Harvey,

---

(1) NASHE. *Works*, I, 169.

indeed, mentions Norreys's expedition in the second of his *Foure Letters*, in a passage which clearly suggests that the time was ripe for an introduction of Henry and the commanders of his army into literature (1).

In the course of his article Professor Charlton repeatedly insists that no references to French events prior to the Essex expedition are traceable in English literature. But then he has evidently overlooked the unquestionably clear allusion Nashe made early in 1591, though it must be admitted that no specific event is mentioned. In Nashe's *Wonderfull . . . Prognostication*, published before March, 1591, there occurs a passage which suggests that the English interest in French affairs was, early in 1591, not as lukewarm as Charlton would have us believe.

Mary, Fraunce is like to haue a great dearth of honest men, if the king preuaile not against these mutenous Rebelles of the League, and Papists in diuers places to be plentye, if God or the King rout them not out with a sharpe ouerthrow (2).

To conclude the first section of his article Charlton points out that Shakespeare probably got his information from a returned soldier of Essex's contingent. Essex knew Biron personally, and the behaviour of the historic Biron corresponds remarkably well with that of Shakespeare's Biron. Furthermore, the lines at IV, i, 21-22

See see, my beautie wilbe sau'd by merrit.
O heresy in faire, fit for these dayes,

can be interpreted as a reference to the activity of the anti-Reformation movement. Henry's conversion was being discussed from March, 1592, onwards, and the lines quoted above again support Charlton's view that the play was written in that year.

These are the essential historical data accounting for the Navarre background of Shakespeare's comedy. It remains to make

---

(1) HARVEY, *Foure Letters*, p. 26 : 'Were I of sufficient discourse, to record the valiauntest, and memorablest actes of the world; I would count it a felicity, to haue the oportunity of so egregious, and heroicall an argument : not pleasurably deuised in counter-faite names, but admirably represented to the eie of France, and the eare of the world, in the persons of royall, and most puissant knightes : how singularlie worthy of most glorious, and immortal fame?' See H. B. CHARLTON, *MLR*, XIII, 265.

(2) NASHE, *Works*, III, 386-7. Compare also III, 383 : 'Beside that by all coniecturall argumentes the influence of Mars shall be so violent that diuers souldiers in partes beyond the seas shall fall out for want of their paye, and heere in our meridionall clyme great quarrelles shal be raised between man and man, especially in cases of Law.'

an additional remark. The 'civil' war in France suggested to Harvey that there was a 'new' one brewing when he remarked in his second letter that 'here is matter inough for a new ciuill war, or shall I say for a new Troyan siedge, if this poore Letter should fortune to come in print' (1). And Shakespeare, it is worth remarking, apparently followed suit and had the Princess say in *Love's Labour's Lost*, II, i, 225-7:

> Good witts will be iangling, but gentles agree,
> This ciuill warre of wittes were much better vsed
> On *Nauar* and his Bookmen, for heere tis abused.

The main feature of Act V, discussed in the second section of Professor Charlton's article, can also be fitted into the chronological scheme. Having sent fairings to their sweethearts the King and his companions appear disguised as Muscovites. This Muscovite masque can be related to the interest in Russian affairs that had recently been awakened by the diplomatic activity of Elizabeth's court with the Czar, and especially to the publication in 1591 of the elder Giles Fletcher's *Of the Russe Common Wealth*. In his book Fletcher gives an account of Russian ways of life and expatiates at length on the low intellectual and moral level of the Russians. What is particularly striking about the whole book is Fletcher's ridicule of the pomposity 'Of the maner of crowning or inauguration of the Russe Emperours.' This love of verbal pomposity is, according to Charlton, 'the official counterpart of those literary affectations which are the main theme of the play.' A point of incidental interest, perhaps not yet noted hitherto, is that this pompous style can be paralleled closely in the speech the Russian ambassador addresses to the 'Prince of Purpoole' in the *Gesta Grayorum* (2).

There is one textual peculiarity in the Russian masquerade that demands further attention, because there is reason to suppose that it may imply or involve an allusion to Lord Strange. On the arrival of the maskers Rosaline asks 'What would these stranges?' (V, ii, 174), a question in which the original Quarto reading may or may not be a misprint for 'strangers.' If not, the word may imply 'those who come in the company of Strange.' A few lines further down King 'Ferdinand,' on requesting Rosaline's love, gets the reply

---

(1) HARVEY, *Foure Letters*, p. 14.
(2) Compare G. FLETCHER, *Of the Russe Common Wealth* (London, 1591), sig. D₃ r⁰, and *Gesta Grayorum*, ed. W. W. GREG, pp. 45-6.

that he 'requests but Mooneshine in the water,' which draws the
following repartee from his lips (V, ii, 209-10):

> Then in our measure, do but vouchsafe one change,
> Thou bidst me begge, this begging is not strange.

And 'change-strange' is again played on two lines further:

> *Kin.* Wil you not daunce? How come you thus estranged?
> *Ro.* You tooke the moone at ful, but now shee's changed?

And a little further, at V, ii, 218-9, Rosaline says:

> Since you are strangers, and come here by chance,
> Weele not be nice, take handes, we will not daunce.

Of course, Russians *are* strangers, but in a play of which 'Ferdinand,'
King of Navarre, is one of the chief characters, and in which the
claims of the learned are trifled with, it does not seem hazardous
to suppose that the 'strange' lines refer to Ferdinando Stanley
Lord Strange; and 'strange-change' occurs in the conversation of the
King. It will be remembered that Nashe in 1592 and Chapman in
1593 exalted Lord Strange as a man of supreme intellectual endow-
ments, and to find Shakespeare hinting at the same nobleman, in a
play probably written in 1592, is surely not surprising.

The three following sections in Professor Charlton's article
comprise, first, one on contemporary social allusions; then, one
on allusions to books; and next, one on verbal and stylistic echoes.
Most of the material dealt with in these sections will be found
discussed in recent scientific editions of the play. And this material,
on which I can offer no fresh comment, supports the view that
Shakespeare wrote his comedy in the latter half of 1592. Charlton's
sixth section, then, bears the title 'Possible Allusions to the Harvey-
Nashe Quarrels.' His verdict on the possible echoes of this quarrel
is merely negative. He concludes that 'the play was written before
the quarrel was of any moment' and that the only 'discoverable
reference' to it 'was not originally intended' (1). I hope to show
that such a view requires considerable qualification. Let us first
discuss the only reference discoverable.

At IV, ii, 89, we find 'Of persing a Hogshead,' both in the

---

(1) See H. B. CHARLTON, *MLR*, XIII (1918), 396-7.

Folio and in the Quarto (in its modern reading: 'Of piercing a hogshead'). Here is the context of the expression (IV, ii, 84-100):

Enter Iaquenetta and the Clowne.

Iaquenetta. God giue you good morrow M. Person.

Nath. Maister Person, *quasi* Person? And if one shoulde be perst, Which is the one?

Clo. Marrie M. Scholemaster, he that is liklest to a hoggshead.

Nath. Of persing a Hogshead, a good luster of conceit in a turph of Earth, Fier enough for a Flint, Pearle enough for a Swine: tis prettie, it is well.

Iaque. Good M. Parson be so good as read me this letter, it was geuen me by *Costard,* and sent me from *Don Armatho:* I beseech you read it.

Nath. Facile precor gellida, quando pecas omnia sub vmbra ruminat, and so foorth. Ah good olde *Mantuan,* I may speake of thee as the traueiler doth of *Venice, vemchie, vencha, que non te vnde, que non te perreche.*

In the speeches of this part the Quarto version confuses the speech-headings 'Nath.' and 'Holo.,' Nathaniel being often substituted for Holofernes. All editors now follow Rowe in the correct re-distribution of the speeches. Let us now examine 'of persing a Hogshead.'

'Person' suggests the pun 'pers-on' (= pierce one), and Shakespeare is quick to explain it himself. 'Pierce' in its turn is a term for broaching a cask and this brings along the expression 'piercing him that is likest a hogshead.' As Shakespeare develops his ideas logically Charlton maintains that the phrase 'of persing a Hogshead' was not written to incorporate an extraneous allusion. But both Charlton and H. C. Hart, the Arden editor of the play, point out that 'of' is a deliberate device for drawing attention to the phrase. Hart held in 1906 that Shakespeare borrowed the jest from the following passage in Harvey's *Pierces Supererogation,* and his suggestion has been accepted by many others (1).

She knew what she said, that intituled Pierce, the hoggeshed of witt: Penniles, the tospot of eloquence: & Nashe, the verye inuentor of Asses. She it is, that must broach the barrell of thy frisking conceite, and canonise the Patriarke of new writers (2).

---

(1) H. C. HART, ed. *LLL,* p. 78. Accepted by A. QUILLER-COUCH and J. DOVER WILSON, edd. *LLL,* pp. 126, 155.

(2) HARVEY, *Pierces Supererogation,* sig. F$_4$ r^0 (*Works,* II, 91).

To accept Hart's view would involve that Shakespeare wrote his play after *Pierces Supererogation* had been published, and this is why Professor Dover Wilson and others have argued that the play was written in 1593. Harvey's sadly laboured pamphlet probably became available about October. The probability is, however, that Harvey was the borrower, and if not, that there was neither borrower nor lender. Harvey certainly and Shakespeare probably had Nashe in mind and they both relished a jest on 'Pierce,' a term definitely associated with Nashe through the publication of *Pierce Penilesse*. A first explanation why 'of persing a Hogshead' is connected with Nashe is offered by Harvey, but his authority does not shed light on the composition date of *Love's Labour's Lost*. It will be recognized that the passage from *Pierces Supererogation* states in merely different terms Harvey's tediously repeated argument that Nashe's invention is of poor quality. Harvey, in fact, again insists—to borrow a few expressions of his in *Pierces Supererogation*—that Nashe fights with 'piercing aquafortis,' and not with the 'trickling water of Helicon'; that Nashe is one whose style is the 'very hart-blood of the Grape' and whose frisking pen plays the 'Sprite of the buttry.' To put it in a pregnant mythological formula: the fountains of Helicon are contrasted with the wine-casks (= hogsheads) of Bacchus. The terminology of Harvey's invective probably throws a fresh light on the meaning of Shakespeare's words. It seems now clear that Holofernes' amusement at Costard's jest is occasioned by the fact that Holofernes believes the jest to be connected with poetic invention. Jaquenetta has just addressed Nathaniel, the curate, as 'Person-parson,' then Holofernes asks who should be pierced, and Costard's hogshead jest brings in its train a whole string of comparisons. Holofernes is also interested in 'invention' in the ensuing conversation with Nathaniel where he criticizes Berowne's poetry as 'neither sauouring of Poetrie, wit, nor inuention' (IV, ii, 165).

But how could Shakespeare come by the hogshead jest before Harvey? So far from being conclusive, one may note that Nashe held in 1589, in the preface to *Menaphon*, that it was 'for a Poet to examine the pottle pots, and gage the bottome of whole gallons.' We have much better proof, however, that comparisons relating to 'gallons,' 'hogsheads,' and the like, did not pass unnoticed in Nashe's works, and in the Harvey-Nashe controversy generally. In the epistle 'To the Gentlemen Readers' prefixed to *Strange Newes*, apparently written early in December, 1592, Nashe explains why he decided to rail against Richard Harvey in *Pierce Penilesse*. Two main reasons are adduced: that Richard barked against him as one of the enemies of the Lamb of God and that he 'fetcht allusions out of the Buttery to debase' him. The statement is important for the light it throws on the origin of the quarrel.

> Say I am as verie a Turke as hee that three yeeres ago ranne vpon ropes, if euer I speld eyther his or anie of his kindreds name in reproch, before hee barkt against mee as one of the enemies of the Lambe of God, and fetcht allusions out of the Buttery to debase mee (1).

With 'heere beginneth the fray' Nashe starts his next paragraph. Let us now investigate what the 'allusions out of the Buttery' may reveal.

The only allusion directly related to 'buttery' that the prefatory epistle to the *Lamb of God* yields, is found in the passage where Richard Harvey says that Nashe was 'one whome I neuer heard of before (for I cannot imagin him to be *Thomas Nashe* our Butler of *Pembrooke Hall*, albeit peraduenture not much better learned).' It is true that the butler of Pembroke Hall is a real person (2), but apart from the phrase 'both matter and manner flowe alltogether in that mad ruffianly veine and drunken stile' (3), 'butler' is the only offensive term connected with 'buttery' that Richard's epistle contains. The 'butler of Pembroke Hall' turns up whenever Nashe or Gabriel Harvey are railing against each other (4). When the allusions 'out of the Buttery' are seen in conjunction with Nashe's enthusiastic praise of Bacchus in *Summers Last Will* (composed about October, 1592), it can hardly be doubted that it was the association Nashe-drunkenness which suggested to Shakespeare the association 'Pierce'-'hogshead.' Furthermore, it is illuminating to find the following 'person' passage in the epistle to the *Lamb of God*:

> The Lamb of God make him a better Lamb heereafter then he hath beene heeretofore, and teach him now to dispute rather *ad rem*, then *ad personam*, especially till he hath reformed his owne person, as corruptible, on my word and his owne proofe, as the person of any his mard Prelates (5).

It has become clear, I believe, that Shakespeare did not need

---

(1) NASHE, *Works*, I, 262.
(2) This was THOMAS NASH of Eltisley, Cambridgeshire (see MCKERROW, ed. *Nashe*, IV, 123).
(3) R. HARVEY in NASHE, *Works*, V, 178.
(4) See NASHE, *Works*, I, 197, and G. HARVEY, *Foure Letters*, p. 51.
(5) R. HARVEY in NASHE. *Works*, V, 179.

to borrow his hogshead jest from *Pierces Supererogation*. In that pamphlet there are plenty of 'allusions out of the Buttery' to debase Nashe, but the person who first used them—as we are told in *Strange Newes*—was Richard Harvey. And this is why Holofernes' allusion could be understood by any audience in the early nineties. It was in the latter half of 1592, apparently soon after *Pierce Penilesse* and the *Foure Letters* had been published, that the most opportune moment had come for inserting a jest on 'Pierce' and 'hogshead' into an undoubtedly topical play.

The passage at IV, ii, 84-100, quoted in full above, exhibits one more textual peculiarity which allows us to determine the composition date of *Love's Labour's Lost* with a high degree of probability. It is the Latin and Italian phrases closing the quotation which now demand consideration.

While Nathaniel reads Berowne's letter—Jaquenetta, of course, has made the audience and the other characters believe that it is Armado's—Holofernes is giving vent to his learning and finds nothing better than a Latin and an Italian phrase. 'Facile precor gellida, quando pecas omnia sub vmbra ruminat' is a misquotation of the beginning of the first eclogue of Mantuanus. Baptista Spagnuoli (1448-1516), commonly known as Mantuanus, was the author of *Bucolica seu Adolescentia* (earliest edition before 1502), a work ordinarily called the eclogues of Mantuanus. The *Bucolica* gradually became a school text-book in regular use all over Europe. In England the work was translated by G. Turberville in 1567, while many Latin editions appeared, in England as well as on the Continent. The first line of Mantuanus's work runs 'Fauste, precor gelida quando pecus omne sub umbra Ruminat.' Shakespeare's distortion of 'Fauste' to 'Facile' is deliberate, for Holofernes professes his fondness for 'facility' twice elsewhere. At IV, ii, 578 he says that he will affect the letter 'for it argues facility,' and a little later, at IV, ii, 125-7, we find: 'Here are onely numbers ratefied, but for the elegancie, facilitie, and golden cadence of poesie *caret: Ouiddius Naso* was the man.'

The quotation from Mantuanus's eclogue has a bearing on the date of *Love's Labour's Lost*. Hart (1) rightly asks why the line is thrust in head and shoulders, apropos of nothing, and points out that the words were classified by Harvey and Nashe, two of the

(1) H. C. HART, ed. *LLL*, p. 79.

chief writers before the public between August and December, 1592, as the especial property of the pedant. In the *Foure Letters* we find:

> He tost his imagination a thousand waies, and I beleeue, searched euery corner of his Grammar-schoole witte, (for his margine is as deepelie learned, as *Fauste precor gelida*) to see if he coulde finde anie meanes to relieue his estate, but all his thoughtes, and marginal notes consorted to his conclusion, That the worlde was vncharitable, and he ordained to be miserable (1).

And Nashe replies:

> With the first and second leafe hee plaies verie pretilie, and in ordinarie termes of extenuating verdits *Pierce Pennilesse for a Grammer Schoole wit;* saies *his Margine is as deepelie learnd as* Fauste praecor gelida, that *his Muse sobbeth and groneth verie piteously, bids him not cast himself headlong into the horrible gulph of desperation,* . . . (2)

Again it may be remarked that the topic of invention is broached. Shakespeare's use of the line from Mantuanus, though admittedly a line widely known, is probably due to Harvey's ridiculing Nashe with it. In other words, the same chronology would seem to be applicable to the tag from Mantuanus as to 'of persing a Hogshead': in both cases Nashe's *Strange Newes* sheds an immediate light on why Shakespeare introduces such allusions, and in both cases there is evidence showing that they were relevant to Nashe ever since *Pierce Penilesse* and the *Foure Letters* were published.

And more interesting still, Mantuanus's line occurs in English in Nashe's preface to Greene's *Menaphon*. Nashe there says of Seneca in connexion with the writer of the old *Hamlet* play—perhaps written by Shakespeare himself—'if you [dramatist] intreate him [Seneca] faire in a frostie morning, hee will affoord you whole Hamlets, I should say handfuls of Tragicall speeches' (3). McKerrow (4) says that the first half of this quotation is a meaningless tag, but, as Professor Baldwin (5) first recognized, 'if you intreate him faire in a frostie morning' is precisely identical in meaning with 'precor gelida.' Baldwin also observes that the line was

---

(1) HARVEY, *Foure Letters*, p. 45.
(2) NASHE, *Works*, I, 306.
(3) NASHE, *Works*, III, 315.
(4) R. B. McKERROW, ed. *Nashe*, IV, 449.
(5) T. W. BALDWIN, *Small Latine & Lesse Greeke*, I, 643-45.

evidently used to characterize a beginner in poetry. On the assumption that Shakespeare is the author of the old *Hamlet* the expression is relevant to him.

A few words must now be said about the Italian proverb. It has long been recognized that the correct rendering of it is found in the *First* and *Second Fruits* of John Florio, as well as in James Sandford's *The Garden of Pleasure* (1573), a work translated from the Italian. The correct proverb runs: 'Venetia, Venetia, Chi non ti vede, non ti pretia,' and as such it is printed in all modern editions of *Love's Labour's Lost*. Many critics have argued that Shakespeare used the proverb to suggest Florio as the pedagogue caricatured in Holofernes.

So far an attempt has been made to disprove the theory which holds that IV, ii, 84-100, could not have been written prior to the publication of *Pierces Supererogation*. But the theory can be proved wrong on the strength of much more cogent reasons. The material to be presently set forth will demonstrate conclusively, I hope, that Shakespeare, in 1592, could well dispense with the information contained in *Pierces Supererogation*, although that pamphlet has once again been drawn on to assign *Love's Labour's Lost* to 1593. In Act V, i, 61-84, there occurs the following conversation between Armado ('Brag.'), Moth ('Page.'), Holofernes ('Peda.'), and Costard ('Clow.') :

Brag. Now by the sault waue (1) of the meditaranium, a sweete tutch, a quicke venewe of wit, snip snap, quicke and home, it reioyceth my intellect, true wit.
Page. Offerd by a childe to an old man : which is wit-old.
Peda. What is the figure ? What is the figure ?
Page. Hornes.
Peda. Thou disputes like an Infant : goe whip thy Gigg.
Page. Lende me your Horne to make one, and I will whip about your Infamie *vnu cita* a gigge of a Cuckolds horne.
Clow. And I had but one peny in the world thou shouldst haue it to buy Ginger bread : Holde, there is the verie Remuneration I had of thy Maister, thou halfepennie purse of wit, thou Pidgin-egge of discretion. O and the heauens were so pleased, that thou wart but my Bastard ; What a ioyfull father wouldest thou make me ? Go to, thou hast it *ad dungil* at the fingers ends, as they say.
Peda. Oh I smell false Latine, *dunghel* for *vnguem*.

---

(1) Q. 'wane.'

Costard apostrophizes Moth as 'thou halfepennie purse of wit, thou Pidgin-egge of discretion,' and probably puns upon 'Pierce (= purse) penniless.' It is striking that this apostrophe comes from the same mouth as 'of persing a Hogshead.' Sir Arthur Quiller-Couch and Dover Wilson (1) hold that Costard's words suggestively echo an outburst by Harvey in *Pierces Supererogation*, wherein we are told:

> ... *Astra petit disertus:* the very starres, are scarres, where he listeth: and a hundred such, and such Particularities; that requier sum larger Discourse; shew him to be a youngman of the greenest springe, as beardles in iudgement, as in face; and as Penniles in witt, as in purse. It is the least of his famous aduentures, that hee vndertaketh to be *Greenes aduocate*: as diuine Plato assayed to defend Socrates at the Barr: and I knowe not whether it be the least of his dowtye exploites, that he salueth his frendes credit, as that excellent disciple saued his maisters life. He may declare his deere affection to his Paramour; or his pure honestye to the world; or constant zeale to play the Diuels Oratour: but noe Apology of Greene, like Greenes *Grotes-worth of witt:* and when Nash will indeede accomplish a worke of Supererogation, let him publish Nashes *Penniworth of Discretion* (2).

To assume, as the New Cambridge editors do, that Shakespeare echoes Harvey involves necessarily that *Love's Labour's Lost* was written after October, 1593. It can hardly be doubted, however, that Shakespeare had got wind of Nashe's indiscretion from quite other, and far more reliable, sources, namely Nashe's writings themselves. The anti-Martinist pamphlet *An Almond for a Parrat*, bearing as its motto *rimarum sum plenus*, had acquainted its readers by means of a universally known line from Terence that Nashe was going to perform an indiscretion. But the liveliest interest in it had been aroused in 1592 by the allegorical beast fable in *Pierce Penilesse* a fable in which a Fly, presumably Nashe himself, was said to have divulged the malpractices of the Puritan faction to the High Commission. And this is why 'discretion' was also mentioned in the third of the *Foure Letters* when Harvey said that 'There is a certaine thing, called Modestie, if they coulde light vpon it: and by my younge Masters leaue, some pritty smacke or discretion would relish well' (3). Harvey's reference, it will be recognized, offers one more reason to support the view that Shakespeare did not need to

---

(1) Edd. *LLL*, p. xxii.
(2) HARVEY, *Pierces Supererogation*, sig. E$_2$ r^0 (*Works*, II, 75).
(3) HARVEY, *Foure Letters*, p. 50. See also *ante*, p. 163.

read *Pierces Supererogation* for *his* allusion to 'discretion.' It is further noteworthy that Shakespeare follows Harvey in stressing Nashe's youthfulness in the passage from *Love's Labour's Lost* we are analysing ('childe,' 'Infant').

It seems quite evident that the point of 'of persing a Hogshead' and of 'Pidgin-egge of discretion' would be most effectively appreciated in October-November, 1592, when Harvey had just issued three of his *Foure Letters* under the title *Three Letters*. Shakespeare, no doubt eager to court the success recently scored by Nashe, could hardly avoid introducing topical hits into his play and this is why two clear allusions to Nashe came to be inserted. He was even enticed to portray Nashe himself in the figure of Moth. It may sound funny, perhaps even ludicrous, but the idea seems to have crossed Shakespeare's mind that the surest means of calling forth widespread response was to follow an established practice and to designate Nashe by means of an insect name. It was thus, apparently, that 'Moth' became an integral part of the constructive design of *Love's Labour's Lost*. Moth was a name, moreover, which suggested 'Thomas' as clearly as might be wished.

Having recognized that the portraiture of Moth owes something to Nashe, it is tempting to suppose that Armado's language reflects the pomposity of Harvey's prose style. Professor Taylor (1) has collected from the writings of Nashe and Harvey an impressive number of phrases and words which can be paralleled in Shakespeare's play. The echoes from the third of Harvey's letters outnumber all the others, a circumstance which again points back to the date October-November, 1592. There are many clues in the speeches of Armado suggesting Harvey, but the more convincing ones, also relevant to the chronology, are to be found in I, ii, where literary affectations are ridiculed. The scene opens with a discussion of 'melancholy,' a malady, as we know, to which Harvey seems to have been particularly liable. At I, ii, 14-18, we find this:

Arm. I spoke it tender iuuenal, as a congruent apethaton apperteining to thy young dayes, which we may nominate tender.
Boy. And I tough signeor, as an appertinent title to your olde time, which we may name tough.

'Apethaton' reads like a deliberate blunder for 'epitheton' and the

---

(1) R. Taylor, *The Date of Love's Labour's Lost*, pp. 34-51.

error is no doubt due to the need for an alliteration with 'apperteining' and 'appertinent.' 'Congruent,' an adjective not used in the other plays of Shakespeare, is a current grammar school term, but it is perhaps significant to find Harvey in *Pedantius*, V, ii, 2467-8, saying: 'odi enim ego omnem incongruitatem,' while Nashe calls his antagonist a 'Cardinall Corrigidore of incongruitie' in *Strange Newes* (1). As to 'appertinent,' this can be paralleled closely in the following conversation between Pogglostus and the 'pedant' in *Pedantius*, I, iv, 648-51 (italics original):

> *Pog.* Non multum refert, si tradas *cum appertinentibus* etiam.
> *Ped.* Quoniam ita vis, trado. Dij hunc cum omnibus pertinentibus eradicent.

Furthermore, Huanebango in Peele's *The Old Wives' Tale* has long been recognized as a satire on Harvey (2). *The Old Wives' Tale* was probably written about 1592. In this comedy a clown retorts to Huanebango's pompously worded assertion that a beautiful wench is his: '*O falsum Latinum!* the faire maide is *minum, cum apurtinantibus gibletes* and all' (3). 'Appertain' and its derivatives seem to have been deliberately used to suggest Harvey to an Elizabethan audience.

The new material I have to offer on the chronology of *Love's Labour's Lost* has now been presented. During the period when the Harvey-Nashe quarrel was coming to a head, Shakespeare's memory must have been filled with the imagery and the striking allusions currently used by the most prominent writers of the day. Being at work on *the* topical play of his whole dramatic output, Shakespeare introduced such topical allusions as could most effectively enhance the appeal of his work. If Charlton maintains that *Love's Labour's Lost* was written before the controversy was of any moment, he seems not to make sufficient allowance for the fact that Nashe must have been writing *Strange Newes* some time before its publication in December, 1592.

Taken singly the arguments advanced here may not carry conviction, but surveyed as a whole they render it increasingly probable that the play was originally written in 1592. A chrono-

---

(1) NASHE, *Works*, I, 290.
(2) For convincing arguments see P. H. CHEFFAUD, *George Peele* (Paris, 1913), pp. 122-125.
(3) PEELE, *The Old Wives' Tale*, ed. W. W. GREG (London, 1909), ll. 348-9.

logically acceptable explanation has been offered for precisely those allusions which have been relied on by other critics to argue for the date 1593. Purely literary material can hardly be expected to yield absolutely conclusive evidence since it is almost necessarily liable to divergent interpretations. Be that as it may, the political and literary events of the year 1592 seem to me to furnish all the elements conducive to that state of mind from which a play such as *Love's Labour's Lost* could originate.

SHAKESPEARE'S REVISION OF
ACT IV, iii, 290-365 (1)

The leading idea of *Love's Labour's Lost* is that the pursuit of love is incompatible with that of learning, an idea which determines the pattern of Shakespeare's thought. The incompatibility is an old one but about 1590-1592 the rival claims of love and learning seem to have been debated so passionately that they inspired Shakespeare's imagination to write a play whose main theme was precisely that love, compared with the attraction of learning, is an irresistible and overpowering influence in man's life. There is no clearer statement of the leading idea of *Love's Labour's Lost* than the famous speech of Berowne in Act IV, a speech which also affords the clearest indications of the play's being revised some time before its publication. Berowne's lines stand out from the rest of the comedy for their lyrical beauty and the concentrated vigour of their imagery as those which would be most readily chosen for improving in a revision. The whole speech is worth examining in some detail. In the following quotation the Quarto reading is followed verbatim, which entails the inclusion of a half-line before IV, iii, 317.

> Haue at you then affections men at armes,   290
> Consider what you first did sweare vnto:
> To fast, to study, and to see no woman:
> Flat treason gainst the kingly state of youth.
> Say Can you fast? your stomacks are too young:
> And abstinence ingenders maladies.   295

(1) The purely bibliographical signs of the revision, such as the Katherine-Rosaline confusion in II, i and V, ii, are not discussed here. Readers interested in these features are referred to H. B. CHARLTON, "A Textual Note on *Love's Labour's Lost*," *The Library*, 3rd Ser., VIII (1917), 355-370; J. DOVER WILSON, ed. *LLL*, pp. 117-125; and J. SPENS, "Notes on *Love's Labour's Lost*." *RES*. VII (1931). 331-4.

And where that you haue vowd to studie (Lordes)
In that each of you haue forsworne his Booke.
Can you still dreame and poare and thereon looke.
For when would you my Lord, or you, or you,
Haue found the ground of Studies excellence,   300
Without the beautie of a womans face?
From womens eyes this doctrine I deriue,
They are the Ground, the Bookes the Achadems,
From whence doth spring the true *Promethean* fire.
Why vniuersall plodding poysons vp   305
The nimble spirites in the arteries,
As motion and long during action tyres
The sinnowy vigour of the trauayler.
Now for not looking on a womans face,
You haue in that forsworne the vse of eyes: 310
And studie too, the causer of your vow.
For where is any Authour in the worlde,
Teaches such beautie as a womas eye:
Learning is but an adiunct to our selfe,
And where we are, our Learning likewise is   315
Then when ourselues we see in Ladies eyes,
With ourselues.
Do we not likewise see our learning there?
O we haue made a Vow to studie, Lordes,
And in that Vow we haue forsworne our Bookes:
For when would you (my Leedge) or you, or you?   320
In leaden contemplation haue found out
Such fierie Numbers as the prompting eyes,
Of beautis tutors haue inricht you with:
Other slow Artes intirely keepe the braine:
And therefore finding barraine practizers,   325
Scarce shew a haruest of their heauie toyle.
But Loue first learned in a Ladies eyes,
Liues not alone emured in the braine:
But with the motion of all elamentes,
Courses as swift as thought in euery power,   330
And giues to euery power a double power,
Aboue their functions and their offices.
It addes a precious seeing to the eye:
A Louers eyes will gaze an Eagle blinde.
A Louers eare will heare the lowest sound.   335
When the suspitious head of theft is stopt.
Loues feeling is more soft and sensible,
Then are the tender hornes of Cockled Snayles.
Loues tongue proues daintie, *Bachus* grosse in taste
For Valoure, is not Loue a *Hercules*?   340
Still clyming trees in the *Hesperides*.
Subtil as *Sphinx*, as sweete and musicall,

As bright *Appolos* Lute, strung with his haire.
And when Loue speakes, the voyce of all the Goddes,
Make heauen drowsie with the harmonie,   345
Neuer durst Poet touch a pen to write,
Vntill his Incke were tempred with Loues sighes:
O then his lines would rauish sauage eares,
And plant in Tyrants milde humilitie.
From womens eyes this doctrine I deriue.   350
They sparcle still the right promethean fier,
They are the Bookes, the Artes, the Achademes,
That shew, containe, and nourish all the worlde.
Els none at all in ought proues excellent.
Then fooles you were, these women to forsweare: 355
Or keeping what is sworne, you will proue fooles,
For Wisedomes sake, a worde that all men loue:
Or for Loues sake, a worde that loues all men.
Or for Mens sake, the authour of these Women:
Or Womens sake, by whom we Men are Men.   360
Lets vs once loose our othes to finde ourselues,
Or els we loose ourselues, to keepe our othes:
It is Religion to be thus forsworne.
For Charitie it selfe fulfilles the Law:
And who can seuer Loue from Charitie.   365

Most critics believe that Berowne's duplicating his own ideas
after line 317 is evidence of revision, but Chambers (1) suggests
that the imperfectly cancelled passage, namely lines 296-317, can be
just as well interpreted as a false start at the time of original writing.
Whichever explanation may win final acceptance, the duplication
proves that Shakespeare attached great importance to what Berowne
had to say at this point of the action. Several features of the revised
text demand our attention.

First a small stylistic detail: the revision, starting at line 318,
opens with an exclamatory 'O,' which the original version does not.
This detail may reveal Shakespeare's intention to slight a contemporary stylistic trick (note the 'O' at line 348 too). It is much
more interesting, however, to notice that the function of the imagery
in the revised passage is not merely to elaborate the earlier
comparisons more effectively, but to exalt the beneficial powers of
love in a digression of great lyrical beauty. Love is celebrated as
an emotion which spreads through the human body with an extra-

(1) E. K. CHAMBERS, *Shakespeare*, I, 333. J. DOVER WILSON, ed. *LLL*, p. 106,
supposes that the revised passage was not written in the margin of the original manuscript,
but on a separate sheet of paper.

ordinary swiftness. It breaks through the narrow limits of the prison-like brain, the dwelling-place within which learning is confined, and then lavishes its benefits upon man. The elaboration of the idea that love is a liberating force, an idea just casually touched on in the original lines, affords a remarkable illustration of Shakespeare's wonderful poetic gift to develop sequences of images, one image generating the next or liberating a whole train of ideas. The lyrical effect is further heightened by the use of mythological comparisons, while the similes with which Shakespeare supports his argument are all finely touched up in the revision. It does not seem possible to read the lines as records of an intensive and genuine experience, for Shakespeare, one feels, is only half-serious and deals with his subject lightheartedly. Nor is there, as yet, that turgidity of diction which is so characteristic a feature of the style of Shakespeare's later period, and which betrays an intense emotional strain in the poet.

But the revision was apparently not undertaken exclusively for the sake of exalting love. It also contains two passages related to the writings of others. Berowne's speech closes on a religious note, which seems to adumbrate Weever's allusions to Shakespeare's play in *Faunus and Melliflora*. On the other hand, two lines in the revised portion are probably related to the following couplet in Chapman's *Hymnus in Noctem*, 376-377:

> No pen can any thing eternall wright,
> That is not steept in humor of the Night.

A. Acheson (1) was the first to point out that Berowne's

> Neuer durst Poet touch a pen to write,
> Vntill his Incke were tempred with Loues sighes:

may be interpreted as a refutation of Chapman's words. Sir Arthur Quiller-Couch and Professor Dover Wilson have subscribed to Acheson's contention and they hold that 'the retorting challenge of *Love's Labour's Lost* nails itself precisely home' (2). No less an authority than Chambers has accepted the 'probability' of the allusion,

(1) A. ACHESON, *Shakespeare and the Rival Poet* (London, 1903), p. 89.
(2) Edd. *LLL*, p. xxxi.

but it has again been questioned by Professor Baldwin (1). Baldwin argues as follows:

It will be seen that the arguments, as such, of Shakspere and Chapman are not either parallel or perpendicular to each other. Chapman is praising Night against Day as an inspiration for writing; Shakspere is praising Love. The arguments themselves follow entirely unrelated lines, even though there is an eye or so somewhere in each. Chapman finally works up to his couplet conclusion that every pen, therefore, must be steeped 'in humour of the Night,' for which he is arguing as against Day. Shakspere is arguing for love in a wholly different sequence and form; and one of his items consists of four lines, two of which are those quoted as parallel; the other two are pretty certainly suggested by Ovid, as the whole may well be. Shakspere said the true poet's ink must be tempered with sighs; Chapman said his pen must be steeped in humour of the Night, that humour being inky, of course. Shakspere has the conventional figure of pen and ink in the service of Love; Chapman has the same conventional figure, but in the unconventional service of Night. If there were any connection, the unconventional application of Chapman would clearly be the borrowing. But there is not the slightest indication of any direct relationship.

I do not think that these arguments are justified. In the first place, Shakespeare as well as Chapman, so far from being exclusively concerned with the ideas of Night and Love, also deal with the theme of learning, a point Baldwin refuses to consider since he does not discuss the parallels in their relation to the context. Chapman regards learning as an apanage of Night, whereas Shakespeare, reversing the argument, regards it as really resulting from the pursuit of love. Baldwin's refusal to admit any connexion between the lines in question forms part of his general endeavour to minimize, indeed ignore, the bearing of *Love's Labour's Lost* upon contemporary literature. The implications of the allusion require further inspection. In his *Shadow of Night* Chapman exalts Night to the detriment of Love and attacks 'passion-driuen men, reading but to curtoll a tedious houre, and altogether hidebownd with affection to great mens fancies.' He also insists quite clearly that Love is a petrifying force, paralysing the activity of the brain. Here, too, the arguments of Shakespeare and Chapman contradict each other. Now, the parallelism between Chapman's couplet and Shakespeare's lines is at first sight only syntactical. The first line of each quotation

---

(1) T. W. BALDWIN, *Shakspere's Five-Act Structure*, pp. 610-611.

starts with a negation, this being tied to a condition which clearly limits the range of its application. For Chapman the poet does not steep his pen in ordinary ink but in humour of the night; neither does Shakespeare's 'poet,' he needs ink tempered with love's sighs. One can hardly expect Shakespeare to abandon his customary non-committal attitude in order to meet Chapman's argument squarely. And scholars will always continue to question each other's conclusions. Considering the contexts in which the alleged parallels occur, however, it seems to me reasonable to regard Shakespeare's words as a refutation of Chapman's. And if so, we are faced with the further problem of the date of the rewriting of Berowne's speech. Though, in the absence of any relevant material, everything is again open to doubt, it may be supposed that Shakespeare was familiar with Chapman's *Hymnus in Noctem* before it was published. It is therefore possible that the rewriting was undertaken in the latter half of 1593 when Chapman was preparing his *Shadow of Night* for publication. But this is mere conjecture.

It stands to reason that the present treatment of *Love's Labour's Lost* is very far from exhausting all the problems raised by the play. A full study of it would have required a separate volume and my aim has rather been to approach the play from the point of view of its literary background, a background of which it is such a characteristic product. And it is hoped, in so approaching it, that new light has been thrown on some of the more significant allusions in the play. In *Love's Labour's Lost* we see Shakespeare rise to the occasion in slighting intellectual arrogance and in exposing the vanity of scholarly pursuits. As such the play is perhaps a salutary warning to those Shakespeareans who are apt to forget to read Shakespeare now that the scientific literature on the poet and his age has grown to huge proportions. Scholarship is, indeed, merely a means to a better understanding of what Shakespeare originally intended to convey. I dare hope that a small part of that ambitious purpose has been achieved.

CONCLUSION

One of the most interesting methods of literary investigation seeks to determine the conditions of poetic creation and to examine what was in the poet's mind when he wrote his work. No critic has been more successful in applying this method than Professor J. L. Lowes, whose brilliant study *The Road to Xanadu* (1927) supplied all the material, literary and otherwise, that went to the making of Coleridge's two most famous poems *The Rime of the Ancient Mariner* and *Kubla Khan*. Far be it from me, of course, to assert that I have succeeded in providing a similar study of the conditions amid which the young Shakespeare began to write. Yet, however imperfect, an attempt has been made here to gather together a number of elements from Shakespeare's reading in order to establish in what respects some of his plays can be related to the contemporary output.

The preceding chapters have made it probable that *Love's Labour's Lost* and *As You Like It* were originally written in the years 1592-1593, during or just after the very period that the popular interest in the pamphlets of Greene, Nashe, and Harvey reached its high-water mark. These writers had all three been taught by the Marprelate controversy how an opponent could be most effectively disposed of. To Shakespeare the controversy merely meant the introduction of a few echoes in both *Love's Labour's Lost* and *As You Like It*, echoes which nevertheless confirm what other material provides in the matter of date-ascription. Greene, who had begun his career as a writer of romances, closed it with a series of highly sensational cony-catching pamphlets. His later activity practically coincided with Nashe's, but the fame of the latter in the field of satire seems to have grown so prodigiously that it went near eclipsing that of the older writer. Nashe rejected Greene's smooth and easy-flowing style. Lacking a refined taste and being inspired by a 'vulgar Muse,' Nashe tended to interlard his pamphlets with colloquialisms and daring out-of-the-way imagery. Merely for the sake of cultivating obscurity he wilfully modified the structure of the language and indulged in the use of far-fetched and unusual coinages so that the final impression Nashe's style leaves is one of carelessness, a carelessness which is apparent in the rambling construction of his work as well.

After Nashe and Greene it was Harvey's turn to enter the

ranks of a 'scribbling generation.' In September-October 1592, just after Greene's sensational death, there appeared upon the scene a writer, a Cambridge don of considerable reputation and literary ability, pedantic and yet truly learned in the eyes of many, who had a marked taste for 'thrice-piled hyperboles' and who proclaimed —to paraphrase his own words—to solace his miraculous self, and to cheer the Muses in cheering his dainty soul, sweetly drunk with their delicious Helicon. Harvey, too, contrived to forge a completely personal style, as obscure as Nashe's, but charged with learned allusion and characterized by a more deliberate 'artistry.' If Nashe's diction is far from pleasing, Harvey's occasionally succeeds in captivating his audience by his bold exploitation of consciously laboured syntactical patterns. And amid all that bustling literary activity Shakespeare was coming to maturity.

Of course, it is important to recognize that the final stage of the evolution of Tudor English had just been reached when Greene, Harvey, and Nashe were making their impact upon the imagination of the Elizabethan public. Nashe and Harvey were among the first to exploit the new possibilities of the language, they introduced pedantic borrowings and coinages most of which have remained strange to this day, but they also invented some which, thanks to their efforts, have struck root in the language. Of the latter category 'capricious' is a notable instance. They gave a new flexibility to the English tongue and they showed their admirers what it was capable of. Among these admirers was no doubt Shakespeare, and omnivorous reader as he was, his imagination was bound to be affected by the new linguistic experiments to which the pamphlets of three of the most popular writers of the day bore witness. More important still, it must be remembered that literary men lived in close contact with each other, and that the subjects of most books that were being printed were already discussed in taverns before the books reached their public. Furthermore, most works circulated in manuscripts before they went through the press.

A subject in which readers and writers seem to have been deeply interested was that of poetic inspiration. It is an admittedly commonplace subject, but even so there can be little doubt that Shakespeare (1) was bound to get more interested in it in view of the fact that it was one of the principal controversial issues in a famous

---

(1) For a general survey see E. C. PETTET, "Shakespeare's Conception of Poetry," *ESEA*, New Series, III (1950), 29-46.

literary duel, that between Harvey and Nashe. The controversy regarding 'Art' was conducted with a considerable degree of animosity and those concerned brought into the lists all the resources of their verbal skill. Renaissance artists generally had at their disposal an important conventionally accepted system of symbols to enhance the beauty of their works: that of mythology. The interest in mythology, by no means uncommon in the Middle Ages, had in the sixteenth century been revitalized under the influence of the emblem writers and mythographers of Italy, and literary men were not slow to recognize the efficient use they could make of the symbolism of classic myth. In the early nineties, however, mythology was not used merely to lend charm and beauty to literature. Harvey and Nashe, as we have seen, were often concerned to develop their arguments in terms of mythology, and a study of these has yielded a satisfactory key to some of the more involved statements of either writer.

There was one author, namely Abraham Fraunce, who was a professed student of allegory and classic myth. Although in his *Third part* he did no more than industriously compile what information the mythological handbooks of the time could supply, his work nevertheless deserves to be rescued from the neglect into which it has fallen practically ever since it was published. I have tried to indicate to what extent Fraunce's manual often throws an interesting light on the mythological symbolism of his immediate contemporaries. Fraunce borrowed his 'explications' from a wide variety of authorities. Quite apart from the interest that the explanations have for source-hunters, it is also clear that they reveal Fraunce's concern to draw in passages to explain the meaning of the mythological symbolism used by the writers of his day.

It is not a matter for wonder that an artist like Shakespeare did not share Fraunce's veneration for the 'mysteries' that lay beneath the veil of classical fables. Professor R. K. Root (1) has pointed out that 'Shakespeare felt that mythological allusion was out of keeping with the highest seriousness of thought and passion,' and that 'a striving after a deeper meaning or greater appropriateness . . . marks the allusions in the plays of the latest period.' Shakespeare's mythology, it need hardly be said, is in substance traceable to his familiarity with the works of Ovid and Vergil. As

_____

(1) R. K. ROOT, *Classical Mythology in Shakespeare* (Yale, 1903), pp. 8, 13.

yet scholars have been unable to discover any direct proof of Shakespeare's acquaintance with the mythological manuals of the time, though it is but reasonable to assume that he knew them. Whatever the origin of his knowledge, the classical allusions in *As You Like It* indicate that the allegorization of the Ganymede myth had presumably reached him by the intermediary of some contemporary work on the subject. In his early plays Shakespeare treated his mythology in a spirit of raillery and *As You Like It* is no exception in this respect.

To give a general survey of Shakespeare's use of classical mythology falls beyond the scope of the present work. I have little doubt, however, that an examination of the contexts in which he refers to Pegasus, Helicon, Cerberus, and Mercury-Hermes, will prove worth while in the light of the foregoing chapters. Furthermore, the theory that the use of mythological terms sometimes implied a personal allusion in the early nineties finds further support from the fact that Shakespeare may well be the 'Phaëton' who wrote a commendatory sonnet for Florio's *Second Fruits* (1).

As we have seen, a rich variety of kinds of evidence—ranging from mythological allusions, points of contact with the works of Greene and Harvey, subject matter, to the use of a peculiar word— strongly suggests that the initial draft of *As You Like It* was written in 1593. *Love's Labour's Lost*, on the other hand, is best assigned to 1592, one of the most sensational years in the annals of Elizabethan literature. The comedy should come, I think, at the culmination of that series of events which embraces the later stages of the Marprelate controversy, the astrological pamphlets of Munday and Nashe, and the rise of the Harvey-Nashe polemic. *Love's Labour's Lost* seems to be very much like a piece of bravado and it has all the appearance of being composed in the nick of time in order to give Shakespeare full scope to show that he had powers quite beyond the range of that of the language-creators of his day. In other words, *Love's Labour's Lost* is Shakespeare's deliberate and eminently successful attempt to rival the contemporary output in linguistic ingenuity. And the play again warrants the conclusion—so often arrived at by the students of his works—that Shakespeare was firmly rooted in his age.

---

(1) For a full and, to my mind, convincing argument see W. Minto, "An Unrecognised Sonnet by Shakespeare," in *Characteristics of English Poets* (Edinburgh, 1885), pp. 371-382.

The present study of Shakespeare's early contemporaries cannot, of course, lay claim to completeness. Any form of investigation is, indeed, but a renewed attempt to make the conditions of problems clearer, and to bring them some steps nearer to a final solution. I can only hope, in all due humility, that the present volume may enable future students of the period to evaluate the literary production between 1589 and 1593 in a clearer perspective.

BIBLIOGRAPHY

(Unless otherwise stated, the place of publication of books is London.)

I.—PRINCIPAL PRIMARY SOURCES

ALBERTI, LEONBATTISTA, *L'Architettura*, transl. C. BARTOLI (Florence, 1550).

ALCIATI, ANDREA, *Emblemata* (Leyden, 1591).

ARBER, EDWARD, *A Transcript of the Registers of the Company of Stationers of London: 1554-1640 A. D.* (1875-1894, repr. New York, 1950).

ARISTOTLE, *Problemata*, transl. E. S. FORSTER (Oxford, 1927).

BOCCACCIO, GIOVANNI, *Genealogia Deorum* (Cologne, s. d.).

BRETON, NICHOLAS, *Bowre of Delights (1591)*, ed. H. E. ROLLINS (Cambridge, Harvard Un. Press, 1933).

BRUNO, GIORDANO, *Opere Italiane*, ed. G. GENTILE (Bari, 1907).

CARTARI, VINCENZO, *Imagines Deorum* (Lyons, 1581).

CHAPMAN, GEORGE, *The Plays and Poems*, ed. T. M. PARROTT (1910-1914).

—, *The Poems*, ed. P. B. BARTLETT (New York, 1941).

CHETTLE, HENRY, *Kind-hartes dreame*, ed. G. B. HARRISON (1923).

COMES, NATALIS, *Mythologiae* (Padua, 1616).

DANIEL, SAMUEL, *The VVorthy tract of Paulus Iouius* (1585).

—, *Works*, ed. A. B. GROSART (1885-96).

DEKKER, THOMAS, *News from Hell* (1606).

EDWARDS, THOMAS, *Cephalus and Procris*, ed. W. E. BUCKLEY (1882).

ELIOT, JOHN, *Ortho-epia Gallica* (1593).

FELIPPE, BARTOLOME, *The Counsellor* (1589).

FICINO, MARSILIO, *Theologia platonica* (Paris, 1559).

FLETCHER, GILES, *Of the Russe Common Wealth* (1591).

FLORIO, JOHN, *Second Fruits* (1591).

FORMAN, SIMON, *The Groundes of the Longitude* (1591).

FORNARI, SIMON, *Spositione sopra l'Orlando Furioso di M. L. Ariosto* (Florence, 1549-50).

FRAUNCE, ABRAHAM, *The Lawiers Logike* (1588).

—, *Insignium* (1588).

—, *The Countesse of Pembrokes Yuychurch* (1591).

—, *The Third part of the Countesse of Pembrokes Yuychurch* (1592).

—, *Victoria*, ed. G. C. MOORE SMITH in *Materialien zur Kunde des älteren Englischen Dramas*, XIV (1906).

—, *The Arcadian Rhetorike*, ed. E. SEATON (Oxford, 1950).

FULGENTIUS, *Mythologia*, ed. R. HELM (Leipzig, 1898).

Gesta Grayorum, ed. W. W. GREG (1914).

GREENE, ROBERT, *Works*, ed. A. B. GROSART (1881-6).

—, *The Plays & Poems*, ed. J. C. COLLINS (Oxford, 1905).

—, *A Groatsworth of Wit*, ed. G. B. HARRISON (1923).

—, *A Quip for an Upstart Courtier* (1592).

HAKLUYT, RICHARD, *The Original Writings & Correspondence of the two*

Richard Hakluyts, ed. E. G. R. TAYLOR (1935).
HARINGTON, Sir JOHN, Orlando Furioso (1591).
HARVEY, GABRIEL, Rhetor (1577).
—, Musarum Lachrimae (1578).
—, A New Letter of Notable Contents (1593).
—, Pierces Supererogation (1593).
—, The Letter-Book of Gabriel Harvey. A. D. 1573-1580, Camden Soc.
    Publ., XXXIII (1884).
—, Works, ed. A. B. GROSART (1884-5).
—, Marginalia, ed. G. C. MOORE SMITH (Stratford-upon-Avon, 1913).
—, Foure Letters, ed. G. B. HARRISON (1922).
—, Ciceronianus, ed. H. S. WILSON and transl. C. A. FORBES, University
    of Nebraska Studies, Studies in the Humanities, No. 4 (Nebraska,
    1945).
HARVEY, RICHARD, The Lambe of God (1590).
—, Philadelphus (1593).
—, Plaine Perceval (?-1590).
HERMES TRISMEGISTUS, Poemander, transl. M. FICINO (Paris, 1554).
HEYWOOD, THOMAS, The Dramatic Works (1874).
HILL, THOMAS, The Schoole of Skil (1599).
HOMER, Opera, transl. J. SPONDANUS (Basle, 1606).
HORUS APOLLO, Hieroglyphica, ed. F. SBORDONE (Naples, 1940).
JONSON, BEN, Works, ed. C. H. HERFORD, P. and E. SIMPSON (Oxford,
    1925-1952).
KYD, THOMAS, Works, ed. F. S. BOAS (Oxford, 1901).
LYLY, JOHN, The Complete Works, ed. R. W. BOND (Oxford, 1902).
HALL, JOSEPH, The Collected Poems, ed. A. DAVENPORT (Liverpool, 1949).
LODGE, THOMAS, Wit's Misery (1596).
MARLOWE, CHRISTOPHER, Works, ed. C. F. TUCKER BROOKE (Oxford,
    1910).
—, Doctor Faustus, ed. W. W. GREG (Oxford, 1950).
MARSTON, JOHN, Works, ed. J. O. HALLIWELL (1856).
—, The Plays, ed. H. HARVEY WOOD (Edinburgh, 1934).
MARTIN MARPRELATE, The Epistle, ed. E. ARBER (1895).
MARTIN SENIOR, Just Censure and Reproof (Wolston, 1589).
MERES, FRANCIS, Palladis Tamia (1598).
MONMOUTH, GEOFFREY OF, Historia Regum Britanniae, ed. A. GRISCOM
    (1929).
NASHE, THOMAS, Works, ed. R. B. MCKERROW (1904-1910).
OVID, Metamorphoses, ed. G. LAFAYE (Paris, 1928).
PEELE, GEORGE, Works, ed. A. H. BULLEN (1888).
—, The Old Wives' Tale, ed. W. W. GREG (1909).
—, The Life and Minor Works, ed. D. H. HORNE (Yale, 1952).
PONTANUS, JOAN. JOV., Amores (Paris, 1791).
SCÈVE, MAURICE, Delie, ed. E. PARTURIER (Paris, 1916).
SHAKESPEARE, WILLIAM, Loves Labors Lost, a facsimile in photo-lithography
    by W. GRIGGS (s. d.).
—, Love's Labour's Lost, ed. H. C. HART (1906).

—, *Love's Labour's Lost*, ed. A. QUILLER-COUCH and J. DOVER WILSON (Cambridge, 1923).

—, *Love's Labour's Lost*, ed. R. DAVID (1951).

—, *As You Like It*, ed. A. QUILLER-COUCH and J. DOVER WILSON (Cambridge, 1926, repr. 1948).

SMELLKNAVE, SIMON, *Fearefull and lamentable effects of two dangerous Comets* (1591).

SPONDE, JEAN DE, *Poésies*, ed. F. RUCHON and A. BOASE (Geneva, 1949).

TASSO, TORQUATO, *La Gerusalemme liberata e l'Aminta* (Paris, 1882).

TORRIANO, GIOVANNI, *The Italian Tutor* (1640).

—, *Piazza Universale* (1666).

TYARD, PONTUS DE, *Discours Philosophiques* (Paris, 1587).

VALERIANO, PIERIO, *Hieroglyphica* (Basle, 1556).

WEEVER, JOHN, *Faunus and Melliflora*, ed. A. DAVENPORT (Liverpool, 1948).

II.—MODERN STUDIES

ACHESON, ARTHUR, *Shakespeare and the Rival Poet* (1903).

ALEXANDER, PETER, *Shakespeare's Henry VI and Richard III* (Cambridge, 1929).

—, *Shakespeare's Life and Art* (1939, repr. 1946).

ALLEN, Don CAMERON, "Ben Jonson and the Hieroglyphics," *PQ*, XVIII (1939), 290-300.

—, *The Star-Crossed Renaissance* (North Carolina, 1941).

ALLEN, J. W., *A History of Political Thought in the Sixteenth Century* (1928).

ARBER, EDWARD, *An Introductory Sketch to the Martin Marprelate Controversy. 1588-1590* (1879).

ATKINS, J. W. H., *English Literary Criticism: The Renascence* (1947, 2nd ed. 1951).

AUSTIN, W. B., "Gabriel Harvey's 'Lost' *Ode* on Ramus," *MLN*, LXI (1946), 242-247.

—, "Spenser's Sonnet to Harvey," *MLN*, LXII (1947), 20-23.

BABB, LAWRENCE, *The Elizabethan Malady. A Study of Melancholia in English Literature from 1580 to 1642* (Michigan, 1951).

BALDWIN, T. W., *William Shakspere's Small Latine & Lesse Greeke* (Un. of Illinois Press, 1944).

—, *Shakspere's Five-Act Structure* (Urbana, Illinois, 1947).

—, "Respice Finem: Respice Funem," in *Joseph Quincy Adams Memorial Studies* (Washington, 1948), pp. 141-155.

BARTLETT, P. B., "Chapman's Revisions in his Iliàds," *JELH*, II (1935), 92-119.

—, "The Heroes of Chapman's Homer," *RES*, XVII (1941), 257-280.

—, "Stylistic Devices in Chapman's *Iliads*," *PMLA*, LVII (1942), 661-675.

BASSE, MAURITS, *Stijlaffectatie bij Shakespeare* (Ghent, 1895).

BATESON, F. W., *The Cambridge Bibliography of English Literature* (Cambridge, 1940).

BATTENHOUSE, R. W., "Chapman's *The Shadow of Night:* An Interpretation," *SP*, XXXVIII (1941), 584-608.

BENTLEY, GERALD EADES, *The Jacobean and Caroline Stage* (Oxford, 1941).

BERLI, HANS, *Gabriel Harvey. Der Dichterfreund und Kritiker* (Zürich, 1913).

BLACK, J. B., *The Reign of Elizabeth 1558-1603* (Oxford, 1936).

BOAS, F. S., *University Drama in the Tudor Age* (Oxford, 1914).

—, *Christopher Marlowe* (Oxford, 1940).

—, "Informer against Marlowe," *TLS*, Sept. 16, 1949, p. 608.

BOER, C. DE, ed. *Ovide Moralisé* (Amsterdam, 1915).

BRADBROOK, M. C., *The School of Night* (Cambridge, 1936).

BRADLEY, A. C., *Shakespearean Tragedy* (1904).

BRIE, F., "Shakespeare und die Impresa-Kunst seiner Zeit," *Shakespeare-Jahrbuch*, L (1914), 9-30.

BROOKE, C. F. TUCKER, *The Life of Marlowe* (1930).

—, "Sir Walter Ralegh as Poet and Philosopher," *JELH*, V (1938), 93-112. Reprinted in *Essays on Shakespeare and Other Elizabethans* (Yale, 1948), pp. 121-144.

BROWN, HUNTINGTON, *Rabelais in English Literature* (Cambridge, Mass., 1933).

BUSH, DOUGLAS, "Notes on Shakespeare's Classical Mythology," *PQ*, VI (1927), 225-302.

—, *Mythology and the Renaissance Tradition in English Poetry* (Minneapolis).

—, *English Literature in the Earlier Seventeenth Century 1600-1660* (Oxford, 1945). *OHEL*, V.

CAMPBELL, O. J., "*Love's Labour's Lost* Re-Studied," in *Studies in Shakespeare, Milton and Donne* (Univ. of Michigan, 1925), pp. 1-45.

CHAMBERS, Sir EDMUND K., *The Elizabethan Stage* (Oxford, 1923).

—, *William Shakespeare. A Study of Facts and Problems* (Oxford, 1930).

—, ed. *The Shakspere Allusion-Book* (Oxford, 1932).

CHARLTON, H. B., "A Textual Note on 'Love's Labour's Lost'," *The Library*, 3rd Ser., VIII (1917), 355-370.

—, "The Date of 'Love's Labour's Lost'," *MLR*, XIII (1918), 257-266 and 387-400.

CHEFFAUD, P. H., *George Peele* (Paris, 1913).

CHURCHILL, G. R. and W. KELLER, "Die lateinischen Universitäts-Dramen in der Zeit der Königin Elisabeth," *Shakespeare-Jahrbuch*, XXXIV (1898), 221-323.

CLARK, A. M., *Thomas Heywood, Playwright and Miscellanist* (Oxford, 1931).

COLE, G. W., "Bibliography—A Forecast," *Papers of the Bibliographical Society of America*, XIV (1920).

COLERIDGE, S. T., *Biographia Literaria* (1906).

COOKE, J. D., "Euhemerism," *Speculum*, II (1927), 396-410.

Coulter, C. C., "The Genealogy of the Gods," in *Vassar Mediaeval Studies* (Yale, 1923), pp. 317-341.

David, Richard, ed. *Love's Labour's Lost* (1951).

Duhamel, P. A., "The Ciceronianism of Gabriel Harvey," *SP*, XLIX (1952), 155-170.

Ebisch, W. and L. L. Schücking, *A Shakespeare Bibliography* (Oxford, 1931).

—, *Supplement for the Years 1930-1935 to A Shakespeare Bibliography* (Oxford, 1937).

Elton, Oliver, "Giordano Bruno in England" in *Modern Studies* (1907), pp. 1-36.

Fay, H. C., "Chapman's Materials for his Translation of Homer," *RES*, New Ser., II (1951), 121-8.

Feasey, L. and E., "The Validity of the Baines Document," *NQ*, 194 (1949), 514-7.

Festugière, J., *La philosophie de l'amour de Marsile Ficin et son influence sur la littérature française au XVIe siècle* (Paris, 1941).

—, *La Révélation d'Hermes Trismégiste* (Paris, 1944).

— and A. D. Nock, edd. *Corpus Hermeticum* (Paris, 1945).

Feuillerat, Albert, *John Lyly* (Cambridge, 1910).

Fleay, F. G., *A Biographical Chronicle of the English Drama, 1599-1642* (1891).

—, "Shakespeare and Puritanism," *Anglia*, VII (1884), 221-231.

Fonblanque, E. B. de, *Annals of the House of Percy* (1887).

Forest, L. T., "A Caveat for the Critics against invoking Elizabethan Psychology," *PMLA*, LXI (1946), 651-672.

Freeman, Rosemary, *English Emblem Books* (1948).

Fripp, E. I., *Shakespeare Man and Artist* (1938).

Giehlow, Karl, "Die Hieroglyphenkunde des Humanismus in der Allegorie der Renaissance," *Jahrb. der kunsthistorischen Sammlungen des Allerh. Kaiserhauses*, XXXII, pt. I (Vienna, 1915).

Gordon, "Chapman's Use of Cartari in the Fifth Sestiad of 'Hero and Leander'," *MLR*, XXXIX (1944), 280-5.

Gray, A. K., "The Secret of *Love's Labour's Lost*," *PMLA*, XXXIX (1924), 581-611.

Green, H., *Shakespeare and the Emblem-Writers* (1870).

Greg, W. W., ed. *Henslowe's Diary* (1904).

—, *Two Elizabethan Stage Abridgements: The Battle of Alcazar & Orlando Furioso* (Oxford, 1923).

—, "The Evidence of Theatrical Plots for the History of the Elizabethan Stage," *RES*, I (1925), 265.

—, *Dramatic Documents from the Elizabethan Playhouses* (Oxford, 1937).

—, "Principles of Emendation in Shakespeare," in *Aspects of Shakespeare* (Oxford, 1933), pp. 128-201.

—, *The Editorial Problem in Shakespeare* (Oxford, 1942).

—, "Was the First Edition of *Pierce Penniless* a Piracy," *The Library*, 5th Ser., XXXIII (1952), 122-4.

—, *A Bibliography of the English Printed Drama to the Restoration* (1939-1951).

HARBAGE, ALFRED, *Annals of English Drama, 975-1700* (Un. of Philadelphia, 1940).
HARRISON, G. B., ed. *Willobie his Avisa* (1926).
HART, H. C., "Gabriel Harvey and Marston," *NQ*, 9th Ser., XI (1903), 201, 281-2, and 343-5.
HART, H. C., ed. *Love's Labour's Lost* (1906).
HIGHET, G., *The Classical Tradition* (Oxford, 1949).
HJORT, G., "The Good and Bad Quartos of *Romeo and Juliet* and *Love's Labour's Lost*," *MLR*, XXI (1926), 140-146.
HOLMES, E., *Aspects of Elizabethan Imagery* (Oxford, 1929).
HOPPE, HARRY R., "John Wolfe, Printer and Publisher," *The Library*, 4th Ser., XIV (1933), 241-288.
—, *The Bad Quarto of Romeo and Juliet* (Cornell Un. Press, 1949).
HORTIS, A., *Studij sulle opere latine del Boccaccio* (Trieste, 1879).
HOTSON, L., *The Death of Christopher Marlowe* (1925).
—, *Shakespeare's Sonnets Dated* (1949).
—, *Shakespeare's Motley* (1952).
JACQUOT, JEAN, *George Chapman* (Paris, 1951).
JOHNSON, F. R., *Astronomical Thought in Renaissance England* (Baltimore, 1937).
—, "The First Edition of Gabriel Harvey's Foure Letters," *The Library*, 4th Ser., XV (1934), 212-223.
—, "Gabriel Harvey's *Three Letters:* A First Issue of his *Foure Letters*," *The Library*, 5th Ser., XXVII (1946), 134-6.
—, "Elizabethan Drama and the Elizabethan Science of Psychology," in *English Studies Today*, ed. C. L. WRENN and G. BULLOUGH (Oxford, 1951), pp. III-9.
JUNG, C. G., *Psychology and Alchemy* (1953).
KIRSCHBAUM, LEO, "Is The Spanish Tragedy A Leading Case? Did a bad quarto of *Love's Labour's Lost* ever exist?", *JEGP*, XXXVII (1938), 501-512.
KNOBEL, E. B., "Astronomy and Astrology," in *Shakespeare's England* (Oxford, 1916), I, 444-461.
KOCHER, PAUL H., *Christopher Marlowe. A Study of his Thought, Learning and Character* (North Carolina, 1946).
—, "John Hester, Paracelsan (fl. 1576-93)," in *Joseph Quincy Adams Memorial Studies* (Washington, 1948), pp. 621-638.
KOEPPEL, EMIL, "Die englischen Tasso- Übersetzungen des 16. Jahrhunderts," *Anglia*, XI (1888), 11-38 and XIII (1889), 103-142.
KRISTELLER, P. O., *The Philosophy of Marsilio Ficino* (New York, 1943).
LEE, SIDNEY, "A New Study of *Love's Labour's Lost*," *Gentleman's Magazine* (1880).
—, *The French Renaissance in England* (Oxford, 1910).
—, *A Life of William Shakespeare* (1925).
LEFRANC, ABEL, "Marguerite de Navarre et le Platonisme de la Renaissance," in *Grands Écrivains Français de la Renaissance* (Paris, 1914), pp. 63-249.
—, "Le Platonisme et la littérature en France à l'époque de la Renais-

sance," in *Grands Écrivains Français de la Renaissance* (Paris, 1914), pp. 63-249.

—, *Sous le masque de 'William Shakespeare'* (Paris, 1919).

—, *A la découverte de Shakespeare* (Paris, 1945).

LEISHMAN, J. B., ed. *The Three Parnassus Plays (1598-1601)* (1949).

LEMMI, C. W., *The Classic Deities in Bacon: A Study in Mythological Symbolism* (Baltimore, 1933).

LEVER, J. W., "Shakespeare's French Fruits," *Shakespeare Survey*, 6 (1953), 79-90.

LEWIS, C. S., *The Allegory of Love* (Oxford, 1936).

—, *English Literature in the Sixteenth Century excluding Drama* (Oxford, 1954). *OHEL*, III.

LIEBESCHÜTZ, H., *Fulgentius Metaforalis. Ein Beitrag zur Geschichte der antiken Mythologie im Mittelalter* (Leipzig, 1926).

LOTSPEICH, H. G., *Classical Mythology in the Poetry of Edmund Spenser* (Princeton Un. Press, 1932).

LÜHR, WILHELM, *Die drei Cambridger Spiele vom Parnass (1598-1601) in ihren litterarischen Beziehungen* (Kiel, 1900).

MCCLENNEN, J., *On the Meaning and Function of Allegory in the English Renaissance* (Michigan, 1947).

MCGINN, DONALD J., "The Real Martin Marprelate," *PMLA*, LVIII (1943), 83-107.

—, "Nashe's Share in the Marprelate Controversy," *PMLA*, LIX (1944), 952-984.

—, "The Allegory of the 'Beare' and the 'Foxe' in Nashe's *Pierce Penilesse*," *PMLA*, LXI (1946), 431-453.

MCKERROW, R. B., *A Dictionary of Printers and Booksellers, 1557-1640* (1910).

—, *Printers' & Publishers' Devices in England and Scotland, 1485-1640* (1913).

—, *An Introduction to Bibliography for Literary Students* (Oxford, 1927).

—, "The Elizabethan Printer and Dramatic Manuscripts," *The Library*, 4th Ser., XII (1931), 253-275.

—, *Prolegomena for the Oxford Shakespeare* (Oxford, 1939).

MCMANAWAY, J. G., "Latin Title-page Mottoes as a Clue to Dramatic Authorship," *The Library*, 4th Ser., XXVI (1945), 28-36.

MILLER, E. H., "Deletions in Robert Greene's *A Quip for an Upstart Courtier* (1592)," *HLQ*, XV (1952), 277-282.

—, "The Sources of Robert Greene's 'A Quip for an Upstart Courtier' (1592)," *NQ*, 198 (1953), 148-152 and 187-191.

MINTO, WILLIAM, "An Unrecognised Sonnet by Shakespeare," in *Characteristics of English Poets* (Edinburgh, 1885), pp. 371-382.

NICOLL, A., *Shakespeare* (1952).

OPPEL, H., "Gabriel Harvey," *Shakespeare-Jahrbuch*, LXXXII/LXXXIII (1946-47), 34-51.

ORSINI, N., "Gabriel Harvey, uomo del Rinascimento," in *Studii sul Rinascimento Italiano in Inghilterra* (Florence, 1937), pp. 101-120.

PANOFSKY, E. and F. SAXL, *Dürers 'Melencolia. I.' Eine Quellen- und*

Typengeschichtliche Untersuchung, Studien der Bibliothek Warburg, II (Leipzig, 1923).

PANOFSKY, E., *Studies in Iconology* (New York, 1939).

PEEL, A., ed. *The Notebook of John Penry 1593, Camden Third Series,* LXVII (1944).

PETTET, E. C., "Shakespeare's Conception of Poetry," *ESEA,* New. Ser., III (1950), 29-46.

PIERCE, W., *An Historical Introduction to the Marprelate Tracts* (1908).

POLLARD, A. W., *Shakespeare Folios and Quartos* (1909).

—, *Shakespeare's Fight with the Pirates* (Cambridge, 1920).

POLLARD, A. W. and G. R. REDGRAVE, *A Short-Title Catalogue of Books Printed in England, Scotland, & Ireland. And of English Books Printed Abroad 1475-1640* (1926, repr. 1950).

PRAZ, MARIO, *Studies in Seventeenth-Century Imagery* (1939).

—, *A Bibliography of Emblem Books* (1947).

—, "Petrarca e gli emblematisti," in *Ricerche Anglo-Italiane* (Rome, 1944), pp. 303-319.

PRUVOST, RENÉ, *Robert Greene et ses romans (1558-1592)* (Paris, 1938).

RALEIGH, W., *Shakespeare* (1907).

RICH, T., *Harington & Ariosto* (Yale, 1940).

ROOT, R. K., *Classical Mythology in Shakespeare* (Yale, 1903).

ROWSE, A. L., *The England of Elizabeth* (1950).

RUBOW, PAUL V., *Shakespeare og hans samtidige* (Copenhagen, 1948).

SAITTA, G., *Marsilio Ficino e la filosofia dell'Umanesimo* (Florence, 1943).

—, *Il pensiero italiano sull'Umanesimo e nel Rinascimento,* Vol. I, *L'Umanesimo* (Bologna, 1949).

SANDERS, CHAUNCEY, *Robert Greene and the Harveys, Indiana University Studies,* XVIII (1931).

SARGENT, R. M., *At the Court of Queen Elizabeth. The Life and Lyrics of Sir Edward Dyer* (Oxford, 1935).

SAULNIER, V.-L., *Maurice Scève* (Paris, 1949).

SCHMIDT, A.-M., *La poésie scientifique en France au seizième siècle* (Paris, 1938).

SCHOELL, F. L., *Études sur l'humanisme continental en Angleterre* (Paris, 1926).

SCHOEMBS, J., *Ariosts Orlando Furioso in der englischen Litteratur des Zeitalters der Elisabeth* (Soden a. T., 1898).

SCHRICKX, W., "Shakespeare and the School of Night," *Neophilologus,* XXXIV (1950), 35-44.

—, "George Chapman's Borrowings from Natali Conti," *English Studies,* XXXII (1951), 107-112.

—, "The Portraiture of Gabriel Harvey in the Parnassus Plays and John Marston," *Neophilologus,* XXXVI (1952), 225-234.

SEZNEC, JEAN, *La survivance des dieux antiques* (1939). Transl. by B. F. SESSIONS as *The Survival of the Pagan Gods* (New York, 1953).

SIMPSON, R., *The School of Shakspere* (1878).

SINGER, D. W., *Giordano Bruno* (New York, 1950).

SMITH, G. C. MOORE, ed. *Pedantius*, in *Materialien zur Kunde des älteren Englischen Dramas*, VIII (1905).

—, ed. *Gabriel Harvey's Marginalia* (Stratford-upon-Avon, 1913).

SMITH, G. GREGORY, ed. *Elizabethan Critical Essays* (Oxford, 1905, repr. 1950).

SPENCER, T., *Shakespeare and the Nature of Man* (New York, 1943).

SPENS, J., "Chapman's Ethical Thought," *ESEA*, XI (1925), 149-169.

—, "Notes on Love's Labour's Lost," *RES*, VII (1931), 331-4.

STOPES, C. C., *The Life of Henry, Third Earl of Southampton* (Cambridge, 1922).

—, "Thomas Edwards, Author of 'Cephalus and Procris'," *MLR*, XVI (1921), 209-223.

STRATHMANN, E. A., "The History of the World and Ralegh's Skepticism," *HLQ*, 1939, No. 3.

—, "Sir Walter Ralegh on Natural Philosophy," *MLQ*, I (1940), 49-61.

—, "The Textual Evidence for 'The School of Night'," *MLN*, LVI (1941), 176-186.

—, "Robert Parsons' Essay on Atheism," in *Joseph Quincy Adams Memorial Studies* (Washington, 1948), pp. 665-681.

—, *Sir Walter Ralegh, a Study in Elizabethan Skepticism* (New York, 1952).

SUMMERSGILL, T. L., "Harvey, Nashe, and the Three Parnassus Plays," *PQ*, XXXI (1952), 94-95.

SWINBURNE, A. C., *Contemporaries of Shakespeare*, ed. E. GOSSE and T. J. WISE (1919).

TAYLOR, RUPERT, *The Date of Love's Labour's Lost* (New York, 1932).

THOMAS, SIDNEY, "New Light on the Nashe-Harvey Quarrel," *MLN*, LXIII (1948), 481-3.

TILLYARD, E. M. W., *The Elizabethan World Picture* (1943).

TRAMER, IRMA, *Studien zu den Anfängen der puritanischen Emblemliteratur* (Berlin, 1934).

TURNER, CELESTE, *Anthony Mundy, An Elizabethan Man of Letters* (Univ. of California Publ. in English, No. 2, 1928).

VAUTIER, CLÉMY, *Les théories relatives à la souveraineté et à la résistance chez l'auteur des Vindiciae contra tyrannos (1579)* (Lausanne, 1947).

VOLKMANN, LUDWIG, *Bilderschriften der Renaissance. Hieroglyphik und Emblematik in ihren Beziehungen und Fortwirkungen* (Leipzig, 1923).

WADDINGTON, CHARLES, *Ramus* (Paris, 1855).

WARD, Sir A. W. and A. R. WALLER, edd., *The Cambridge History of English Literature* (Cambridge, 1907).

WENTERSDORF, K., "Shakespeares erste Truppe," *Shakespeare-Jahrbuch*, LXXXIV/LXXXVI (1948/50), 114-130.

WILSON, FRANK PERCY, " 'A Wonderfull Prognostication'," *MLR*, XIII (1918), 84-5.

—, "Some English Mock-Prognostications," *The Library*, 4th Ser., XIX (1939), 6-43.

—, *Elizabethan and Jacobean* (Oxford, 1945).

—, "Shakespeare and the New Bibliography," in *Studies in Retrospect* (1945), pp. 76-135.

WILSON, FRANK PERCY and BONAMY DOBRÉE, edd., *Oxford History of English Literature* (Oxford, 1945-   ).

WILSON, HAROLD S., "Gabriel Harvey's Orations on Rhetoric," *JELH*, XII (1945), 167-182.

—, "The Humanism of Gabriel Harvey," in *Joseph Quincy Adams Memorial Studies* (Washington, 1948), pp. 707-721.

WILSON, JOHN DOVER, "The Marprelate Controversy," in *CHEL*, III (1908), 374-398.

—, "Anthony Munday, Pamphleteer and Pursuivant," *MLR*, IV (1908), 484-490.

—, *The Essential Shakespeare* (Cambridge, 1932).

—, "The Origins and Development of Shakespeare's *Henry IV*," *The Library*, 4th Ser., XXVI (1945), 2-16.

—, "Malone and the Upstart Crow," *Shakespeare Survey*, 4 (1951), 56-68.

WILSON, MONA, *Sir Philip Sidney* (1950).

YATES, FRANCES A., *John Florio* (Cambridge, 1934).

—, *A Study of Love's Labour's Lost* (Cambridge, 1936).

—, "Giordano Bruno's Conflict with Oxford," *Journal of the Warburg Institute*, II (1939), 227-42.

—, *The French Academies of the Sixteenth Century* (1947).

YSSELSTEYN, G. T. VAN, "L'auteur de l'ouvrage Vindiciae contra tyrannos publié sous le nom de Stephanus Junius," *Revue historique*, CLXVII (1931), 46-59.

ZANDVOORT, R. W., *Sidney's Arcadia. A Comparison between the two Versions* (Amsterdam, 1929).

III.—DICTIONARIES

BARTLETT, JOHN, *A Complete Concordance or Verbal Index to Words, Phrases and Passages in the Dramatic Works of Shakespeare* (1894).

LEE, SIDNEY and L. STEPHEN, edd. *Dictionary of National Biography* (1908-9).

MURRAY, J. A. H. and H. BRADLEY, W. A. CRAIGIE, and C. T. ONIONS, *The Oxford English Dictionary* (Oxford, 1933).

ONIONS, C. T., *A Shakespeare Glossary* (Oxford, 1919, repr. 1951).

ROSCHER, W. H., *Ausführliches Lexikon der griechischen und römischen Mythologie* (Leipzig, 1884-1937).

SCHMIDT, A., *Shakespeare-Lexicon*, 3rd ed. (Berlin, 1902).

SMITH, W. G., *The Oxford Dictionary of English Proverbs* (Oxford, 1935).

TILLEY, MORRIS PALMER, *A Dictionary of the Proverbs in England in the sixteenth and seventeenth centuries* (Ann Arbor, 1950).

LIST OF ABBREVIATIONS

CHEL   = *Cambridge History of English Literature.*
ESEA   = *Essays and Studies by Members of the English Association.*
HLB   = *Huntington Library Bulletin.*
HLQ   = *Huntington Library Quarterly.*
JEGP   = *Journal of English and Germanic Philology.*
JELH   = *Journal of English Literary History.*
MLN   = *Modern Language Notes.*
MLQ   = *Modern Language Quarterly.*
MLR   = *Modern Language Review.*
MP   = *Modern Philology.*
NQ   = *Notes and Queries.*
OED   = *Oxford English Dictionary.*
OHEL = *Oxford History of English Literature.*
PMLA = *Publications of the Modern Language Association of America.*
PQ   = *Philological Quarterly.*
RES   = *Review of English Studies.*
SP   = *Studies in Philology.*
TLS   = *Times Literary Supplement.*

INDEX

A., L. T., 157
Académie Françoise (L'), 245
Acheson, Arthur, 26, 264
Achilles Shield, 52-3
Acontius, Jacobus, 155
Admonition to the People of England (An), 171
Aduertisement for Pap-hatchet and Martin Marprelate (An), 145-6, 177, 180-5, 186n, 188, 191, 193, 196, 213, 215
Aeneid, 79
Aeschylus, 218
Aesop, 23, 166
Agrippa, Henry Cornelius, 233
Alarum against Usurers (An), 198
Alba, or the Months Mind of a Melancholy Lover, 241
Alberti, Leonbattista, 106
Albricus, 5
Alciati, Andrea, 9-11, 74-5, 105, 209, 220
Alcida, Greenes Metamorphosis, 137-8
Aldus Manutius, 7
Alexander, 95n
Alexander, Peter, 23-5, 237
Alexandro, Alexander ab, 8
Alleyn, Edward, 16-8, 21, 24, 67, 68n, 69-71, 71n, 221n
Allot, Robert, 21
Almond for a Parrat (An), 83, 85-6, 89, 144, 147, 149, 156, 166, 168-9, 173, 176n, 192-6, 203
Amadis de Gaule, 157
Aminta (Tasso), 64, 68, 78
Amores (Ovid), 49, 161
Amores (Pontanus), 38n
Amyntas (Watson), 62-3
Amyntas Pastorall (Fraunce), 63-4, 73, 77, 203
Anatomie of Absurditie (The), 87, 136, 138-9, 142, 143n, 156, 169, 196, 208n
Anatomy of Abuses (The), 198
Anthologia Planudea, 9
Anticosmopolita, 97, 98n
Antonio and Mellida, 58
Apollonius Tyaneus, 119, 183
Apuleius, 8, 121
Aratus, 40
Arber, Edward, 146
Arcadia (The), 157-9
Arcadian Rhetorike (The), 61-2, 149
Archimedes, 106
Architectura, 106
Aretino, Pietro, 90-2, 90n, 140, 142, 143n, 150, 170, 196, 224
Argall, Thomas, 40

Ariosto, L., 2, 12, 67, 102, 144
Aristophanes, 121
Aristotle, 114-5, 114n, 116, 119, 197n
Arius, 181, 181n, 182
Armenini, G. B., 6
Arthur, King, 156
Artis Analytica Praxis, 31
Ascham, Roger, 122, 194, 214
Asclepius, 230
Astrological Discourse (An), 153, 197, 201
Astrophel and Stella, 87, 157, 159
As You Like It, 34n, 66-7, 71-2, 200, 221-7, 267, 270
Athanasius, 191
Atkins, J. W. H., 142
Aubigné, Agrippa d', 244
Austin, W. B., 100
Avalos, Alfonso de, *see* Vasto, marquis of
Avicenna, 161

B. R. 128
Babb, Lawrence, 113
Bacon, Francis, 5
Baines, Richard, 27, 32, 32n
Baker, George, 128
Baker, Thomas, 100
Baldwin, T. W., 105n, 178, 256, 265
Bancroft, Richard, 171, 175
Banister, John, 128
Bargaglio, Scipio, 63
Barnaud, Nicolas, 184
Barnes, Barnabe, 148, 151
Baro, P., 183
Barrow, Henry, 183
Bartas, Guillaume Salluste Du, 245
Bartlett, P. B., 52
Battenhouse, R. W., 38
Bebel, Heinrich, 150
Belleau, Remy, 78
Belt, T., 18
Bestrafte Brudermord (Der), 48n
Beza, T., 183
Bird, Christopher, 163
Biron, 243, 249
Bishop, George, 217
Blount, Sir Charles, 87, 138
Blundeville, T., 118n
Boccaccio, Giovanni, 4, 6, 220n
Bocchi, Achille, 9
Bond, R. W., 153n, 186
Bowes, T., 245
Bowre of Delights, 159, 160n
Bradbrook, M. C., 26, 29, 34-5
Brahe, Tycho, 35
Braunschweig, H., 99

French Academie (The), 245
Friendly Admonition to Martin Marprelate (A), 146
Fripp, E. I., 178
Frysar, Ingram, 225
Fulgentius, 2, 2n, 4
Fulke, Dr. W., 97
Furio Ceriol, Federico, 118n
Furness, H., 222
Furnivall, F. J., 51

Galen, 114, 128-9, 164
Gallathea, 135, 153n
Garden of Pleasure (The), 257
Genealogia Deorum, 4, 6n, 220n
Genialium Dierum libri sex, 8
Gentile, G., 107n
Gesner, Conrad, 90, 92
Gesta Grayorum, 236n, 250
Giehlow, Karl, 9
Giovio, Paolo, 10-12, 63, 103
Gontaut, Charles de, 243
Goodale, T., 18
Gower, John, 143
Gracchus, 139
Gratulationes Valdinenses, 96
Greene, Robert, 12, 16, 21-6, 51, 62, 66-9, 71, 74, 77-8, 81, 87, 89, 94, 109, 126, 136-9, 141-2, 155, 162-3, 167-9, 175, 186, 190n, 196-202, 197n, 199n, 207, 214-216, 221-2, 221n, 224, 227, 256, 258, 267-8
Greg, Sir Walter W., 19, 19n, 21, 21n, 23, 33, 68, 71, 71n, 160
Greville, Fulke, Lord Brooke, 98n, 107, 157-8
Groatsworth of Wit (A), 22, 78, 162, 258
Grosart, A. B., 94
Groundes of the Longitude (The) 231
Gubbin, Thomas, 62
Guevara, Antonio de, 137
Guise, Henri de, 243
Gwinne, Matthew, 107
Gyraldi, Lilio Gregorio, 5, 5n

H., G., 105
Hacket, Thomas, 136
Haddon, Dr. W., 194
Hakluyt, Richard, 28, 45
Hamlet, 48n
Hamlet (old Hamlet play), 48n, 257
Hanmer, M., 182
Harington, Sir John, 12-4, 21, 102, 104
Harman, Thomas, 198
Harriot, Thomas, 28, 31-3, 52-5, 245
Harrison, G. B., 31
Hart, H. C., 106, 252, 255
Harte, Lord Mayor, 16
Harvey, Gabriel, 19, 61-2, 71, 71n,

81-2, 84-5, 89-93, 94-135, 98n, 99n, 105n, 106n, 108n, 117n, 125n, 141, 145-9, 151n, 154-6, 160, 162-4, 166-8, 171, 177-186, 181n, 188-193, 186n, 190n, 193n, 195, 197-8, 201-2, 203, 205-7, 210n, 211-216, 218-220, 221n, 222-7, 235-6, 246, 249, 251-5, 258-260
Harvey, John (father), 95, 178
Harvey, John (brother to R. and G. Harvey), 119, 124, 177, 199, 201, 231
Harvey, Richard, 89-92, 90n, 119, 124, 144, 152-3, 155-6, 166, 171, 177, 182, 185-9, 191-6, 197n, 199-202, 204-210, 212, 224n, 254-5
Harvey (Kingston usurer), 173-4, 174n
Hatton, Sir Christopher, 96, 174
Have with you to Saffron Walden, 103, 109, 151n, 169
Hay any worke for Cooper, 171
Hebraeus, Leo, 79
Hecataeus Milesius, 80
Hécatomgraphie, 9
Heminges, John, 18-9, 19n
Henry III, King of France, 52, 107, 229, 244
Henry IV, King of France and of Navarre, 185, 243-4, 247-9
1 Henry IV, 210
2 Henry IV, 210-1, 218
Henry V, 218
1 Henry VI, 17, 20
3 Henry VI, 23
Henslowe, Philip, 16-7, 21, 48n
Herbert, Henry, see Pembroke, Earl of
Herbert, William, 158
Hermes Trismegistus, 8, 36-7, 42, 43n, 84, 229-238
Hero and Leander, 32, 42
Herodotus, 229
Héroët, Antoine, 137n
Herostratus, 210n
Hesiod, 42
Hester, John, 128
Heth, Thomas, 197
Heywood, Thomas, 124
Hierocles, 182-3
Hieroglyphica, 7
Hill, Thomas, 40, 45, 50, 50n
Historia Naturalis, 8, 84
Historia Regum Britanniae, 204, 207
Holland, John, 18
Homer, 2, 49, 52-4, 70, 75, 85, 90n, 126, 228
Hone, Dr., 173-4
Honesta Disciplina (De), 7
Honorable Historie of frier Bacon (The), 16, 22
Honour of the Garter (The), 231

Taylor, John, 83n
Taylor, Rupert, 246, 259
Terence, 110, 148, 168, 189, 258
Terrors of the Night (The), 30, 169
Textor, Ravisius, 5
Theater of fyne Devises (The), 9
Theatre des bons Engins, 9-10
Theobald, Lewis, 73
Theodosius the Great, 90n
Theologia mythologica, 4
Thesaurus Linguae Latinae, 230
Theses Martinianae, 171
Third part of the Countesse of Pembrokes Yuychurch (The), 13-4, 64, 78, 92, 148, 203, 220, 234-5, 269
Thomas Sidney, 205-6
Thorius, John, 118, 145-6
Three Letters, 162, 259
Three proper, and wittie, familiar Letters, 97, 100, 177
Thynne, Francis, 198
Tilley, Morris Palmer, 88
Titus Andronicus, 17
Tofte, Robert, 241
Tom Nash his Ghost, 83n
Torriano, Giovanni, 88, 235
Tractado de Conseio, 118
Treatise of Melancholy, 113
Tristia, 161
Troublesome Reign of King John (The), 20
True Tragedy of Richard Duke of York (The), 23
Turberville, G., 255
Turner, Celeste, 176n
Turner, George, 106n
Twelve Books of his Iliades, 52
Two Gentlemen of Verona (The), 240
Two other, very commendable Letters, 97
Tyard, Pontus de, 56, 114
Tyrtaeus, 228
Udall, John, 172-4
Underhill, J., 108n, 111n
Univers, ou Discours des parties et de la nature du monde (L'), 114
Valeriano, Pierio, 7, 10, 59, 80
Valois, Marguerite de, 243
Vasto, Marquis of, 220, 220n
Vautrollier, Thomas, 217
Venus and Adonis, 46, 66n, 78, 217, 237
Verderius, 5
Vergil, 2-3, 63, 269
Vergil, Polydore, 7

Verres, 139
Very briefe treatise declaring howe many counsells, 118n
Victoria, 61n
Vie de Gargantua et de Pantagruel, 218
Vindiciae contra tyrannos, 184
Volkmann, Ludwig, 9

W., I., 99, 128-35, 202
W., N., 10, 112n
Waddington, C., 62n
Waldegrave, Robert, 83, 146, 172, 176
Walsingham, Sir Francis, 157
Warner, 31
Waterson, Simon, 159
Watson, Thomas, 62-3
Weever, John, 241, 264
Wentersdorf, K., 25
White, E., 216
White, William, 240
Whitgift, John, 82-3, 87, 172, 206
Whitney, Geoffrey, 10-11
Willet, Andrew, 10-11
Williams, Sir Roger, 248
Willobie his Avisa, 31
Wilson, F. P., 150, 150n, 223
Wilson, H. S., 95
Wilson, John Dover, 24, 26, 33, 45, 66-7, 73, 140, 176n, 200, 200n, 224, 227, 237, 240, 252n, 258, 261n, 264
Windet, John, 52
Wingfield, Antony, 101-2
Wit's Misery, 91
Wolfe, John, 62, 86n, 88, 118, 145-6, 157, 160n, 162, 172-3, 184-5, 189, 196, 198, 204, 217 221n, 223
Wonderfull Strange and Miraculous Astrologicall Prognostication, 149, 150-1, 196, 249
Woodcocke, Thomas, 78
Worlde of Wordes, 159n
Worthy Tract of Paulus Jovius (The), 10
Wright, Leonard, 146
Wright, William, 149

Xenocrates 116
Xenophon, 49, 90n

Yates Frances A. 26, 29-30, 35, 104n, 123, 134, 147, 155, 217, 218n, 229, 235, 246
Young, Dr. John, 95